A Language of Song

Samuel Charters

A Language of Song

＊

Journeys in
the Musical World of
the African Diaspora

＊

Duke University Press Durham and London 2009

The photographs from the Bahamas are
by Ann Charters, and the captioned photographs from
Trinidad are by Nora Charters-Myers. All
other photographs are by the author.

All historical materials are from the Samuel
and Ann Charters Archive of Vernacular
African American Music and Culture at
the Dodd Research Center, University of
Connecticut, Storrs.

"No Woman No Cry" is published by Bob
Marley / Blue Mountain Music Ltd. All rights
reserved.

"Columbus Lied" by Winston Bailey,
issued by Straker's Calypso World,
copyright controlled.

✳ for Annie, of course

✳ Contents

I think of this as a book about music, but it is as much a book about the journeys I took to find the music. I realized more than half a century ago that I couldn't write about music in northeast Brazil or on an island in the Bahamas, or in Trinidad, Jamaica, New Orleans, Harlem, or the Georgia Sea Islands unless I'd made the journey there. I couldn't write about a place if I didn't know what the sun felt like on the streets, how the food tasted, what the earth smelled like, how couples moved when they danced. I took along the usual traveler's guides, dictionaries, and phrase books, and since each journey was in search of music, I also had any notes I'd found to recordings, along with any books or articles or pamphlets that had something to do with the music I hoped to find. I've cited in the bibliography the materials I took with me or consulted, including books that I found in later years that helped me understand what I had heard.

A helpful companion for many of the things I was looking for was John Storm Roberts's *Black Music of Two Worlds,* and I would have missed many things in the Carnival season in Trinidad without Dr. Hollis Liverpool's rich history of calypso, *Rituals of Power and Rebellion.* I often encountered newer writing that appeared after I had returned from my journeys, and there was useful information I wish I'd had at the time. An example of this is Michael Tisserand's fine *The Kingdom of Zydeco.* My journeys in western Louisiana went on for more than ten years beginning in the 1970s, but Tisserand's book wasn't published until 1998.

I also later drew on the notes I'd made on many of the trips when I was either recording the artists I was meeting or talking with record company owners and studio engineers who were involved with the music I was interested in. Anyone who has read my earlier books or notes to the recordings will recognize the source of some of the incidents I included here. Of all the writing I found, two very different sources were most helpful. One was the letters written in 1838 from a Georgia Sea Islands plantation by the English actress

Fanny Kemble, published under the title *Journal of a Residence on a Georgia Plantation* in 1863. Her insights into the psychological damage that the conditions of their bondage had inflicted on the slaves around her made me conscious of much that I was seeing and hearing. The other useful source was the three volumes of his collected interviews with living calypso artists that were transcribed, edited, and published by Rudolph Ottley in Trinidad in the 1990s. Ottley's love for his subject and his objectivity in his writing about the artists remained the standard I tried to maintain for myself.

I can only extend my thanks to everyone who has made some of the same journeys and who left a chronicle of their experiences for readers like me. I also hope that they enjoyed the music as much as I did.

SAMUEL CHARTERS
Stockholm, 2008

Beginnings. Roots. Sources. Every story has a beginning. Every story has its roots. Behind every story is a source. In the story of the music that was part of the long African journey in the New World, there must be a beginning, and it must be a beginning in Africa itself, since so much of what the journey has yielded has its sources there. Even now, when so many centuries have passed, the roots of the journey lie in Africa.

Many of the things that travelers have written about Africa—that it is large, that it is a continent of contrasts, that the land is hard, that it is beautiful, that it is cruelly poor, that its cultures are rich, that it is fascinating, that it is ancient, that it is new, that it is dangerous, that there is no way to understand Africa and its people without having been there—these things have been written again and again for hundreds of years, and they still are just as true. Traveling in Africa continues to be a thicket of experience that leaves everyone who journeys there in some way changed.

The mass of land that is Africa is almost large enough to contain the United States and Western Europe, and there is nothing in the barren mountains that enclose the Sahara Desert in the north to prepare you for the broad, grassy plain along the Niger River at Bamako or the choked mangrove swamps of the Guinea coast, hundreds of miles to the south. The vivid contrasts of colors of the African landscape become enough in themselves to change your perceptions of color—the gaudy flowers dangling over the walls of Dakar, the gray, thorny brush of the savannah, the green of the forests of Ghana, and the red of the earth where roads have been slashed through the stands of trees. It is the flaming colors of the African mornings that many travelers remember—the abrupt blaze of the sun flaring through the morning mists, the pale rim of the horizon flushing from faint yellow to orange, the endless blue of the sky as the sunlight floods the land.

The story of the African journey to the continents and the islands to the west across the Atlantic, however, is only closely linked to one clearly demarked area of Africa—the coast of West Africa. It was along that coast that the slavers' ships waited offshore for the African rulers who controlled the commerce to bring them their cargoes. The long miles of the coast still mirror the mingling of the languages and the customs of the European nations that at some point considered the lands to be part of themselves. The coast of the northern desert had Spanish rulers, south of it, in Senegal and Guinea—inland to Mali—the rulers were French. Farther to the south it was the British, their "protectorate" beginning at Sierra Leone, in an effort of slave repatriation, then following the curve of the coast to Ghana, and ending in Nigeria. The Portuguese, still farther south, were the rulers of the last decades of slave commerce, with their stretch of coastline in Angola. It is that coast that was the source of the African peoples who became part of the journey to the new Americas. When I journeyed to Africa, it was that crescent of coast line that was my destination.

I flew to West Africa in the early spring of 1974, and my journey began in the city of Banjul, the capital city of what was still known as The Gambia. My travels led me from Senegal to Mali, and south to Sierra Leone, Ghana, and Nigeria in search of anything I might learn about the sources of the American blues. Of course, what I found was much more than what I was searching for, and in the usual ironies of travel I learned that the sources of the blues itself were somewhere else. The first blues that I had already heard in Memphis or St. Louis, Alabama or Mississippi, were as close to a source as I would ever come. What I found in Africa were a gathering of cultures and a continuing history that lay behind the flood of musical expression I encountered everywhere in the lands across the Atlantic Ocean—from Brazil to Cuba, to Trinidad, to New Orleans, to the Bahamas, to dance halls of west Louisiana, and the great churches of Harlem. What I would learn in The Gambia, as one of its singers told me, was the story of everything.

The Gambia is a thin sliver of land stretching inland along the banks of the Gambia River, in some places no wider than the mounded earth of the banks and a strip of fields on either side of the muddy current. Banjul, which is two hundred miles south of Dakar on the Atlantic coast, was then small and still. A commercial traveler I met later on a coastal ferry shook his head when I said I'd been staying in Banjul. "That's a sleepy little place!"

The city had spread without plan or order along the banks of the Gambia River, and across the battered wharves along the water's edge I could see the line of surf where the river—almost a mile wide at its mouth—surged out into the sea. The struggle between them, the river and the ocean, went on through the rise and fall of the tides as the river's ribbed, murky flood pushed tirelessly against the dazzling gleam of the ocean's turquoise blue swells.

The bare, cement-walled room I rented in an empty hotel a block from the river smelled of wet plaster and disinfectant, and from the open door to my little balcony I could hear the distant crash of the surf. The room had so little furniture that my notes, my tape recorder, and its jumble of accessories were spread out over the tile floor. I usually worked in the late afternoons in Banjul's one room library, making notes from the early records of the country's upriver English trading post. The commercial venture's storeroom inventories and yearly sales summaries had been turned into a thick-volumed "history" of the country. Banjul itself had been built at the mouth of the river early in the nineteenth century to assist the British Navy in its efforts to stamp out the slave trade, and in its years as an outpost of the British Empire the city's name had been Bathurst. When it became the capital of the newly independent country, its name was changed to Banjul, the native word for a tall cane reed that grows along the riverbanks.

It was too hot to go out in the sun in the middle of the day, so when I had to shop in the noisy covered market I joined the streams of people in its dank passageways in the hours after dawn. By 10:30 the streets were almost empty and lazily silent. What music I heard came over radios, or followed me in the dark passages of the market where three or four stalls sold 45 rpm singles. Most of the recordings were South African hi-life bands. I was conscious that the other music, the music of the older traditions I was listening for, was there somewhere, and as the days passed I began to hear its echoes. Sometimes the echo was faint and uncertain, other times it was loud and jarring.

Late one morning I became conscious of the sound of voices and the rattle of cars on the street below me, and I went to my balcony and looked down. Despite the heat, the street was filled with people in richly colored robes—the women with their heads wrapped in turbans sewn of the same dyed cloth as their robes, and the men in the sober skull caps they wore of the mosque. The people were streaming toward the small park in the center of the city. I had forgotten that it was the country's independence day. It had been nine generally peaceful years since the last British governor had turned the country over to its first African government. Though it was almost noon, and the sun was at its most intense, the government had organized a celebration that included groups from all of the tribal villages up and down the river.

The afternoon passed with speeches by conscientious men in dark suits and sun glasses who addressed the crowds from a newly erected wooden platform on the dry grass of a soccer field in the center of town. When the speeches ended there were processions of self-consciously proud children in their stiffly ironed school uniforms, accompanied by loud shouts from their equally proud parents pressed against the iron fence that kept them out of the soccer field. There was a continual fluttering of people fanning themselves in a futile gesture of protest against the blazing heat. Following so closely behind the school children that they bumped against the last lines of marchers, the dancers and musicians from The Gambia's native peoples hurtled onto the field. In their flapping, swirling, brightly colored robes they looked like large, exotic, excited birds.

As the hours passed there was music everywhere around me. Processions of drummers swept through the streets, followed by lines of serious-faced men and women swaying in time to the music. Beside a gritty wall a trio of ragged musicians playing slim, curved native flutes entertained shrieking crowds with suggestive acrobatics. Drifting with the rhythms I suddenly began hearing a new ensemble of instruments. The sounds filled the air with the nervous pandemonium that European travelers in West Africa had described hundreds of years before. In a street close to the soccer field a group of thirty or forty men were milling in a patch of shade with impatient energy, trying to maintain some semblance of an organized procession. At the same time they were impatiently expressing their feelings about being made to wait there on the sticky macadam pavement by the arm-banded marshals who were keeping order for the day. The noise they were making was enough to make me forget the heat. It was a shattering crash that rang in my ears for most of the next week. In the hours I had spent following the drums and the rattles of other tribes as they worked their way toward the gates in the fence to make their appearance down the wobbly chalk lines on the scrubby grass, the musical excitement had been measured and restrained. Now I found myself squeezed into the middle of an irregular procession of Fula musicians.

The Fulas—or Fulanis—there are many spellings and variations of the name—were one of the tribes that had won great victories in the religious wars of West Africa in the centuries before the imposed stewardship of the Europeans, and in the steaming heat on the jammed street I could almost believe that they had defeated their enemies by deafening them. The men clustered together on the street were tall, muscular figures, swathed for the day in formal, long, white robes. They had traveled from their isolated villages in the dusty, dry, backcountry thickets of spindly trees and brush where they tended herds of scrawny cattle, and they still had the edgy saunter of men who spent their lives in the sun. As I wrote in *The Roots of the Blues*,

> In the dense press of white robed bodies I could have been present at any moment in the hundreds of years since Europeans first met the Fulas. The dark faces, the tall sharpness of the bodies, the swaying robes, the din of the instruments—it resembled a scene from the earliest descriptions . . . somewhere in the procession there was every kind of Fula instrument. Men were carrying deep, bowled drums with strips of thin metal nailed to the rims to add to their thudding tone. Behind them were a row of men with xylophones strung from their necks. There were also the one-stringed fiddles, the riti that I had heard the Fula jelefo play.
>
> Close to me were four or five flute players, their hand-carved wooden instruments more than a foot long with a high, sweet tone. I could see five-string harps made from a curved piece of wood—see them, but not hear them, any more than I could hear the one-stringed fiddles in the din . . . [1]

In the dense crowd around me some of the musicians were playing curved trumpets fashioned from the horns of their cattle—blowing long blasts of a single note, in no sequence or pattern that I could ever work out. They took a breath, lifted their much handled instruments, and blew as loudly as they could for as long as their breath held out. I realized that if they hadn't blown their notes with such insistence they wouldn't have been heard over the swollen calabash drums that some of the men had strapped to their stomachs and played with metal rings on their fingers. The noise of the calabash drums, though, had to fight against the thunder of the elongated wooden drums that other men were carrying with worn leather shoulder straps or had set up on the street. Their instruments had been carved out of tree trunks, and the deep, throaty sounds were like the grunts of a large animal emerging from the depths of the earth.

But even standing a few feet from them it was hard to make out what the drummers were playing, because closer to me were several men energetically shaking rattles made of dried pieces of calabash. The rattles were constructed from long, bent sticks, with a coarse string tied from the bent tip to the sweat stained handgrip. Dangling from the string were large, flat, square pieces of dried calabash, the large gourd that is an indispensable part of West African life. The skin of the calabashes dries hard and it lasts for years, and dried calabashes turn up used for everything from water bottles to hand rattles. The thunderous, clattering sound as the men shook their sticks energetically would have drowned out jackhammers.

The musicians filling the street around me wouldn't have been out of place in one of the battles that travellers in West Africa described in the 18th century. Godfrey Lovar heard one of these assemblies of musicians playing during a battle on the Guinea coast in 1701, not far to the south of the Gambia River, and he wrote,

> During the Combat the Drums, Trumpets, and other Instruments in their way continually sound; which joined to the cries of the Negroes, make a Noise louder than Thunder. Their drums are a Piece of Wood, hollowed at one end only and covered with the Ear of an Elephant, tightly bound over the mouth. Their sticks are two Pieces of Wood shaped like a Hammer, covered with Goat's Skin, which give a dull, hoarse Sound . . . [The musicians, including boys playing trumpets made out of elephant's teeth, blasting out a single tone, stayed close to the combatants.]
>   To this . . . They add an instrument as remarkable for the Simplicity of its Construction, as it is hard to be described. It is of Iron, shaped like two small concave Fire-Shovels, about a foot long, soldered together, and which form a kind of oval Belly. A boy holds this instrument by the small end, and with a Stick of half a foot long strikes on it according to the Cadence of the Drums and Trumpets, who are always near the General, while the Fight lasts . . . [2]

Usually European travellers didn't come so close to a crowd of musicians, since it was a battle they were witnessing, but even from their safe distances they generally used the same word, "din," to describe the noise, and for once the travelers got it right.

A Fula named Musa Camara was helping me find the older musicians I was looking for. Musa was young and enthusiastic, and he was planning to use the money I was paying him to add to his small salary from Radio Gambia to accumulate a "bride price" so he could get married. I would also take tapes to the small compound where he lived with his two sisters and they would lie giggling and sprawled on the sagging bed, slowly working out rough translations of the songs I was recording. Although they were Fulas, they also were fluent enough in Mandingo, or Mandinka, as the word is often spelled, the language that was spoken by most of the people in the small city. It was also the language of the most important praise singers, the *griots*, and at the end of the afternoon I would have enough notes and suggestions from the words and lines they called over to me that I could assemble a text. With the text of the song and the tape I would then spend an hour with a retired school teacher who, though he was Serrahule, was completely fluent in Mandinka, and his considered responses and polite corrections would give me some assurance that what I had put together was the song I'd heard.

Usually I would hear brisk footsteps on the concrete floor in the empty corridor, then I'd hear a sharp knock on my door. Musa stood out in the corridor, always in a hurry to return to his job. He would propose a time when he could help me and tell me a little about the musician he would take me to meet. Musa was slim, muscular, and strikingly good looking, with dark skin and a vivid smile, usually contrasting with his bright red or yellow shirts. He always made it clear that his role was only to tell me how to find the musicians, and to sit with them and enjoy the music. To emphasize that what I was paying didn't oblige him to help me carry any of the recording equipment, he hurried far enough ahead that I had to struggle to keep up with him. I had cables, plugs, and microphones in the bags draped over my shoulders, and a sagging case with tapes and the tape recorder. If we were in one of the areas of "bush" outside of Banjul I was left to trail after the back of his shirt as he strode ahead of me on the meandering paths through the waist high grass. He always managed a few moments of talk with the people in the compound before I struggled up, my face red and my shirt soaked with perspiration.

One night after I'd eaten in a noisy restaurant close to the market streets I came back and found that Musa had left a note under my door. It was a sketch of a part of the city where I'd never been, with a mark for the compound of the most important of The Gambia's Mandingo griots. A note explained that the singer had just come back to his city compound from the village, and he was willing to see me. Musa would be there waiting.

I walked through the dirt streets following Musa's directions to the section of Banjul known as Brikama. Like everywhere else in the cities along the coast, Brikama was crowded. I had to stop again and again to look at the rough map. I was walking in a haphazardly laid-out area of one-story stucco buildings and the corrugated iron fences of the compounds. Most of Brikama was a collection of small compounds that were composed of a few small stucco buildings around a dirt courtyard swept with a twig brush every morning to keep down insects and rats. The compounds were separated from each other by sagging, shoulder-high fences made of woven sticks or rusted sheets of corrugated iron, and they were strung along dirt pathways that in some places had been widened enough for cars to make their way around the piles of garbage that had accumulated every thirty or forty yards. Dusty trees among the houses gave some shade to the compound yards, and hanging over the edges of the fences were clusters of leafy bushes and vines.

The narrow dirt streets served to give the neighborhood of the compounds a loose coherence. There were the usual smells from small fires and the heaped rubbish that blocked many of the small streets, and there was a stronger stench from the open sewer that ran through the center of the area. The occasional single houses I passed had been built out of boards against the side of the street, and the windows were open. I could see inside the cramped rooms, with their unmade beds and rough furniture.

I found the singer's compound at the end of a street that had been once paved with a layer of crushed shells but was yielding to the usual crumbling ruts. Inside the fence was a long, low building with a row of doors that opened onto the sleeping rooms. Like all of the buildings, there was a veranda with an overhanging roof that gave it some protection from the sun. There were wooden benches set out beside the doorways, but the only privacy was from flowered hanging curtains that swung languidly in the afternoon heat. Musa was waiting for me outside the compound, and with a pleased smile, he led me inside. Women were pounding millet outside in the sun, and they stopped for a moment, nodding to us, but too shy to say anything beyond a murmured greeting to Musa.

The singer came out of one of the small buildings and stood silently waiting as Musa introduced us. He nodded, and said in uncertain but emphatic English, "I would not come except this man ask me." He gestured toward Musa. "It isn't because you pay me that I will sing for you, but I would like to come to your country as the representative of the Mandingo people." Musa made it clear that the man, whose name was Alhaji Fabala Kanuteh, was one of the two griots in the service of the President of The Gambia, and when he had sung for me he was to go to the Presidential Palace to discuss his performance for the Independence celebrations.

Alhaji Fabala was a tall, imposing man, wearing a dark brown robe His face was strongly molded, and his expression was guarded as he studied me through gold rimmed glasses. His head was covered with a white skull cap. He led us to a corner room in the long building in the compound yard, sat on a mat on the floor with an imperious swing of his robe and pulled a handmade *balafon*, the African predecessor of the marimba, against his bare feet. I had seen the larger versions of the instrument that were played for ceremonies and dancing, but this was a

Bakau Village.

smaller instrument to accompany singing. It had nineteen hand-carved wooden keys tied to a frame of thick sticks, and it was small enough for him to hang it from a leather thong around his neck if he performed when he was standing.

Since Musa and I both had also taken our places on the mat on the floor, the room's handmade chairs had been pushed back against the wall. Two of its walls opened out to the courtyard to catch whatever breeze might drift in from the sea, and the bright cloth curtains swayed behind me with any breath of the wind. There was a large double bed, and the walls were decorated with family photographs. As Alhaji Fabala waited for me to set up the recording machine he played lightly on the balafon with wooden mallets. His mood became more serious as he glanced up at me. "Playing is my job."

His first "song" was a long, half-recited, half-sung narrative about one of the renowned warrior figures of the history of the region, Almami Samory Toure. His voice was light, thoughtful, almost as though he were considering the story himself as he related it. The accompaniment was a pattern of light rhythmic tapping on the small wooden keys, with interjected runs and flourishes as he gave himself a moment to think of what came next. The dry sound of the balafon was a delicate foil to the tone of his voice. Even though I couldn't understand what he was singing, he told the story so compellingly, with a veteran storyteller's pauses and emphases, that I found myself concentrating on every word, certain that I was understanding at least some of what he was telling me.

It was his next song that brought me to the source of what I'd come to Africa to find. I didn't know if there was any such song, but after a moment of hesitation I asked him if he knew a song about the first coming of the Europeans and the first meetings with them. He held up his hands, as though he were surprised that I would ask such a foolish question.

"I can tell you the history of everything. Africa, India, China, everything. But you must come back when you have time to listen."

He sat for a moment, tapping delicately on the balafon. "The Europeans? It is a hard song to do and goes on for a day and a half. I don't sing it often."

The song was "Toolongjong."

As he sang, in the background other sounds filled the afternoon. Outside in the compound the women of his family had gone back to the day's work that our arrival had interrupted. They were pounding millet in a large, much used wooden mortar with heavy pestles that they swung with steady, practiced movements. There were three women, their robes wrapped loosely around their bodies so their arms were free, lifting the pestles in a flowing rhythm, murmuring in low voices as they worked. Inside the small hut, as the curtains began to stir with a fresh breeze, the short sticks in Fabala Kanute's hands moved almost in a reverie over the keys of the balafon on the floor in front of him. The sticks were short handled, cloth tipped mallets he held between his fingers as he played a repetitive, dry, ticking pattern of notes over and over in a gentle, wooden tapping sound. When he paused in the recitation to rest his voice and to think about what he wanted to tell me next, he shifted to the highest tones of his little instrument and played scurrying, descending patterns of notes that were almost freely structured in their rhythmic cadence. His voice was as casually phrased against the fleeting accompaniment.

Toolongjong is the song that was sung for Sunyetta,
   the king of Fuda.
This same Toolongjong was also sung for the great soldiers of Sunyetta.
This Toolongjong was sung for Musa Molo, the king of Fuladu,
for Seneke Jammeh, this Toolongjong was sung for the Koree Danso
for the Sang Kala Maran,
this Toolongjong was sung for Mansa Demba of Berending,
this Toolongjong was sung for Wals Mandiba.

Now I will tell you how slaves came to be sold to the Europeans.
How it came about is what I'm going to tell.

In that time Mansa Demba was the king of Nomi
And Seneke Jambi was at Bakindi Ke.
There were two wharves, one at Jufreh Tenda and the other at
Albreda Tenda,
and anyone who went there, to Youmi Mamsa, went to the king there,
that is the king Mansa Demba, and to the woman king
called Kodending.
If they got hold of any slaves they took them to Mansa Demba
and sold them to him.
At this time Han Sunyetta was the leader of the world.
He made another king for the village of Sillia,
and made another king at Salum,
and made another king at the village of Baul.
Another king Murujang and Gao,
Before that Satifa Jawara and Fakolly Kumba,
And Komfatta Keying and Nana Jibril. They were the strongest
of Sunyetta's soldiers.

Then the Europeans came from Europe,
and at that time the only Europeans were the Portuguese.
    (A long interlude of praising)

When the Portuguese came they brought their ship
to Sani Munko and they left the ship at Sani Munko and
    raised their flag there.
Mansa Seneki Jammeh, a king, sent people to Sani Munko to see them.
The messengers arrived at Sani Munko and they found the
Portuguse there and the Portuguese asked them questions.
The first man they saw was Kambi Manneh and the Europeans
asked him what was the name of the place
and he told them "My name is Kambi," and they wrote
the name of the place down, Kambi.
And they came to this place and they found people cutting
these sticks called the "bang," and the Europeans asked them
"What are you cutting?" and they said they were cutting the
sticks called bangjolo, and the Europeans wrote that down
    for the name.
Then the Europeans said to Seneke Jammeh, "We are looking
    for something,"
and Seneke Jammeh asked them, "What is it?"
And they told him, "We are looking for slaves."
Seneke then went to Tambana and fought with the people of
Tambana, and fought with the village of Baria,

and then fought with Jokadu Dasalami.
When he had these slaves he went
and sold these slaves to the Europeans.
    (A short instrumental interlude)

Then he sold the slaves to the Europeans,
and the leader of the Europeans was called Wampiya,
and he took the slaves to the city of Salamki Joya.
He went with the slaves to the Walendeya,
that is to the people of Holland,
and he sold the slaves to the Walendeya,
then the walendaya took the slaves to America.
    (A short instrumental interlude)

Then Musa Molo, the king of Fuladu, took four slaves
and gave them to the men called Dikori and Dansa.
He told Dikori and Dansa to take the four slaves
to the place called Youmi Mansa, to Seneke Jammeh,
then the two messengers said to Seneke Jammeh
that we were sent by Musa Molo to bring these four slaves
to you and sell them to you, to sell them to you for
gunpowder and white cloth.
Seneke Jammeh said, "Well it's true we sell slaves
to the Portuguese," then the Portuguese took the slaves
to the Walendaya, the people of Holland,
and the Walendaya took them to America.
    (A long instrumental interlude)

So then they took the four slaves and sold them to the
Portuguese and the Portuguese took them on their ship
and sold them to the Dutch—the Walendaya—and the Dutch took them
to America, and when they got
to America they sold the slaves there.
Then Dansa and Dikori returned to Musa Molo and told him
that they sold the slaves at Youmi.
And Musa said, "Is that so?"
Then he said, "I would have taken my army to the people
of Youmi and fought them."
Then Musa went with his people to Kunti Wata, to Mansa Burekamara.
Mansa Burekamara gave Musa Molo 300 and 3 slaves,
and then Musa Molo left again.
He went to Almam Basise of Yani, who was together with
Bamba Esa Jamili,
and each of them gave Musa Molo 300 and 3 slaves.

Alhaji Fabala Kanuteh.

Then he went to Lyama Banta, to Ngari Sabally of Kachamb.
Ngari Sabally gave him 1000 slaves.
He then went to Jatta Sela at Toro Koto with those 1000 slaves
and when he came to Jatta Sela, then Jatta Sela told him,
"I will give you 400 slaves."
And then they went to Samkarangmarong
and he, too, gave Musa 300 slaves.

Then Musa crossed the river.
He left the Jokardu district,
he came to the village of Tambara,
and to the villages of Baria and Darselami,
and he sent a message on to the village of Bakindiki,
and the drum was beating there.
The drum was beating at a village called Berehkolong.
Another drum was beating at Berending and at Jinakibarra,
and another drum at Tubabu Kolomb.
    (An instrumental interlude)

When they arrived they sent a message to the lady king
Musa Mansa Kodendng and to Seneke Jammeh
and another message to Bumyadu
and another message to Berending
and another message to Sangako
and another message to Misseramding
and another message to Missiraba
and another message to Jinakibara
and another message to Jinaki Kajatta,
and they said Musa Molo the king of the East has arrived
and come to visit the king of the West, Mansa Demba.
Then Mansa Demba said, "I will send a message to Seneke Jammeh,"
And they sent a message to Bakindi Ke.
When the message came to Bakindi Ke the people then
got ready, and they said,
"Musa, we know what you want," and they gave him 100 slaves.
100 young girls. 100 women. 100 young boys.
Money, 100. Gold, 100. Cows, 100. Goats, 100. Sheep, 100.
Musa then said, "If there is to be a war you can see that
it is only because there is something we want to have."
Then he said to the people of Bakindi Ke,
"There is no fight between us."
He told the people, "You have divided your land between the
two villages, Albadar and Jufering,

and these two villages took slaves and sold them
to Sanneh Munkujoyeh. Since you have been doing this,"
Musa told them, "I would like to meet the Dutchmen themselves."
And the people told him that it was the Portuguese who came,
and not the Dutchman himself.
"But when the Portuguese come we will take you to the place,"
then they took the Portuguese to a river place,
the place they called Jang Jang Bure, that is the name
of two brothers there.
    (An interlude of praising)

Then when Musa Molo came he collected all the people
of Fuladu, from Ndorma up to Santangto Bubu Tabanding.
up to Santangto Wuruma. Up to Chargel.
He collected them all and he told them,
"Let us build a house at the place of the brothers
Bure and Jang to put slaves in,
and then sell them to the Europeans.
If we build that slave house then we can
sell the slaves when the Portuguese come
with their ships to sell them to America."
Then the people said, "Yes, we're going to do it."
Then they built the house, and up to now
the house is still there,
the kind of house the Europeans used to call
"Slave House."
The building is still at Jang Jang Bure.

At that time when they sold the slaves
the people who caught the slaves for Mansa Musa Molo
were Dikori, Dansa, Malam Buletema, Yungku Mandu,
Kemo Sarata, Funjungu Kemo,
they were the people who got all the slaves,
And Dembo Danso was also among them.
    (An instrumental interlude)

When the Europeans came,
when they brought their ship from Portugal,
the ship used to start its journey from Banjul,
then it went to Sanemunko Joyo to collect slaves there
in the presence of Senneke Jammeh, and Mansa Demba Sanko,
and Samkala Marong, and Wali Mandeba, and Jata Sela.
And anyone who had slaves they collected them all together

and took them to the places called Aladabara and Jufure
to sell them to the Portuguese.
Then the Portuguese put them in their ship
and left there and went to Jang Jang Bure.
When they arrived there they went
right to the slave house to collect the slaves there,
    and take them to the Dutch.
Then the Dutch collected them and sent them to America.
It is because of this
that slaves were plenty in America.

They call them American Negroes.

I heard the final words as the song ended—"Portuguese," "America,"
"Negroes." Musa had listened as intently as I had, and when Alhaji
Fabala leaned back and laid his sticks on the balafon Musa burst out,
"You must have my shilling!" and he stood up, reaching into his pocket
for the ceremonial payment for a particularly moving performance. As I
left him, Alhaji Fabala Kanuteh shook down the sleeves of his robe and
said in a tired voice that the song had come from "his father's father
and his father's fathers." The last thing he told me as I went through
the opening in his compound's fence, sweating with the weight of the
microphones and the recording equipment, was to repeat that the slave
house was still there, up the river.

The slave house is there. If you want to know about slave times you
go to that place.

A few days later, I traveled on a dusty road in the back of a small, jolt-
ing truck fitted with wooden benches, crammed with passengers, and
trailed by a choking cloud of dust up the Gambia River to the island that
in his song was called Jang Jang Bure. I looked for its "Slave House," but
I found only the ruin of the nineteenth-century warehouse of the British
commercial outpost. If there had once been a slave pen built by Mansa
Musa Mola at what was then called Jang Jang Bure, it had been lost for
so many centuries that no one in the village had ever heard of it. The past
of the small gathering of worn stucco buildings at the edge of the dry,
spindly, empty brush lived only in the art of the griot's song.

A New Music in an Old World

Off the west coast of Africa, north of the bulge where the continent widens out to the barren stretches of the Sahara Desert—where the coast line is divided into the modern countries of Morocco, Mauritania, and Senegal—the sun seems to draw the color out of the sea. The choppy current has a pale, drained, soft blue color, and the swells surge toward the land with an uneven, white crest topping the sharp, ribbed waves. As you fly above them, the clouds move in a slow procession, some days a heavy, muffled covering, on clearer days marking the space of the sky like scattered puffs of smoke. It is only as you keep scanning the drifting lines of the clouds that you notice, idly, that the shape of one of the clouds has altered. Instead of the domed crest there is a higher, lifted point to it, as pale and as colorless as the clouds, but with a soft dusting you see more clearly as you drift closer. When you go back to something else you've been thinking about, then look up again a half an hour later you can see that the crested cone that lifted above the clouds has broadened out, with a wide, heavy base that edges out of the fog, its shape as vague as one of the conversations you barely hear from the seats behind you. The shape rising out of the ocean below the clouds is the first of the Canary Islands, only sixty miles from an African coast that is as dust-brown as the spent volcano that formed the island.

The shape of the islands seems to be so much part of the drift of the sun and clouds that for more than a century voyagers were certain that there eight large islands clustered off the dry coast. The position of one of them on the old maps, the island of San Borondón, was less definite than the position of the other seven, shifting with each traveler's account. It was north and west of the small island of La Palma, at the western edge of the Canaries, itself mostly a dry, barren volcanic cone jutting up into the Atlantic. San Borondón was somewhere farther west. The only points of agreement between the early accounts of the different parties of Portuguese and French mariners who claimed to have landed on the island's shores or sailed close to it in the sixteenth century were that a strong current made it a challenge to bring a ship in for a landing, and that there were forests of tall, verdant trees that reached the shore. The force of the currents kept many ships off, but they also provided a protection for the pirates—Portuguese, French, and English—who were said to use the island as a refuge.

Among the romantic artifacts of the period were several maps of San Borondón. One, by an Italian military engineer named Giovanni Torriani was the most detailed, showing two large rivers and several important cities. The size of the island was, on his careful chart, more than two hundred and fifty miles north to south, and almost a hundred miles east to west, which would give it the greatest mass of all the islands. It was only with considerable reluctance that after a hundred years of tracing the island's shape on their maps, the sea captains who sailed west of La Palma finally accepted the fact that there was no eighth pale cone shape rising out of the procession of clouds over the Atlantic. There are only seven major Canary Islands—Lanzarote, Fuerteventura, Gran Canaria, Tenerife, La Gomera, La Palma, and El Hierro. San Borondón never existed.

Perhaps the most difficult thing to anticipate about the Canary Islands today is that the stark landscape could give any hints of a more exotic past. Below the clouds, as you descend toward the crumbling slopes of Gran Canaria, the island containing Las Palmas, the largest city of the Canaries, the dun-colored drift of clouds and haze at the horizon gives way to the gray-brown fields of crumbling lava and the stone-filled ravines of the Canarian landscape. Then the bare landscape gives way to jumbles of stucco buildings, streaks of paved motorways, and dark, tent-like cloth-covered patches where dwarf banana plants are huddled in dense clumps in concrete-block enclosures. The plants are tented under the cloth to fight the steady evaporation in the dry air. However softly muted and outlined in haze the land of the islands looked from the clouds, there is nothing vague about the city you approach as you drive north away from the airport. Las Palmas has more than four hundred thousand people, and most of the building and expansion has come in the last fifty years. Once you're in the city, it seems even larger, since at any moment the island is also the temporary residence of armies of tourists from the countries of northern Europe, where it is usually never as hot as the Canaries on an ordinary cloudy day.

It would make no sense to come to the Canary Islands if you lived in Italy or Greece or Spain, since they share their mild winters with the islands, but the beach cities on the Canaries, the crammed tourist resorts stretching along the south coast of Gran Canaria, and on the nearby large island of Tenerife are a noisy congregation of Germans, Swedes, Danes, Norwegians, Dutch, Belgians, and English, spending part of their mornings reading their own country's newspapers, and large parts of the rest of the day steadily drinking tax-free liquor to help them deal with the dust, or lying in the sun on the sand and tending the flocks of children who splash at the water's edge. Any sun, even on days when the skies are thick with clouds over the Canaries, is better than the dreary winter fogs of Berlin, Hamburg, Manchester, Helsinki, or Oslo. On the wind-swept airport runway I noticed a plane from Iceland, emptying out its pale, sun-starved cargo from Reykjavík.

After the silent drift of the clouds outside the windows of the airplane, the road into the city is another reality. Lines of traffic, a string of businesses along the roadside, small manufacturing plants producing dinner dishes, the Swedish furniture department store IKEA, rows of offices and gaudily decorated restaurants. Insistent advertisements, road signs, battered apartment blocks line the shore. The highway follows the coast to the city—only a dozen miles—and the inland side of the highway is hemmed in by gray, sloping hillsides. There perhaps are more barren slopes somewhere on the earth, but these certainly hold their own among the bleakest. The hills were once volcanoes, and the soil is a crumbling deposit of lava that has eroded to gray stones and dust. Not even Iceland, with its dark fields of lava that stretch away on either side of the highway from its airport to Reykjavík seems as bare. I couldn't see any sign of trees or brush on the Canarian hillsides, just the dense gardens of the banana plants, shadowed under their dirty coverings. Even though it was spring there was only a faint hint of green in the thin scattering of weeds in the ravines that the sporadic rains have worn into the hillsides.

When I arrived, the airport was jammed with tourists. Several planes from northern Europe had landed in the early afternoon, but the busses that pressed patiently against the barriers of the parking area were waiting to take them to the south coast of the island, to the newly built colonies of beach resorts and—hopefully—days of sun. Only a handful of us climbed into the mini-van that would take us to Las Palmas, and certainly I was the only one who had come to the Canaries to look for music.

It was only chance that had brought me to the islands. I had never been conscious of any African-derived music that had its roots in the Canary Islands. One morning I turned on my kitchen radio to a classical radio station while I clattered with pans and dishes cooking myself breakfast.

It was an ordinary morning, and I was only half listening to the music. I was vaguely aware that I was hearing a selection of instrumental pieces performed on a baroque guitar by the estimable Swedish musician Jakob Lindberg. Then as I was standing by the sink I heard a different rhythm, a different melodic shape in the new piece he had begun. I carefully shut off the water and stood silently with the sauce pan I was holding in my hand, waiting for some announcement when the music was finished. Instead of the measured seventeenth-century polyphony and the complex chordal structures of the other pieces Lindberg had played, this was a little melody that repeated itself over and over against a steady pattern of minor harmonies. The melody itself never felt tightly bound to the chords or the rhythms in the bass strings, and for stretches of the piece the harmonies were plucked with lightly syncopated accents. The piece was like melodies I had heard often before, but always on new recordings, and almost never on a program of classical music. What I was hearing, however stiffly it was woven into the studied phrasing of the guitar transcription, was an African-derived reshaping of a European musical dance form.

The short piece ended, and the one that followed it was in the familiar baroque dance mode, with regular harmonies and the rhythms marking out a precise cadence. I had to wait for two more short pieces before an announcer read the titles of what I had heard. It was a composition by a Spanish composer named Sanz, and the piece that had made me stop what I was doing in the kitchen was called "Canarios." The Canary Islands, at that moment, became somewhere I had to visit.

I found, as I came to know Las Palmas, that I had never experienced a place that seemed so far from any hints or suggestions of music of the African diaspora, even if the Moroccan coast was only sixty miles from Fuertaventura, the closest of the islands. As the Canary Islands have experienced the tourist boom of the last thirty years, the city's past, and the past of the islands themselves, have come to reflect much that has been saved, but as much that has been lost. Entire peoples have been lost in the Canaries. Although some island families claim ancestry that links them to the original inhabitants through early intermarriage, there are as many local historians who insist that the Guanches, the tribes who were living on the islands when the Spanish landed, were entirely destroyed. The only agreement seems to be that except for a few place names the culture of those early people has been entirely lost. The Africans who were carried to the islands to take the place of the first inhabitants have also disappeared, leaving only the rhythm of their way of playing the dances I had come to Las Palmas to find.

It was sugar that had brought Africans to the Canaries, just as it brought them to so many other scattered islands in the new Western worlds, and most of what is known about their early presence comes down through the writings of travelers and merchants involved with sugar. One of the first English traders to visit the islands, a sixteenth-century sugar merchant named Thomas Nichols, published a work titled *A Pleasant Description of the Fortunate Islands*, and for many years the term "Fortunate Islands" was used to characterize the Canaries. The islands had been vaguely known from ancient times as blessed lands beyond the Pillars of Hercules, the Greek term for the Straits of Gibraltar, and both of the classic Greek poets of the eighth century B.C., Hesiod and Homer, wrote of beautiful islands in the Atlantic, sometimes called the Hesperides. The Canaries could be what they meant. Although English speakers associate the name of the islands with the name of the bird, the canary, the birds were probably named for the islands. That is the only thing that is reasonably certain about the use of the word "canary" for the islands or for anything found on them. One common theory for the name is that it comes from the Latin word for dog, "canes." The islands were known to the Romans in the pre-Christian era, and in an account written by the historian Pliny the Elder he referred to the islands as "Canaria, so named from the great number of dogs (canes) of very large size."

Pliny was reporting on the journey to the islands by a King Juba II, who had been designated as monarch of Numidia and Mauritania, areas at the fringes of the Roman Empire, and who in 25 B.C. had sailed to the islands. Earlier Phoenician voyagers had discovered that a lichen that was common on the islands, called *orchilla* by the Spanish, was useful as a purple dye, and Juba attempted to establish centers for gathering the dye on the islands closest to the coast of Africa. His own name for them was *Insulae Purpuriae*, Purple Islands. To the Romans, impressed by stories of the sun and the continual summer, they were *Insulae Fortunatae*, Fortunate Islands, and the Spanish also used the term *Islas Afortunadas* for several centuries. For Pliny the limit of the known world was the island of El Hierro, the westernmost of the group.

To add to the confusion it also seems that Juba was in error when he said the islands were uninhabited. Archaeological excavations have found that there were early settlements of a Berber people of North Africa living in caves on the slopes of the hills, and they were known as Canarii, members of a tribe in Morocco. The name of the inhabitants could have been passed on to the islands. The islands were finally mapped by a fleet of three caravels with Portuguese and Italian commissions in 1341, although the existence of San Borondón would continue

In the Old Town, Las Palmas.

to tantalize seafarers for another hundred and fifty years. There is more agreement about the presence of people on the islands after May 1, 1402, when a Norman adventurer named Jean de Bethencourt landed with a small party and commenced the tragic struggle that ended in 1496 with the native population dead, enslaved, or scattered. Although they were all called Guanches they were probably from several different cultural groups. They were usually described as of light brown complexion, with blue or gray eyes, and blondish hair that they wore to their waists. In a park in downtown Las Palmas there is a Victorian-style bronze statue of Guanches playing in a pool and waterfall. Their cheerfully skinny, naked appearance is as much a product of a later imagination as the flowing water in the fountain.

Las Palmas is crowded and it is losing its struggle with the relentlessly increasing traffic, but it is also a beautiful city. It probably should be described as more than one city, since its major areas are so different from each other. The Old City, which was constructed even before the destruction of the Guanches was complete, was walled and fortified, and it is still largely contained within itself; its short streets lined with closed, austere stucco houses fronting against narrow stone sidewalks, with small wooden balconies on the upper stories, which nobody seems to use. On his first voyage to the unknown western ocean in

1492, Columbus was forced to leave one of his caravels, the Pinta, in the primitive harbor of Las Palmas to have the rudder refitted, and he completed the preparations for his voyage on the island of La Gomera to the west. It is probable that he also stayed briefly in Las Palmas. A small, austere church and a house nearby are the legendary sites of his visit.

The well-known tourist beaches are spread along the southern coast of the island, but Las Palmas has developed its own long sweep of beach on an extended peninsula that separates the open ocean from the harbor. The section of the city along the beachfront is a maze of narrow streets all more or less leading to the new, broad brick and stone promenade that stretches along the entire two and a half miles of beach. It is a noisy area crowded with long-term tourists, many of them from Sweden and Finland, who settle in for the winter to take advantage of the cheap prices. There are also noisy crews in off the freighters in the harbor, with the usual scattering of the gaudily dressed women waiting for them in the brightly lit doorways of the bars and restaurants. On weekends, when the weather is hot, the entire city seems to descend on the beach, and the narrow streets take on some of the gaiety of an unending, laughing family party.

With the land of the Old City already filled, the port area completed, and the neighborhoods along the water between them crowded with shops and apartment buildings, there was no way for Las Palmas to continuing growing except by going up, so a new city has grown on the stony ridges above the harbor. At any hour of the day or night people toil up long flights of stairs built into the steep hillside, though for most of the people who work in the businesses and shops closer to the harbor, the neighborhood buses grind up twisting streets to the new areas of modern, high-rise apartment blocks.

The simplest way to begin looking for the musical composition I had come to find was obviously to ask musicians about it, and it was because of this that I had journeyed to Las Palmas, instead of to one of the smaller cities on another island. I found the new, dour, gray stone building that had been designed as the city's Conservatorio Superior de Musica on a narrow back street close to the Old City. The looming structure had more of the atmosphere of a municipal office building than it did a busy music school, but its steps were crowded with students in jeans and shirtsleeves. At the head of the steps inside the door was a bulletin board with a clutter of announcements for student recitals and rehearsals pinned between handwritten notes offering rooms for rent, cheap music lessons, and instruments for sale. There was a reception desk along a corridor and using my uneasy schoolbook Spanish I spoke to the women behind the desk, asking if there was anyone there who might be familiar with a style of music called *canarios*. One of the women, hesitating, called out to a young instructor who was talking to a friend. He answered my question by smiling, humming a few measures of a lightly skipping *canarios* melody and asking me in English, "Is that it?"

I'm sure that I showed my surprise as I nodded, yes, that was it. There was a consultation among several people who were standing in the corridor. A young woman who I thought must be an instructor, with the Canaarian women's beautiful clear skin and austerely combed dark hair, studied an article I had copied from the Spanish music encyclopedia about *canarios*; then turned to speak with one of the women behind the desk. I should call someone else, a guitarist who also taught at the conservatory, but who didn't have any classes that day. One of the women dialed a number on the desk phone and handed me the receiver. "Yes," the man I spoke to responded, "Yes, we can meet. Not today, but tomorrow."

The next day I waited for him in an old square, the Alameda Colon. Around the open space there were the ornate, formal façades of nineteenth-century buildings, and tables from two open-air restaurants filled most of the sidewalk space across the street from the small park that was the center of the square. I was anxiously watching people sitting at tables around me or hurrying past on the pavement, since I had no idea what the man I'd spoken with looked like. Then a tall, broad-shouldered, good-looking man, perhaps in his late twenties, wearing a casual T-shirt and dark, unironed trousers, hurried up a side street, and I realized from his relaxed smile, that he was Carlos Oramas, the guitarist I'd been told about.

Since the day was warm, we stayed outside at one of the tables on the sidewalk. We sat at a breezy table covered with my notes and papers, and glasses of Tropical, Las Palmas's fine local beer. Carlos had an open, engaging expression, and it was obvious that the music I had come to find was something he knew about and enjoyed. He wore his curly black hair long and tied in a bushy tangle at the back of his neck. We had enough language in common to talk about his music and music in the Canaries. He was thirty, and he worked part of the week teaching classical guitar to eighteen students at the Conservatorio. He had spent many years playing only the classical repertory, but there were so many of kinds of music that interested him now. He had recently toured Europe with the excellent Gran Canary Symphony Orchestra, performing the Joaquín Rodrigo guitar concerto, *Concierto de Aranjuez*—twenty concerts in almost as many days, and I had the impression that for the moment the tour had been enough classical guitar for a few weeks. He knew of the old music called *canarios*; but for someone like him, who had grown up in the islands, it wasn't a style of classical music, even if the first time I'd heard it had been on a classical music station. "Una música clásica o una música folclórica?" "Classical music or folk music?," I asked.

He grinned and shrugged apologetically, "For us it is folkloric."

Some of the pages I'd copied from the music encyclopedias had examples of *canarios* from the sixteenth and seventeenth centuries and he hummed melodies and counted out rhythms on the worn wooden table top. Carlos was thoughtful for a moment and looked away across the square.

"We are part of Africa—we are so close—but we say there is no influence on our culture from Africa. Not only music, but all of our culture." He bent over the pages and studied one of the melodies again. "The things that are African were changed here. It isn't African music any more. It's Canaries music. Then the Europeans took it and changed it again, but it still is our music."

Finally he looked at his watch. We had talked most of the afternoon and it was almost five. He had to get to a dress rehearsal for a concert of folk music and dance that was going to be presented that evening in a new theater close to the beach. Did I want to come to the concert? Of course. He would arrange for a ticket. Then suddenly he remembered something and began to laugh.

"Tonight I am going to play one of the pieces we talked about—the piece by Sanz! It's a *canario* we play for a dance!"

Had I come any closer to the little piece I'd heard on the radio only a few months before? Gaspar Sanz, I had learned by turning to the *Grove Dictionary of Music and Musicians*, was the figure whose name was associated with two of the small pieces still played today. The dates of his birth and death are uncertain, but it is known that he studied music, and became a skilled guitarist in the middle of the seventeenth century. At the same time he studied theology at the University of Salamanca. When his university studies were completed he entered the priesthood and traveled to Italy to continue his musical studies. His two *canarios* were included in a guitar instruction manual he published in Zaragoza, after his return to Spain. There were two editions, the first in 1674, and the second, which has been reproduced in modern facsimile, in 1697.

Sanz's instruction manual was so popular that there were several subsequent printings, and other musicians were inspired to create their own collections. The book is an oblong, hand-drawn collection of pieces in tablature titled *Instrucción de música sobre la guitarra española*. In his

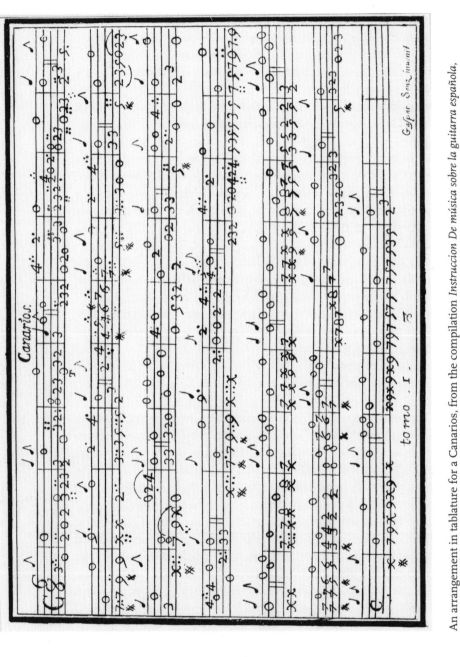

An arrangement in tablature for a Canarios, from the compilation *Instruccion De música sobre la guitarra española*, by Gaspar Sanz (Zaragoza, 1674).

introduction to the second edition Sanz described himself as coming from the province of Aragon and mentioned his studies at Salamanca. He then discussed the way of tuning the guitar—double strung, with five "courses"—and described the most common playing techniques, the *rasqueado* or strummed style, and the *ponteado* or plucked style. He also wrote charmingly about the guitar as an instrument, and about the music that can be performed on it. Much of what he wrote is still valuable for guitarists today, and his treatise on playing techniques has been a priceless source for anyone studying early music. The pieces were written out in guitar tablature, instead of musical notation, but Carlos, after a moment of fingering some of the measures of the old tablature, said excitedly, "It's just the same today. I can read it!"

What you hear in the *canarios* as the form was taken up by other composers are the lilting, gently syncopated accents of the rhythm and the harmonies. The melodies generally consist of simple repetitive patterns. None of the other dance pieces in Sanz's collection suggest these same characteristics or the same musical sources. It is in the layering of the rhythms and the tonal scale of the melody that the African roots are most strongly suggested. The melodies and the accents reflect the familiar patterns of adaptation and assimilation that the small dances share with many of the other African-influenced musical styles that emerged in Europe and the Americas. Also, like so much of the music that has Africa as one of its sources, the *canarios* have an infectious swing.

The earliest forms of the dance which would become the distinct Canarian adaptation may have been brought in the baggage of adventurers from the north of Spain in the early years of the conquest. By the time the island's dance had become known in Europe, less than a century later, however, it had been transmuted by the musicians of the Canaries, many of them slaves. What surprised me at first was that until I heard the little piece by Sanz and became curious enough to spend an hour in the library, I had never thought of the Canary Islands as part of the world of slavery. It was the word "sugar" in the early histories that told me that there had been a period of slavery in the islands. In those early centuries of sugar production the labor of cutting the cane and boiling the juice was so brutal and debilitating that only slaves could be forced to do it. The Spaniards introduced sugar cultivation in the islands even before the wars with the Guanches had ended, and the islands' first significant exports were refined sugar shipped in crude barrels to Spain.

In a useful pamphlet by Jose Miguel Alzola, *A Brief History of the Canary Islands*,[1] I found a more detailed account of the early years of slavery in the Canaries.

A racial contribution (to the island's population) with an unhappier origin was that of the slaves acquired by the landowners for the cultivation of their estates and the work in the sugar refineries. There were frequent expeditions to Barbary, on the nearby African coast, for the purpose of obtaining cheap labor. These expeditions were encouraged and supported by the Crown. Many black slaves were also brought to the islands. In Gran Canaria alone, there were, in 1677, 6,468 black and mulatto people, some free and some slaves. To cite an example of slave trading, in 1653 a boat loaded with two hundred blacks arrived at Las Palmas harbour, and within a few days all of these had been sold at a good price.

There was so much contact between Africa and the islands that in the middle of the sixteenth Century on the two islands closest to the African coast, Fuerteventura and Lanzarote, there were more people characterized as Moors than Spaniards. In the writings about the Canaries from this period I found the terms Berber, Moor, and African used freely, sometimes interchangeably, although the Moors were well known to the Spaniards. It was only in 1492 that the Spaniards succeeded in driving the last of the Moors from the parts of southern Spain that had been occupied for eight hundred years. It is perhaps the confusion over these terms that has caused the *canarios* to be generally overlooked as one of the earliest examples of the music of the African diaspora which reached every part of the European musical world. With almost disbelief I read that sometimes when the pieces were danced in Europe the performers not only dressed in what were considered African costumes, they blackened their faces and sang and spoke in an imitation of African languages that could be considered a foreshadowing of the nineteenth-century minstrel show!

It is generally thought that the *canario* made its way to Spain with the slaves who sailed to the peninsula (as Spain is called by Canarians) as part of the crews of trading vessels, or who were brought to work as slaves in Spanish households in the middle of the sixteenth century. By the time Sanz compiled his collection, the melodies of the *canarios* had been known in Europe for more than a century, and like all musical traditions transmitted aurally the idiom had undergone many changes. What is surprising about the islands' little dance pieces is that they continued to have a distinctive character, even if they inevitably became more Europeanized. By the end of its long reign of popularity, in the middle of the eighteenth century, the dance had been stylized into something like a jig, but it was still characterised as a "canary"—the English term—or as the French "canarie" until early in the nineteenth century.

The earliest mention that has been found of the dance and its music is from 1552, in the history of the first years of the conquest, *Historia general de las Indias* by Francesco Lopez de Gomera. In nearly every subsequent reference to the melodies they are described as coming from the Canary Islands, and often the description includes a reference to African antecedents. In the collection *Intavolatura de liuto* published by the Italian lutenist Giulio Cesare Barbetta in Venice in 1585, the music for a *canario* is described as "Moresca detta la cabarie," by which he meant "A Moorish piece called 'a canary.'" The best known of the early descriptions of the music and the dance appeared in a widely circulated treatise on the art of the dance by a French cleric named Thoinot Arbeau, who was born in Dijon in 1520 and died in Langres in 1595. In his *Orchesographie*, published in 1588, he included a melody for a canary, and with each note he also indicated the step or movement of the dance.

Especially interesting is Arbeau's discussion of the dance.

> Some say that it originated in the Canary Islands—others—whose idea I share, say that it originated in a ballet composed for a masquerade where the dancers were dressed as Kings or Queens from Mauretania, or else as wild people, colored and wearing feathers . . . A man takes his woman and they dance together to the rhythm of the music to the end of the room. He leaves her there and dances back to the place where they started, looking back at her all the time; after that he dances to the woman again and does various dance combinations and then dances back again. The woman now dances forward in the same way . . . The combination of steps should be lively, but strange and fantastic with a strongly barbaric character.[2]

I also learned from my reading that the *canario* was so well known in European musical history, and it was so firmly embedded in the European classical repertoire over such an extended period, that most modern music dictionaries include entries describing the music and the dance, and Arbeau and Sanz are frequently quoted. What was more interesting for me was that the most comprehensive work on the *canario*—a long article bringing all of the sources together and discussing their significance—had been done by Lothar Siemens Hernandez, a musicologist who works at the National Museum of the Canary Islands—El Museo Canario—in Las Palmas.

I found that although he was close to retirement age, Siemens was still working at the museum, and when I reached him by phone he said that he would be glad to talk to me. The city has retained many of its Spanish customs, even with its floods of tourists, and it still closes down for a two or two and a half-hour siesta in the afternoon. He asked me to meet him in the museum at 5:30, when the streets came to life again. Siemens was a plump, pale, affable man in his sixties, his hair graying, his expression at the same time friendly and anxious. He was wearing a light suit and a tie. When I came to the door of the museum he was waiting for me in the bare entrance hall, talking to a guard at the ponderous wooden desk that stood against one wall.

Siemens, like anyone connected to a large museum anywhere in the world, had many things on his mind, but he was pleased at being asked about his work on the *canario*, and in a moment he was speaking volubly in excellent English, his hands moving expressively as he spoke. He led the way into the museum's quiet bookshop. In what I now recognized as the very distinct Canarian accent he asked the director of the shop if there were any copies of the offprint pamphlet the museum had done of his article. After some rummaging in the shelves, a copy was found and he presented it to me with a modest flourish. *Orígenes y devenir del baile llama do "el canario"* (Origins and Transformations in the Dance Called "The Canario").[3]

Siemens pointed to the date on the cover of the pamphlet, 1998, shook his head, and laughed loudly.

"I began to think about this in 1963, and I was looking for one thing, the date of the first time the name of the dance the canarios appears in Spanish history." It was Siemens who had supplied the date I had found in my reading. "1552. It is in 1552. I looked for that for thirty-five years."

He took the pamphlet for a moment, glancing at some of the pages, then he shook his head again and handed it back.

"Thirty-five years! But this is what I have decided about the canarios after so many years."

We stood talking, voices echoing in the shadowy corridor. For Siemens the important question had been the possible connection between the dance and the older Guanche culture.

"The dance originally came from the north of Spain with the conquest," he said emphatically. "That is where the men came from. You read about it there. I put everything in that I know."

For me, however, what was important was that even if the dance might have been originally Spanish, the music and the way the dance was performed could have been transformed by the decades in which the Canaries had large numbers of African slaves. I asked him this question, and he was thoughtful for a moment, then he nodded agreeably.

"Some acculturation was possible."

The entry in Grove's dictionary for the Canary, written by Richard Hudson and Meredith Ellis Little, mentions numerous descriptions of the dance, "11 choreographies, including three by English choreographers, are extant . . . Most are difficult theater dances employing virtuoso steps such as cabriolets."[4] As we talked in the corridor Siemens had also mentioned the difficulty of the dance, as a further indication that its ties to the islands' slave culture were tenuous. Following the success of the dance in the court ballets composed by Jean-Baptiste Lully in the 1660s, the *canarios* became popular as an energetic, demanding dance for stage performance, with athletic leaps and heel stamps. In recent years, however, we have seen the same phenomenon with Irish folk step-dancing. The success of Michael Flatley and his theatrical versions of the folk style have completely altered the popular conception of the old native dance. Siemens himself cited early travelers in his article on the *canarios*, and they described it as "sweet"—"dulce son canario"—writing that it was a popular dance of the islands' courtesans, and that it was precise and witty, not immodest, and performed with "politeness."

The hotel where I was staying was the cheapest I'd been able to find through the travel agent. It was, the woman had said with a hopeful smile, a little noisy, but it was close to the beach, and she was certainly right about that. The popular wide promenade that hugged the two-and-a-half-mile crescent of sand was only two hundred yards down a narrow street from the hotel entrance. On warm afternoons the crowds at the beach were loud enough, but aside from the beach's pleasures, the neighborhood was noisy and rundown, and the hotel itself was a second-class version of the kind of Spanish establishments you usually find close to a railroad station. The nights were a persistent whine of motor scooters, a rumble of garbage trucks, and shouting in several languages, though once a family in the next room varied the monotony by arguing all night in shrill torrents of what sounded like Chinese as I pulled the pillow over my head and tried to sleep.

The concert of folk music and dance that Carlos had told me about was in a new auditorium building at the distant end of the beach, and since the evening was still sunny I decided to take the half-hour walk to get there. The tide was streaming in, and the low, eddying waves had flowed up onto the narrow strip of beach, but there were still shouting clusters of skinny boys kicking footballs and runners stoically splashing barefoot through the wash of the surf. The auditorium for the folk concert was in a new building beside the city's even newer concert house, the Alfredo Kraus Concert Hall, named for the celebrated opera singer, who was a native of the islands. It had been designed by a Basque architect to suggest the austerity and the rigors of the old cities along the desert coast. It was a high, daunting stone edifice, gray-brown, almost windowless, as barren as a desert fortress, with deep, sharply refined terraces that lent a harsh geometry to the rising walls. It was a stunning architectural achievement, and the auditorium inside had been finished with rich wood and burnished metal. On the sunset of the first day I was in Las Palmas, I walked to see it, and I spent an hour sitting on one after another of the paved terraces surrounding its walls, studying its severities from one angle then another.

The auditorium where the folk concert was being held shared some of its blend of austerity and opulence, though it was designed for less ambitious presentations. There was a low stage, without a curtain, and the stage had been decorated with antique farm implements and old musical instruments. When the musicians and the dancers made their entrance from a doorway at the side of the stage it was clear that the folklore that survived in the Canaries today was Spanish. Carlos and the other were dressed in costumes that had their origins in rural Spain. Blue collarless shirts with baggy sleeves, gray trousers with broad strips of black cloth for a belt, soft, light-toned leather shoes and brown fedoras for the men. The women were in a variety of rural dresses and skirts, with wide brimmed, floppy straw hats, aprons, and a cloth tied at the back of their necks to keep the sun off.

The program was ambitious, with a large and enthusiastic group of amateur performers. Twenty-five musicians accompanied almost as many dancers, who filled much of the open stage in front of the orchestra. Several of the men and women also sang as a chorus. The instrumentalists entered with four different kinds of guitars, a tambourine, a large, venerable bass drum that a serious-faced woman in a stiff, wide brimmed hat thumped with a padded stick, and an accordion that was used for a late-nineteenth-century couples dance. Carlos was playing a thin, five-stringed guitar-like instrument which I recognized as the Canaries' version of the small guitars of Spain and Italy called a *timple* (pronounced *teem*-play). After a friendly introduction by one of the instrumentalists, the program began with a simple group dance that was titled "El Canario." As two guitarists accompanied him with simple harmonies, Carlos stepped forward and played the little Sanz piece over and over for the swaying dancers. As the dance ended there was loud, supportive applause from the audience.

The narrow-bodied timple that Carlos had played with such rhythmic freshness, has been the subject of much speculation. Its shape is different from instruments on the "Peninsula," but the question of why it is different has troubled people for some time. In the notes to an album of traditional timple pieces played by Totoyo Millares, one of the modern masters of the timple, Lothar Siemens, who had also written so much about the *canarios*, suggested that one possibility for the source of the distinctive narrow, deep body of the timple was an African instrument. After discussing the old Spanish *vihuelas* as the possible antecedent, he wrote:

> But we add a second possibility. In the areas of Africa close to us there exists a type of Moorish guitar with a sound box incredibly similar to our timple. In an area of Africa, effectively from Mauritania to Guinea along the Atlantic, as as we enter the heart of Africa to Mali and Niger, there exists this curious instrument with a thin neck, but with a sound box very similar to the timple: right handed, long, and curved on the back. With this in mind we should formulate here another hypothesis which might be considered more closely in the future. It is the following: It is known that in the past many slaves were brought to the Canaries from Africa. In the middle of the sixteenth century Fuerteventura and Lanzarote had more Moors than Spaniards. Many times these islands were raided by Berber pirates and repopulated with a profusion of Africans captured along the Atlantic coast. We ask ourselves today if the construction in the Canaries of the classic small guitar the timple, with its sound box inspired by these Moorish guitars . . . is not the consequence of the African traces that remain in the easternmost islands of our Archipelago.[5]

When I talked with Siemens in the corridor of the museum I asked him about the notes he'd written. He looked surprised and asked to see them.

"That was long ago!"

He pointed to the date of the album. It had been released in 1973.

"I don't think that way now," he said briskly. "It's all Spanish. The timple is nothing more than a little Spanish guitar."

As the evening of folk dance drifted past with flushed dancers filling the stage, the audiences continued to express their enthusiastic appreciation for the exhibition that was being presented by performers who I realized were friends and family members. After I had watched several of the dances I understood why there was so little interest in an African presence in the islands' heritage of cultures. Whatever the slaves had been called—Moors, Berbers, or Africans—they had become lost early in the Canaries' history. Some of the dances I was watching imitated the movements of the work on the farms, and they mimicked the usual digging, planting, and harvesting motions I had seen in other places. The cruelties of sugar planting and cane cutting never came into the dance movements. At the end of the performance, as all of us stood and applauded noisily, I spent a moment with Carlos, meeting his wife, and we watched the excited families gather around the dancers. We agreed that we would talk again, then I walked slowly back to the hotel along the beach. The flood lights were still shining over the sand and the boys were still playing football, and in the restaurants I could see young couples dancing the latest international disco styles, the rhythms of their African past overlaid with modern sounds and interpretations. Elderly Swedish couples, their bodies as brown as weathered boards from the sun, dined slowly, with quiet laughter, under the night sky.

The Canary Islands Room in the large Victorian building at the back of the small square where I had met Carlos a few days before had the very reasonable explanation for the disappearance of African culture from the islands. Sugar, once again, had decided what happened to people's lives. Despite the early success of the small sugar plantings, the Canaries have very little water. The landscape is a brushy desert. Even if there had been more rain five hundred years ago there still wasn't much. When the conquest of the West Indies opened the island of Santo Domingo for sugar cultivation, the growers immediately recognized that this new land—fertile, hot, and wet—would give them higher yields, and in the forests was enough wood for the endless fires needed to refine the raw cane syrup. Slaves were simply part of the work process, and when the planters boarded the small ships to cross to the West Indies their slaves went with them. The slaves were not only the raw labor force that dug the soil, chopped the cane, turned the wheels of the mills, and tended the fires of the refinery pots—they were also seasoned specialists who knew *how* to do all these things. It has been so long since those of us who live in industrial societies have worked field crops by hand that we've forgotten how much of the work that goes on in these unyielding conditions demands skill and technical knowledge. Africans had grown and harvested sugar for hundreds of years, and when there were new lands to be cleared and planted, it was African slaves who were driven to do the work.

With the early generations of slaves disappearing from the Canaries, and with no need for large numbers of new slaves, the free people of color were slowly assimilated into the larger population, or they traveled the short distance back to the cities along the African coast. The Spanish had set up courts of the Inquisition in the Canaries, just as they had everywhere else where they had established colonies, and the judicial records indicate that the courts were occasionally involved in dealing with the presence of Moors, but they were more seriously engaged in rooting out any Jews who still had not conceded to the enforced conversions to the Catholic faith.

On the weekend after the concert the air was hot, the sun was stifling, and the city came to a standstill. The beach was a long carpet of sweating bodies sprawled on brightly colored towels spread out on the sand. The loudest sound was the squealing of the children splashing in the water. As Sunday afternoon dwindled into a deepening umber sunset, I noticed files of men and boys streaming away from the beach, and followed them back into the maze of streets behind the long promenade. They were on their way to unpretentious open-air bars on the street corners to look at television screens that had been set up on benches. For the first time in the history of Las Palmas football (the game Americans refer to as "soccer"), the city's team was playing in the proud Spanish First Division. The television screens were turned on to the game against the mighty Barcelona team in a packed Catalan stadium. When a lanky Las Palmas forward scored the first goal, it felt as though the entire city was being rocked by a small earthquake. Men with gray hair and large stomachs and boys as skinny as the birds along the beach leaped to their feet, fists waving, and there was so much shouting it was impossible to hear the voice of the announcer on the television. I could hear the roaring from every corner. But it was not to be a day of miracles. As Barcelona went on methodically to score the next four goals the mood became more and more subdued, and by the fourth Barcelona goal the handful of men still sitting at the tables set up on the street corners were idly talking about something else.

When I saw Carlos the next day we didn't talk about the game, though I knew he followed the team. We met in the square again, then walked the two or three blocks to the Conservatorio and he showed me the modest studio where he did his teaching. It was bare and functional; a serviceable desk and two or three chairs, a large mirror on one wall for the students to study their hand positions. Behind the desk was a cassette and CD player for reviewing lessons and lesson materials. He wanted me to hear a piece from a jazz project he was recording with friends for CD release. The music was a beautifully modulating tonal landscape shaped around the sound of Carlos's light-toned timple, but grounded in the textures of the accompanying guitars, a bass, and a muted trumpet. It was modern jazz at its most intelligent, with an understated, compelling swing. At the same time it was distinctly Spanish and completely individual. We talked again about the *canarios* I had come to the island to find, and he took his guitar out of the case. He looked at me and smiled.

"Do you know John Dowland?"

Yes, I knew Dowland's music.

"We know so many kinds of music, and all of it becomes part of what we play ourselves."

He began to play a simple, beautifully phrased dance by Dowland, originally composed for the lute, but as effective in the light legato tones of the guitar. Then Carlos leaned back and talked for a moment about the recent European tour. Finally he picked up the guitar again. Grinning over at me he began to play a *canario*. It was one of the classic melodies, but he played it with the effortless flow of a folk song. He played three or four choruses, improvising melodies over the repetitive harmonies in a style that could only be Canarian. Then he brought the piece to a graceful close and laughed.

"But we don't play like that now. We like to play blues and jazz."

3 ✳ Go Down Chariot

The Georgia Sea Islands and Fanny Kemble.
The Slavery Spirituals, Lydia Parrish
and Zora Neale Hurston

It was Fanny Kemble who brought me to the Georgia Sea Islands. Years before I had encountered the collection of her letters written to a New England friend in 1838 from a plantation on one of the chain of shifting islands stretched along the coast of Georgia south of Savannah. For more than two decades she was forced to delay their publication, but when her book, *Journal of a Residence on a Georgia Plantation*, ultimately appeared, it was instantly recognized as a classic depiction of slavery in the American South. No one had ever described the privations of early plantation life and the harsh conditions that were the daily experience of the slaves with such a flood of detail. Her wrenching anguish at what she was witnessing filled the letters, just as she was again and again left almost speechless by the beauty and the tranquility of the wild growth, the light and the smells of the earth around her.

Although Kemble made an effort to conceal the name of the owner of the plantation where she had lived, it was an open secret that it had been the property of her husband, and even after he divorced her and took their children from her, his determined efforts to stop the book as well as her consciousness of the effect its publication could have on her family, succeeded in suppressing it for twenty-five years. Although friends who knew of what she had written pleaded with her to speak out, the book was not published until 1863. When I picked it up again, years after I had first read it, I found myself turning its pages with renewed excitement. I realized now that what she was describing was a living landscape, and her descriptions of the slaves around her were portrayals of people who had lived on that land with her. Would there be anything left of it today, I thought? Was it now only a lingering shadow of history? So many years later, could there still be some trace of the people and the island she had experienced?

In part Kemble's letters were also the story of her journey, both the physical journey as an English woman traveling with two small children, one only a baby, her luggage weighted with enough clothing and housing utensils for her and Irish girl who was the baby's maid to remain on the plantation for several months, as well as the emotional journey of trying to find who she would become in her months of isolation. On the first days of the journey from Philadelphia, where she had been living with her husband, the tired and increasingly grimy small party traveled by train, but train travel late in 1837 was only a little better than journeying by stagecoach, with the added discomfort of the perpetual shroud of soot from the wood fired engine. From Savannah, she was rowed south in a flat supply barge out through the maze of shapeless mud islands that lined the coast to her husband's plantation on Butler Island.

Although Kemble had traveled by boat in 1838, there are fewer boats now, and since I wanted to know something about the land that surrounded the closest settlement to her, what was then the crude frontier town of Darien, Georgia, I made the journey by car. Driving south from New York in the first weeks of early spring I followed the traffic on the interstates to Savannah, then turned off toward the coastline. Within a few miles I could see that the salt marshes along the sea were still a half world that hovered unsteadily between land and water. The roads I was driving grew smaller and narrower as I entered the separate world that skirts Georgia's flat coastal plain, and the edges of the plain itself were a shadowy contour of low dirt hills that hovered over my right shoulder as I drove. The hills were thinly covered with stands of pine and leaf trees, clearings of wild grass and thick leaved brush, with overgrown paths that meandered off into the brush. Along the creek beds there were scattered houses in pinched openings cut out of the growth of the trees.

On the other side of the road, toward the gray slick of the Atlantic, I could see beyond the salt marshes to the last points of land where wind-worried sentinels of trees clustered on half-submerged shelves of earth. There were scenes that could have been lifted from her book's pages. I sometimes glimpsed short stretches of beach, but for miles along the coast the marshes themselves were the shoreline. No paths crossed them. The road had to be lifted over them on pilings. The marshes nudged out into the ocean in a monotonous, unvarying rich green tone. A land of tough sea grass, with roots in black, slick mud that floated with the tides two times each day. Only a kind of grass with roots stubborn enough to cling to the earth through the ceaseless floods could live there. Where they met the sea, the shape of the marshes was a dark curve of grass standing two feet above the water, the curve spreading away in a series of long, rounded crescents, as guileless as a child's drawing.

As gaps in the sea of grass opened beneath the road ahead of me, I realized that to bridge these openings, the roads had to be lifted above the marshes. There were pathways around her, but if on her walks

The Sea Island
salt marshes.

close to the rough plantation cabin Kemble did find traces of one, it
was a woodland trail, and she was continually warned to look out for
snakes. The real pathways of the marshes were the inland rivers and
creeks, threaded into a maze of channels by the thick burden of earth
that they'd carried with them across the inland coastal plain. It was this
burden of earth that became the flat, sandy soil of the sea islands. Carrying the earth of the new banks and the new headlands with them after
each inland rainfall, the streams wandered in shapeless configurations
that shifted with the cycle of seasons as they struggled to free themselves
from the marshes and come to the sea. The shallow banks of the streams
I crossed on the road's bridges were sloughs of brown mud that turned
and twisted on themselves as the river's currents tried blindly to find a
new way to the ocean that had to be somewhere on the other side of this
sea of dark grass.

On her first days on the island Kemble was as struck by the evanescent
nature of the earth around her, though she expressed herself in terms
appropriate to her time.

. . . The two elements are so fused hereabouts that there are hardly such things as earth or water proper; that which styles itself the former is a fat, muddy, slimy sponge, that, floating half under the turbid river, looks yet saturated with the thick waves which every now and then reclaim their late dominion, and cover it almost entirely; the water again, cloudy and yellow, like pea-soup, seems but a solution of such islands, rolling turbid and thick with alluvium, which it both gathers and deposits as it sweeps along with a swollen, smooth rapidity that almost deceives the eye.[1]

As I drove slowly, winding the car window down so I could smell the laden spring air, it was clear that I had found the land Kemble had written about, but what was left of the people who had been such a vivid presence in her letters? The older wood-framed houses I passed seemed to be empty, or lived in only part-time. There were no signs of gardens or even flowers planted around them. After a few hours of driving, however, I became conscious that what she had seen was all around me in the coarse thickets. I stopped the car on the shoulder of the road and climbed to a small rise. As I shaded my eyes and studied the overgrown vegetation stretching away from me, I could see that I was driving over abandoned fields. Beneath the covering of grass and tangled weeds I could make out the scars of irregular ridges dug into the earth. Under the weeds were the signs of eroded furrows and dikes, almost obliterated now, but still visible in the afternoon light as the sun slanted across the fields in a darkening, golden flood that cast rows of shadows where the furrows had been dug so long ago. The ragged lines were a sign that once this land had held the people who filled her pages.

For the historians who write about her, and for the biographers who have turned to her life again and again, it is, in part, Kemble herself that they find so fascinating and the contradictory roles her life demanded. She had grown up in England as a *Kemble*, one of the most famous English theatrical families, and whatever her misgivings about a life in the theater—and she had many—she made her début as Juliet in the family's London theater at the age of seventeen to help her father through financial difficulties. She caused a sensation, and when she and her father toured America a few years later she became even more celebrated. Sometime histories of Georgia in the troubled years before the Civil War include a well-known portrait of her. She is leaning toward the artist, her face a blend of innocence and careful, watchful intelligence. She was already known as a woman who would say what she felt, and who was difficult to convince of anything she didn't believe. She was wearing a light colored gown, bare over her neck and shoulders, and her waist, as a concession to the tastes of the day, was bound into a corset that looked so tight that she must have had trouble breathing. With her dark hair in loose ringlets and her face dominated by her clear eyes and a suggestion of a smile, the portrait presented a woman of distinctive beauty and an only half-concealed individuality.

Perhaps because she didn't intend to spend her life on the stage, she allowed herself to fall in love with a tall, thin, darkly good looking southerner named Pierce Butler whom she met while she was performing in Philadelphia. What she didn't know, or understand—or wasn't told during their brief courtship—was that Butler's fortune came from two plantations his family owned on the Georgia Sea Islands. One plantation, within sight of Darien on a small island that came to be called Butler Island, grew rice. The other, on St. Simon's Island close to Brunswick, fifteen miles to the south by waterway, grew cotton. The work on the plantation was performed by more than seven hundred slaves who, like the land, were Butler's property.

When they had been married for three years and already had their first child—a daughter named Sarah—Butler made his first winter visit to the plantations. Because of the dangers of disease, as well as the stifling discomfort of the summer heat, the white plantation owners remained past the month of March only at considerable risk. In the exchange of infectious diseases that followed the conquest of the new continents, the slaves had brought yellow fever and a common form of malaria. In the thousands of years that Africa had struggled with these diseases Africans themselves had built up a partial immunity, though their bloodstream still contained the sources of the fevers. Within a few years the diseases had become so prevalent that most of the owners made determined efforts to stay away from the infected areas in the most dangerous months.

The next year, in December 1837, when Butler again made the journey, Kemble, who had only a few months before given birth to their second daughter, Frances, insisted on going with him, even though the only place for them to stay on the island was a cramped and uncomfortable cabin. Kemble was twenty-nine, her husband a year younger, and their daughter Sarah was three. For most of the year the only white people on the plantation were the overseer and his wife, and he maintained order through a handful of "drivers," slaves themselves who could flog the field workers—but only with a prescribed number of strokes. The heavier flogging—up to fifty strokes—was left to the overseer. Among their friends in Philadelphia there was criticism of her plans to stay on the plantation, since she went there already prejudiced against slavery, but she answered sharply, "Assuredly I *am* going prejudiced against slavery. For I am an Englishwoman, in whom the absence of such a prejudice would be disgraceful."[2]

What made her book distinctive in the flood of writings that came out of the abolition movements of the early 1800s was her determination to write honestly about what she found on the plantation. Other travelers to the South in the antebellum years had recorded their impressions, but generally their descriptions of southern life were closer to the style of the popular books by Frederick Olmstead, who focused on what he perceived as the economic weakness of slavery. His arguments were used by southerners to justify the system of forced labor that dominated the South. In contrast, her descriptions of her daily encounters with the realities of the life in the slave cabins were as despairing as they were sharply observant. The deeply disturbing glimpse of slavery that I had absorbed when I first encountered the book, her letters' visceral reaction to the filth, the cruelty, and the hopelessness of the slaves' situation, had never left me.

Kemble understood that the slaves had been brutalized both physically and emotionally by their lives in enforced servitude, and of all the writers who responded to the realities of slavery, she was the only one who showed an understanding of the psychological effects of their bondage on the slaves. She was aware that what had happened to them had caused a pervasive emotional trauma, which would take years to heal, if it could be healed at all. She didn't sentimentalize what she was seeing, as Harriet Beecher Stowe had done in her fiction when Stowe created the slave archetype in her novel *Uncle Tom's Cabin*. Stowe created fictional characters that were, in every important aspect, simply projections of herself and her own emotional verities. The strength of what Stowe did was in her ability to personify the characters she described in emotional situations that her white readers could understand.

In her letters Kemble wrote candidly that the slaves in her husband's plantation cabins were dirty, that they smelled, that she often couldn't trust what they told her, and she remarked again and again that they felt such despair at their lives that they made only half-hearted efforts to make use of even the few liberties that were allowed them, like growing food in their own gardens. In her despair she finally began giving the women pennies to wash their children's hands and faces. At the same time, she was conscious that the situation she found was less destructive than in many other areas of the South. Like on the other plantations on the islands, the Butlers' slaves worked on a "task" system—a set task was to be performed, and when it was finished the slaves were free for the rest of the day. For most of the year the island's slaves finished their tasks by mid-afternoon, and the men spent some of the time gathering moss, which they rowed over to Darien along with whatever produce they had grown in their gardens, to exchange with merchants for printed cloth and kitchen utensils.

This passage relating one of Kemble's first visits to the slave huts only a few hundred yards from her family's own rough dwelling is typical of what confronted her in her first weeks.

These cabins consist of one room, about twelve feet by fifteen, with a couple of closets smaller and closer than the state-rooms of a ship, divided off from the main room and each other by rough wooden partitions, in which the inhabitants sleep. They have almost all of them a rude bedstead, with the gray moss of the forests for mattress, and filthy, pestilential-looking blankets for covering. Two families (sometimes eight and ten in number) reside on one of these huts, which are mere wooden frames pinned, as it were, to the earth by a brick chimney outside, whose enormous aperture within pours down a flood of air, but little counteracted by the miserable spark of fire, which hardly sends an attenuated thread of lingering smoke up its huge throat. A wide ditch runs immediately at the back of these dwellings, which is filled and emptied each day by the tide. Attached to each hovel is a small scrap of ground for a garden, which, however, is for the most part untended and uncultivated. Such of these dwellings as I visited to-day were filthy and wretched in the extreme, and exhibited that most deplorable consequence of ignorance and an abject condition, the inability of the inhabitants to secure and improve even such pitiful comfort as might yet be achieved by them. . . . Firewood and shavings lay littered about the floors, while the half naked children were cowering around the two or three smouldering cylinders. The moss with which the chinks and crannies of their ill-protecting dwellings might have been stuffed was trailing in dirt and dust about the ground, while the back door of the huts, opening upon a most unsightly ditch, was left wide open for the fowls and ducks, which they are allowed to raise, to travel in and out, increasing the filth of the cabin by what they brought and left in every direction. In the midst of the floor, or squatting around the cold hearth, would be four or five little children from four to ten years old, the latter all with babies in their arms, the care of the infants being taken from the mothers (who are driven afield as soon as they recover from child labor), and devolved upon these poor little nurses, as they are called, whose business it is to watch the infant, and carry it to its mother whenever it may require nourishment.[3]

Beyond her appalled reaction to the realities of life on the island, what had been most useful for me when I first looked into her book

The ruins of the rice mill, Butler's Island.

were her attentive descriptions of the music she heard on the plantation. She was a professional performer, so her descriptions of the slaves'
singing, even though these were only scattered paragraphs through the
letters, are the most detailed we have from any part of the South in these
pre–Civil War years. I quoted a passage describing the singing of her
boatmen in the book *The Country Blues* in 1959.

While it is true that what Kemble wrote about the music of the slaves
has become an important source of our knowledge of their music, what
is also significant is the music that she *didn't* hear. With several hundred
people between the two plantations, the small island was dotted with
clusters of slave cabins. Her husband had constructed settlements everywhere, and in the long winter nights it was silent, except for the noises
of animals and night birds stirring in the swamps. If there had been
any drumming or instrumental music, even any singing, she would
have heard it. She describes a plantation dance with a banjoist playing,

but she only mentions hearing distant singing from a prayer meeting on one clear, moonlit night, and she emphasized that it was an English hymn.

Most of the slaves who were shipped to the Sea Island plantations already had a rudimentary knowledge of the complicated rhythm of flooding and draining that rice required, and they were sold for higher prices because of their experience. Despite threats and beatings, they were unwilling to do the grueling work of ditching and maintaining the system of dikes that kept the tidal rivers out of the rice paddies, perhaps because in Africa they had left these tasks to their own slaves. On the plantations around the island this heavier work was performed by a gang of itinerant Irish laborers who slept on the riverbanks and worked for pay. Most of the hoeing and digging in the rice fields was performed by the slave women, generally forced back into the fields only three weeks after delivering their latest child. They continually came to Kemble begging to be allowed more time for their bodies to recover.

What Kemble heard daily was the singing of the crews of ragged boatmen as they rowed her to Darien in the plantation's primitive boats, most of them canoes hollowed out of logs. Darien was only a half-mile east of Butler Island, but to reach it by boat meant rowing against the current around the western end of another island shaped by the river's deposits of mud. In later weeks she took trips in a larger boat that was used to haul supplies between Butler and St. Simon. Often she had her daughters with her—Sarah, called Sally by the slaves, and the younger baby, Frances, as well as the baby's Irish nurse. Sally and the nurse, and Kemble's tight corset, were sometimes the subject of the improvised verses of the boat's singers.

Rowing yesterday through a beautiful sunset into a more beautiful moonrise, my two sable boatmen entertained themselves and me with alternate strophe and antistrophe of poetical description of my personal attractions, in which my "wire waist" recurred repeatedly, to my intense amusement. This is a charm for the possession of which M- (my white nursemaid) is also invariably celebrated . . . Occasionally I am celebrated in these rowing chants as "Massa's darling," and S—(Sally) comes in for endless glorification on account of the brilliant beauty of her complexion; the other day, however, our poets made a diversion from the personal to the moral qualities of their small mistress, and after the usual tribute to her roses and lilies came the following rather significant couplet:

"Little Missis Sally.
That's a ruling lady."[4]

In a later passage she wrote of her husband's departure with the plantation's rowers for St. Simon's Island, and her professional consideration of the rowers' style of singing is one of the book's best-known episodes.

The boat he went in was a large, broad, rather heavy, though well-built craft, by no means as swift or elegant as the narrow eight-oared long-boat in which he generally takes his walks on the water, but well adapted for the traffic between the two plantations, where it serves the purpose of a sort of omnibus or stage-coach for the transfer of the people from the one to the other, and of a baggage-wagon or cart for the conveyance of all sorts of household goods, chattel, and necessaries. Mr. —— sat in the middle of a perfect chaos of such freight; and as the boat pushed off, and the steersman took her into the stream, the men at the oars set up a chorus, which they continued to chant in unison with each other, and in time with their stroke, till the voices and oars were heard no more from the distance. I believe I have mentioned to you before the peculiar characteristics of this veritable negro minstrelsy—how they all sing in unison, having never, it appears, attempted or heard any thing like part-singing. Their voices seem oftener tenor than any other quality, and the tune and time they keep something quite wonderful; such truth of intonation and accent would make almost any music agreeable. That which I have heard these people sing is often plaintive and pretty, but almost always has some resemblance to tunes with which they must have become acquainted through the instrumentality of white men; their overseers or masters whistling Scotch or Irish airs . . . the tune with which Mr. ——'s rowers started him down the Altamaha, as I stood at the steps to see him off, was a very descendant of "Coming through the Rye." The words, however, were astonishingly primitive, especially the first line, which, when it burst from their eight throats in high unison, sent me into fits of laughter.

> "Jenny shake her toe at me,
>   Jenny gone away;
> Jenny shake her toe at me,
>   Jenny gone away.
> Hurrah! Miss Susy, oh!
>   Jenny gone away;
> Hurrah! Miss Susy, oh!
>   Jenny gone away."

. . . Except the extemporaneous chants in our honor, of which I have written to you before, I have never heard the negroes on Mr. ——'s plantation sing any words that could be said to have any sense. To one, an extremely pretty, plaintive, and original air, there was but one line, which was repeated with a sort of wailing chorus—"Oh! My massa told me, there's no grass in Georgia." Upon inquiring the meaning of which, I was told it was supposed to be the lamentation of a slave from one of the more northerly states, Virginia or Carolina, where the labor of hoeing the weeds, or grass, as they call it, is not nearly so severe are here, in the rice and cotton lands of Georgia.[5]

In her first weeks she found that she recognized the source for many of the songs she heard, but later she wrote:

My daily voyages up and down the river have introduced me to a great variety of new musical performances of our boatmen, who invariably, when the rowing is not too hard, moving up or down with the tide, accompany the stroke of their oars with the sound of their voices. I told you formerly that I thought I could trace distinctly some popular national melody with which I was familiar in almost all their songs; but I have been quite at a loss to discover any such foundation for many that I have heard lately, and which have appeared to me extraordinarily wild and unaccountable. The way in which the chorus strikes in with the burden, between each phrase of the melody chanted by a single voice, is very curious and effective, especially with the rhythm of the rowlocks for accompaniment.[6]

Kemble had inadvertently come closer to the African roots that lay just below the surface of the slaves' way of making music, and much of what she heard can be interpreted as characteristic of the adaptations that Africans made in their new world to create a music that would come to occupy a continually shifting middle ground between the two cultures. In her transcription of the words to the boatmen's "nonsense" song based on "Coming through the Rye," it is clear that it is being sung in a call-response form, which she also describes in her note about "the way in which the chorus strikes in with the burden." Her comments on the clarity of the rhythm and the musicality of the voices have been confirmed by the descriptions of many other travelers. The rhythms of rowing were easily adaptable to African singing styles, and once the land had been cleared there was little use of gang labor, so rowing would have been the one opportunity for singing that Kemble would have heard. Even in this early writing it is clear that there was a language of song which drew the slaves, from whatever tribal background, into a common musical expression.

With its unprepossessing air of a sagging backwater—there are two home-style restaurants on a wide, gawky main street, a dispirited antique shop in one of the buildings by the river, a modest fleet of shrimp boats that ties up along the town's wharf, and a warehouse filled with repair parts and gear for the fishing boats—Darien wouldn't have tempted me to turn off the highway, except that it was the only village in the marshes when Kemble spent her winter on the plantation, and she mentioned it often in her letters. When I walked along the riverfront I would often stop at the bridge that had been built across the marshes, and from it I could see, a half-mile away, the tall, ruined brick chimney of the Butler Island rice mill.

I felt some of the same stir of emotions when I drove over the Altamaha River (locally pronounced al-ta-ma-HA) and got out of the car at the site of the plantation buildings to look back at Darien. The town still has some of the unfinished character Kemble described in her letters. The water that encircles the island is as swollen with mud as her descriptions from 1838, but drainage has sunk some of the inland marshes, and I could see the water level was lower since I was standing on the river bank in late spring, and she had come to the island in the winter. But if the ground was drier, the season has its own torments. May is the season of stinging flies the size of yellow jackets. Darien people had different names for them—horse flies, cow flies, or May flies—and after a few moments in the brush by the river I was driven back to the car, stumbling and waving my arms to drive off the buzzing cloud.

A few days later I left Darien and drove the twenty miles along the coastal road south to Brunswick, where there is now a causeway over to the southern tip of St. Simon's Island. St. Simon's was almost as well known to me as Butler Island because of the work of another of the indefatigable women who played a central role in preserving so much of early black song in the South. Lydia Parrish's *Slave Songs of the Georgia Sea Islands*, published in 1942, had been almost as useful to me as Kemble's volume of letters.[7] Of all the books that have been published of collections of African American song material, Parrish's remains the most intensely researched and lavishly presented. It is still one of the most important contributions to our knowledge of the songs from the islands, known today as the Sea Island spirituals.

St. Simon's Island, where Kemble was rowed on a clumsy, flat-bottomed freight boat to join her husband on the cotton plantation on the island's northern tip, was briefly so well known for its long-fiber cotton that in the early nineteenth century the yearly harvest was sold by name in the London markets. Cotton, however, devours the soil, and continually needs new lands. By the late 1830s the declining fertility and the competition from the new cotton growing areas of Mississippi and Alabama were pushing St. Simon's into an economic slide from which its cotton economy never recovered. One of the most difficult things for me to imagine as I drove along the coast was what this monotonous, brushy landscape of new growth forest and dense salt marsh grasses would have looked like when Kemble first saw it.

As she was rowed along the muddy channel she would have passed land that was crowded with people. Already, by 1838 much of the land had been cleared, and on Butler islands and the sea islands close to it the new fields were planted with rice. As in rice farming everywhere, the land was divided into paddies by the earth dikes that were an integral part of the flood control system that was essential to rice cultivation. The cotton fields on the drier islands were kept clear all year around, and the land was relentlessly hoed and weeded. If I had been traveling then I would have passed miles of tilled fields and hundreds of workers dressed in rags gouging at the dirt with crude hand tools. I would have seen the scattered hovels of the slaves, the occasional more substantial wooden houses of the overseers, and a handful of the larger dwellings occupied by the plantation owners. In most of the slave huts there would have been a small, smoky fire sputtering all day for the children who tended the babies. Many of the plantations had wood-fired boilers to provide steam for the machinery that milled rice or sawed lumber. A smudge of smoke lay continually over the countryside, and Kemble writes of a brush fire that raged for days in the uncleared land beside the salt marshes.

I wouldn't, however, have seen much of this if I had tried to go inland. The only roads were the rough, meandering dirt tracks through the scrub forests. The wide, almost panoramic views I might have had of the rice fields would only have been possible from the glistening channels of one of the mud filled rivers, and its surface would have been busy with a continual traffic of small boats and handmade dugout canoes moving people and supplies from plantation to plantation.

As I came closer to the new causeway to St. Simon's Island, I quickly left any trace of the old Sea Island life behind me. The town of Brunswick has become a small city, now at the entrance of a modern causeway that has opened up St. Simon's to vacation living. Sprawled over its old fields are condominiums, watered golf courses, shopping centers, gated communities, and tourist shops. The only trace I could find of Fanny Kemble and her husband were two streets that had been named for them in a luxurious development built on the site of their old plantation. Where two tree lined, gracious streets crossed I found myself at the corner of Fanny Kemble Street and Pierce Butler Drive.

Lydia Parrish's book on the St. Simon's Island songs was printed in large format, with several pages of photographs, a prestigious publication by a New York press. It was the result of twenty-five years of work on the island by Parrish, who from her photos was a tall, dignified society woman, with a thin, stiffly composed face and a serious expression. She was best known on the island as a vacationing visitor, the wife of the successful artist Maxfield Parrish, whose paintings and illustrations with lushly imagined themes from myth and legend had widespread popularity everywhere in the United States. She had grown up in a Quaker community south of Philadelphia that did not accept music as a form of worship, and she wrote in the introduction to the book that the descendents of slaves she encountered there "and some ex-slaves themselves—were the only singers. Theirs was the only music worthy of the name that I heard in my youth." The island's plantations had already lost their economic struggle against the cotton cultivation in the Mississippi states, and the old way of life had disappeared when she first came to St. Simon's in 1912. At first, it seemed to her that the musical culture of the slave cabins had been lost at the same time.

> When I arrived on St. Simon's in 1912, the stillness of the Negroes was puzzling until questioning brought out the fact that the island was a summer resort, and contact with city whites and their black servants had had its numbing influence; that the old-time singing had gone out of style, and spirituals weren't sung any more. After three musically barren winters I discovered, however, that a few Negroes remembered their old songs and could be induced to sing for me if I could make it worth their while. This was in 1915, and, ever since, I have been doing just that: making it worth their while. During the bleak winters of the depression, some of the singers literally sang for their supper—which, they thankfully observed, the Lord had provided . . . [8]

Parrish's book shows the long labor that went into it. She seemed to have found every reference to slave music that had made its way into print in the years before the war, and she had also combed the travel literature of the slave areas of West Africa. In her presentation of the songs and the old life styles on St. Simon's she also traced whatever could be found linking the music and the customs to the African cultures from which the slaves had descended, and these sections still have a remarkable relevance. In one of the chapters she quoted an account of a visitor to Butler Island in 1845, Sir Charles Lyell, who was met at Darien by a local man who came down the river "in a long canoe, hollowed out of the trunk of a single cypress and rowed by six negroes, who were singing loudly and keeping time to the stroke of their oars." In Lyell's writing she found a comment that agreed with her own observations, and could help explain the strong survival of slave songs on the islands.

It is evident that on these rice farms, where the negroes associate with scarcely any whites, except the overseer and his family, and have but little intercourse with the slaves of other estates, they must remain far more stationary than where, as in a large part of Georgia, they are about equal in number to the whites, or even form a minority . . . In Glynn Country, where we are now residing, there are no less than four thousand negroes to seven hundred whites, whereas in Georgia generally there are only 281,000 in a population of 691,000 or more whites than colored people. I give these figures because they explain why more distinctive slave songs can be found in the rice swamps and cotton plantations of the adjoining sea islands than in the Piedmont section where Anglo-Saxon influence has always predominated. In all probability we have the malaria mosquito and the absentee landlords to thank for this.[9]

In a note Parrish added that the proportion of the races was similar when she first came to the island, and that in 1810, when all of St. Simon's had been cleared for cotton, there were fourteen plantations with about 1,200 slaves. Parrish's research had been patient and exhaustive, and if there had been other work done like this everywhere in the South we would have had an unparalleled picture of the music that was a continual presence in southern life.

Parrish's labors to save the culture of the island led her to build—with the help of her singers—a small, primitive cabin, blessed with the proper exhortations to the spirits and lined with newspapers on the board walls.

In the papering of the Cabin, on my own initiative, I took another precaution which has afforded the singers much amusement. The walls of many small cabins are covered with newsprint, because the prevailing idea in the old days was that a hag (an evil spirit) had to read every word before she could work evil on you. I used the financial section of *The New York Times* for good measure.[10]

The musical transcriptions in Parrish's book, like everything else in the volume, were given much attention, and they were a long step beyond what the editors of almost all of the earlier collectors of southern song had attempted. Included were the kind of call and response songs which were missing from many of the earlier collections, with the chorus response annotated. In the transcription of one of the most widely known island spirituals, "Plumb De Line," there was a notation for the rhythm of the singers' stamping feet. Despite Parrish's intentions, however, the transcription is once more an indication of the difficulty of presenting African American musical idioms in European notation. The rhythms of the voices, if they are sung against a loud stamping by the singer's feet, do have the feel of the polyrhythms characteristic of all the music from African America, and there is a repetition of the call and response in the chorus responses of "Plum de line." It is in the use of harmonies in some of the transcriptions that they come closer to the arranged spiritual that followed the success of nineteenth-century singing groups like the Fisk Jubilee Singers. The distinct intervals of the African pentatonic scales have been blurred. Parrish's notations could as easily have been sung by a local amateur choir, if they had been skilled enough to count the rhythms of the vocal entrances.

Parrish's book was a remarkable achievement, if only for the wealth of song material she documented, but in many ways it marked the end of a long era of study and collecting of the spirituals. One reason, of course, was that at this point, almost a hundred years after Emancipation, there were so few older singers who still knew spirituals and ballads that hadn't already been collected. Also, although the transcriptions are of considerable value for someone studying the way the songs are shaped—which has always been the justification for notation, even with the limitations which were freely admitted by everyone trying to gather the music—recordings now made it possible to capture the essence of the performance in a way which the transcriptions could only suggest.

In 1960 Alan Lomax recorded a version of one of the signature pieces of Parrish's performers, the song that customarily ended the evening for visitors at The Cabin, "Good-Bye Everybody." If you listen to Lomax's recording with the transcription from her book in front of you, you are immediately conscious that a crucial element of the song's effect which is missing from the notation is the complex pattern of handclapping that gives the melody its strong propulsion. You immediately become conscious that for many songs the handclapping was a substitute for the drums that were forbidden on the plantations. The transcription doesn't attempt to capture the energy of the performance, and you sense only hints of the subtleties of the vocal melody.

The painstaking scholarship of Parrish's book, her conscientious effort to save a part of the slave legacy, and her personal involvement with the singers she knew for so many years make the book still a landmark today, though there is sometimes a tone of propriety that can be uncomfortable for a modern reader. Some of the singers worked for her as servants, and what is always an expression of genuine sympathy on her part almost never becomes empathy, which might not have been possible on St. Simon's island nearly a century ago. I drove over the causeway from Brunswick, inching toward the toll booth in my air-conditioned car in a line of vacation traffic, in the hope that I might find "The Cabin" Mrs. Parrish had built with her singers, but no one I spoke to, as I went from one of the town's offices to another, could tell me where it might have been. The island's library had a worn copy of the book, which one of the librarians held up proudly for me to see. It looked like an artifact left over from another world.

Sympathy. Empathy. The two emotions are so close, and at the same time so distant from each other. In the book there is a picture of Lydia Parrish sitting on the school steps in a severe print dress and coat, posed with one of her singers, standing beside her in a servant's shapeless housedress with a simple hat covering her hair. In another book, recently published, *Go Gator and Muddy the Water*, there is a photo of a younger folklorist who was also collecting African American songs and tales in the South at about the same time.[11] The photo was taken in one of the rough camps of the turpentine workers in Florida. She is also a woman, but all similarities end there. It is a hot afternoon, she's in the shade on a crude porch. She's wearing a light, open work dress, she's smoking a cigarette, and her expression is wary, knowing, and watchful. She is a woman who wouldn't be easy to fool. She is at home on that porch, and she is easy with what she is doing at that moment on that porch because she is a black woman, and she knows just about everything there is to know about black men. The woman is Zora Neale Hurston.

By the time she was photographed on the porch of a shack in a turpentine camp Hurston had already traveled a long and eventful road. Her life had veered through so many changes and directions that it is difficult to know how to describe her. She was one of the most talented writers associated with the Harlem Renaissance in the 1920s, and at the same time she was studying anthropology with Franz Boas at Columbia University. She was then already in her mid-thirties, and she had been publishing stories and poems for several years, mostly supporting herself by working as a waitress. For three decades she continued to be a volatile, creative force in African American culture, usually with little money, always with large projects, working in the theater as a writer and producer of staged presentations of everyday American black life. She sometimes sold her small store of possessions to bring something she believed in to the stage. She was also unpredictable, emotional, and complicated in ways that didn't always help her achieve what she wanted. Married and divorced in her thirties, when she was in her late forties she married a WPA worker who was twenty-three, and she gave her own age at the ceremony as twenty-nine.

Most of Hurston's work in southern folklore was done for various government Depression programs. There were few jobs for anyone, but she was temperamentally suited to the hard traveling and the interviewing that was part of the research, and her writing about black culture was colorful and animated. Most of her work was popular journalism, rather than academic scholarship, and her articles and retelling of southern folk tales appeared in many leading magazines. She had already traveled widely in the South, and in her later field work she spent considerable time in Jamaica and Honduras, as well as Haiti, where she learned Creole.

Hurston was particularly suited to write about the music of the black church, since she had grown up in Eatonville, Florida as the daughter of a Baptist minister. Her father, John Hurston, was pastor of the town's Zion Hope Baptist Church and the Macedonia Baptist Church, and he went on to become active in church associations in south Florida. Her mother was superintendent of the Sunday school. In her writing Hurston expressed her own personal response to the efforts to preserve the slave spirituals, which had been the concern of the song collectors like Parrish. Hurston, with her typical forthrightness, was less than enthusiastic about what seemed to her to be a waste of time and effort. What she insisted was that the spiritual, as a true expression of black religious faith, could never be presented as a concert performance.

There never has been a presentation of genuine Negro spirituals to any audience anywhere. What is being sung by the concert artists and glee clubs are the works of Negro composers or adaptors *based* on the spirituals. Under this head come the works of Harry T. Burleigh, Rosamond Johnson, Lawrence Brown, Nathaniel Dett, Hall Johnson and [John] Work. All good work and beautiful, but *not* the spirituals. These neo-spirituals are the outgrowth of the glee clubs. Fisk University boasts perhaps the oldest and certainly the most famous of these. They have spread their interpretation over America and Europe. Hampton and Tuskegee have not been unheard. But with all the glee clubs and soloists, there has not been one genuine spiritual presented. To begin with, Negro spirituals are not solo or quartette material. The jagged harmony is what makes it, and it ceases to be what it was when this is absent. Neither can any group be trained to reproduce it. Its truth dies under training like flowers under hot water. The harmony of the true spiritual is not regular. The dissonances are important and not to be ironed out by the trained musician. The various parts break in at any old time. Falsetto often takes the place of regular voices for short periods. Keys change. Moreover, each singing of the piece is a new creation. The congregation is bound by no rules. No two times singing is alike, so that we must consider the rendition of a song not as a final thing, but as a mood. It won't be the same thing next Sunday.

Negro songs to be heard truly must be sung by a group, and a group bent on expression of feelings and not on sound effects.

Glee clubs and concert singers put on their tuxedoes, bow prettily to the audience, get the pitch and burst into magnificent song—but not *Negro* song . . . [12]

I had come to Butler Island and the other islands along the coast prepared to accept disappointment that I wouldn't find any of the old music on the islands. Certainly not the living music that Kemble had encountered, and that had been part of Hurston's childhood. I hadn't found anything of the old life on St. Simon's Island—only landscaped estate houses and shopping malls—and on Butler Island, only a ruined chimney and the buildings of the state animal protection service. I had heard that there was still a native community on Sapelo Island, as far north of Butler as St. Simon's was to the south, but when I drove to the landing where the ferry to Sapelo docked, I learned that the island has been owned for some years by the University of Georgia, and it was being used for research into the ecology of the salt marshes. Access was limited to small groups of tourists, or to guests in the two or three houses that offer bed-and-breakfast facilities. I still was interested in seeing what was there, so I took the small, modern ferry through the marshes, then across a wider stretch of open water to the small dock at the edge of Sapelo's sparse forest.

The ferry trip was noisy and excited, not for the view of the marshes stretching in the morning mist around us, but for the meetings inside the crowded cabin. An African American extended family was holding a reunion in Darien, and they had taken the trip to Sapelo together to get acquainted. Children ducked their heads shyly as they were lifted up to be inspected by cousins they had never seen before. A gray bearded man in a wrinkled shirt pointed out of the windows at the islands and told about trips he'd taken on the ferry as a boy. A woman in a brightly colored jumpsuit went down the aisle with an older woman, pointing. "My daughter Althea, my daughter Vermaine, my adopted daughter Josephine." Laughter and greetings. Outside the cabin's windows the sun was stripping the mist off the marsh grass, and the boys who had chosen to stay out on the deck ducked and twisted to get away from the flies.

On the island we creaked over dirt roads in a rattling bus, with a woman from the island community telling us about the trees and the

The Altamaha River where Fanny Kemble was rowed by her boatmen
across to Darien.

animals, and the occasional buildings where we stopped. The land was
flat and sandy, wide stretches of it covered with a thin forest. As I had
been told, there was a native community on the island. Sixty-eight people
lived in modest houses in a cleared area called Hog Hammock. The one-
story frame wooden buildings and mobile homes were scattered across
small fields and under the shade of the oaks. What I hadn't understood
was that although the people still living on the island were descended
from slaves who had worked in the plantation fields, the island had been
a private summer retreat for wealthy white owners almost since Emancipation, and for most of this century it had been owned by the family of
R. J. Reynolds, founder of the North Carolina tobacco company. There
was a tackily furnished mansion where we were left to look at the so-
larium with an obtrusive new floor covering what had been a small
swimming pool, then taken to a shabby room in the basement with
a much-used one-lane bowling alley and a billiard table, and a grimy,
cramped "ballroom" upstairs done up in a kindergarten circus decor.

The people who remained on the island worked for the Reynolds family, either in the house as servants, or in the large cattle barn or gardens.
Their children today take the ferry every morning to go to school on the
mainland, and now two or three of the men have also taken mainland
jobs. It has been many years since there had been any life on the island
that was dependent on the land or the waters around it. I didn't see a
kitchen garden beside any of the houses of Hog Hammock. For some

of the visitors in the group there was a lingering interest in the Gullah language, the old dialect that had been compounded on the islands from African speech. As we straggled out of the mansion one of them asked the woman from Hog Hammock who had been guiding us what Gullah sounded like.

The woman, dark-skinned and with a cheerful, round face, wearing a khaki state employees uniform, laughed indulgently.

"You been listening to it for two hours."

"It's like English!"

"Just like English," the woman agreed, "Only some words that's different for things we have out here."

Even if I hadn't found anything left of the old culture on the nearby islands, I still was drawn to Darien. The low line of brick buildings I could see from the ruins of the Butler Island rice mill had some of the distant promise for me that they must have had for Fanny Kemble and the slaves of the island. In her book she had been curtly dismissive of the town of Darien. She wrote,

> How shall I describe Darien to you? The abomination of desolation is but a poor type of its forlorn appearance, as, half buried in sand, its tumble-down wooden houses peer over the muddy bank of the thick slimy river. The whole town lies on a bed of sand: side-walks, or mid-walks, there be none distinct from each other; at every step I took my feet were ankle deep in the soil, and I had cause to rejoice that I was booted for the occasion. Our worthy doctor, whose lady I was going to visit, did nothing but regret that I had not allowed him to provide me a carriage, though the distance between his house and the landing is not a quarter of a mile. The magnitude of the exertion seemed to fill him with amazement, and he over and over again repeated how impossible it would be prevail on any of the ladies there to take such a walk. The houses seemed scattered about here and there, apparently without any design, and looked, for the most part, either unfinished or ruinous. One feature of the scene alone recalled the villages of New England—the magnificent oaks, which seemed to add to the meanness and insignificance of the human dwellings they overshadowed by their enormous size and grotesque forms.[13]

After a few days in the town I found myself wondering what Darien had thought of *her*. Kemble had continued to delay publication of her book because of her concern for its effect on her daughters, but by 1863 her anxieties over the mood in England toward the Civil War caused her to change her mind. At this point, with the outcome of the war still undecided, the book's harsh descriptions of the cruelties of slavery were intended to bolster English support for the North. Everywhere in the industrial areas of England workers were suffering severe economic difficulties because of the Union naval blockade, which had cut the English mills off from southern cotton. She appended two long letters specifically attacking slavery which she had previously published in London journals to her original manuscript, and the book's publication in London and New York added its weight to the public mood that had already been shaped by Stowe's *Uncle Tom's Cabin*. *The Journal of a Residence on a Georgia Plantation* appeared in the New York stores in June of 1863, just weeks before the battle of Gettysburg. It is clear that the writings of Stowe and the raised voices of other writers like Kemble helped create the public sympathies that kept England neutral in the early years of the struggle, and with hindsight it seems almost certain that without the assistance or open support of a European power the South had little chance of winning the war.

There is a small, new public library on Darien's main street, and—despite Kemble's disparaging remarks about their town—Darien's library had two copies of a recent edition of her book, one copy in the reference section and one in circulation. I could see that the circulating copy had been off the library shelves almost continuously since the book had come into the library. No comments had been made on the pages where she described the dreary aspects of Darien, but the material she had added attacking slavery had aroused some emotional responses in the page margins. The lines "Southern aristocracy, thanks to the pernicious influences by which they are surrounded, are unfit to be members of a Christian republic," had roused a Darien reader to add, "What about the bastards in Britain and Northern U.S., who originated slave trade in America?" [sic] Another statement by Kemble had ruffled southern vanity: "the New York men, owners of the fastest horses and finest houses in the land" was also underlined and in the margin was the protest, "Another statement showing ignorance of fact about America, as the best and largest houses were in Ga., Louisiana, Mississippi, and horses in Kentucky & Tenn." Kemble's description of the slaves who persisted in coming into the room to watch her while she was eating breakfast caused the annotator to rejoin, "This cannot be less than a patent fabrication, as such conduct would not be tolerated, by any white master."

Whatever Darien thought of Kemble, the plantation had been closely bound to the town's everyday life. Several times she described the slaves rowing over from the island with moss or produce from their small gardens to exchange for cloth and utensils. On Sundays several of the slaves rowed over for church services. After the war her younger daughter Frances returned to the plantation with her father, for the first time paying wages and attempting to operate it as a commercial farm. In these struggling reconstruction years the newly freed workers on Butler Island and the small African American community in Darien became even more closely linked.

Behind Darien's old brick city hall is the white wooden building of the First African Baptist Church, and although the building itself is newer, the congregation has held services in the town since the slavery years. Services are now held in the church every second and fourth Sunday in the month, and I was in town on a fourth Sunday. The church has an almost modern appearance from the outside—a stately, clapboard building with a tall steeple, newly painted and the parking areas neatly trimmed—but inside I felt as if I had stepped back into another century. The pews were ornamented with wood carvings that must have come from the older church, and in front of the altar was a circle of antique formal chairs, newly reupholstered in crimson cloth, with large bouquets of crimson flowers beside them. Behind the altar, and on the walls around me there was new plywood paneling, but on the balconies above us there were still the older framed wood panels, painted a light apple green. Above the center aisle there were hanging lights and old, large-bladed fans, but with the building's new air conditioning the fans were still. In the wall beyond the altar there was a decorated window with an image of Jesus. The light inside the church had its own distinct softness. Glass painted in broad, vertical stripes of red, green, and blue had been mounted as windowpanes, and the mingled tones of light gave the space a muted calm.

Although the congregation seemed small—about twenty people when the services began—there was a formal printed program including a Mission Offering, Selections from the Choir, an Altar Call, and Holy Communion. I didn't know what kind of service I would hear, but I felt that I had come closer to what I had been looking for in the Sea Islands simply by sitting quietly in the pew on a still Sunday morning. The minister of the congregation, Rev. George E. Clark, a tall, elegant, imposing man with gold rimmed glasses, was sitting in one of the red chairs making notes on his program. He was dressed in a long black cassock with silver crosses on the lapels that emphasized the dignity of the morning. In front of the altar two deacons, in black suits, white shirts, and dark ties, had begun prayers. In the front pews I could see several women, some of them older, all of them in white dresses. Suddenly, almost without any sign of what was to come, the younger of the two deacons ended a prayer; then in a new tone of voice began the word "Je-," and before he had time to finish the word the women and others in the congregation around them burst into the old hymn "Jesus On the Mainline, Tell Him What You Want." Hands clapped, voices came forward to join the responses of "Tell Him You want," feet tapped on the wooden floor, shoulders swayed, and one of the women lifted her waving arms over her head as she sang.

As I listened I realized in surprise that I had been wrong in my assurance that the music of the islands had been forgotten. What I was hearing was the music I had known only from recordings, or from festival appearances by island groups years ago, or from the printed spiritual collections. Music with its roots in the years of slavery was still a living presence in this modest Georgia church! If I had spoken to anyone as I found a seat in a pew, if I had asked about music, the spontaneity of the moment, the surprise that caught my breath, would have been lost. The second deacon led a longer and even more emotional prayer, and this time the women in the front pews burst into another of the Sea Island spirituals, "Go Down Chariot." Worshippers sitting around them added their own voices, clapping their hand, their arms reaching up like flowing banners. It was not, as Hurston had insisted, a way of making music that was meant to be performed for an audience—it was music that was meant to be sung together, the voices free to enter and drop out, the clapping as unexpected as the wind. The song became, as Hurston insisted, a new creation, at the same time that it was an affirmation of the strength of a long, well-worn tradition.

When the song ended the women stood up and walked to the back of the church. What they had sung was a kind of informal prelude to the formal service. After a moment they came back down the aisle in a solemn procession as the church's choir, and for an hour there was a service as genteel and restrained as the printed program. Then Reverend Clark stepped forward and began to speak quietly about "Zechiah," who was short, and with his handicap he couldn't see God, but he didn't let his shortness keep him from taking his place with other worshippers. After a few sentences the minister was chanting, a few more sentences and he was prowling the stage, his arms waving, the long robe flapping around his body. His voice became incantatory, incandescent. Long rhythmical chants broke off with his plea, "Can I have a witness?" then returned with a renewed level of tension. Other voices joined in; people stood in the pews clapping, arms again thrusting up into the air. Finally, when it was palpably obvious that the minister had come to the moment of emotional revelation where he was leading us, his voice flattened into a shrill repetition. Around me it felt as though there had been a surge of light in the church. For the congregation, the power of his voice had summoned the Spirit into the building, and for all of us in the pews it was as though we were suspended in space. With the moment of grace achieved his voice slowly altered, the chant-like rhythm unwound its tight coils, he spoke about "consolation," and after a few moments he invited the members, in a quiet voice, to prepare themselves to receive Communion.

An hour later I was in the car, driving again. I had run out of time, and I had to leave Darien behind me. But as I drove into the stream of traffic filling the interstate on the way north, I found that it was only the physical presence of the town and the marshes that I was leaving behind. So much of what I had found in the ruins on the empty island and in the silence of town's streets still hung in the air around me.

Good Time Music before the Blues

If you travel far enough south in Alabama, you come to Mobile, the striver port city that for years contended with New Orleans for its ocean traffic. Mobile is in Alabama's deepest South, on the Gulf Coast. The summers are hot and steamy and wet, and the harbor's surface is as slack and stained as spilled gasoline on a filling station's driveway. When I came into Mobile in the early summer of 1952 it was dusk, and the streets were wet and sticky from an early rain as my bus approached the downtown business district. Dark eddies of shadows bunched under the trees, and there were so few cars that there were only brief bursts of illumination from their headlights. But there were enough cars to stop us in a line of traffic at a red light two blocks from the bus station. I had slept for only a few hours since I'd begun hopping rides on military cargo planes the day before to get to New Orleans, and I was leaning my head against the window trying not to perspire too freely and find a few moments of sleep somewhere before the bus would let me out into the muggy heat of the street. If I'd had more sleep, I would have understood more quickly what I was seeing out of the bus window.

Over the idling of the bus's motor I suddenly thought I heard music. I sat up and stared out through the rain-flecked windowpane. The bus had stopped on a nearly deserted street, beside a line of shops that had closed for the day. I couldn't see any people on the sidewalk, but in the dimness I found myself looking at a black street string band playing in the recessed doorway of one of the shops, between its two display windows. I caught my breath. I wondered if they were still playing for their own pleasure as much as they were playing for anything else, since no one besides me seemed to be listening. Nobody in the seats around me had turned to look out the window. With the bus's windows shut, what I could hear of the music was half-lost in the motor's idling, but I realized that this was music that came from some moment in the past that I had only known about from stories.

I still see the little band in memory, at least as clearly as I could see them in the fading light on the Mobile street. Seated on a stool in the center of the doorway was a man who was stroking a washboard with flourishing gestures. His instrument was held out in front of him on a rough, perpendicular wooden frame, and the pieces of board had clattering attachments nailed to them. The metal ridges of the board were bowed with hard use. The two guitar players standing on either side of him were playing battered country guitars, and a fourth man was playing a bass fashioned out of a washtub, a stick, and some clothesline.

All the musicians were dark-skinned, wearing rumpled work clothes, and it was obvious, from the first notes I heard, that they had been playing together most of their lives. I still can see the guitarists in much worn hats that they'd pulled down on their foreheads, and the washboard player staring intently in front of him, as if there were more of an audience than the side of an idling bus. He was humming into a kazoo and the others were singing in low, relaxed voices, a harmony that seemed to be ordained with the piece they were playing. Whatever the song was, it wasn't a blues. It was a party song with a loose, juke-joint chorus, and the washboard player nudged the rhythm with the relaxed ease of someone opening his shirt to scratch his stomach. It was a style of "jump-up" blues that I was certain had died out years before—and here it was, in a shadowy storefront on a street in downtown Mobile.

I had only a small duffle bag with me and I dragged it out of the luggage rack and stumbled up the aisle of the bus, still only half-awake. I called to the driver to let me out, but just then the light changed, the cars in front of us moved ahead, and we slowly followed them. When I reached the front of the bus I leaned down and begged the driver to open the door and let me out, but he only shook his head and pointed ahead. We'd be at the depot in two more blocks. I could get out there. When he finally rolled to a stop I was standing on the bus's steps and the moment the door opened I was running back to the storefront. When I found the place where I'd heard them only a few moments before, the band had gone. I told myself that they hadn't had time to go far, and I began to crisscross the empty downtown streets in the dusk. Still half-asleep and soaked with perspiration, I rounded corners and ran down alleyways, but there was no one on the streets. The band had disappeared.

As I finally fell asleep on another bus a few hours later, swaying along the dark coastal road to New Orleans, I found myself wondering numbly if I had even seen the washboard player and the others in the band there in the doorway. Could it only have been something I'd dreamed about so often, and half-awake in the bus I had only thought I'd heard them playing? In my sweaty struggle with the heat had I made them up? I thought of them often, sometimes listening to the music again in my ear, trying to decide if I really *had* heard the sound of their music through the bus window.

It was the Army that kept me from returning to Mobile to look for my storefront band. I had made the summer trip to New Orleans on a short leave, and I still had a year of service ahead of me. I knew the term that described what I'd glimpsed in the dusk—it was a "skiffle" band. The term "skiffle" had become popular among folk musicians in the early 1950s to describe an instrumental group using guitars, washboards, harmonicas, and kazoos—sometimes adding a jug or washtub bass. The bands played with loose, loping rhythms, noisily presenting songs that came out of their country backgrounds. I didn't receive my Army discharge and return to the United States until the summer of 1953, but the following year I enrolled at Tulane University for the spring semester. Before I returned to New Orleans I had acquired an early model tape recorder, a clumsy, bulky Pentron, with a wavering green eye to indicate the level of the volume on the tape. When I go through the boxes of tape I preserved from New Orleans during these months it seems that I must have held out my microphone to anyone I met who sang or played an instrument. A friend, a violinist and tennis player from California named Clarence White who had also just finished his military service, drove to New Orleans to spend the summer, and finally my first wife Mary and I found a free weekend and crowded into his small coupe, with the tape recorder and some clothes in the car's trunk. We drove on the coast road east through Biloxi to Mobile to look for the musicians I had lost that sweaty night two years before.

Mobile in the early 1950s was still a rundown port city, although with some signs of the relative prosperity of the Second World War decade. It also still preserved some of the less strict attitudes toward life in port that had given New Orleans its old gaudy reputation. The hotel we found close to the Greyhound depot was decorated with strips of blue and red neon around the doorway to welcome anyone just in from the sea. The rooms could be rented by the hour, and the tired stairway had a steady traffic of sailors and women in short, flowery dresses. There was no air conditioning, and our drab room had a large, creaky double bed facing an equally large, stained mirror. There was a narrow cot for Clarence against the wall. With our suitcases and the tape recorder pushed into a closet we got back in the car and drove toward the part of the city where we might find some trace of the musicians I had seen.

By this time I had already been in the South on several visits since December, 1950, and I'd spent many months in New Orleans and in the countryside outside the city interviewing older jazz musicians. I had quickly learned that I could find the African American neighborhoods by looking for streets that the towns and cities hadn't bothered to pave. The streetlights would be out of order, and the sidewalks—if there were any—would be cracked and broken. If the town did provide a school in the section it would be a shabby building on a patch of bare dirt. This was the era of what the U.S. Supreme Court defined as "separate but equal" opportunities and facilities for African Americans.

I had also found that because of the constant pressure of fear that surrounded the black community I could think of myself as "safe." No one in the black districts would harass a white man who wasn't drunk, wasn't looking for women, and who seemed to have legitimate business in the neighborhood. When Mary, Clarence, and I parked his little coupe on Davis Avenue, the main business street of the African American section of town, it was Saturday night, there were crowds surging along the sidewalks, and the bars were jammed. Everyone was in far more sophisticated, prettier clothes than our chinos and T-shirts, and Mary's blouse and 1950s "pedal pushers." But the people we passed who were clustered against the building fronts carefully took no notice of us, except to slide out of our way. Their noisy, teasing conversations were silenced until we had continued a few steps farther along the street.

I had also learned in my months of looking for older musicians in New Orleans that any queries I had were passed on through several intermediaries, and often it was only after some time had passed that I would hear something about the person I was seeking. With Mary and Clarence nervously following me—Mary, a slim, pale, light haired woman who was quiet and shy, and Clarence, a year younger than I was, slight and apologetic in his white T-shirt and chinos—we walked into teeming bars and pool halls, asking if anybody had seen the little band I had heard playing on the street two summers before. People stopped their card games or their noisy conversations and listened—all of us sweaty and uncomfortable in the steamy night. Sometimes the people we approached were drunk enough to shake their heads and laugh at the sight of the three of us with our earnest smiles.

It had been about ten o'clock on Saturday night before we found our way to Davis Avenue, but at midnight a woman in the back room of one of the bars decided there wouldn't be a problem if she told us about the band. She called out from a group around one of the tables that they were in town, she'd seen them drive by in their truck, and if we came back in the morning we'd find them. We thanked her, nodded to the wary faces that had glanced up from their intent card game spread out on a table against the wall, and edged through the crowded room back toward the street.

As we got closer to the door, walking by rows of people in their best clothes lined alongside the bar, we realized that the room had suddenly fallen silent. Couples at the small tables stared into their drinks, whatever they had been laughing about forgotten for a moment. When we came out onto the sidewalk we found the Mobile police waiting for us at the curb in a patrol car. Didn't we know it was dangerous around here? The officers surrounded us. Those people were just waiting to get their hands on strangers like us. We could get our throats cut hanging around here. They blocked us off from the door we'd just left. Mary, Clarence, and I shifted our feet, our heads down, nodding respectfully. I had also learned not to argue with southern policemen.

The officers emphatically adjusted their holsters, leaned against their cruiser with its lights flashing, and waited while we walked back to Clarence's car where we'd parked it a block down the street. Halfway there we passed a man standing against a post, his head leaning drunkenly on top of it. I could hear he was singing a mournful field holler to himself and I hesitated, trying to listen, but I could see the police motioning impatiently, and with Mary and Clarence a step behind me we hurried to the car.

It had been years since I had heard the band, but I knew now that I *had* heard them. The moment of surprise on the sweaty bus had been real. The next morning we found two of the men from the group in wrinkled work shirts and loose trousers, standing beside an old, rusted flatbed truck, a few blocks from Davis Avenue. One of them, a heavy man named Moochie Reeves, seemed to be the leader. He was in black trousers with thin suspenders over his shirt and he was wearing a dark, sweat-stained fedora hat. The other man, Ollie Crenshaw, was shorter, with an unbuttoned cloth vest over his shirt sleeves and khaki trousers. I could see that under his hat his expression was nervous and worried. Yes, they had been playing in Mobile most of their lives, but there was a "whole gang" of them in the band, and maybe they had been the ones I had seen on that steamy summer night, but they had so many musicians in the band that I might have seen somebody else. The washboard player had moved to Texas, but they had continued making music without him. They had moved up to Selma after I'd heard them. They were sharecropping out in the country, but they'd come down to Mobile for the weekend with the truck to move some furniture. It was only chance that had brought us all into the city at the same time. I could see they were uncomfortable, however, and they finally told us that they were uneasy about another musician, their washtub bass player, Tyler Jackson, who had come down in the truck with them. Tyler had gone out drinking on Davis Avenue and he'd been picked up by the police. If I wanted to do any recording I'd have to go and get Tyler out of jail.

The whole jumbled, chaotic day in Mobile began as an uneasy was a long replication of the role that southern blacks had learned to play, and which southern whites had been exploiting since the collapse of Reconstruction. I had never been to a city jail in the South, but I was aware that any white person, even someone as unlikely as I was, could get a black prisoner released by simply telling the desk officer that the man or woman being held was "their nigger" and by paying whatever fine the police had decided on. Tyler had been picked up as drunk and disorderly, and the fine was $12. A few moments after I paid it Tyler was turned over to my custody. He was ushered down the corridor by a bulky officer in a tight uniform. He was a slight, light-skinned man in a neat dress shirt with the sleeves rolled up and pressed dark trousers. I was relieved to see that he hadn't been worked over, and he was simply anxious to get away from the jail. He worked as a bricklayer in Montgomery, and he'd come along with Moochie and Ollie to play a little music for friends. He was too nervous to say more than a few words, but his expression lightened when he understood that what I wanted was simply for him to play music with the band. Then he stammered apologetically. There was another problem.

The problem was that when the police had picked him up they'd taken his washtub bass and they hadn't given it back to him when he was released. We'd have to find him a new instrument. After driving around the empty Sunday morning streets for half an hour we found a store open on a side street close to Davis, with washtubs stacked on the sidewalk outside. A new galvanized washtub cost me one dollar. He and Ollie found a broomstick, and a length of rope to go with the tub, and we were ready to record.

With Moochie, Ollie, and Tyler leading in the rattling truck, and the three of us following in Clarence's coupe, we turned off of Davis and drove deeper into the black neighborhood. After two or three blocks the city gave up any pretense of paving the streets and we lurched over rutted dirt tracks. Moochie stopped the truck in front of a row of sturdy, small wooden houses with metal chairs and benches set out in the shade of the front porches. He came back to the car to say that he knew some people in the neighborhood, then disappeared up the street. A few minutes later a dark-skinned woman in a yellow sleeveless dress came out from behind one of the houses, and walked over to us with Moochie beside her. I could see she was determined to make us feel as much at home as possible, since white people didn't get to that part of Mobile often, and she wasn't entirely sure what to do with us.

Of all the things that outsiders could ask of African Americans in the South during these years, music caused the fewest problems. Everyone accepted the notion that white folks thought of black music as a recipe for gladness, and when the woman found out we only wanted to do some recording, her smile relaxed. She could help us with that. I lifted the tape recorder out of the trunk of Clarence's car, then I talked again with Moochie. The tape recorder had to be plugged in somewhere. I didn't have one of the battery-operated machines that were just becoming available. By this time several people had gathered and someone suggested we could use one of the houses close to where the band had parked their truck. The woman hesitated, then led us onto the porch, opened the door, and waved us inside with the same welcoming smile.

Most of the neighbors followed us into the neatly furnished living room, and we found that before we could do any recording we had to push most of the furniture out of the way. Some of it finally had to go out on the porch. I now had a name for the band—they were called the Mobile Strugglers—and we could begin to record. It was hot in the crowded room, but we had to keep the windows closed to muffle the street noises. I didn't often use a microphone stand then, usually holding the microphone in my hand so I could move it from a singer's voice to his guitar for a solo. With three of them singing, though, I had to find some other way to hold the microphone. After rummaging in the kitchen the woman came back with an ironing board. We opened it up and put the microphone of top of it.

In the 1950s it still was possible to find musicians in the South like Moochie, Ollie, and Tyler. They weren't blues singers, though they knew several blues and recorded them for me. Ollie's most memorable blues, I found later, was an emotional version of "Broke Down Engine," one of the early recordings of Georgia singer Blind Willie McTell. Ollie and the others had grown up in a different musical era, when local singers were expected to be ready to play whatever anybody asked them for. The term they used for themselves was *songsters,* and it wasn't until I met musicians of the next generation that I ever heard anyone use the term *blues man.* Along with their blues they knew party songs, minstrel songs, and even performed a heartfelt version of the children's favorite "My Bonnie Lies over the Ocean." If I had asked them for hymns they would have obliged. Their music was simple and effective, never losing its dance beat, with vocal harmonies honed over long years of street practice. It was a quiet Sunday afternoon on a Mobile back street, and as far as the people who had crowded into the little room were concerned this was as close to a party as a hot Sunday afternoon allowed. I had brought a small bottle of whiskey, and we'd picked up some beer in a grocery store, and even with the band drinking most of what we'd bought, the stifling room rang with noisy, pleased, spontaneous applause.

Then after an hour the door opened, and a nicely dressed, middle-aged couple stepped inside, a second man a step behind them. They looked around at us wide-eyed. Who were we? After a silent moment of confusion I realized with a sinking feeling that it was their house. The woman who had led us inside was only a neighbor who knew they had gone out for part of the afternoon. With red-faced embarrassment I began an apology, but I was conscious that the family who owned the house was hesitant to say something that might upset three young white people, whatever they were doing in the family living room. Mary, Clarence, and I hurriedly began pushing the furniture back, the neighbors streamed noisily out into the sunlight, and by the time we'd folded up the ironing board, the woman of the house was able to laugh a little at the situation. She kindly allowed us to photograph the band in a formal pose on the porch, with the woman in the yellow dress who had led us inside smiling cheerfully, hands on her hips, standing between the guitar players.

In a collection of remarkable recordings made with women prisoners in Mississippi's notorious Parchman Farm the song collectors John A. Lomax in 1936 and Herbert Halpert in 1939 discovered a wealth of song material that opens a window on this world of the pre-blues. The women they recorded worked in the sewing room at Camp 13, where their portable recording equipment was set up. In her helpful notes to the collection Rosetta Reitz, who released the songs on her Rosetta Records label, explained that the women's work "was making clothes for the prisoners, mattresses and bedding for 3,000 beds, and field sheets for collecting cotton. The women also did the canning, and in 1935 they canned 15,000 cans of produce from the prison gardens. They also helped out in the fields."[1] The songs that were recorded, particularly in the Halpert sessions in May and June 1939, were so distinctive that there is every reason to believe that this was the archetypal form of what had become the much more widespread commercial blues idiom at about the same time many of these women were sent to prison.

The songs they performed were titled "blues," but stylistically there were distinct differences between what we think of as the commercial blues and what they were singing. Their songs had only two line verses, and they were sung in an extended, slow rhythm that was obviously accappella in its origins. There was no space in the vocal line for an accompanying instrument. The women's songs were in a repetitive melodic form, based on pentatonic scales that clearly suggested an African melodic memory. Textually they contained the germ of so many verses

The "Mobile Strugglers" on the porch with neighbors, Mobile, Alabama, Sunday afternoon, July 18, 1954. Left to right: Moochie Reeves, Ollie Crenshaw, Tyler Jackson.

Moochie Reeves.

recorded in the 1920s in Mississippi in the newer three line verse form. The material was released by the Mississippi Department of Archives and History on an emotionally wrenching LP titled *Jailhouse Blues*, marketed by Rosetta Records in 1987.

A selection of verses shows the clear connection to the moods and expressions of the earliest blues songs. The names of the women who sang were Beatrice Perry, Elinor Boyar, and Evie White.

Beatrice Perry:
I ain't gonna tell my man what my kid man do for me.
Ain't gonna tell my man what my kid man do for me . . .

Oh baby, you got a head right on your head and pains all in your thigh.
Now woman you ain't gonna do nothin' but walk the road and die.

Elinor Boyar:
When the sky rose this morning I was lyin' down on my clothes.
I was screamin' 'n' hollerin,' baby please don't go.

I said take me back, baby, try me one more time.
If I don't do right, break my poor head tryin'.

I said it's alright, baby, you gonna need my help some day.
I said it's alright, baby, you gonna need my help some day.

Say I hate to see the risin' sun go down.
Baby, I hate to see the risin' sun go down.

Evie White:
Don't tell me the moon looks pretty, shining down through the willow
     tree.
I can see my baby, but my baby can't see me.

No mo' freedom! No mo' good times in this wide, wide world for me.
Oh I'm beat from my feelin, and I'm sick as I can be.

But someday, yes, someday some day I will go free.
I'm gonna treat all you people just like you treated me.

The immediacy of the verses and the unadorned tone of the women's voices had the emotional authenticity I also heard in the music of Moochie Reeves and Ollie Crenshaw and their country skiffle band. If I had to characterize the kind of music I found in this world-before-the-blues, "authenticity" would be the word that encompassed what I was seeking.

Coming to the South in the winter can be an unforgettable experience of waking to blues skies and an eddy of light wind swaying the green trees.

It can also mean waking up in a raw, cold room under leaden skies, and since the South is so little prepared for the numbing air that can drift down from the North, bedrooms and bathrooms fill with a damp chill that gnaws at the bone. Outside the windows the sky is as leached of color as a page from a newspaper thrown in a pond. It was November of the next year, 1955, when Mary and I returned to the South, driving from California through Texas. I had bought a pre-war Packard sedan for $150 in Berkeley, where I'd been going to school, and with five of its eight cylinders functioning we traveled slowly through a gray, colorless Texas landscape. Coming from California, we hadn't thought about the Texas winter. The lack of gloves was only one of many problems, but since I had to grip the steering wheel the cold was always with me.

We felt the cold most intensely in the first streaks of morning light. We had so little money that some nights we slept in the car. The Packard was roomy enough for us to stretch out, and we had packed some blankets in the trunk so we'd have something to keep out the cold when we got to New Orleans. But in the car the cold seeped around us and we woke up stiff from curling up on the seats. In the small towns where we parked we took the chance that the police would pick us up, but if we moved on early we could stay out of trouble. We always drove off as soon as the first light woke us. Down the road we'd find coffee for Mary, and a package of sticky buns to hold us until lunch.

Our afternoon in Mobile with Moochie Reeves and the skiffle band had only been a small taste of the other styles of black music that were still everywhere in the South in the 1950s. The music had been shaped by the harrowing social conditions in the years after the Civil War, and by the sharecrop system that left the ex-slaves technically free but as tied to the cycle of cotton harvests as they had been during the decades of slavery. Many of the musicians performed for white audiences, and the music they presented to their fitfully attentive listeners was an informal collection of jaunty, reassuring songs and instrumental pieces. Some of these verses that everyone knew were humiliating racist carry-overs from the minstrel-show stages. It was already a world of music that was fading, but I still could imagine what it had once been, as individual faces and voices emerged from a countryside that was only beginning to be familiar.

My memory of those small Texas towns is the hardscrabble dirt beside the car when we woke up, the bleak, stippled layers of clouds that separated reluctantly for the pale sun, the brown-pebbled stretches of poor farmland that stretched away from the road as we began driving again, the small, poor houses inside their squares of rusted fence wire in the little towns. On other trips when I'd driven across Texas, the towns had been ordinary road stops and I'd only measured my way from one to the other to keep track of how far I'd driven. But on these pinched winter days in 1955 the towns were beginning to take on their own character.

For the first time I had a route I was trying to follow, even if the route was only a guess, or a suggestion, or an undependable memory that was leading us from town to town. The African American musical styles that I knew, the blues, the country breakdowns, the guitar evangelists and gospel congregations, had come almost entirely from phonograph records, and at first I hadn't realized that the music on the worn discs I found in used furniture stores in New Orleans had been recorded less than a generation earlier. Some of the songs I was listening to had made their way onto disc only a few years before. I had suddenly become conscious that many of the musicians who made the records were still living in the city ghettos or along backcountry roads everywhere in the South. If I followed the suggestions of the first musicians I encountered they might lead to so many others.

In the 1940s I had been moved by the music of two rural artists—musicians about whom nothing was known, except for the cold, unadorned facts taken from company ledgers and record master numbers of where they had done their recordings and the dates when they'd sat down in front of a microphone. One was a blues singer, someone named Robert Johnson, who had done a song that I knew from an acetate copy, "Stones in My Passway." The other was a guitar evangelist named Blind Willie Johnson, who had recorded a solo guitar instrumental, "Dark Was the Night, and Cold the Ground." His hummed vocal, blended with the keening legato tones of his slide guitar was one of the most emotional moments I knew in American music. A traditional jazz group I sometimes rehearsed with in Berkeley in 1948 usually ended the night's work by playing one of the pieces—the blues one night, the gospel instrumental the next. We knew nothing about the musicians who had made the records.

In New Orleans in the spring of 1954, a few weeks before Mary, Clarence, and I drove to Mobile, I spent an afternoon with a blind evangelist who had been playing on the street for nickels and dimes at the busy bus stop at the corner of South Rampart and Canal. His name was Dave Ross, a heavyset, middle-aged man, who always wore the customary dress shirt, necktie, and jacket, though his clothes were worn and faded, and it was obvious that someone else had knotted the tie for him. He was also a warm, friendly man, and what had interested me about his playing was that he knew some of the songs of Blind Willie Johnson. A few days later, in his kitchen, with the microphone propped up on a chair and his wife washing dishes in the background, I asked him about

Willie Johnson and his music. Without hesitation he answered that he'd met Willie in Beaumont, Texas, in 1929, then he'd met him again later that year in New Orleans.

"He came down here and he made a record, I believe, in '29, down here on Canal Street. See can I think of that song he sang—I forget. It's a song I know. Anyhow, I believe that's the last trip I knowed of him being down here. In '29, and I haven't met him since"

"Have you heard from him recently?" When I listen again to the album that documented that journey across the Texas winter I still can hear the surprise in my voice that I could even consider asking that question.

"No I haven't. Now and then I'd hear. He's still alive last time I heard from him, he's still living, but he's up there around I think Dallas or in that section there around Dallas."

It was Dave Ross's tentative suggestion that we might find Blind Willie Johnson in Dallas that led the next year to the pale sunrises in the harsh cold of the Packard, and to a Lighthouse for the Blind in the country-side outside of Dallas on a barren winter day with ice on the puddles beside the road. The director of the Lighthouse, a middle-aged, pleasant man named Abbie Lewis, was working patiently with an older man on a machine lathe that was winding wire, their faces turned away from the noise of the old machine, their hands guiding their movements. Like Dave Ross, both of them were blind. The workshop was a litter of shelves that were stuffed with tools and spools of wire. Walkways had been left open from the doorway to the lathe, and from the lathe to the shelves. The two men laughed to each other as they worked, moving confidently around the lathe. They had obviously spent many hours finding their way in the crammed room.

Again, as I'd found before, there was no irritation that we'd interrupted them, or that they thought there was anything unusual about people whose voices identified them as young, white, and northern asking about a black evangelist. With his fingers still carefully spread over the spooled wire and the mechanism of the lathe so he could go back to the work without danger, Lewis thought about where we might look next.

Brenham, Texas, was his suggestion. A small cotton town on a country road ninety miles west of Houston on the flatlands of south central Texas. He knew of a preacher in Brenham, someone called Adam Booker. What I had already learned in the South was despite the decades of the sharecropping, which had scattered the former slaves across the countryside in isolated cabins or lonely rows of "quarters," there was a deeply rooted sense of community that held people together despite the continual difficulties that they faced. If someone knew something that would lead us to the next town or help us find an address on the next street, they would finally tell us. In those years I found that even though I was learning so much about songs and guitar styles, I was learning much more about the resilient, determined people who had created this almost forgotten music.

We found Adam Booker living in a small, dark cabin on the outskirts of Brenham. We were sent from one cabin to another by nervously helpful women who stood behind closed screen doors as I explained why we wanted to talk to him. He was an old man who lived alone, small and stooped, but he was stubbornly taking care of himself. He drew his own water, tended his own stove, fixed his own meals, even though, like everyone else I'd talked to about Willie Johnson, he was blind. He was proud of his independence.

"I finished up in school. Like you, I finished thirty-two books. I'm a broom maker, bed mattress, doormats, pillows, collars, taught school four years in the state blind school, piano player, tune pianos, repair organs, cut cordwood, pick cotton, pull corn, anything!"

As we sat in the shadows of his cabin I could feel him slipping back to his youth, when he was preaching in the crossroads town of Hearn, Texas. With quiet laughter he let us follow in his footsteps as he remembered the busy Saturdays when the families who were bringing in their crop came into town to shop, and playing on the streets were blind singers like Willie Johnson with a tin cup wired to the neck of their guitars.

"Well, he was there, you know. He came to see his daddy, and while being there, you know, that being good cotton country, people were all there picking cotton and they would come on the streets every Saturday and he'd get on the streets and sing and pick the guitar, and they would listen and would give him money."

"Every Saturday he'd come in?"

"Well, yes sir, every Saturday. He wouldn't hardly miss."

In a final question I asked Booker if he knew what Willie Johnson looked like.

"No sir. I couldn't see well enough to tell his color."

Like Dave Ross, he hadn't heard that Willie Johnson had died, so he might still be living somewhere. He suggested that we try Beaumont.

In those years, if you wanted to find out about something in another town, along another road, there was no way to know whom you might ask. It was still impossible to believe that Blind Willie Johnson might be living—that there could even be a connection with that other world of recordings that had been done two or three decades before—so it was with a mixture of anticipation and resignation that we climbed back in the Packard and made our way across the drab countryside hoping to find someone to ask about a man who might have lived in the black section of Beaumont twenty years before. Beaumont is a medium-sized city close to the Texas coast, east of Houston near the state line with Louisiana, and it had once been a wealthy shipping and manufacturing center. But in the district where we stopped by grocery stores and barber shops to ask about Willie Johnson, there was no sign that there had ever been any wealth in the town. Across the South black neighborhoods were a different world. Segregation and economic discrimination had left their indelible marks on every street.

As we walked from one shop to the next, we were back in the same shabby squalor we had found in Mobile. The streets were unpaved, sidewalks non-existent. Rusty metal chairs sat on sloping wooden porches. The small frame houses needed paint, and behind the sagging chain fences scruffy, bristling dogs watched us narrowly. Outside of a seedy row of glass-front commercial buildings on Forsythe Avenue, the handful of businesses were mostly small grocery stores and ramshackle fenced yards that took care of auto repairs. The ground was frozen hard with the cold.

As we walked along Forsythe in the bright November afternoon we asked people if anyone had seen a blind gospel singer.

"Which one?" they asked.

I said he was an older man who played a guitar.

They asked again, "Which one?"

Late in the afternoon the druggist in Fowler's Pharmacy, at the corner of Neches Street, realized who we were looking for, and he sent us to a woman named Angeline who lived in a small house at the edge of town. We had to ask along the street for her, and we interrupted three or four young men with loose jackets pulled around their shoulders, sitting in a wood-frame shack stuffy with the heat from an iron stove. They shifted awkwardly and looked at me closely when I took a step inside. Yes, there was a woman in a little house down the street. She used to live with the man I was asking about. What did we want with her? I realized that white people sometimes came looking for the woman in the house they pointed out. I didn't ask what they wanted her for, but we found later that Angeline sometimes scraped together a poor living as a midwife and day nurse.

When she opened the door to her house Angeline looked at us without expression. She looked to be in her fifties, and was wearing a loose, faded dress with a sweater over her shoulders, her hair in a dark bandana. Her body was shapeless, and she stood waiting with her hands crossed in front of her waist. She had gold-rimmed glasses and her face was lined and tired. Then as we asked her about Blind Willie Johnson her expression changed. We had come too late, but we had come close. She was his widow, and even though we didn't find Willie Johnson himself she gave us her rich memories of the man we had come so far hoping to meet.

In the 1950s perhaps the most important thing we learned about the music we had grown up with on phonograph records was that the recordings were only a glimpse into the creative expression of an entire community. For every singer who was brought into the makeshift studios that were set up in the southern cities there were dozens of others who never were in the right place at the right moment. Angeline's shack had no electricity, but a neighbor let us use her front room for the tape recorder, and for the rest of the afternoon, with the microphone set up on a tabletop, Angeline created some of this world of music we had missed. To her it seemed that we had missed Blind Willie Johnson by only a few years. There had been a fire in their house.

"He died from pneumonia. We burned out there in the North End. 1440 Forest. And when we burned out we didn't know so many people and so I just, you know, drug him back in there and we laid on them wet bedclothes with a lot of newspaper. It didn't bother me, but it bothered him."

(She remembered the year as 1949. A search by researcher Randy Harper in the Texas state archives in the 1990s turned up a death date of September 18, 1945, and the official cause of death was listed as malaria.)

As Angeline described hearing Blind Willie singing on the street her guarded expression suddenly became animated, her voice warm with her youthful memories.

"He was singing on the street and he was singing 'If I hadda my way I would tear the building down,' and I went walking behind him [she sings] 'If I hadda my way, oh lordy lordy, if I hadda my way, oh, I'd tear the building down.' And I went on to, you know, talking with him and I asked him, I said, 'Say, are you married or single?' He says 'I'm single.' So I say, 'Come go to my house, I have a piano, and we will get together and sing.' And he says, 'Have you ever singed anywhere?' 'Well,' I say, 'I sing over the radio. Our church.'

"And he says, 'Alright.' And he went on over.

"Well, we went on over to the house and we sit down and taken a few drinks, you know, and played, and he played his guitar and I got up to the piano and I went to playing 'If I hadda my way.' He say, 'Go on gal! Tear it up!'

Well, we went on back and so he says, 'Well, let's get on the street,' and I said 'Well, look, don't you want something to eat?' He says, 'What have you cooked?' I said, 'Well, I have some crabs. We're making the old-time nigger gumbo.' I said, 'Don't you want some?' And he says, 'Well, yes, I'll take some.'

"So he went in there and accepted a bowl of gumbo and I broke it up, you know, the claws, so that he could enjoy. And then we sit down and eat."

As she talked and sang gospel pieces she knew from her church she was filling in the blurred sketch of the man I had known only as a voice on a phonograph record. In her voice and her memories of Willie and other street singers she had heard they became living figures. She leaned toward the microphone with her head to one side, hands clasped on her lap, often smiling to herself and gently shaking her head. In the neatly furnished room where we sat for the rest of the afternoon she opened the door to her young memories of the old street singers and let us know them almost as well as she had known them herself.

Of all the Texas cities, Houston in the 1950s was the most like New Orleans and Mobile. Not in the sterile, lifeless business district that began its steady growth a few years later, but in the noise and the vigor of the sprawling ghetto along Dowling Street. And the weather. Houston can be as stultifyingly hot as the Gulf Coast, but the city is without the beauty of the beaches or the blue shading of the Gulf itself. Houston is shapeless, flat, congested, and hot. It is also a very large city, and it would have been difficult for me to find anyone without some help. Once again I had the benefit of a community that continually knit itself together as quickly as it was pulled apart. The country skiffle band I'd recorded in Mobile had talked about the washboard player I'd heard out of the bus window. His name was Virgil Perkins, and his sister had her brother's address in Houston. The city was also too much for us to deal with by sleeping in the car so we found a cheap downtown hotel before I called the number she'd given me.

Virgil was wearing a suit and a buttoned shirt without a tie when he opened the door to his downstairs apartment on a side street close to Dowling. He surprised me by seeming to be nervous, not only because he had two white strangers in his living room, but because I was asking him to play the washboard. It was easy for me to forget that for the musicians I talked with there was the other side of the equation—they were uncomfortable that their neighbors would see them with white strangers, and they were self-conscious because their neighbors could think that they were putting on airs. There was finally some uncertainty about whether I'd like their old style of playing. Often there *were* difficulties with neighbors. At this hard-pressed economic level there were many unresolved jealousies and disappointments. I was simply happy that I'd been able to find him so easily, and in a city the size of Houston I felt certain that the police wouldn't be paying us much attention. Virgil was short and thin, a careful, friendly man, despite his nervousness. He worked as a gardner in the city and his hair was neatly trimmed short. Living with him in the simply furnished, tidy apartment was his wife Ethel, and her sister Equila Hall. They were attractive, middle-aged women, who would be part of the audience for Virgil while he was playing, and perhaps contributed to his nervousness.

He wasn't sure who had been playing the night I had seen him Mobile.

"Sometimes, you know how fellas are, when you say six, a couple of them, sometime the other fellas, you know, get boozed up over night. They wasn't no one compelling them to play and they just—they wouldn't show up, so whoever be there, they'd just go, make a little change or something."

He smiled self-consciously at the memory. "Some nights we average ten or twelve dollars on a busy night."

But the moment I heard him play a single rhythmic phrase on his washboard I was certain that he had been there in the shadowy Mobile storefront. I had never heard someone approach the washboard with his finesse. I knew about washboards and jugs, kazoos and combs. When they were introduced into the comedy blackface routines in the nineteenth century, at one level of the audience's perception, they were still another way to depict the African American as a childish buffoon. At the same time there was a centuries old tradition of music on homemade, improvised instruments. Rhythm on a washboard, melodies on a jug, the rasp of the kazoo, the thump of the clothesline on a washtub bass! What happened as the black musicians picked up the instruments, instead of the repetition of old racial stereotypes, was one more demonstration of the musicality of the performers, who could make music on whatever they played. Something that had been intended as a cruel joke had metamorphised into a new country music idiom.

As Virgil played the washboard with the set of thimbles he slipped onto his fingers, his "jazz horn" kazoo held stubbornly between his teeth, I was aware with the subtle shadings of the rhythm and complex variations in the song's basic pulse that he was conscious of how good he was. At the same time I sensed from the nervous tone of his voice when we talked that he wasn't sure that I also knew it.

There was also other music on the tapes from the night in Virgil's apartment. Sometime later, when we'd put the guitar and the washboard aside, his wife and her sister asked if they could sing into the microphone. Their music was in many ways completely different from the party songs and ballads we had been playing, though they drew from the same deep well of melody and rhythm. The songs they performed were from the oldest gospel traditions—the slow, intensely emotional "surge songs," sung in a breathy half whisper. The two voices were like parts of the same single melody, and at the same time they continually drew responsive inflections and phrases from each other. It was some of the most beautiful, most pure music I had ever recorded.

I would have to wait forty years before their songs finally were released on an album, but as they sang in the apartment that night, Ethel sitting forward on the edge of the chair, Equila on the apartment's couch, eyes shut, their concentration totally turned inward on their music, I could feel the walls falling away, as they had in Evangeline Johnson's little house when she remembered following Blind Willie Johnson along the street, singing his song with him. Like Virgil, like Angeline, like Moochie Reeves and Ollie Crenshaw and their jump-up blues, the two women were letting us hear still another accent of this continuing language of song, another dimension of the music I had first heard out of a bus window only a brief handful of years before.

In the late afternoons, when I flew into New Orleans from New York in the 1970s and the 1980s, a haze always softened the horizon. The slackening sun turned to a flat glare that slid across the city's outstretched palm of land, and the shining bend of the Mississippi River that holds New Orleans in its close embrace had dulled to a dirty gray. The crescent of the river drew so tightly around the city that the hints of its relentless power often stirred uneasy misgivings. If I was in one of the neighborhoods close to the levees, I could see even more clearly the edgy balance between the river and the city. The water level was dozens of feet above the land. The houses and their gardens, the streets, the lines of trees, were spread below the glistening surface, and it was obvious that if the levees gave way, or the massive system of pumps malfunctioned, the city would drown. Until August 29, 2005, I was somehow certain that it would never happen. Then the winds of hurricane Katrina swept in from the Gulf, its surge of water breeched the levees, and as we had known it could happen, the city drowned.

It was probably something in their nature that allowed for New Orleanians to ignore the weight of the water that was continually flowing against the earthen levee walls. The city had burned and it had been laboriously rebuilt, again and again winds had torn off roofs and uprooted trees, but the historical center of the city, the French Quarter and the Garden District, had never suffered serious flooding. Even the continual hurricanes from the Gulf of Mexico had generally come ashore to the east or the west of the city, battering New Orleans and leaving its earth black with spewing rains, filling its streets with water that somehow had to be made to flow uphill to fall back into the river, but with its buildings still standing. The pumping system, with its maze of pipes and drains, is one of the largest in the world, and it can pump up to twenty-five million gallons of water in a day. Until Katrina it had held the water away.

Three hundred years earlier, the land where the city's first streets were laid out in optimistically elegant rectangles was flat and featureless, home to a small band of Native Americans and a portage trail they followed from the Mississippi to Lake Ponchartrain to the north. It was a brush-choked swamp, pestilent in the soaked winters and almost as sickly for the rest of the year. It was land without any particular characteristic to set it apart from the other settlements that were being hacked out of the Louisiana wilderness—except the crescent shaped curve of the river that enclosed it.

The threat of flooding that always lingered at the edge of the city's consciousness helped give New Orleans a little of its fatalistic acceptance of life's vagaries. In the 1970s and the 1980s the city met its chronic difficulties with a casual shrug. The problems went beyond the threat of the water to the persistent unemployment, poverty, crime, and the still painful aftermath of the racial segregation that continued to divide the city into black, white, and Creole communities, each with its own complicated attitudes toward its role in the city's culture. But even with this uneasy legacy, New Orleans was still a city unlike any other.

In those calmer moments of New Orleans' recent past, to walk on the quiet streets in the Garden District, with their old wooden mansions settled in their broad gardens, or drive along the breakwater at Lake Ponchartrain to the restaurants on the old piers built out over the lake at West End, was to feel that the steady growth and progress that the rest of the country was experiencing had been left at the city limits. The traffic that choked the downtown business streets hadn't spread out to the older neighborhoods, and under their leafy arcade of branches the side streets along St. Charles Avenue were still empty except for occasional delivery trucks or children on bicycles. The city, on a summer day, seemed to breath with a satisfied stillness.

As pleasant as so much of New Orleans still was then, though, it was even pleasanter in the 1950s. At least I tell myself that it was, and certainly one of the reasons I remember it with such nostalgia is that I was on Red Clark's list. Red Clark's list? I have to make it clear that I'm not someone whose name turns up on lists. It was the only list I've been on in my life. Because of that heady experience from the 1950s, though, I do have some intimation as to how it felt to be given the special treatment I always envied in old Hollywood movies—the nod of recognition from the maitre d' when the leading man swept into a gilded night club with an equally gilded model on his arm. For all of us who were on Red Clark's list it meant we had been granted a special privilege that meant more to us than any of the other possible rewards those years offered—it was like being invited to a Hollywood star's birthday party.

Who was Red Clark and what was his list? Red was the sousaphone player and the manager of the Eureka Brass Band, and during those years the band was the city's most distinguished African American musical organization. If you were on his list he called you to let you know every time the band was hired to play a job.

Red Clark's formal name was Joseph. He was the son of a brass band musician, Joseph Clark Sr. His light skin had a reddish tone, so he was called Red, just as many other "high colored" men and women have been given the same nickname. He was sixty-one in the spring of 1954, when I made it on to his list, a large, round shouldered man with a seamed, friendly face and sorrowful eyes. His mouth was shaped by his missing teeth. He walked with a kind of loose shuffle, careful and plodding, but he also possessed a serious sense of dignity. When the phone would ring in the mornings in the stifling, high-ceilinged apartment in the old building at 728 Dumaine Street where my first wife, Mary, and I had a balcony apartment, I would hear Red's earnest, wheezing voice.

"Sam, got a funeral" or "Sam, we got a Sunday school. I think you know the people I'm talking about." After a few phone calls, if he said, "It's the Olympians this time," I knew he meant the Young Men's Olympians, a social organization in the black community with a revered history, and a membership that was steadily aging.

With the same breathy tone he would tell me the time the band was going to start and the day of the job. Then would come the more complicated business of telling me just where the band was meeting. He had grown up in New Orleans, and beneath the wheeze of the teeth that weren't there any more I could hear the rounded edges of the city's laid-back accent. He knew every street and corner in the neighborhoods where he'd been following the brass bands since he was a child, skipping along as his father marched with his baritone horn. For someone like myself, who had been in the city only three or four years and lived in the French Quarter, the directions often took a little time to get straightened out—at least as straight as I was able to get them.

"I can't tell you the name of the street there," Red would begin, "I forgot it if I did know. I know there's a sign for the street there somewhere and you can look around for it. But where we going to be—it's by that grocery store on the corner just down from Liberty with the awnings with the stripes and you walk along the fence until you come to a wall. The last time I saw it it was painted white. You look along the wall and that's where the church building for the Sunday School is. You come out that way and you'll find it."

In the quiet back streets, the bands and the little parades were still a part of the community's everyday life. There was always at least a small, straggling group of "second liners," the band followers who danced along the sidewalks or trailed the processions down the streets. Usually there were even more people standing on their front porches or on the

The Eureka Brass Band, mid 1950s. Red Clark is playing the sousaphone at far right; the two trombonists are (left to right) Sonny Henry and Albert Warner; the tenor saxophonist is Emanuel Paul; the alto player, Ruben Roddy, is concealed by Albert Warner; the bass drummer is Robert Lewis; and the three trumpeters are (left to right) Percy Humphrey, Kid Shiek Colar, and Charlie Love.

front steps of the old frame houses, and they simply waved with a casual familiarity as the bands passed in a loose marching order, led by a stern, ornately sashed grand marshal down the mostly unpaved streets. Sometimes I followed the Eureka to one of the cemeteries outside of town and as the parade passed along the crushed shell shoulder of the road the only people we saw along the route were sitting in their cars.

The parades went on even if there was rain. The musicians had plastic covers that fastened to their caps with elastic. One of the people from out of town who followed the parades whenever they were in New Orleans in the 1950s was photographer Lee Friedlander, who brilliantly caught the mood of the bands and the parades in his nostalgic book *The Jazz People of New Orleans*.[1] In one of the photos Alfred Williams, playing the snare drum with the Young Tuxedo Brass Band, is marching calmly in the last row of musicians despite a gray scattering of rain, and a young, thin, serious-faced fan is holding an umbrella over the drum to keep the skin head dry. The band enthusiast is me.

I learned from Red's phone calls that I could never anticipate what kind of a job the Eureka might be playing, since people hired the bands for almost any kind of occasion. Usually it was a funeral or a Sunday school parade. Often some of the band's musicians were fellow members of the venerable fraternal lodges whose funerals were part of lodge ritual. The Sunday school parades were an opportunity for parents and church elders to show off the young members of the congregation. The boys and girls were dressed in spotless white shirts and white dresses and they marched in self-conscious files behind the band, trying, with very little success, not to grin happily when they saw someone they knew waving from the curb. The parades never went on for very long, since the short legs wouldn't last for more than the familiar neighborhood streets. The bands that played for Mardi Gras parades were usually the large local high school bands, but in the noisy confusion of carnival day itself I would often see some of the Eureka members mingling with musicians from the other brass bands, playing on the streets with pick-up groups.

Red could usually tell me what city bus line would get me close to where the band was going to meet, but when I left the French Quarter I always gave myself thirty minutes more than he thought I'd need so I could find the street or the corner. If I'd gotten the directions wrong I would search the streets until I found the band sitting on the steps outside a grocery store, or standing out of the sun against the side of a building. If it took me too long to find the address Red had given me and they'd already moved off, then I'd walk a few blocks in the direction that neighbors pointed out to me and I would stop and stand still to listen. New Orleans is laid out on flat, featureless land and away from the downtown business streets it's a city of one- and two-story houses. In the older African American neighborhoods, with their chalk white curbing of crushed shells and rows of old wooden "shotgun" houses built one against another, the streets where the parades passed were generally drowsy and quiet. The Eureka's leader, trumpeter Percy Humphrey, had a high, piercing tone, and if I stood still and listened long enough, through the green canopy of leaves from the trees along the streets I would hear the sound of a trumpet somewhere around the corner.

I never asked Red how many names were on his list. There couldn't have been too many of us. Sometimes Mary and I would be the only ones standing in the shade of the grocery store's rusted awning, sipping a beer, and listening to the casual talk of the band members as they waited for Percy to blow the little two note call that signaled them out onto the hot pavement. The musicians always dressed in dark trousers and white shirts with formal black neck ties. Dark band jackets if it was a winter parade, sometimes with a sweater buttoned up under the jacket. If it was the summer they were in shirt sleeves, but the sleeves were usually not rolled up. If it was a parade they wore white caps with the name *Eureka* on a cloth strip above the stiff visor. For a funeral the caps and the name strips were black.

I could always laugh and joke with Red while we waited for a parade to begin, but I would never have thought of joking with Percy. He was a graying, serious-faced man in his late forties, dignified and slow moving. He was the grandson of Professor James Humphrey, who had taught many of the city's finest brass band musicians. Percy had played all his life, but to help with the family's bills he began selling insurance in 1939. He had to spend hours every week going from house to house collecting the small premiums. He would shake his head when he had to postpone a meeting or a rehearsal. "It isn't so much money—sometimes just a quarter or fifty cents, but I got to go round when they just been paid, so they don't spend it on something else."

For Red, it was a pleasure to see any of us who turned up, and he never seemed to notice if we got into any "second lining" ourselves as we followed them along the sidewalk. Percy, however, expected us to behave with some decorum. One sunny afternoon when the band was playing with even more than its usual loose swing, I drifted out into the street to join a gathering of second liners from different neighborhoods who were showing off their own styles of footwork and I fell in with one of the shuffling dance steps that involved a lot of hip swinging. In the middle of a slide I glanced up and saw Percy staring narrowly at me in stern disapproval, stiffly shaking his head. Chagrined, I retreated to the sidewalk, and with Mary resumed the casual, floating rhythmic step alongside the band that everyone who grows up in New Orleans, white or black, knows how to do from the day of their birth.

Mary had a day job and often she couldn't get away for the music and sometimes I was the only one of the French Quarter people who managed to find where the band was starting. Most of the time another French Quarter dweller, Dick Allen, who had been interviewing musicians for several years and was to go on to help develop the oral jazz history archives of the William Hogan Collection at Tulane University, would be there, and since Dick seemed to know every New Orleans jazz enthusiast in the world, he would often have three or four visitors with him. Other friends from the Quarter had weekday jobs, so I could only count on seeing them on weekends. To help Red out we also had our own phone network. The moment we hung up the phone after Red called us we were back on the phone, calling the people on our own lists. It was clear that we were being granted an opportunity that wouldn't come again, and we prized what had been granted us.

When I look back on those years, it is the funerals that I remember the most of all the jobs the Eureka played. Of the rich profusion of musical forms that have found an expression in the African diaspora it is probably the New Orleans brass band funerals that are the most often described, even if the ceremony itself sometimes has lost a little in the myriad translations. Newer research also suggests that the city's first marching band funerals were performed by the German bands that were a part of the city's cultural mix after the waves of immigration in the mid-1800s, but in the succeeding decades the city's black musicians adopted the tradition as their own.

In the classic descriptions of a New Orleans music funeral the band follows the body with its sorrowing marches to the cemetery, the body in its hearse with the family following in two or three other cars. When the ceremony is over at the graveside, the drummer tightens up his snares, the bass drummer pounds out a syncopated rhythm, and the brassy roar of a street dance takes the mourners back to the starting point of the march in a celebration of the triumph of faith over death. For most of the funerals I followed with the Eureka, however, the day was longer and more crowded, and the musical sequence was more complicated. Instead of two intervals during the funeral when there was music, there were actually three long sections of the ceremony when the band was expected to play.

If the Eureka was playing for one of the lodges who used them regularly, like the Young Men's Olympians, the meeting place was the sidewalk outside of the lodge headquarters. The music would begin there with the solemn procession of the lodge members in their dark suits and hats through the streets to the church. The Eureka played a restrained group of street pieces; hymns and marches, danceable for the small crowds who immediately fell in with them along the sidewalks, but there was a mood of respect for the deceased. Anyone seeing the parade pass would immediately know from the furled black banners the lodge members carried, the black gloves and sash of the grand marshal, and the black bands on the caps the band were wearing, why they were marching. Then they would scatter along the street outside of the church for the long pause of the church service. It was usually an hour's wait, and most of the band members would sit and join us for a bottle of beer.

When I think of those afternoons it is the easy languor of the long waits outside the church, the New Orleans' smells of damp wooden buildings, mildewed stucco, flowering gardens, and dark earth that stays in my memory. As the hour passed it was usually one of the best opportunities I had to ask questions, to write down addresses and phone numbers, and to hear more of the endless stream of slow, rambling reminiscences of the early days of jazz and the brass bands in the city as the musicians sat talking to each other as much as they were talking to us.

The first break in the day's slow mood would come as the church doors swung open with a swell of song from the choir inside. The sobbing family members were led out to the line of cars that would take them to the cemetery and the service beside the waiting grave. Then came the casket, the pallbearers often as old as the person they were burying. The band members stood up, stretched, and lined themselves up behind the grand marshal in their accustomed order of the two trombones and sousaphone in the front line, then the two saxophones, behind them the snare drummer and the bass drummer, and finally the band's three trumpet players. The snare drummer slackened the snares on the drum to muffle the sound, at a signal the bass drum beat out the somber funeral cadence, and with the slow, studied half-step/ half-march that was part of the funeral tradition, the band's trumpets began one of the older hymns, often "What a Friend We Have in Jesus," as they moved away down the street.

If the deceased lodge member had been particularly fond of the Eureka's music, the band would save one of their complicated, arranged dirges for the final blocks before the cemetery. The music for the dirges was mounted on small, much-handled cards about four by six inches that Percy Humphrey carried in a worn canvas bag around his shoulder. In the early years, to prevent other bands from copying their most acclaimed pieces, the tops of the arrangements with the titles and composer credits were cut off, and despite exhaustive research the titles of some of the pieces in the band's repertoire remain a mystery. The dirges were long, multi-strained compositions that had complicated changes of key. They were difficult to play, and they featured sorrowing solos by the trumpets and saxophones. It was music that sobbed and wept over the thudding beat of the bass drum. One of the most ambitious of the dirges, "Eternity," with its throbbing melodies by the trumpets playing in duets and trios often brought the procession to the gates of the cemetery.

We didn't have to wait as long outside the cemetery. At some of the older cemeteries there was no room among the crumbling crypts for more than the family members, the lodge banners, and the minister. The musicians found themselves balancing on the worn edges of the older grave plots as they waited for the ceremony to be over. A short eulogy, the lowering of the coffin, the cries of the mourning relatives and the newly bereaved widow or widower; the despair of the confused, wildly sobbing children. Then came the third act of the musical drama, the march back to the lodge headquarters where we had begun hours before, the band's musicians finally allowing themselves to swing out freely. In the sudden brassy flash of the music there was the symbolism of the glorious afterlife that followed death, but for the tired musicians there was also the encouraging prospect that after a few more blocks they could finally pack away their instruments and go home. The funerals offered such a feast of music that we counted them like shining beads on a golden chain. All of us who had trailed along for the afternoon would return to the French Quarter, stiff and sunburned, drowsy with the beer, our ears still ringing with the glories of the music, and as sweaty and almost as tired as the Eureka's musicians themselves.

The abrupt change in the musical style in the homeward journey of the funerals could be considered the religious equivalent of the sacred and profane—the sacredness of the ceremony, and the Dionysian celebration of the return from the cemetery, but in musical terms a more complicated shift was occurring. While the music of the formal dirges was European, the loose, noisy street pieces expressed the persistent strains of the African American musical culture. The brassy, drum-punctuated *sound* of the band was the same, but the street style took on the rhythmic layering and the shifting accents of their African antecedents. The New Orleans street bands like the Eureka were one of the most vivid expressions of the city's complicated social structure, and their skilled melding of the two musical cultures was to have a long-lived effect on the jazz styles that flowed from them.

What was immediately obvious in the mingling of the cultures were the drum rhythms. For the occasional composed marches that were still part of the Eureka's repertoire the bass drummer and the snare drummer played a straight, unaccented beat, with the strong pulse on the first count of the measure to cue the marchers. In a decided contrast, the bass drum rhythm for the street pieces changed to a syncopated dum-dum-dum-de-dum-dum, and the drummer added an offbeat with a bent coat hanger on a cymbal mounted on the drum's shell. At the same moment, the snare drummer switched his unaccented rhythm to the offbeat, and instead of a march the beat was now accompanying a loose-jointed dance. Against this less restricted rhythm the horns blazed with a new freedom, and there was an immediately perceptible vocalization of the tone of Percy's ringing solos as he trailed a step behind the other trumpeters, giving himself a little room to hear what he was playing.

Often during one of these afternoons as we sat talking with the musicians, someone would solemnly declare that this was a moment that would soon be lost and that this music and its rich traditions would disappear from the city. The reality, however, is that in New Orleans a half century later, before Katrina struck, there were probably more bands out on the streets than at any other time. The new bands performed on the streets and in local clubs, and some of the young musicians spent more time in the recording studio than all the bands of the 1950s did throughout their careers. It was, however, a music that had been created in a changed city. The *sound* of the new generation of bands had clear affinities with the older bands, but it was a different musical idiom, with roots in a different tradition, and with ambitions and dimensions beyond the modest dirges and hymns and marches of the older style music. The differences between the older bands like the Eureka, and the younger bands that began to replace them are a vivid chapter in the long story of the New Orleans street rhythms. At the same time, they mirrored the social changes and the shifting racial realities that were a product of the city's complicated history.

From its beginnings, New Orleans has had its own distinctive character. For the first forty-five years after its founding in 1717 it was French, but French with an admixture of peoples and cultures from every part of North America, the Caribbean, and Europe. A French military engineer laid out the city's first plan. The city, however, failed to develop economically, though it was named the capital of the Louisiana colony in 1722. In a census done the year before, its population was only 470 people; a majority, 277, whites; with 172 African slaves, and 21 enslaved natives. Then in the tumult of the European dynastic wars the city for a brief period, 1763 to 1800, was ceded to Spain. It was the only time during its colonial era that it was efficiently governed, and under Spanish rule the population growth was more robust. In 1803, when *La Nouvelle Orléans* became American, its population was estimated at about 8,000, of whom 4,000 were white, 2,700 were enslaved Africans, and 1,300 manumitted slaves, designated as freed "persons of color." Before it was incorporated into the United States as part of the Louisiana Purchase in 1803, large areas of the growing city were destroyed by raging fires in 1788 and 1794, and the Spanish rebuilt it in the style of their colonies to the south. It is this Spanish section that in characteristic New Orleans fashion is called the "French" Quarter.

The New
Orleans
levee in the
1890s.

In its first unsteady decades as part of the United States the city continued to develop in its own distinct way. Across what was called the "commons"—now known as Canal Street—an ambitious business section spread along the riverbank and slowly became identified as the "American" section of New Orleans. As capital of the state, and with its site close to the mouth of the Mississippi River, the city was the terminus for the river's growing traffic from the states to the north, many of them southern states, like Louisiana, implacably committed to slavery. In the city, however, the French had left not only their language and their legal system, they had also bequeathed to the city their more liberal attitudes toward freed Africans. New Orleans had a large French upper class, the Creoles, with jealously guarded social privileges, and allied with it was the large French-speaking population of freed slaves who occupied a vaguely defined social space somewhere between the aristocratic French, the newly arrived white merchants from the states to the north, and—at the bottom of the social pyramid—the Africans who were still enslaved. It wasn't unusual for wealthy freed blacks to have slaves of their own.

The New Orleans brass bands reflected the cultural diversity that is at the heart of the city's uniqueness, with the usual New Orleans diversions from all accepted paths. A white bass drummer, Jack Laine, one of the most active of the city's brass band musicians at the end of the nineteenth century, lived into his nineties, and he was always ready to talk to anyone who came up his front steps and asked him about the early years of jazz and the city's brass band traditions. In the 1890s he worked during the day as a blacksmith for a cartage firm, but on weekends he played the bass drum in his marching band, and on three or four nights a week he played the trap drum in his dance orchestra. It was a common solution to the problem that musicians didn't make much money. What Laine remembered from his early years of playing on the streets was that there weren't significant differences between the repertoire of the city's African American marching bands and its European-influenced white bands. All of the band musicians played from written parts, and they took considerable pride in their musical skills.

Many of the members of the two best-known African American marching bands, the Excelsior and the Onward, came from the Creole community. Often they were music teachers as well as performers, and they passed on their musical traditions to generations of younger musicians. They also took part in many of the city's ceremonies and celebrations that included music. During the months of the Centennial Exposition and Cotton Festival that opened in Audubon Park in mid-December, 1884, there was often work for the band members. The Excelsior Band played at the ceremony opening the "colored" exhibits on February 23, 1885, and the *Daily Picayune* described them as "the well-known Excelsior Cornet Band of the city."[2] A crowd of more than four thousand listened to their program of light concert music.

Laine's earliest memories of having a drum of his own dated from 1885, at the summer closing of the Exposition, when his father bought him one of the instruments that was auctioned off. What the Exposition also left was a variety of new dance rhythms and a new concept of the role of a brass band which were to have a lasting effect on the music that would develop in New Orleans over the next decades. "Jass" music, as New Orleans's style of band ragtime came to be called, probably would have emerged eventually from the city's mix of cultures, but the effect of the "Mexican Band" that performed in the Exposition, certainly hastened the process of change.

The Mexican government considered the Exposition an opportunity to demonstrate the country's progress since its independence fifty years before, and also to honor the inauguration of the country's new president, Porfirio Díaz. The Mexican pavilion was large and lavish, and to provide entertainment the officials sent one of their best-known musical ensembles, the band of the Eighth Regiment of Mexican Cavalry. The number of musicians varied, but there were always at least sixty to eighty instrumentalists available to perform, and they appeared everywhere in the Exposition. In their varied programs the musicians performed as the entire band or as smaller ensembles that played for less formal events, including dances and light entertainment.

For the city's African American musicians there was not only the startling sight of a highly trained musical group with a range of skin colors from white to black, they were impressed by the obvious level of the Mexicans' musicianship and the wild enthusiasm that greeted their playing. Even more important, however, were the syncopated rhythms the Mexicans included in many of their arrangements. It was perhaps these new rhythms that more than any other element of their musical style gave the musicians in orchestras everywhere in the city the impetus to experiment with a freer syncopation in their dance rhythms. Among the pieces listed on the concert programs the Mexicans played were *dansas*, a syncopated rhythm that was derived from the same *habanera* that was at the center of a variety of Latin dance rhythms.

The influence of the Mexican musicians in the local musical world was reinforced when a few of them remained after the band returned to Mexico in the summer. The band had been in New Orleans for several months, and some of the performers had formed attachments and found bands that would hire them. In the complicated New Orleans balancing between the races they were generally designated "Creoles." As the new ragtime style became more popular, the Creole musicians, with their concert training, found themselves marginalized. Though they made every effort to maintain their privileged position, the legal basis for their distinctive life style was stripped away by changes in the city's racial codes in the 1890s. When I lived in the French Quarter in the 1950s, however, the differences between the city's black, white, and Creole societies were still clearly defined.

What a band like the Eureka represented, with the worn little canvas bag of music parts Percy Humphrey carried on his shoulder, and its dedication to regular rehearsals to be able to perform pieces like the complex dirge "Eternity," was this still French-speaking Creole society. Because of skin color, however light, the Creoles had been denied any real role among the city's elite, but they were determined to maintain the separation between themselves and what they perceived as the crude, unassimilated Africans. On those afternoons, when Red Clark called to tell me where the Eureka was going to play, I often saw the city's racial debate acted out on the streets.

The clearest glimpse I had of the tensions the music represented was at a casual neighborhood parade back of Claiborne Avenue on a hot, sun-bleached Saturday afternoon. On the weekends any sort of parade picked up a crowd, since most people were home from their jobs. By the time the band had gone three or four blocks there would be a crowd of second liners strung out along the sidewalk and the streets, dancing along with the music. There was usually an obstreperous cluster of young men, shirts off, arms waving, who gave off a heavy smell of wine. Even with two or three policemen walking along at the head of the parade there were often sudden flare-ups of temper that could lead to street fights. I remember once or twice a flash of knives between one of the stumbling dancers and someone who had accidentally bumped against him on the sidewalk.

The Eureka stubbornly maintained its role as the last of the reading bands, carrying on the traditions of the Excelsior and the Onward bands, but they also played the popular songs and the familiar gospel melodies that the crowds danced along with. The rhythm for these pieces was the loosely swinging pattern stressing the second and fourth beats of the measure that had been introduced by the more casually organized bands that began to appear on the streets when ragtime held its place in the repertoire. The bass drummer announced the street pieces with an abrupt cadence that began as a simple, unaccented count, then veered into the syncopation that signaled to the crowd that this was going to be one of their street melodies—an old rag tune like "Panama" or "You Tell Me Your Dream." Often it was one of the gospel standards that were first recorded as street pieces by Sam Morgan's jazz band in the 1920s, something like "Sing On" or "Over in the Glory Land." The bass drum's introduction was the familiar dum-dum-dum-de-dum-dum, which was enough to bring a shout from the crowds.

At the sound of the new beat the street came alive with dancing. The arrangements for these melodies were spontaneous and direct, the entire band playing uncomplicated versions of the familiar songs in unison harmonies. The trombones, Sonny Henry and Albert Warner, blared out their loud two horn solos, Percy Humphrey's trumpet soared out over the tumult of the street with his cascading choruses, Emanuel Paul, who played the tenor saxophone with a throbbing vibrato, repeated the melody, with a lilting, lighter-toned counterpoint from the alto saxophonist, Reuben Roddy, who had come to New Orleans from an early apprenticeship in Kansas City with Walter Page's Orchestra. At the left front corner of the band Red Clark stomped stolidly on with his sousaphone. The two drummers marched in front of the three trumpet players: Percy, Willie Pajeaud, and usually George Colar, known as "Kid Sheik."

The snare drummer could be any one of several who played with the band, but the bass drummer was generally a tall, serious-faced man named Robert Lewis, who was always called by his nickname "Son Few-clothes." The bass drum had a battered cymbal mounted on the top, and Son played the offbeats on the cymbal with a twisted metal coat hanger that had a handmade taped handle. The snare, the bass drum, and the cymbal built a steadily shifting, irresistible rhythm that drove the second liners into looser and wilder bursts of excitement. The surge of bodies along the sidewalk often pushed people standing in front of their houses back against the fences or into the gardens. If anyone pushed back, the volatile, half-drunk mood, in a moment, could take on a threatening tone.

On this Saturday afternoon's parade Percy realized that the band was approaching one of the city's more despairing housing projects, with even more unpredictable crowds. Around him the glistening, sweat-soaked second liners were already jostling against each other in unsteady clashes. Some of the crowd was stumbling against automobiles that had been trapped in the rush, the passengers inside turning their heads nervously to see how long the parade would go on. On the sidewalks, children in their mothers' arms who felt themselves being squeezed in the press began to cry. Their mouths were open, but no sound was audible in the thunder of the music and the shouting dancers.

After another look around him, Percy fumbled in his canvas bag and pulled out a much-fingered set of band parts that he passed out to the other musicians. As they marched out from under the shadows of the underpass, the snare drum and Son's bass drum tapped out a new rhythm, and the band burst into a John Philip Sousa march in a precise 6/8 time.

Sousa's marches are a unique part of American culture and they are brilliantly conceived small compositions for brass bands—but you can't dance to them. The only thing you can do is march. There was a frustrated roar from the crowd. The second liners surged in protesting groups alongside the musicians, and for a moment I thought the crowd might attack them. It was not only the change in tempo that upset the dancers. What Percy had done to cool down the mounting excitement was to insist, for a moment, on cultural values that were already disappearing from the culture of New Orleans' streets. Part of the anger I could sense was that some of the young men who had been sweating and shouting around the band as they danced alongside understood the implications of Percy's gesture.

When the musicians marched steadily on, ignoring the tumult, I could see the loudest of the protesters peeling off to sprawl on low porches and steps. Waving arms and fingers in broad, emphatic gestures they let the Eureka go on past them. It wasn't until the band was a few blocks beyond the housing project that Percy softly blew the two note call that signaled a new piece. Son Fewclothes beat the familiar syncopated bass drum introduction to a free-swinging street performance of the old vaudeville number "Down in Honky Tonk Town," and in a moment the glowering mood of the crowd still with them turned into shouts of excitement.

It's probably not too much of an exaggeration to say that without the brass bands there wouldn't have been the style of early jazz that emerged in New Orleans. One night in a large, elegant auditorium in California in the mid-1950s, at the height of the New Orleans jazz revival, I managed to squeeze into the crowd at a concert with Louis Armstrong and His All-Stars, the small group he toured with for the last twenty-five years of his career. For the concert they were appearing with the band led by trombonist Kid Ory, who had known Armstrong from their New Orleans days and recorded the classic Hot Five and Hot Seven sides with him in Chicago in the 1920s. The promoter had decided that the most exciting way to open the concert would be with an old style brass band parade up and down the aisles of the auditorium.

With easy laughter and a flourish of the white handkerchief that he always had with him when he played, Armstrong fell into line beside Ory's trumpeter, Ted Buckner, and with as comfortable grace Louis's trombone player, the affable Jack Teagarden, lined up behind them with Ory. Behind the two trombones were the clarinetists, Ory's Joe Darensbourg and Armstrong's Barney Bigard. The drummers had to struggle with harnesses for their ordinary dance band instruments, but after much encouraging whooping from the crowd the trumpets led the band off in a reasonably well-ordered march up the main aisle, playing the street favorite "High Society." The only thing we didn't have with the parade was second lining. The ushers managed, more or less, to keep us at least close to our seats as the band surged past, all of the musicians somehow grinning a little as they played. When they finally got back to the stage after the ringing, brilliant improvised choruses of the march, the routine shows they offered us with their usual bands seemed almost anti-climactic.

The history of jazz wouldn't be the same without the New Orleans brass bands, but for many of the city's young musicians the bands were also a place to sharpen their technique and practise their reading skills. Willie

Pajeaud, the Eureka's second trumpeter and soloist for the dirges, often reminisced about their challenges to each other.

> You'd be in the barber shop and you'd see somebody who was learning to play there getting a hair cut and you'd go over to him and say, "Give me all the notes of the scale of A-flat relative minor." And he'd open his eyes and tell you the notes. Just like that. And they had this test they'd give you if you played the trumpet. They'd hang the trumpet up on a string and they'd tell you, "Now you go and you don't touch your horn with your hands and you play me a high-C." What they meant by that, you couldn't get help—you had to make that note with only your lips. How many trumpet players can do that if they haven't studied?[3]

When the musicians left the discipline of the brass bands they generally had the skills to handle any kind of music. In New Orleans, with its Mardi Gras parades, there were as many white brass bands as there were black, and most of the younger white jazz musicians of the 1920s, including many with Italian backgrounds, like Nick LaRocca, Tony Sparbaro, and Tony Parenti, grew up playing on the streets. One of the most important figures of the New Orleans Revival, the clarinetist George Lewis, spent years with the brass bands. He was an early member of the Eureka, beginning with them in 1923, and he was included in the band, playing an E-flat clarinet, when they made their first recording in 1951. Many of the brass band musicians were continuing a family tradition. Red Clark's father, Joseph Clark Sr., played the baritone horn in the Onward Brass Band and the Excelsior Brass Band, two of the leading bands in the city.

In the early years of the Eureka it was already considered a "reading" band. The Allen Brass Band across the river in the Algiers neighborhood was more casually organized, and many of the younger jazz musicians, like Armstrong, were hired for the parades and funerals. The leader was cornetist Henry Allen Sr., and his son, Henry Allen Jr., "Red" Allen, went on to a brilliant career in New York as trumpet soloist first with the Luis Russell Orchestra, then as leader with his own small groups for another thirty years. He began playing with his father's brass band when he was still in short pants, and once in the late 1940s, when he was back at home visiting his family, he found that his father's band was playing a Sunday afternoon parade in Algiers. Resplendent in his New York clothes he went back to the house for his trumpet and walked for a few blocks playing beside his father, reviving his memories of his first jobs in the streets.

Percy Humphrey, the Eureka's musical leader and trumpet soloist was also from one of New Orleans' musical dynasties. His grandfather, Jim

Humphrey, who lived in a white house at the corner of Valas and Liberty streets, taught many of the finest musicians in the city, and also traveled by horse and buggy out into the countryside to instruct the local players. He taught the entire Eclipse Brass Band at the Magnolia Plantation, and as its musicians moved into the city they found their way into some of the finest New Orleans bands and orchestras. His son, Percy's father Willie Sr., was a clarinetist, and his daughters Lillian and Jamesetta both played bass. Three of his grandsons played important roles in New Orleans music. Earl played the trombone and took his love for bands to the traveling circuses. He and his father were in the band for the Al G. Barnes Circus in 1919. When Earl was in the city he played with the Onward and the Eureka. His younger brother Willie, also a clarinetist, played with the Excelsior Brass Band. Percy, three years younger than Willie, began playing with the Eureka in the 1920s.

The Eureka itself had a long tradition of musicianship. It was formed about 1920 as the Hobgoblin Band, the club band for a lodge called the Hobgoblin Club, an uptown marching group. The Hobgoblins asked them to play oftener than there were the resources to pay them, and when the Odd Fellows Lodge asked them to become their band under a different name the band's leader, cornetist Willie Wilson, agreed. The newly named band had a christening party in Wilson's backyard. There was a cake with the new name, Eureka, written on it in icing.

In the summer of 1954 the jazz historian Frederic Ramsey Jr. came to New Orleans with his wife, Amelia, and their one-year-old son, Locke, to spend a few weeks in the city. Fred found a stuffy, low-ceilinged apartment for rent close to Coliseum Square, on the other side of Canal Street. He was passionately interested in New Orleans and its music. He was tall and jowly, usually in rumpled shorts and a short-sleeved shirt. Fred had been one of the editors of the most influential history of jazz that had been written up to that time, *Jazzmen*, published in 1939. It was the earliest study of jazz that placed the beginnings of the music in New Orleans, and the colorful introductory sections written by his close friend Charles Edward Smith portrayed the mystique of New Orleans and its musicians and musical styles with so much emotion that for many years jazz historians never seriously questioned the role of the city in their iconography.

Fred and his family were traveling in the South on a Guggenheim Fellowship, the first awarded for research in jazz. They were documenting what they could find of African American musical roots, both with portable recording equipment and Fred's 35 mm Leica camera. They had worked extensively in Alabama, then shifted to Mississippi, and in New

Orleans they intended to catch their breath, listen to some of the music in the city, and go through what they'd already collected. It was so hot in the city, though, and they were so tired from their months of traveling, that after a few days Amelia returned with Locke to their home in rural New Jersey. Fred stayed on in the apartment, with his tape recorder set up on a table and his notes spread on every available surface. The room was sticky and musty with the classic New Orleans smell of mold and damp, and Fred spent most of the time without a shirt as he went through the tapes they'd recorded.

In Mississippi only a few weeks before, Fred had made one of the most surprising discoveries of his trip. He had stumbled across two rudimentary brass bands in the countryside, the Lapsey Brass Band and the Johnson-Laneville Brass Band. Neither of the bands had a surviving trumpeter, so there was no distinct melody in their music, but there were vigorous cross-rhythms in the drumming and accented offbeats of the trombones and alto horns of the surviving band members. The musicians had no formal training of any kind. The trombone player for one band had simply taken his father's trombone and gone off to play for a picnic when his father couldn't turn up for the job. In his Guggenheim study Fred was searching for jazz roots, and in this rough music he was certain he had come close to the beginnings of the New Orleans brass band tradition.

One night he asked me if I would take him to one of the Eureka's rehearsals. We put the tape recorder and the Mississippi tapes in the car and drove to the Union Hall on Jackson Avenue where the band was rehearsing. It was a substantial one-story brick building, with a roomy meeting hall that was used as a rehearsal space by several of the local bands. It had no air conditioning and we were soaked with perspiration by the time we had the tape recorder set up on a bench against a wall. Fred explained what he'd found to the band members who had circled around him, and then he turned on the tape recorder.

The first piece was determinedly rhythmic, and there was the semblance of the melody in the tones of the blaring horns, but mostly it was cacophony. Fred turned off the machine and looked around. There was a stunned silence from the Eureka musicians.

"Do you feel that's the background of the kind of music you play with your band? Is that where it all started?" Fred asked with some excitement.

There was no answer. Two or three of the men shook their heads. I could see Percy studying Fred's face with some curiosity. He was obviously wondering what was in Fred's mind.

"I'll play you another piece and you tell me if that's what you remember from the old days."

They circled the tape recorder again, listening to another grinding, rough, rhythmic piece from one of the country bands. The melody-less ensemble sounded like their model might have been an old time country string band, but with the music coming out of breathy horns and thudding drums.

"Is that what you remember?" Fred asked again.

Percy finally shook his head firmly, "I never heard anything like that in all my life," and beside him Emanuel Paul nodded in emphatic agreement.

"What does that make you think about when you hear it?" Fred asked finally.

This time it was Red Clark who spoke up; generous, earnest Red Clark. "I think we could help those boys. I think if you just brought them here we could show them how to play so they'd know how to make a sound on those horns. You just bring them here and we'll help them."

Percy hesitated, still not certain what Fred was thinking. Finally, he held up a hand in agreement with Red.

"We could give them a little help," he agreed firmly.

There was much nodding of heads, and with a bemused expression Percy turned away, fingering his trumpet. It was time to resume the rehearsal. Fred smiled ruefully at me and began putting his machine away. It was clear that the roots he was searching for lay somewhere else, not in the proud traditions of the city's great marching bands.

There were other, less polished brass bands also playing in the streets in the 1950s, and it was their freer improvised styles that led to the change in the new brass band music that has revitalized New Orleans music. The Young Tuxedo Brass Band, which had taken over from the classic, older Tuxedo Band that had included the young Louis Armstrong and Papa Celestin, was especially popular. It had a gifted trumpet soloist, Thomas Jefferson; an inventive sousaphone player, Wilbert Tillman; and—most important for us—the band was led by the city's last active E-flat clarinet player, John Casimir. This instrument is pitched higher than the B-flat orchestra clarinet. It is shorter and has a squalling, piercing tone that was audible from even farther distances across the city blocks than Percy Humphrey's trumpet. The Young Tuxedo was not a reading band, but there was great dignity in their hymns, and the piercing sound of the E-flat clarinet as John marched slowly forward in a somber, twisting half-step was one of the memorable experiences of the 1950s. In the traditional bands, however, what lingered was the past, and it was the past that so many of the people who were interested in New Orleans music were drawn to. In the rougher music of the

The Rebirth
Brass Band
playing at the
Rock 'n' Bowl,
December 2005.

younger pick-up groups like Harold DeJan's Brass Band or the Gibson Brass Band, however, was the music of the future.

In the street music there was room for a communal response to the bands. A piece that all of them played was a blues tune that had many names, but was often recorded as "Holler Blues." It got its name simply because the second liners had a chance to holler in the arrangement. The band played a ringing rhythmic figure, then paused and the dancers circling them in the street hollered out a resounding "Yeah!" It wasn't a classic call and response, but it was a moment when everyone could join in the sound.

One night in the 1970s, when I was passing through New Orleans on the way to Houston to record the Texas blues artist Lightnin' Hopkins, Lars Edegran, a young Swedish musician who had made his home in New Orleans and was leading the traditional-styled New Orleans Ragtime Orchestra, asked me to come with him to one of the small clubs in the uptown district. The street outside was empty, but inside the club I found myself in a packed, dark room, its most distinctive feature its mirrored walls. But as distinctive was the musical group lined up against one wall. It was an eclectic, tightly rehearsed brass band, with a repertoire that stretched from traditional street pieces to contemporary bop instrumentals. Everything was played with a precise, bright musical sound, and they were at ease with a wide ranging repertoire that ranged from Armstrong to Dizzy Gillespie to Thelonious Monk. The group called itself the Dirty Dozen Brass Band, and it was obvious from the noisy response of the crowd that they were the new voice of the city's streets.

What groups like the Dirty Dozen have done is to explore the rich heritage of African American music, adding Latin American rhythms and even African pieces like the irresistible South African melody "Eyonmzi" recorded on their album *What You Gonna Do for the Rest of Your Life*, from 1991. Their sound is based on the concepts of the brilliant sousaphonist Kirk Joseph and the baritone and soprano saxophone soloist Roger Lewis. In the notes to the album Lewis described the hours of work he put in with Joseph to create their style.

> Kirk and I used to shed a lot. We burned a lot of midnight oil together. He would play the chord changes while I would play the lead, or he would play a bass line complementary to what I was playing, or sometimes I would work out a bass line, turn him on to it, and he would take that bass line and take it totally someplace else while I would continue what I was playing. My concept was for Kirk to play the tuba like a string bass. That's what I had in mind . . . [4]

The emphatic, intricate lines of Joseph's sousaphone style have almost no similarities to the earnest chord progressions that Red Clark played with the Eureka, and the Eureka, even at its best, never matched the precision of the Dirty Dozen. The new band has some of the warmth and lyric quality of the old bands, but the *sound* of the arrangements, with their emphasis on the sousaphone, is a new dimension in New Orleans' music. In their eclecticism and their confident range through the repertoire of bop, soul, and contemporary rhythm and blues, the Even Dozen are more reminiscent of the Chicago "new jazz" groups like Henry Threadgill's orchestras, Ernest Dawkins's New Horizon Ensemble, or the Ethnic Heritage Ensemble, which also confidently stride across stylistic boundaries. Threadgill's group especially, with its own tuba virtuoso Bob Stewart, often seems to be working the same side of the street as the New Orleans bands.

The city's new bands like the Even Dozen are comfortable on festival stages and just as much at home, as I heard them the first time, playing

The Hot 8
playing at Café
Brasil, December
2005.

their Monk arrangements in a jazz club. Many of their members have also spent some time playing with the bands on the streets. They generally restrict their street repertoire to the jump tunes of the down-home bands. In the continual debate between the city's two musical cultures, the older musicians who would assimilate with the larger society and the younger performers who would use music as an expression of their own racial self-identity, the younger musicians have won. Whatever a proud group like the Eureka represented, with its earnest dirges and hard learned Sousa marches, it is part of New Orleans's past. Perhaps to an extent this is because younger, ambitious African American musicians now can find a place in the city's symphony orchestra, or play chamber music or opera with any of the other musicians who make New Orleans their home. It may have been, in part, the role of the Eureka to prepare the way for the new generation to go beyond what they were permitted to accomplish themselves.

In his notes to a 1984 album by the Rebirth Jazz Band, one of the new street groups, Jerry Brock listed some of the other bands who were crowding after the Dirty Dozen, whose musicality and flair had already taken them everywhere in the world of festival jazz. Among the bands he listed were the Roots of Jazz Brass Band, the Charles Barbarin Memorial Brass Band, Tuba Fats and the Chosen Few, the Pinstripes, the West End Jazz Band, the All Stars Jazz Band, the Young Men Jazz Band, and Leroy Jones and the Hurricane Brass Band. He went on to list some of the older bands who had added new members with their roots in the new eclecticism: Doc Paulin's Brass Band, Floyd Anckle and the Majestic Brass Band, Harold DeJan and the Olympia Brass Band, the Onward Brass Band, the Imperial Brass Band, the Spirit of New Orleans, and the original Sixth Ward Dirty Dozen Kazoo Band.

The name that was missing from the list was the Eureka Brass Band. The band members I followed on the streets have all died, and although there have been efforts to continue the band's name and musical identity, it may be that the older style of street music that the band represented finally has no further role to play in the continuing story of the city's music. The name of the Eureka Brass Band, however, will continue to be a revered symbol of the city's timeless musical legacy.

"Shake the World's Foundation with

the Maple Leaf Rag!"

It is a slow climb up the narrow stairs in the old red-brick house on Delmar Avenue in a neighborhood of scattered buildings and stretches of grass on the north side of St. Louis. The stairs are narrow, you hold tightly to the wooden banister, and the floors, when you reach the second floor, are still as rough and as splintered as they were a hundred years ago, though they have been newly painted. You walk along a shadowy hallway toward the room that looks down on the street, with its old-fashioned curtained windows facing north in the afternoon's soft sunlight and you find yourself in a quiet front parlor, with modest secondhand furniture from the period of 1900 to 1910. The room is unassuming, but with a quiet atmosphere of solid domesticity. There is an ornate piano against one wall, the room's only expensive piece of furniture. The pleasant, knowledgeable young African American woman, Chantelle Moten, who is one of the curators of the house, has followed you up the stairs. She gestures to the furnishings and the view out of the window and smiles when you play a few notes on the piano and look up inquiringly.

"We always keep it tuned," she nods. "Every piano in the house is in tune. So many people who come are musicians, and they want to play something."

There are few places we can visit that will bring us closer to one of the figures who was of decisive importance in the development of an African American musical idiom, but it was in this modest second floor apartment that the ragtime composer Scott Joplin lived with his first wife Belle at number 2658A of what was then called Morgan Street from 1902 to 1907. Belle, who was older than her husband, was the widow of the older brother of Scott Hayden, an aspiring young composer Joplin had met and befriended when he lived in Sedalia, a busy small city in western Missouri. The two men—Joplin was fourteen years older—might have met in the music classes Joplin took at Sedalia's George R. Smith College. Hayden, who in his one known photograph was slim and boyish, had collaborated on a rag with Joplin, "Sunflower Slow Drag," which was offered for sale by Joplin's publisher, John Stark, in 1901. At the time its popularity rivaled Joplin's classic "Maple Leaf Rag," which had been published two years earlier and helped ignite the country's excitement over ragtime.

In part, the two musicians probably moved to St. Louis to continue their relationship with John Stark, who had just shifted his operation from a music shop in Sedalia to the city. Joplin, however, had also decided to continue his musical studies with a German-born musician named Alfred Ernst, who was the director of the St. Louis Choral Symphony Society. In an enthusiastic article published in the *St. Louis Post Dispatch* in February, 1901, Ernst wrote of the thirty-four-year-old Joplin:

> I am deeply interested in this man. He is young and undoubtedly has a fine future. With proper cultivation, I believe, his talent will develop into positive genius. Being of African blood himself, Joplin has a keener insight into that peculiar branch of melody than white composers. His ear is particularly acute. . . . The work Joplin has done in ragtime is so original, so distinctly individual, and so melodious withal, that I am led to believe he can do something fine in compositions of a higher class when he shall have been instructed in theory and harmony . . . The soul of a composer is there and needs but to be set free by knowledge of techniques.[1]

Hayden left Sedalia with his wife Nora at about the same time as Joplin also decided to move, and the two couples shared the second floor of the building, which was owned by an elderly German doctor who rented out part of his home and office space. In the middle room upstairs there is a photo of Belle Joplin on the wall between the windows. It is an original photo, which was found in recent years, and it is the only authentic survival from Joplin's years on Morgan Street. Although the furniture in the rooms and the piano convey an atmosphere that reflects the life he must have lived there, everything was found in homes and antique shops in the area. It was only a few months after he and Belle moved into the apartment that W. H. Carter, who published Sedalia's African American newspaper the *Sedalia Times*, dropped by for a visit while he was in St. Louis to visit the famed Exposition. Carter also played valve trombone in Sedalia's brass band, The Queen City Concert Band, which once had included Joplin as a cornetist. Carter's note appeared in his newspaper on April 26, 1902:

> The editor and publisher of the Times spent Monday and Tuesday in St. Louis, and while there called on many Sedalia boys, who appear to be

doing well. Our first visit was to Mr. Scott Joplin, who is gaining a world's reputation as the Rag Time King. Mr. Joplin is only writing, composing, and collecting his money from the different music houses in St. Louis, Chicago, and a number of other cities . . . [2]

It was almost impossible for me to sort out all of my emotions as I stood in the place where Scott Joplin had lived and composed some of his finest pieces. His music, and Joplin himself, had been part of my life since I'd first heard one of his rags as a teenager, and in the winter of 1947 I spent long hours laboriously teaching myself to play "Maple Leaf Rag." For me, it felt as though the charming, quiet rooms of the Joplin apartment still echoed with the presence of the couple who once lived there, but in reality there is almost nothing left that allows us a closer look into Joplin's personal life. Only three photographs, badly reproduced on sheet music covers, and one letter have survived of his thirty-year career. The rooms themselves tell so little of the difficulties he experienced while he lived there. Hayden's young wife died in child-birth; the child Joplin and Belle had together died while still a baby and a sorrowing Belle returned to Sedalia. Despite the tragedies, Joplin's years in the upstairs rooms on Morgan Street were productive. The rags he composed there, including his well-known "The Entertainer," as well as the ambitious "Elite Syncopations" and his "Ragtime Dance," are among his most optimistic and ebullient pieces. It was also on his piano in the front room that he created a composition that has haunted scholars since its existence became known in the 1950s. Perhaps as a response to his studies with Alfred Ernst, Joplin wrote his first opera in the apartment, a still-lost composition titled *The Guest of Honor.*

Since it's a Sunday afternoon there is little traffic on the street outside. Chantelle Moten walks slowly through the rooms with me, past the brass bedstead in the middle room, with its hand worked quilt and the framed photo of Belle Joplin on the opposite wall. We stop in the room at the back that looked down on the spring garden. She points, laugh-ing, at a brass bound chest in a corner.

"That was what they had as an ice box then!"

Even if more is known about Joplin's music than about his life, there still are corners that won't come into focus. Chantelle and I linger in the fading afternoon light, talking about the first opera. She throws up her hands in frustration.

"We know *The Guest of Honor* was composed. We *know* it was on the stage. In the newspapers we have thirty-two listings of performances around the state! Little theaters and music societies. We even have re-views. Somebody sang it and played it and they had to have music. But we've never found it. How that could be—even with the times Joplin moved—I just don't know!"

The next day, as I left St. Louis to drive west to Sedalia, where Joplin's career had begun, I found myself in a countryside that seemed empty of anything that could have nurtured the unique syncopations of ragtime. When the car reached the top of a rise on the back road I was following through the Missouri farmlands, the view ahead was only of the tops of more rises. A line of ridges stretched endlessly in front of me. The road I'd taken was a narrow, grayish strip of pavement that led straight through the featureless landscape. It was only in the fading afternoon light as I drove toward the west that the lowering sweep of the sun threw lengthening shadows that lent more shape to the land's contours. I could see distant silhouettes of houses and silos—sharp, dark forms in a land of smoothed hills and undulating fields. From the patches of forest in the meandering creek beds I saw that the land had once been forested, and it had been laboriously cleared before the first plows could break up the earth. The unending work of the clearing had been done by slaves, but I could see no signs that they ever had lives or homes here. The landscape was almost deserted, and in the small crossroad towns I noticed only a line of stores along the road and two or three filling stations. There were no dirt streets behind the stores, or the rows of sharecropper shacks that would have been part of a Mississippi landscape.

I wanted to get some feeling of the land that lay between the upstairs apartment in St. Louis and Sedalia, across the state, so I stayed off the crowded interstate highway. After several hours of casual driving, I reached the outskirts of Sedalia, and I found myself on a solidly built residential street with a sign pointing toward the business district. A billboard along the road claimed that there were 20,399 people living in Sedalia in 2003, but it wasn't until I'd driven through the areas of farmland at the edge of the city a day or so later that I could account for so many people.

As I turned off onto Ohio Street, the main street of the business section, I could see the debilitating effects of the downturn in the rural economy everywhere I looked. Although the street was lined for three or four blocks with dark brick buildings, four and five stories high, they were relics of the previous century's prosperity. The buildings were shabby, most of their windows blank, and the worn doors and window frames in need of paint. As far as I could see, the main business activity seemed to be a row of "antique" shops that filled the shadowy display windows with Sedalia's discards. I had driven to Sedalia for the annual festival honoring Scott Joplin and his compositions, but as I left the car in an empty lot behind the main street and stood at a corner waiting for some other traffic to pass me, I wondered how Joplin's exhilarating music could have flourished in these unwelcoming streets.

But had Sedalia been so unwelcoming to someone like Joplin a hundred years before? After I'd been there for a few days I understood that the music I'd come to hear needed small cities like Sedalia. On my first morning in the motel where I'd finally found a room after driving up and down the roads for two or three hours, it was hard to see much difference between Sedalia and a hundred other small Missouri towns— except for the faint sound of someone playing an unsteady version of Joplin's "Stop Time Rag" on the piano in the motel lobby—but ragtime is a social music, a music of polite gatherings and social dancing, and it needed a social setting.

When I came down for breakfast the next morning the tables in the coffee shop were crowded with Midwestern families and couples who had made the trip for the festival. It was the kind of social moment that has become the world of ragtime today. All of the faces were white, except for the man sitting with me, a friendly, enthusiastic man named Donald Ryan, who was appearing at the festival as a pianist. He had grown up in Toronto, but he'd moved to Tulsa, Oklahoma and he was active in the ragtime society there. When I asked if he was one of the festival's regular performers, he shook his head.

"They've tried to get me here so many times, but this is the time of year when I have the most work in Tulsa—you know how it is in June and July. Weddings—dances—that's when they need pianists. But this year I decided to drive up and do what I could. Their grants from the state have been cut way back and they have such a problem with money."

"And they need to have an African American in the program?"

He grinned comfortably. "That's right. When you think about ragtime there aren't too many of us."

Although in his early years in Sedalia, friends remembered Joplin as quiet and retiring, it is obvious from the paths he followed in his musical career that he was tirelessly ambitious. With all of his ambition, however, he couldn't have achieved so much in so few years if he hadn't met a man in Sedalia who was as individualistic and as determined as himself. His unlikely ally was a strong-willed and sublimely self-confident music store owner who conducted his small business on a side street in the downtown business area. His name was John Stark, a tall, brusque man with the prophet's beard that was popular in his era.

He was fifty-eight when his association began with the town's most promising ragtime composer. Stark had served in an Indiana regiment as a bugler in the Civil War, and at the war's end, on occupation duty in New Orleans, he fell in love and married a thirteen year old girl from the city. After the war he tried several occupations, but unlike so many restless men in the Reconstruction years he was a success at everything he tried. In 1886, after a period of selling ice cream and musical instruments out of a wagon in the countryside, he bought a music store on East Fifth Street in Sedalia. With his wife and three children encouraging him, he turned to the music business with the same headlong enthusiasm he'd brought to all his other projects. In these decades of family music making, music publishing was a successful sideline for many local music stores.

Perhaps the best introduction to Stark as a ragtime music publisher are the tempestuous advertisements he wrote for the new compositions he began publishing after his meeting with Scott Joplin. In ragtime he had found a righteous cause that would come to dominate his life.

> What is ragtime? Let those who are sure they do not like it think up an answer. In the meantime, let us say that it is a rhythmic treatment of a melody or score, and consists in tying an unaccented note to an accented one. It also intensifies the accent. Why is it bad? Echo answers why? The energetic fight against it by those who cannot play it gets funny when we consider that those syncopations have nothing whatever to do with the genius of melody or the scholarship of its harmonic treatment. . . . The good rag will live and the poor rag will die. It is not a sign of low taste to like ragtime of the better class.[3]

In a later peroration he allowed himself to raise his voice as he attempted to differentiate the "better-class" ragtime compositions he was publishing from the rising tide of novelty imitations.

> Positively if you have never heard "Maple Leaf Rag," "Sunflower Slow Drag" or the other RAGS OF OUR LIST, then you have never heard RAG TIME—the simon pure, the REAL THING. If we simply say to you, that they are fine above all others—then you have heard language as strong from others and the music was weak. If we tell you that these "RAGS" are really startling and thrilling—why this is a bromide, rank, and may not even attract your attention. What shall we say then? Shall we sound the hew gag [sic], blow our trumpet inside out and smash the big bass drum?
>
> It may be that you have heard all the great operas, perhaps have been to Coney and have shot the Shutes and bumped the bumps. Possibly [you]

Main Street, Sedalia, Missouri, 2004.

The Maple Leaf Club Memorial, Sedalia, Missouri.

have visited the art centers of many nations and have blown yourself for all the treasures and pleasures that came in your way, but, if you have never heard these syncopes played with artistic precision and effect, then you are poor indeed, and life's joys have been but meager. No words can describe them. If one falls in a new place it sets the woods on fire. If played by request or as an encore at a concert, it smashes the program and must be repeated to the end of the show. They have actually been known to stop the conversation at a church social. Seriously they are both classic and popular, profound and simple. They please at once the untutored and the cultured. Everybody likes them the first time they hear them played. And they like them still better when they have heard them one hundred times or more. "Age cannot wither nor custom stale their infinite variety." No musician can outgrow them. They will add luster to any repertoire. They are played by the country fiddler and turned loose on the circumambient by the greatest bands and orchestras, in all cases reducing competitive imitations to the cube root of a vacuum.[4]

Perhaps most startling about his eruption was his own estimate of his tone as he concluded his piece: "In thus describing them we are surprised at our own moderation. The half has not been told. If you have heard Maple Leaf, then you know we have many others as good. Send for free catalogue. You cannot do without the entire set."[5]

He was, by his own standards, showing a little "moderation." In this outburst he only dismissed the compositions published by his competitors as "the cube root of a vacuum," but in another outburst, in a more Missouri kind of comparison, he described them as "Molly crawl-bottom stuff posing under rag names." His tone, despite its strident hyperbole, has two reasonable justifications. One is that to this day the music industry continues to hype its products with the same shrill hucksterism. The other is that despite the occasional composition of some musical value published by other firms, he was right. Without Stark and the composers whose music he published, "Rag-Time" might seem, in the musical free-for-all of the early 1900s, something like the "cube root of a vacuum."

At the time that Stark wrote his diatribe, ragtime had already experienced its first decline and rejuvenation. "Maple Leaf Rag," which Stark published in Sedalia in the fall of 1899, and other serious ragtime piano compositions by a new generation of composers that followed the path of its success, had seized the imagination of young musicians and dancers everywhere in the country. Between 1900 and 1914 there were nearly one hundred music publishers announcing new ragtime piano pieces in New York City alone. However, as the renowned bandleader John Philip Sousa complained in 1908,

Ragtime had the dyspepsia or gout long before it died. It was overfed by poor nurses. Good ragtime came and half a million imitators sprang up. Then as a result the people were sickened with the stuff. I have not played a single piece of ragtime this season because people do not want it.[6]

A few years later Sousa would be forced to change his mind. In 1911 an unknown song writer named Irving Berlin published a popular song in the ragtime style titled "Alexander's Ragtime Band," which had the galvanizing effect of "Maple Leaf Rag." John Stark never regained the central position of his "classic ragtime," as it came to be termed, but his compositions were to experience a new swell of popularity before their exuberant offspring "jass" finally swept them into a shadowy corner a decade later.

In the many collections of slave songs that followed the appearance of the groundbreaking *Slave Songs of the United States* in 1867, there was in all of them a lack of everyday music. What the earnest field collectors were missing, as they understood uncomfortably, was the instrumental music that was an integral part of slave life; the "fiddle songs, devil's songs, corn songs and jig tunes" that were mentioned in the introduction to the 1867 collection. It was these missing pieces that were to be the source of ragtime. In the earliest known painting of a slave dance, a watercolor of a slave dance in South Carolina painted about 1780, one musician is playing a small gourd banjo, and behind him a second musician is playing a small drum held between his legs. This is obviously an example of the same musical source that the English ship captain Richard Jobson observed in the Gambia in 1623.

That [instrument] which is most common in use, is made of a great gourd, and a neck thereunto fastened, resembling in some sort, our Bandora . . . In consortship with this they have many times another who playes up a little drumme . . . which he holds under his left arme, and with a crooked stick in his right hand, and his naked fingers on the left he strikes the drumme.[7]

The drum in the painting might have slipped past the general prohibition against drum instruments on the plantations, since it was so small its sound wouldn't have carried over the thuddy plunk of the banjo.

The song collectors in the South might have missed the banjo pieces, but theater audiences in most of the United States had been humming and whistling them for years. Despite their thick tone and crude construction, banjos were a mainstay of the early minstrel companies. Most contemporary accounts suggest that in their early manifestation the minstrel shows were not the viciously racist spectacles that emerged after the Civil War. The first minstrel quartet, the *Original Virginia Minstrels*, with Dan Emmett as fiddler, Dick Pelham playing the tambourine, Frank Brower bones, and the banjoist Billy Whitlock, who made their début at the Bowery Amphitheater in New York in February 1843, had derived at least part of their repertory of songs and dances from slaves. They borrowed not only the instruments and the musical idioms, they also wore plantation clothing, blackened their faces, and wore African-style wigs. The banjoist, Whitlock, performed several African-styled instrumental pieces.

The sentimental songs of Stephen Foster were more typical of the earliest minstrel show offerings, with their unctious portrayal of the "good darkey"—"Old Black Joe" or "Old Folks At Home." Songs like "Coon, Coon, Coon, How I Wish My Color Would Change" or "Every Race Have a Flag But De Coon" came later with the vicious racial stereotyping of the Reconstruction years. Even the Confederate anthem "Dixie," which Emmett wrote in 1859 when he was with Bryant's Minstrels, began as an exuberant marching song popular with troops from both the Northern and Southern armies. Emmett himself was an ardent Unionist who had grown up on an Ohio farm, and he was dismayed when his song became associated with what he always characterized as the southern rebellion.

The immense popularity of the minstrel shows made the banjo a household instrument everywhere in America, but although the rhythms and melodies of ragtime were shaped by the banjo and the violin, the instrument that dominated the domestic musical life of most middle-class families, and also bulked large under handmade lace coverings and ornate ceramic pieces in their best parlor, was the piano. The daughters of the family were expected to play it with some skill. Already by the 1840s and 1850s music publishers were introducing arrangements that adapted the syncopations and catchy repetitive melodic figures of the banjos and violins to the piano, even if in the beginning there was nothing more ambitious than simple collections of dance tunes. The New York music companies announced among their varied wares, medleys of "Ethiopian Airs" published as quadrilles in simple piano arrangements for "polite" entertainment. Since the music was intended for the crowds of young people flocking to the public dancing rooms, or for a gathering of friends in the family parlor, the setting of the melodies were adapted to the familiar set of rhythmic patterns which accompanied the complicated figures of the dance. The melodies of the African-influenced pieces themselves, however, often included measures of repeated melodic figures and a freer use of rhythmic accents. In the shaping of the melodies were indications of ambiguous major and minor tonalities. Even in these simple piano pieces there were the elements of the continual process of adaptation and refiguring that marked the common language of song in the slave world.

The early quadrilles are particularly interesting, since they precede the overwhelming popularity of the minstrel shows, which for several decades affected every level of American musical entertainment. A New York publisher, F. Riley & Co., in 1844 announced on the covers of its "Sets" of *African Quadrilles* that the five pieces that made up each quadrille were "*Selected from the Most Admired Negro Melodies.*" The piano arrangements were in the simplified European idioms of the period, but the melodies selected for their four different sets included "Boatman Dance," "Dandy Jim," "Old Dan Tucker," and "De Old Gray Goose." Another "set" from 1848, *The Ethiopian Quadrilles*, published by the New York firm William Hall & Son, included five popular "plantation aires:" "Gwin ober de Mountain," "Jonny Boker," "De Old Jaw Bone," "Jumbo Jum," and "Jim along Josey."

Ragtime is one of the few African-derived musical styles with roots and antecedents that can be clearly traced to African sources, all of them tied to the banjo. The banjo itself is an African instrument with a line of development that can be followed from its older forms to the more brilliant, staccato-toned instruments played everywhere today. The complex ties between the West Africa instruments and the banjo in the early United States would seem to have been lost in the centuries since a memory of those first instruments came to the colonies with the earliest shipload of slaves. In recent years, however, there has been such intense study of the old accounts in African travel narratives that the links to American antebellum banjo instruction manuals and song collections have been clearly established. The questions that still hang over the exchange—which of several possible African instruments was the model for what became the banjo and how was it played on the plantations—have come tantalizingly close to being answered.

One winter night at an ethnographic concert in a small auditorium in Stockholm I found myself as interested in the instruments scattered across the floor in front of the stage as I was in the two musicians who were carefully tuning them. I could see several African stringed proto-banjos, some with slim, shallow bodies carved from wood, others with deeper, broader bellies shaped out of dried gourds. What they had in common was a skin head, three or four strings resting against it on a carved wooden bridge, and a long neck made from a stick, with the strings tied at varying lengths along it. I recognized the small *halam*

Cover of *The Ethiopian Quadrilles*, 1848. Published by William Hall & Son, New York City.

Opening of "Jumbo Jum," from *The Ethiopian Quadrilles*.

of the Wollof griots I had recorded in the Gambia and the longer-bodied *konting* of the Serrahule griots I had recorded on other journeys to West Africa.

One of the instruments was new to me—a round-bodied, long-necked instrument built on a dried gourd with a shape startlingly similar to the early-styled American banjos that were resting on wire racks beside it. When I asked the solidly built Swede in an African tunic who was presenting the evening what it was, he told me it was an *akonting*, the traditional instrument of a Gambian tribe, the Jolas. The man's name was Ulf Jägfors, and for almost two decades he has been collecting instruments, learning to play them himself, and traveling to West Africa to make a series of remarkable films and recordings of musicians playing proto-banjo instruments. It was impossible not to be drawn to Ulf's enthusiasm and he quickly led me over to meet the Jola musician who was tuning the *akonting*. His name was Daniel Jatta, a slim, wiry man with the dark skin and the strong facial moulding of many Africans from his tribal region. After earning his bachelor's and master's degrees in business in the United States, Daniel has worked for many years in Stockholm as an industrial economist. Ulf shook his head as he introduced us,

"You wouldn't think it could happen like that, but I didn't know anything about what Daniel was doing until I saw a notice in the paper that Daniel was going to talk about the beginnings of the banjo. For ten years we lived ten miles from each other and I didn't know anything about him!"

I learned later that although he had grown up in a village in Gambia, Daniel didn't learn about his tribe's string instrument traditions until long after he had left the country. When I asked him about it later at Jägfors's home, he shook his head, still surprised at how little he'd known. He had first become aware of a possibility that there could be some music like this in his village after he had left the Gambia and become a student in the United States.

"When I came to the junior college in North Carolina," he told me, "I heard music on the radio that was called 'country music,' and it had different kind of instruments. I heard something called a 'banjo,' and somebody at the school told me it came from Africa. When I came back to Gambia on a holiday I said to my father, 'Do you know anything about something like this?' And I told him what I knew about the banjo.

"He said that the Jola people had something like the banjo from a long time back. He told me he played it himself, but I had never seen it when I was growing up. He said he left it in the wine room in the village so it wouldn't bring any trouble to our family.

" 'Men who play,' he told me, 'sometimes they go into the forest and they don't come back. You only find a track where they went, or you only find their shoes.'

"So my father said he would go and get his *akonting*, and he would show it to me and how he played it. He said it was a very old instrument for the Jola people. It goes very far back. So I began to learn from him."

The other musician, who was tuning an old-fashioned five-string banjo so that he could play it together with Daniel's akonting, was Clarke Buehling, an amiable, talented instrumentalist with a large mustache. He was dressed in a vest and jeans that could have come out of a nineteenth-century tintype. Clarke, who lives with his family in Fayetteville, Arkansas, is one of the group of American banjo enthusiasts who have turned to the antebellum minstrel show banjo manuals and songsters to re-create the banjo styles of the 1850s. The instrument he was tuning was a heavy-necked, thick-toned instrument with a broad skin head that he had built himself after a prototype instrument in a museum collection. Daniel and the akonting had been as much of a discovery for Clarke as they were for me. Did he think the akonting was the ancestor of the banjo?

"It's sure one of them! You found those players in Africa, those Wollof players in Africa who played the halam. They played it the same way I play the banjo, and you said in what you wrote that the sound is the same. But the akonting is made out of a gourd, and what they played for you in Africa had bodies made out of wood. Maybe the answer is the gourd that the akonting's made from! The gourd is what we had in American in the beginning! It *could* be the akonting!"

Clarke is associated with a number of dedicated instrumentalists, among them Joe Ayers, Bob Carlin, Bob Flesher, Tony Trischka, and Bob Winans, in the group named the Tennessee Banjo Association. They have been some of the first performers to reconstruct the old slave gourd banjos, both the round-bodied five-string instrument and the smaller four-string *banza*, depicted in the earliest illustrations of the slaves' musical entertainments. As the audience began to fill the rows of the auditorium Daniel called over to Clarke that he had his own instrument tuned and in a moment they pulled chairs close and began playing a soft duet. Ulf stood beside them, eyes closed, smiling to himself as he listened to the cascading notes. The light sound of the African instrument was an intriguing contrast to the heavier tones of its American descendent. First Daniel played, demonstrating his tribe's downstroke, plucking thumb style, and Clarke answered him with the early American downstroke, known as "frailing," with its plucking thumb. It was impossible not to hear the exchange of technique and melody that went from one instrument to the other. For a moment, sitting a few feet from them, I could imagine myself on the porch of a country plantation a century before.

The next morning Clarke performed several of the duets for banjo and piano of ragtime compositions that had been published in the middle of the ragtime craze of the early 1900s. The pianist was a Swedish ragtime specialist named Peter Lundberg, and in the exhilarating musicality of their playing it was impossible to miss the affinity between the ragtime styles that had developed for both instruments. The arpeggiated melodies that lay naturally in the tuning of the banjo strings adapted themselves easily to the arpeggiated chord patterns of the piano. Unlike so many other instrumental styles derived from African sources, the melodies of ragtime were not influenced by singing. The melodic roots were in the rippling finger patterns of the banjo, built on the lilting syncopations that came from the small drums that accompanied the first banjos in the New World.

Before the early banjo melodies could make their way into America's genteel parlors, however, there had to be a more extensive adaptation. The most widespread sound of popular music in the United States in the ragtime era was the brass band, which was part of the life of every American community, whatever its size or race or ethnic background. For ragtime, its breakthrough came when its still nascent forms were adapted to the harmonic, multi-thematic structure of a composed march, which was the staple of the repertory of every local band. It isn't a coincidence that one of the first pieces published as a "ragtime" composition, "Mississippi Rag" in 1897, was composed by a Chicago bandmaster William H. Krell, who assembled vernacular melodic strains that were popular along the Mississippi Valley into a syncopated instrumental piece with a march structure.

Many of the early ragtime compositions offered to the public by companies like John Stark Music were published with the tempo indication "Play in March Time," or "Tempo di Marcia." As Joplin became more and more upset by the fast tempos adopted by the vaudeville pianists who performed his music, he began adding the tempo indications "Slow march time," then "Very slow march time." The march was such a broadly accepted point of reference that Joplin added the indication "Very slow march time" to his beautiful composition "Solace, a Mexican Serenade" which he had written in the syncopated rhythms of a Cuban *habanera*.

Working with old newspaper files, a group of researchers have found a series of articles in the columns of newspapers in eastern Kansas from the late 1880s which use the word "rag" to describe the popular dances in the area, as well as a way of dancing, and in some of the writing the music itself is described as "rags." A writer in the *Kansas City Star* on April 13, 1895, quoted a newspaper column from the *Leavenworth Herald*: "If the present 'rag' craze does not die out pretty soon, every young man in the city will be able to play some kind of a 'rag' and then call himself a piano player. At the present rate Leavenworth will soon be a close second to Kansas City as a manufacturer of piano pugilists."[8]

Many of the newspaper articles mention a piece called "Forty Drops" in connection with the popularity of the new dances, and the title probably refers to the popular medication laudanum, a tincture of alcohol and opium that was sold by the drop. It has been proposed that it was a folk ragtime piece that became identified with "the irresistible hammerings of eastern Kansas' black society girls."[9] An arrangement of the piece was published in 1898, however, and it is clear that the only thing anyone could do with the melody is hammer it out, since it isn't a syncopated piece, and it has none of the repetitive melodic figures that emerged in the ragtime compositions a few years later. The "Forty Drops" melody is in the style of the popular energetic marches of the German-American social lodges that were widespread in the area, and the pieces were typically given thunderous performances. Serious ragtime compositions, as they are defined today, would have to wait a few more years to make their appearance.

It was Scott Joplin who was being celebrated in the Festival in Sedalia I had come to see. He had been born in 1869 in a small town in north Texas, but though his family was poor, his mother was determined to lift him to middle-class status. He had already begun piano lessons with a neighbor when the family moved to Texarkana, where his father found work in the railroad yards. His mother and father separated, and to keep the family going she cleaned houses. There was a piano in the parlor of a white family where she worked, and she arranged for her young son to be able to practice while she was busy in the house. He was also learning to play the banjo, and he worked out banjo melodies at home at night. He was soon taken on as a pupil by one of the German immigrant musicians who were to make a crucial contribution to the rich harvest of Missouri ragtime. It is one of the ironies of the decades following the Civil War that while in the states of the defeated Confederacy African Americans were being systematically denied any rights, or anything more than haphazard, irregular schooling, in Missouri German music teachers were giving their promising young black pupils free piano lessons.

The Scott Joplin Mural Wall, Sedalia, Missouri, 2004.

Joplin's teacher was a neighbor named Julius Weiss, who had found a position tutoring the children of a wealthy family in Texarkana. The German musicians were not only less affected by prejudice than white musicians in the South, they also brought with them their very European belief in music as a moral force for good. In his studies with Weiss, Joplin became a competent pianist—he was never a virtuoso—but what was more important, he absorbed the beginnings of music theory and he was introduced to the European classical repertory. It was almost certainly in these years of early studies that he formed the love of European vocal styles and melody that lasted for the rest of his life.

With her first savings his mother managed to buy him a much-used upright piano for their house, and when he was sixteen he organized his first musical group, a vocal quartet called the Texas Medley Quartet, later including his younger brother Robert as a fifth member. He soon was performing as a pianist for local functions, playing the standard marches, operatic selections, dance pieces, and popular songs that his audiences requested. When he left Texarkana a few years later, it was this diverse musical repertory that he took with him. He had realized that there was already a bustling, optimistic world of black entertainers whose appearances were chronicled in the African American newspapers that were also making their tentative appearance.

In the early 1890s he was living in St. Louis, where he was part of the crowd of young musicians who congregated at the Rosebud, a saloon bar owned by a fellow pianist and ragtime composer, Tom Turpin. When Joplin later moved to Sedalia, he and Turpin continued their friendship. As I got to know Sedalia better I understood why it hadn't been an ill-advised choice. It then had a large railroad repair yard that employed hundreds of African Americans. The passage to a middle-class life that would have been impossible for someone like Joplin in the states of the old South was a distinct opportunity in Sedalia, with its college for African American students, its musical societies, and flourishing social organizations. There was even the enterprising newspaper published by the business man and amateur musician who later visited Joplin and his wife in St. Louis. Sedalia wasn't alone in its relative openness to black musicians. Another in the triumvirate of great ragtime composers whose music was also published by John Stark, James Scott, lived in Carthage, a nearby small city where he played an active role in the city's musical life until his death in the 1930s. Although ragtime has a folk-like exuberance and in its early years it was still associated with the saloons where it was sometimes performed, it is a complex musical style that requires some training in harmony and form, as well as the technical skills to play it. It was a music for the new middle class, and in Sedalia in the 1870s and 1880s it was possible for African American families to take the first steps into American middle-class life.

Joplin probably moved to Sedalia to attend music classes at George R. Smith College, a substantial red-brick building at the outskirts of town that was supported by the northern Methodist churches. To pay for his tuition he gave piano lessons, and one of his pupils was the son of the family where he rented a room in town. The pupil's name was Arthur Marshall, who later collaborated with his teacher in two brilliant rags, "Swipsy—A Cakewalk" and "Lily Queen Rag." Fortunately he was still living when researchers became interested in ragtime's roots in the 1940s, and he reminisced about Joplin's life in Sedalia. Joplin also assembled a new vocal group and began appearing on one of the new entertainment circuits. As a result of his tours, two of his early songs were published in Syracuse, New York in 1895, and the next year a music store in Temple, Texas published two marches and a waltz.

In Sedalia Joplin's life was filled with his music and his friends. He learned the cornet as part of his music studies and for a time he played in the city's African American brass band, the *Queen City Concert Band*. He formed a dance orchestra to play for local entertainments, and with a group of friends he was part of a social institution that was to leave its name in the history of ragtime. For thirteen months they rented the upstairs of a two-story commercial building beside the railroad tracks that divided Sedalia's white and black neighborhoods. It seems to have been typical of the many social clubs that young bachelors who lived in rented rooms created as a gathering place in small towns in this period of American life. Their calling card listed Joplin as the club's "entertainer." Their modest clubroom was on Main Street, with the noisy railroad tracks running behind it. The name they gave it was "the Maple Leaf Club."

Joplin's first rags were composed as early as 1897, but he was unable to place them with the larger of Sedalia's two music stores, A. W. Perry & Sons on West Broadway, so he took them to Kansas City, which was only seventy-five miles farther west across the Missouri fields. One of the music stores there was owned by another German immigrant, Carl Hoffman, who had no knowledge of the new music that was emerging around him, but who trusted the judgement of one of his clerks, Charles N. Daniels, who would go on to a successful career as a composer under his own name as well as several pseudonyms. Joplin's first published rag, "Original Rags," was issued in the spring of 1899, with Daniel's name added to the cover as "arranger." A few months later Joplin stopped in at Sedalia's other music store, John Stark's enterprise on E. Fifth Street. Stark's son remembered Joplin as a quiet-spoken, pleasant-faced, diminutive man, who came into the store holding a small boy by the hand. He asked if he might play something for the proprietor, and when he struck up his piece the boy began dancing enthusiastically. The piece was the "Maple Leaf Rag," and with it a new life was to begin for both Joplin and his new publisher.

In 1951 a jazz writer named Rudi Blesh, and Harriet Janis the wife of the important New York City art dealer Sidney Janis, published *They All Played Ragtime*, the first book that documented early ragtime and its important composers. It was the spark that turned what had been a carefully tended specialists' interest in ragtime into a major musical revival. They managed to locate many of the survivors from the first ragtime era, and they had a sensitive response to the essence of what John Stark had called his "classic rags." In the book they singled out three of Stark's composers as the most significant of ragtime's creators. Of all the forms of African American music developed in the United States, ragtime has the most pervasive European harmonic and structural elements, so it wasn't entirely a surprise that of the three composers they described—Scott Joplin, his Missouri compatriot James Scott, and the New Jersey born Joseph Lamb—one of them, Lamb, was white, and when Blesh and Janis talked with him he was living in Brooklyn. Eight years after the book's publication, when I met him, Lamb was still living in a quiet Brooklyn neighborhood and still composing ragtime.

In the summer of 1959 my wife Annie and I were also living in Brooklyn. It was always hot. The sun hung over the scraggly trees on our street, and the low two-story houses—brick and wood siding—seemed to draw the heat inside them. We had been married only a few months and we had a cellar apartment—a single room with an alcove for a kitchen—with no ventilation, and we had to live with the heat of the house upstairs over our heads. Some of the houses had air conditioning, but we were paying very little rent, and the rent didn't include air conditioning. A fan at night was the best we could do. In the afternoons we left the door open.

One afternoon in August we heard a car stop in the street—our street was only two blocks long so we didn't have much traffic—a car door closed, and a tall, wispy haired man in neatly pressed trousers and a shirt with the collar unbuttoned and the sleeves rolled up burst into our room, went to our piano, and without saying a word began playing a fast ragtime composition. It was "Sensation: A Rag." It had been published by the John Stark Music Company in 1912. The man who was playing it, his face somber with concentration, was Joseph Lamb. When he finished, still without sitting down at the piano bench, he straightened up and smiled broadly at us as we sat startled at the square little table in our cramped kitchen alcove against the apartment's back wall.

"I just wanted you to know I've been practicing."

Lamb had a penetrating accent, half New Jersey and half Brooklyn, and he spoke very loudly, since he was hard of hearing. We jumped up to shake his hand and wave to his daughter, who was waiting in the family car outside. He was tall and still lanky, though his shoulders were a little rounder than they'd been in the photographs we had seen of him from 1915, when he was as tall, but dark haired and a little slimmer. He had been practicing for several weeks to record for us later in the summer. He had first played his composition for Scott Joplin fifty years earlier, and on Joplin's recommendation John Stark issued Lamb's composition a few months later. To smooth its reception, Stark sagely added Joplin's name to the cover as "arranger."

"It's hard to get it right, after all these years," Joe said as loudly, still smiling as pleasantly, "but I told you I'd do it."

Lamb, one of a handful of people still living who had known Joplin and who had composed his own rags in Joplin's style, agreed with the approach to classic ragtime that emphasized the tempos and the scores of the published compositions.

One of few personal glimpses we have of Scott Joplin is Lamb's reminiscence of their first meeting. Lamb was a young New Jersey office worker who composed songs and had ambitions as a ragtime composer. When he met Joplin he had recently returned to the United States after several years in a Canadian boarding school, where he'd been sent following the early death of his father, an Irish immigrant who had made a success of a contracting business and moved his family to Montclair, New Jersey. Lamb had already begun his musical career with instrumental compositions published by a Canadian music company when he was still a student. He had taken an office job with a textile firm in New York City, but in his evenings and weekends he directed amateur music groups in Montclair, and spent what extra money he had on sheet music. He did his shopping at stores where the music was cheaper—five to seven cents a song—picking up anything he saw that looked interesting. It was "Maple Leaf Rag" that hit him, as he told an interviewer, "good and proper," and he continued, "Ninety-five percent of the best rags were written by Negroes, you know, and I seemed to fall right into their things."[10] It was in John Stark's new office on East Twenty-Third Street in Manhattan, close to Broadway, that he found himself face to face with Joplin.

In a burst of optimism as the classic ragtime in his catalog continued to sell to what seemed to be a steadily expanding audience, Stark had moved his office to New York in 1905, and in 1907 Joplin again followed him, though now Joplin was also offering his new compositions to other publishers. As much as he seemed to want to stay close to Stark, he almost certainly felt that in New York he would be able to fulfill his ambitions to complete the score and find a producer for his second opera, the large and challenging work *Treemonisha*.

Lamb's memories of his meeting with Joplin, as he recorded them for us later in the summer of 1959, mirrored not only a consciousness of the racial dialog that ragtime represented, but also the social attitudes that shaped the worlds of both men. The boarding house where Joplin was living when Joe visited him was at 128 W. 29th Street, only six blocks north of the Stark office on E. 23rd Street. One of the indefatigable researchers who are patiently filling in what details can be gleaned of Joplin's life, John Keen, located a photograph of Joplin's address in the New York City Municipal Archives. In the early Depression years it was a small, *rundown* tenement with a flight of stairs up to the doorway. A newer, larger building crowded against it. Thirty years earlier it had been one of a row of similar houses, before that area of New York hadn't yet declined so dramatically.[11]

As Lamb remembered;

> I was in Stark's office one time. I used to go there and get music all the time. He gave me a special price on it, and I went up there looking over the music. Mrs. Stark was there. There was a colored fellow sitting there with his foot all wrapped up and he had his crutches. That didn't mean anything to me, so I kept picking out the music. And I happened to mention to Mrs. Stark that I'd like to get some pretty decent things, especially things that were written by Joplin, that he was my favorite writer. And while I was picking things she was suggesting things and then this colored fellow he started suggesting things. Well, I figured that was natural, being a colored fellow and liking ragtime that he would naturally be able to know a lot of pieces. So anyway he mentioned some pieces and I didn't notice particularly that he mentioned Joplin's pieces. So I got what I wanted, and in the course of the conversation I happened to mention to Mrs. Stark, I said,
>
> "That's one fellow I'd like to meet. I admire him an awful lot and I'd certainly like to meet him sometime."
>
> So she said, "Well, would you really like to meet him?"
>
> And I said, "I certainly would."
>
> So she pointed to this colored fellow, "Well, there's your man."
>
> So I looked at him and I said, "You don't mean to tell me you're Scott Joplin?"
>
> He said, "That's who I am. I don't look like it much now with my foot wrapped up with gout and all that kind of business."
>
> So I said, "That doesn't make any difference to me."
>
> I went over and shook hands with him and told him I was tickled to death to meet him, no matter how he looked or anything. That was one of my ambitions.[12]

Lamb's compositions, beginning with his "Sensation," were all published by Stark, and they reflected his talent for creating flowing melodies in Joplin's style. Lamb joined the melodies to a sophisticated harmonic texture, often creating rags with considerable density and with an unmistakable lyric sense. A half-century later, his memory of the first time he played for Joplin was still fresh.

"Sensation, a Rag." Published by John Stark, 1908.

I called him up one time and made a date to go to his boarding house with the "Sensation," which he wanted me to do. So I went up there and went in the door and there was a big parlor. A lot of colored people were standing around talking and that kind of business and there was a piano in the back and I met Joplin at the door. He took me back to play "Sensation" on the piano. So I sat down and I played it, and as I said before all the people were talking, which I figured was alright, because I was kind of nervous about the thing. I didn't want people to stop and listen to me or anything like that. So I played "Sensation" and before I got finished I noticed there wasn't anymore noise. Anyway, I couldn't stop in the middle, I couldn't get nervous then, so I just plugged ahead until I got finished. So when I got finished they all clapped and some fellow came over and spoke to Joplin and asked him what that was I was playing and all that kind of stuff. Jop told him it was "Sensation Rag."

"He wrote it."

He said, "Well, that certainly is some rag. That's a real colored rag."

Well, that was what I wanted. I figured I was writing real colored rags. That's all I wanted to do. That's all there was to it.[13]

In Sedalia, nearly fifty years after meeting Joseph Lamb, I could hear the light sound of ragtime piano behind me as I waited in line to buy lunch in the downstairs dining room of the Methodist Church. All of us were taking a break from the Joplin Festival concerts, standing by a long table filled with sandwiches and salads, cake and pie, prepared by the Methodist ladies. I had learned long ago that the cooking in these Methodist church basements could always be trusted. The day's specialty was homemade strawberry ice cream, which a white-haired man was scooping onto plates of homemade Angel Food Cake. In the low-ceilinged, white-painted dining room an elderly woman was playing a small Kimball upright piano set close to a wall that divided the eating areas. On the music rack were several well-used music folios. She played almost entirely rags, with one or two familiar popular melodies from the 1930s. She was trim and gray-haired, in a white, three-quarter-length-sleeved knit shirt with small gold figures, neat white slacks and white running shoes. She read her music through modest gold-rimmed glasses.

For several moments I forgot I was in a slow-moving line waiting for my strawberry ice cream. Her playing was light and gently syncopated, and I could hear sensitivity in her shadings of the melodies. She took liberties with the scores from time to time, but her interpolations were always identifiably in the style of older ragtime. Usually it was an embellishment of the melody rather than a speed-up of the tempo or a careless reading of a bass line. Joplin would have been satisfied—nothing she played was too loud or too fast. I took my tray and moved to a table as close as I could find room. The dining room was crowded, but the voices were low so the piano could be heard. I wasn't the only one who was listening; the applause after each piece was spontaneous and pleased. I realized what I was hearing was ragtime that was still close to the parlor setting for which the music had been written. I hadn't understood that this way of playing ragtime was a distinct idiom, with its own clear boundaries. She was putting her music away when I went to thank her, and she smiled politely. Her name was Jean Iuchs, and I was told by a woman standing close to her that she had been playing her rags for years, and everybody in town knew her thoughtful way with the music. Tactfully, I didn't ask her her age, but I questioned the people who looked to be her age who were serving lunch and who had known her all their lives. None of them could tell me. The man serving the homemade strawberry ice cream stopped with a scoop in his hand.

"Now, I don't really know how old Jean is." He looked questioningly at the women around him. They all shook their heads or shrugged. "But she's just like us. We've always known Jean and she's just like us."

The gently lyric moment of parlor music in the Methodist Church base-ment had helped me find my way back to ragtime's social setting. After three days of dropping in on the performance tents set up along Ohio Street for the Scott Joplin Festival, what I realized was that the feeling of the ragtime revival of the 1970s, when the compositions had come alive again through the recordings of the serious new ragtime artists, had passed. After the international success of first the recordings of Joplin's compositions by Joshua Rifkin, then the film *The Sting*, with a multi-million-selling soundtrack album based on Joplin's music, and finally the orchestral recordings of the rags played by the New England Rag-time Ensemble under Gunther Schuller's direction, there were several years when ragtime was performed with the musical integrity and care that Joplin and Stark had fought to achieve in their lifetimes. Joplin's compositions were choreographed by the English Royal Ballet, and they found their way onto concert programs in university music series and on stages in New York and other cities in the United States.

For many of us who had long waited for some recognition of Joplin's genius, the moment culminated with the New York premier of his opera *Treemonisha*, in a stunning production by the Houston Opera Company with an African American cast. The production was staged at the reno-vated Palace Theater on Times Square, and as we streamed out into the street with the opera's triumphant "Slow Drag" finale still ringing in our ears, it seemed that now ragtime would take its place as a colorful and vital aspect of America's musical culture.

Nothing in a living culture is permanent, however. By 2004 the music I was hearing in Sedalia's street tents had reverted to the jingly man-nerisms of the sing-along ragtime of the pre-*Sting* era. Performers came on stage in arm garters and string ties and performed the compositions at tempos that distorted the melodies, playing with a casual disregard for any of the harmonic or melodic subtleties that were written into the printed scores. Invariably the final piece of every set was a rushed 1930s composition in the "stride" style, with its repeated note clusters replacing the melodic flow of the classic compositions, and at a tempo that would have driven the disappointed dancers off the floor in the early ragtime years.

I was also disappointed not to find any of the pianists—with the ex-ception of the Canadian performer Mimi Blaise—performing composi-tions by a group of composers who call the style of their new ragtime pieces *Terra Verde*—"Green Earth." The most prominent of the writers, David Thomas Roberts, Frank French, Scott Kirby, and Hal Isbitz, have extended and enriched the classic ragtime style with works that remain in the ragtime genre but employ new rhythms and more open melodic forms. Roberts has composed a major suite based on impressions of the streets of New Orleans, and one of his pieces, "Roberto Clemente," a tribute to the charismatic baseball player who died in a plane crash attempting to deliver relief supplies to Nicaragua after a major storm disaster, is often performed by other pianists, and was recorded by the Barfota Stompers, a ragtime jazz band in the northern Swedish city of Umeå. Isbitz, a retired computer programmer living in Santa Barbara, California, became so interested in the syncopated Brazilian tangos of Ernesto Nazareth that he composed a group of his own tangos, recorded by the Canadian ragtime pianist John Arpin on his expressive album *Blue Gardenia.* Isbitz has been particularly productive, and he has composed an intriguing body of new ragtime compositions that are innovative and technically challenging, as well as pieces that lie easily under the fingers for ragtime beginners.

I would also like to have heard something by one of the most popular of the ragtime performers, Max Morath, who presented a series of ragtime "entertainments" in the 1960s and 1970s, and who also has composed haunting new ragtime pieces. His affectionate tribute to John Stark and his wife, "Golden Hours," is a modern rag classic. It is also the only rag I know of with measures in the irregular 5/4 time signature. Many in the casual audiences walking along Ohio Street would have been as interested in the ragtime compositions of the young African American composer Reginald R. Robinson, who startled the small ragtime world with an album of his classic style compositions. He was later awarded a MacArthur "genius grant" to pursue his composing career.

As I went from tent to tent along the street, what I heard were hurried tempos, poorly shaped interpretations, and the thundering monotony of the left-hand rhythms. Only a few of the pianists played with a confident level of skill. Notes were missed, left hand passages were a stumbling blur, and there were even moments when the performers simply stopped to remember how the piece was supposed to go. The smiling audiences seated in rows of folding chairs, however, were mostly made up of the agreeable older couples I saw at the other tables when I ate breakfast at the motel. They had driven to Sedalia to see their friends for the weekend and to have a pleasant walk up and down the street on a sunny afternoon. If they could sit and listen to someone play the piano for a moment, that was part of the day's modest pleasures, and the clumsiest performances were applauded with the same cheerful enthusiasm as the occasional performer who got most of a piece right. I also realized, after two afternoons of the tents, that I saw almost no black faces in the small crowds around the pianists. I was attending a festival for a major

African American musical figure, and it was being presented without an African American audience.

Late Saturday afternoon I decided to walk across the railroad tracks to the African American section of town to ask why no one was walking up to the center of Sedalia, even with free music and the low-keyed carnival atmosphere. On Main Street, not far from the open space dedicated to Joplin and the Maple Leaf Club, three African American women had set up a table offering African carvings and ceramics. Two of them were in their twenties, and an older woman, obviously the mother of one of them, was sitting in a car parked at the curb with the door open. One of the women had a baby on her lap, and another child who looked about three or four ran around the table or clung to the other woman's leg when I came closer. We talked about their small stock of merchandise and the lack of people on the street. I asked why they hadn't set up their table on Ohio Street, where there were people strolling from one tent to the other.

The youngest of the women, chunkily built and round faced, and wearing a neatly ironed blouse and trousers, looked up from the baby in her lap, smiled pleasantly, and studied the brightly painted vases arranged on her table.

"There wasn't any room for us up there so we set up here."

I hadn't noticed that the curb on Ohio Street was crowded with street vendors.

Was this their biggest time of the year?

"The State Fair. That's bigger. That's the most we get."

She was still smiling as I looked at the vases. I hadn't seen many African Americans in the audience up there, I said casually—all that going on just up the street and only one or two black couples who looked like they were tourists. The other woman, taller and slimmer, with lighter skin and a more serious expression, spoke up abruptly.

"It used to be right down here—you know—on Main Street. The festival was all around here."

The other chimed in. "We marched with the drill team."

"You marched?"

"Every year, right down the street." I could hear the touch of pride in their voices.

The taller woman nodded emphatically. "This was the part of town where we came. There used to be little shops along the street."

"There was an arcade," the woman with the baby added.

"We could walk over from where we lived to all the places, and this was where we came 'cause we were just over the track."

She hesitated, then studied a building across the street as she talked. "That part of town down Ohio Street that was—you know—they had segregation. It wasn't where African American people went. They started to do the events in Liberty Hall, and that wasn't a place African American people could go. A lot of the older people, they said when they moved the festival up into town they took it away from us."

"Do people like this kind of music?" I asked cautiously.

The younger woman shrugged and smiled again. "Some do. Oh, I like it."

The other woman tried not to laugh. "Some of them call it 'Lily.'"

I hadn't heard the word used to describe music before. "Lily White?"

Laughing loudly now, they nodded in agreement.

Were they proud of Scott Joplin?

The young woman shifted her baby and shrugged. "I feel good about his name and everything and the festival for him—but we don't go into that part of town."

I walked on across the tracks to where the families that remained of the city's black community lived in frame houses along the still streets. No one passed me as I walked, but I could see that chairs had been pulled out into the shade on the sidewalks, and small groups of people sat talking and laughing. The broad lawns were being trimmed, and bent figures in straw hats and work clothes were digging out weeds in the wide swaths of garden that filled the empty spaces where many houses had been demolished. It was an ordinary Missouri Saturday afternoon in a quiet African American neighborhood. The festival across the tracks was another world away.

7 ✳ Gal, You Got to Go Back to Bimini
The Bahamas, Its Rhymers, and Joseph Spence

It was still early in the evening, but darkness had closed in on the little settlement of Fresh Creek on the east coast of Andros Island in the Bahamas. There was no electricity in the settlement in the summer of 1958, and the only lights in the small houses scattered through the brush were the dim yellow shapes of windows opening into rooms with kerosene lanterns set on the wooden planks of the tables. It was only our second night in Fresh Creek, and we hadn't learned our way around the crushed shell paths that led through the spiny brush from one house to another. The young woman stumbling after me in the shadows, whose name was Ann Danberg, had also been a student at the University of California, Berkeley, and we had met in music classes in 1954. We both were studying other subjects, but music in all its forms was a consuming interest for us both, and when we finally began talking after class, music was one of the continual themes of our endless conversations.

We had put a flashlight in the shoulder bags we'd brought with us to Andros, but we had forgotten to bring it on our night walk. It had been left behind in the bare wooden house we had rented in the afternoon from an old woman who lived in another of the houses close to the creek that gave the settlement its name. We were too interested in what we were hearing in the night's mingled buzz of sounds to go back for the flashlight, and we picked our way clumsily through the bushes, waving at the whining mosquitoes that had managed to find us, even if we couldn't see them hovering close in the shadows.

One of the sounds we could hear was the ocean. It drove in a monotonous thudding against the headlands a few hundred feet beyond us in the darkness. We could hear dogs barking—every house had a scarred, wary dog chained in the yard outside the door as an alarm and as protection against the other dogs in the settlement. There was the occasional scrabbling of the goats as they stirred uneasily in the tangled brush that hemmed in the house yards. From one or two of the houses we could hear battery-operated radios. The voice on the one station that reached the island was methodically reading the expected times of the next day's high and low tides in every harbor of the Bahamas. In the night air around us was a hum of other night insects and low piping exclamations of birds darting in athletic sweeps after the insects. But mingling with all of the sounds was something else that was drawing us through the dry brush that lined the paths we couldn't see well enough to follow. There was singing—somewhere in the shadows beyond us.

With the singing as an uncertain guide we picked our way past the scattered lights coming from the houses at the edge of the settlement. We soon were aware that other people also were making their way toward the sound, but they were walking more quickly along what were to them familiar paths. Following behind their dim figures as best we could, we finally found ourselves in a small clearing in front of a weathered, one story wooden house like the others in the settlement. We had come close to the headlands, and the boom of the sea was louder now. The night was a dark curtain that had pulled close behind us, but kerosene lamps were burning inside the house, casting an amber sheen over the room's minimal furnishings and the figures inside.

Through the open door we could see the faces of women in wrinkled cotton skirts and faded blouses slumped on wooden chairs in the center of the room. They were singing in an emotional, ragged chorus, some of them crying as they stared down at the uneven boards of the floor. The dark skin of their faces shone in the gleam of the lanterns. Some were gray-haired, their hair braided and pushed under their stained straw hats. Their tired faces were lined, and their bodies filled out their loose clothes with the shapelessness that comes with the years. One was holding a pipe, but she had let it go out. All of them had handkerchiefs balled in their hands, and they twisted them between their fingers, wringing them convulsively, then using them to wipe the tears from their eyes, as though the moisture were a kind of solace. A woman in a wrinkled long-sleeved shirt who looked older than the others was holding a much fingered hymn book, its pages open, and from time to time she turned it toward the lantern beside her to read silently from the texts.

In the gleam of the lanterns we could also see that the porch was filled with men from the settlement, and we could smell the bottle of raw, coarse rum that was being passed from hand to hand in the shadows. Inside, the women's voices had melded into a rough choir, the words clearly distinguishable as a familiar hymn.

"You go in," one of the men said to me. His voice was thick with rum, but I could see his face was glistening with tears, and the low whisper of his voice was tight with grief. "You go in, they find someplace for you to sit."

I leaned close to him, through a stronger smell of the rum. "What is the singing for?"

There was a sucking sound as he drank from the bottle, then he shrugged and began to cry openly. "The woman in the house, she sick. She goin' die soon."

The voices inside the house went on with the ragged hymn as voices broke in with emotional interjections. "Hear me Lord!" . . . almost a shout, "I'm praying to you, Oh Lord . . ."Oh Lord Jesus, I come to you." A voice broke. "I'm thinking of you, Lord Jesus . . ."

The man's grief-stricken face turned toward us again. "We're havin' a wake for her."

"Is she still alive?" I was leaning closer and my voice had also dropped to a whisper.

"She die tonight maybe. Maybe tomorrow."

In the shadows of the porch it was difficult for us to see anyone's expressions. We could only make out the dark shapes of the men's bodies in their sun-bleached shirts and the splashed pants they had been wearing out on their boats. All of them were fishermen, since it was the only work in the settlement, and none of them had thought of going home to change their clothes. Through the window I could see two or three men hunched in chairs pushed back against the wall of the room. A large, perspiring woman, her hair covered with a flowered handkerchief that she'd knotted at the corners, had turned to one of the men against the wall and she was begging him to sing.

"John Roberts, you must sing. You know it be time for you to sing. John, she be listenin' for you." Grief had shrunk her voice to a thin whisper.

The man leaned forward, his shoulders bowed, staring down at the floor. The black-painted wooden slats of the handmade chair where he was sitting were almost as high as his head. He was slightly built, but I could see that like the men around us his body was compact and wiry. He was dark-skinned, perhaps in his late forties, with a square, serious face and his white hair trimmed short. Unlike the other men he was wearing dark trousers and a white shirt with the sleeves rolled up. In the glimpse I'd had of his face in the lantern light his expression had been self-conscious, his eyes anxious and concerned. He glanced uncomfortably toward the woman who'd spoken to him, then dropped his head and stared down at the floor again. I could see that he was embarrassed by the woman's insistence.

"We must hear a song from you." I could hear the woman's voice rising now as she struggled with her grief. She turned toward him, persisting in her entreaties. "You know she be listenin,' just like she always do."

We could make out the outline of an opened door at the end of the room. The room beyond it was in darkness, but the women kept turning to look toward it as they sang. The dying woman was lying in the next room, and from her bed she was listening to the voices around the kerosene lanterns.

The man who had been addressed, John Roberts, hunched his shoulders, still too self-conscious to lift his head. Finally he cupped one hand against his ear so he could hear the pitch of his notes, and began to sing. The first low notes were the opening line of a simple hymn, like the songs we'd heard as we'd made our way through the brush to find the house, but his voice had an authoritative tone. The sound was rough, with a strong accent, and the words of the hymn suddenly took on a new emotional urgency. In the middle of the verse a second man's voice joined him. In the half-light the new singer standing in a shadowy corner of the room looked younger, with a dark, square-jawed face and bulky shoulders and arms. His voice was lower, and he was adding a simple bass harmony to the hymn melody. A moment later a third voice joined them. Like the other two the new singer had one hand cupped against his ear. He was sitting straight backed in a chair close to the bass singer. He was lighter-skinned and looked younger than either of the others. His eyes were tightly closed, his expression earnest and concentrated. The new singer's melody was a treble harmony above the melody that John Roberts had begun.

Their voices were hard; the tone was coarse and intense. The harmonies echoed in the room and spilled out through the open window into the darkness of the porch around us. In the first lines I recognized that what they were singing was a conventional Anglican hymn melody, but the rhythm was more marked, more decided. Feet were beginning to tap, even though the harmonies themselves were what I would have heard from a choir in an English country church. Then the man who was leading the song for the first time straightened in his chair, and though his eyes were still squeezed shut his head lifted. As he began a new verse his voice took on a stronger timbre and he began to make subtle alterations in the melody. The rhythm of what he was singing suddenly freed itself from the unaccented beat that the people around him were marking with their feet. A moment later he abruptly began improvising a new text to the hymn. His voice was harsher, and he was half-singing, half-chanting new words suggested by the text he'd begun with. From the other side of the room the two men singing with him shifted their own rhythms and harmonic phrases and the verse took on a new dimension as a complex polyrhythmic chant. The women around them swayed in the golden light, sitting forward in the stiff chairs, their feet tapping loudly. The rhythms became more insistent. All three were singing now with their eyes closed, as if they were conscious only of the sounds they could hear in their cupped ears. The women turned from singer to singer in the glow.

The voices on the porch around us had fallen silent. It was still possible to follow the harmonies of the simple hymn that were the unchanging foundation of the melodic elaborations, but each of the singers was improvising now. It was as though they were weaving an elusive, continually changing pattern in the amber light, and if we closed our eyes, we could see the lines of the song weave themselves into a fabric that felt as though it had the strength to bear the weight of the earth.

Then there was an almost imperceptible shift in the intensity of John Roberts's chanting voice, his tone lost its insistent push, and as he came to final lines of an improvised verse, he slipped back to the melody where he'd begun. The two others had caught the slight signal and, following his lead, they picked up the hymn's chords. The lines of their half-chanted, freely fugal singing smoothed themselves into a conscious anticipation of the simple harmonies. At the concluding line, they ended the final word on a major triad. With the last hummed tones they returned us to the stuffy room with its darkened doorway and to the light of the lanterns and the raw smell of rum from the bottle the man beside us clutched in his hand.

As John Roberts ended his hymn, people stirred around me, and there was a murmur of voices. This was what the people who had gathered for the wake had hoped to hear. I could hear the clank of the rum bottle passing from hand to hand. A woman's voice took up a wavering prayer inside the house. I leaned to the man beside me.

"What was that song?"

The man's face was confused as he tried to think of an answer. "Just ordinary. No special."

"But the way they sang it," I insisted.

"That be rhyming." The man still was uncertain about what I was asking him. "John just rhymin' it up."

We took a step back. We could see people moving around inside the house, stretching stiff arms and legs. The singer stood up at his chair, wiping his face with a handkerchief. We suddenly were aware that the cloud of mosquitoes had drifted nearer, and the heavy dampness in the air seemed to be closing in. The sea's pounding had begun again at the headlands, Before we could say anything to him, John Roberts slipped through the door, went down the steps from the porch and disappeared into the darkness.

Along with the other things slavery did to anyone who found themselves in its path, slavery scattered people. It left people scattered over thousands of miles, in places they had never known existed or could imagine that some day they would live, and of all the isolated areas or forgotten backcountry villages where slaves found themselves, Andros Island was one of the most unlikely. It is the largest of the scattering of islands that make up the Bahamas—104 miles long and 40 miles wide—but in 1958 it contained only about 900 people, almost all of them of African descent, living in a string of impoverished settlements along the island's eastern shore line. Each of the settlements was about a day's sailing from the ones closest to it. We never learned how many people lived in Fresh Creek, but it seemed there could only have been a dozen or so families, close to a hundred people. Fishing was the only economic activity, but there was no place to sell the fish, so the crude handmade sloops sailed with their catch to Nassau, the capital city of the Bahamas on the island of New Providence. Their vessels were constructed with a center well, drilled with holes to allow the sea water to flow through them. Without refrigeration, the only way they could bring their fish to Nassau was to keep them alive in the wells.

Fresh Creek and Andros would be transformed within a few years by the spread of tourism to the island, but the only signs of it in 1958 were a newly constructed hotel that sat empty on the other side of the creek, and a few simple frame houses, like the one we had rented, that had been constructed for the workers who built the hotel. The small structures now were also empty as the settlement had gone back to its old life. Most of the houses in the village were without running water or electicity, and ours, like the others, had a smelly privy besieged by hulking land crabs in the bushes behind it. Our bare, two room house had a small porch, giving it some sense of elegance on the path beside the creek, but its windows were simple openings cut into the board walls, and the kitchen had only a hot plate on a wooden shelf. There was no sink or drain. At night one wall would be covered with black moths with wings the size of our hands.

Although I was to read later that the Bahamas was not an ideal place for slavery to take root, we could see that for ourselves when we tried to follow the faint paths that led out of the settlement back to-

Fresh Creek at low tide. *Photo by Ann Charters.*

ward the interior of the island. The paths inevitably led to struggling garden patches, a few hundred square feet of soil hacked out of the growth and planted with vegetables. A few yards beyond the gardens the paths dwindled into the uneven litter of stones and debris. The Bahamas, spread out on a map, cover an area of almost ninety thousand square miles, but only a few thousand square miles of the area are actually land. What land there is is scattered over about seven hundred islands and cays, and at least two thousand low rock formations without vegetation that could also be called islands. Unlike the islands of the Caribbean to the south, like Cuba or Jamaica, the Bahamas have no core of volcanic peaks. The islands are almost flat, formed of porous limestone only a few feet above sea level. There are no rivers, though Andros does have tidal creeks, like Fresh Creek, the wide, fast-running stream in front of our house, and Andros is divided across its waist by wide sluggish bights—tangled passages of clear water that bisect the island's swampy interior and emerge on the mud flats of the western shore that faces Florida, about sixty miles away across the Gulf Stream.

The rest of the Out Islands, as all of the Bahamas islands except for New Providence are termed, were almost as thinly settled as Andros.

Only 30 of the islands and cays were inhabited. The total population of the Bahamas was about 250,000, with more than 160,000 people living in Nassau. Although Andros had seemed large when we looked at it on a map, the interior is a mosquito ridden swamp, and the west coast is a tidal mud flat without usable harbors. The only soil was the fringe of earth along the coast where we had rented our house.

The song we heard the night of the wake, when John Roberts just "rhymed it up," was unlike any other styles of the musical language of the African diaspora, but like the others, it mirrored the particular circumstances of the system of slavery that lay behind it. With so little land, and with no prospects for the kind of large-scale cultivation that gave slavery its economic base, slavery not only came late to the Bahamas, it almost didn't come at all. Only a small number of slaves were imported, and the slaves who did arrive on the islands had Africa only as a distant memory. With only a few exceptions, their homeland was one of the English colonies on the mainland of North America. Most of them had been born in the colonies, and even if Africa was part of their consciousness, it wasn't a living memory.

In the turbulent years of the American Revolution, from 1776 to 1783, revolutionaries continually attacked the loyalists and their property. In the South there was considerably less fervor for the break with England than there was in the northern colonies, which had been settled by people already alienated from England for their religious beliefs. The small numbers of loyalists in the north could flee to Canada, but for southern loyalists the nearest refuge was the Bahamas. Whatever ideas the loyalists had about the possibility of establishing a new life on the islands, they took their slaves with them only because they had a justifiable fear that their slaves would be confiscated, along with the rest of their property, by the new governments. When the war ended in 1783 a surge of loyalists fled with their slaves to the islands. That same year the Crown granted land to 114 of the refugees, the grants parceled out over sixteen separate islands.

Before the Revolution the entire population of the Bahamas was less than five thousand, and a majority of these were domestic slaves. Fifty years later the number of people living on the islands had grown to more than twenty thousand, with slaves now a sizeable majority. In the beginning the settlers found enough land to grow cotton, and with the development of the cotton gin they experienced a few years with a reasonable return for their labors. Cotton, however, quickly exhausted the thin fringe of soil, as it did everywhere it was grown, and it was only a few years before dreams of a new land of large slave plantations were abandoned.

The situation had so little prospect of improvement that slavery ended without turmoil in the Bahamas in the summer of 1834, the day celebrated on the islands as "August Monday." The Emancipation process ended slavery everywhere in the British Empire, and the Bahamian slave holders shared in the twenty million pounds that were paid as compensation for the value of the freed slaves. In an effort both to compensate the slaves in some way and to encourage settlement on the nearly deserted islands, a series of statutes were enacted allowing ex-slaves to purchase a minimum of twenty acres of land for a fixed price of twelve shillings an acre. The promise of "forty acres and a mule" that the newly freed slaves expected in the United States at their emancipation thirty years later was a reality in the Bahamas, in part because the land was poor, and it was scattered across the empty islands. Over the next decades many of the new freemen became holders of large tracts of land, which they in turn divided among their children. On the most hopeful of the islands, Andros among them, small settlements of freed slaves struggled to scratch some kind of living out of the barren soil, and harvest what they found in the surrounding sea.

Fresh Creek had only a scattering of houses, and the next afternoon a question at the nearby shop directed us to the house of the singer we had heard at the wake, John Roberts. We also learned that he had one of the few jobs at the empty hotel. He tended the garden, keeping its spare plantings trimmed in wait for the winter and the hoped-for guests. His house was older, solidly built, with a long porch across the front of the low structure facing the creek. He had just come back from work, crossing the creek on the small dinghy that was sculled back and forth across the swiftly flowing current by a muscled ferryman in a torn shirt and ragged shorts.

Roberts's face was more lined with the weather and the sun than we had been conscious of in the lantern light, and he was as evasive and guarded about his singing as he had been the night before, when it took several entreaties before he overcame his shyness. Yes, he knew old songs, but he insisted that his cousin, a man named Frederick McQueen who was somewhere on the south of Andros, was a better singer and Frederick knew more songs. John's eyes went from one of us to the other as he answered our questions, clearly having difficulty understanding what we wanted from him. When we tried to persuade him that it was his singing that interested us, he was silent, and he shook his head. I said that we had a tape recorder with us and we wanted to record him. Could he do that? He demurred again.

"No, it not be right for me to sing for you. Frederick McQueen, now, Frederick McQueen could do it for you. He be the one to sing for you."

When I asked helplessly where Frederick McQueen was, John shrugged. When his cousin worked he was out at sea, and John hadn't heard anything about him for several years.

I asked, in a last effort, if he knew any more songs like the one he had sung at the wake. The question clearly puzzled him and he studied the boards on the floor of his porch, just as he had stared at the floor in the house the night before. Then he looked off across the clearing, toward the shining surface of the creek. After a pause he tried to make us understand that what he had performed at the wake wasn't any particular song, it was a way of singing.

"That just be rhyming, what you heard."

I still hadn't completely understood what he was trying to tell me. I knew the name of only one traditional Bahamian song, "Dig My Grave." Was it a song he knew?

He still hesitated, surprised, then he slowly nodded. "I know it." But he couldn't sing it for us. "I must have some of the boys sing it with me. You see, the old songs, they take more than one man. You got to have help."

For the first time I could see that he was considering my questions. I sensed that there might be a possibility he would sing for us. I told him we would pay him a little, and we would also pay anyone who sang with him. After a silence he nodded tentatively. If he was just asking the others to do a job with the prospect of a little pay, then it would be alright. It was clearly important for him to insist that he wouldn't agree to record for us out of any kind of vanity or pride in his singing abilities. The community scattered along the creek was too closely knit for that kind of immodest assertion. His dark face was creased in thought, then he finally nodded again with more certainty. He would talk with the "boys"; he would tell us what they said.

It seems completely improbable that I might have heard a traditional Bahamian song in California, where I was going to the university in the mid-1950s, but I had heard "Dig My Grave." I had listened to it so obsessively that as I walked through the settlement I would sometimes find myself singing the words to myself.

Dig my grave both long and narrow,
Make my coffin deep and wide.
You dig my grave both long and narrow,
Make my coffin deep and wide.

Well, it's two two to my head,
Two two to my feet,
Two two to carry me when I die.

A Bahaman work sloop. *Photo by Ann Charters.*

It was fascination with the fragmentary verses of the song that had brought us to Andros and to Fresh Creek.

The folk music collector Alan Lomax had found the song for me, just as he had found—for many of us—ways to hear much of the unique treasure of America's vernacular song. On a trip to the Bahamas with Mary Elizabeth Barnicle in 1936 he had heard a group of Andros fishermen singing on the docks in Nassau, and since there was no electricity on Andros itself, he recorded them in the governor's mansion in Nassau. His collecting was financed by the Library of Congress, and in the 1940s and 1950s, whenever there was enough money, the library would release songs and instrumental pieces on single 78 rpm records. When I was taking music classes at Berkeley in 1954 I would bicycle to the campus early so I could listen to records in the music library, and I found "Dig My Grave" on one of the ten-inch singles the library had purchased.

For weeks I began my mornings with the little Bahamian song. Lomax wrote in his notes only that the singers were sponge fishermen from Andros, and even though I had no definition for the music I was hearing, I was already conscious that in the still little-known world of African American music, there was something that I sensed as a language of song. I was to learn later that at the center of this common language was a continuing process of musical adaptation, and what drew me to the song's rough polyphonic texture was that the voices were creating a sound that could have come from the eighteenth century in England. What I was hearing was a living example of a song from this older English tradition, but as it was sung by the Andros spongers it had become unmistakably altered by its African antecedents in the texturing of the polyphony, in the altered tones of the vocal scale, and in the timbre of the strong voices. This was the song I hoped to find, but already the one we had heard John Roberts improvise made it clear that there was much else there for us.

As the days passed in a glare of unyielding sun and indecisive breezes that filled the nights, we saw John from time to time. The two young singers he was teaching his songs were often out in their boats fishing, and they had only sporadic moments to practice. He explained each time that there was no way he could sing without them, and they didn't know his songs.

"They be so many of the old songs. I know many, many of the old ones—but the young boys here, they sing. But they don't know the old songs." And he added again, in a rueful tone, that his cousin Frederick McQueen, "he could sing them all for you. Frederick, now, he knows them all."

One afternoon, as we stood talking in the shadows under the palm trees that enclosed his house, he tried to explain what the people in the settlement meant by what they called "rhyming," since he realized that we didn't understand the term at all.

"A rhymer, see he rhyme it up. Whatever the song is about, the rhymer he use that to tell a story, and he rhyme up more about it all the time the singing does on. That's what the young boys don't know how to do. They don't know how to rhyme. Now the rhymer, he can't do it all alone. He just singing the ground, and he have to learn the afterbeat from the others that's singing."

"Ground," "Afterbeat,"—terms I'd heard in music lectures before, but here they had taken on new meanings that hadn't been suggested in any of my classes.

In the hot summer days most of the men spent hours out in their primitive boats fishing, and the women tended their vegetables in their stony garden patches. The boats that the men sailed were heavy-bottomed, thirty-foot-long coastal sloops, with ragged sails, a small pit on the open deck for a fire, and a crude space below the deck for shelter in heavy storms. The well for the catch of fish was in the hull's center, and the weight of water made the boats sluggish and hard to maneuver. They had no motors or compasses, and they were at the mercy of the wind and the currents. One week a sloop, trying to come in to the anchorage at Fresh Creek spent six days only a mile offshore, drifting back and forth with the tides, waiting for enough wind to sail through the break in the reef that lined the coast.

The older men in the settlement had spent their youth sponging, and often when they talked I could feel how their life on the boats had helped to create the rhyming song we had heard at the wake. In the long nights they tied the boats together, and with the fires casting a red glow over the decks they spent hours singing, improvising the rhyming texts. One of the veterans of the sponging days, an old man with scarred hands named Captain Ormond Johnson, grew nostalgic as he looked back to those nights. One of the men sailing with him was Frederick McQueen.

> We pull up at night on the sponge beds you know. If it be really calm we let the boats come together, tied up so a man could walk from one boat to another. But we didn't walk over to visit so much. We just want to be close. We run no lights. Only the coals still glowing red in that fire box out there on the deck and we be in our blankets because it be chilly in the night. Then we'd be lyin' there, looking up to the stars, you know, and Frederick would sing. I never heard anything so beautiful.[1]

In his book *Grand Bahama* Peter Barratt gave a useful description of sponge fishing and its importance to the Bahamian economy. In appearance most of the sponges looked like slimy, dark balls dropped on the ocean floor, with patterned openings in the skin. It was the sponge's dried skeleton that became the soft, commercially valuable bath sponge.

> The best sponging grounds were the Andros mud flats and the area north of More's Island at the eastern end of Grand Bahama, appropriately called "the mud." The sponge fishermen usually owned a schooner which acted as a "mother ship." From this pairs of men in dinghies would fan out, the guide sculled and the hooker scanned the sea bottom with a glass-bottomed bucket. When a sponge was spotted the hooker took his long-handled two pronged rake, deftly hooked it from the sea bottom and scooped it into the boat. After the dinghy was filled they returned to the mother ship. Catches accumulated on the deck of the schooner near a good sponging area from Sunday to Saturday, by which time the older people say the boat could be detected by scent faster than by eye.[2]

The sponges were taken to large water-filled corrals, and after soaking for a week, they were cleaned by breaking away the dark outer skin. Barratt notes that in one three-year period, from 1900 to 1903, over one million pounds of sponges were shipped from the islands every year. At the period of the greatest harvest, the Bahamas supplied almost 30 percent of the sponges that reached the world's markets.

By the 1950s the days of the sponge boats were part of Andros's past, but for once the collapse wasn't caused by human interference in the natural chain of survival. Sponges are hardy survivors, but they are vulnerable to parasites, and in 1938 a microscopic blight wiped them out. The collapse of the sponging ended the years of relative prosperity on Andros, and when we came to Fresh Creek the people were still struggling with an economic catastrophe that had lasted twenty years.

Despite the heat we often crossed the creek in the small dinghy to walk to a deserted beach to wash and swim as much as we dared. We saw sharks in the surf almost every day, so we took turns splashing to get some of the perspiration off us while the other watched for the dark shapes that slid closer to the shore when they noticed us. It was on one of our walks across the settlement that we encountered the man who would become the best known of all the Bahamian musicians we recorded that summer. As we were walking along one of the crushed shell paths we heard music from a building site ahead of us. Three or four men were working on the walls of a small house, but it was almost midday and they were working lethargically in the heat. A few feet from them a man with a guitar was sitting on a wall of loose bricks in the shade of a palm tree. There was so much music that I was certain there must be another guitarist on the other side of the wall, and I walked a few steps and leaned over to look. There was no other guitarist. There was only the man sitting on the bricks with a large acoustic guitar that he was playing with strong, agile fingers. We had just met Joseph Spence.

Spence was a broad shouldered, muscular man, with a strongly shaped face and large hands. He had a pipe clenched in his mouth and he growled along with his improvisations in a kind of free rhyming style that functioned as much as an illusion of rhyming as rhyming itself. No one we had talked to had ever told us about Joseph Spence, probably because he wasn't from Fresh Creek. He was from the settlement of Small Hope, fourteen miles north of us along the beach, and he hadn't been living on Andros for several years. He worked as a stonemason, and he lived in Nassau with his wife and family. He'd been laid off his job and had come back to Andros to stay with his sister in Small Hope for a few weeks. He'd been spending most of the time practicing the guitar, and when he decided to sail down to Fresh Creek to see some friends on one of the small sloops that delivered supplies and coconuts and pigs from settlement to settlement, he brought his guitar with him.

The workers were so pleased to see him that the work dwindled to a stop. One of them dispatched a boy to a small shop by the creek to bring back a bottle of rum. Spence sipped on the rum as he talked, nodding and waving to people as they passed us on the path. It was fiercely hot, and we joined him in the shade by the piled bricks. He was in a loose, short-sleeved shirt and khaki trousers, with a straw hat pushed back on his forehead. He looked in his late forties. He'd already talked with the friends he'd come to see, and he hadn't decided what to do with the rest of the day, so without hesitation he agreed to come to our house and record for us. We walked slowly along the dusty paths across the settlement, talking as we went. Since he was carrying his guitar, we picked up a straggling, laughing procession of people who were still in the settlement for the day. We saw many women we recognized, and everyone seemed to recognize Spence.

Though our house only had its two small, bare rooms, we had thought we would record him in the kitchen, since there wouldn't be any noise in the microphone from the wind, and the wooden walls of the room had a natural resonance. So many people had followed us, however, that the only place we could record him was out on the cramped porch, since he clearly intended to play for everyone who'd come to hear him. I brought out one of the wooden chairs from the kitchen, Spence rested his straw hat on the porch railing, tuned his big guitar while I adjusted the microphone, then he laughed in a pleased voice and began playing.

Perhaps because of the crowd around the steps of the porch, what he played for the next two hours was a program of nearly all the varying styles of Bahamian music. There was a breathtaking series of variations on the American popular song "Coming in on a Wing and a Prayer," there were three older style religious "anthems," one in 3/4 time. He included two Bahamian folk songs that I recognized, "Jump in the Line" and "Brownskin Gal." There was another folk song I remembered by the line "gal, you got to go back to Bimini." The women teased him, demanding to know why he didn't sing as well as play. He protested that he wasn't a singer, he didn't sing, but one of the women shouted scornfully,

"What do you mean you don't sing? You got a mouth to talk!"

Spence did his best for her on the next piece, a spiritual from the islands titled "I'm Going to Live That Life." He sang and rhymed on the verses as he played, but he was right, he wasn't a singer. He didn't bother to take his pipe out of his mouth, and what he did for the pleased crowd of women was a syncopated growling that had the rhythm of the piece but only phrases and mumbled lines of the text. What he was playing on the guitar was so startling in its inventiveness that he didn't need to sing, and giving any attention to a song would have gotten in the way of the inventive rush of his improvisations. The large-bodied guitar he was playing had a wide neck, so he had room for his thick fingers, and he'd dropped the bass string of the guitar from E to D, which gave him more flexibility in the chording on the upper strings. He played flowing streams of melody with his fingers, setting them rhythmically against the moving bass patterns he played with his thumb. At some moments he seemed to be improvising simultaneously on the bass, the melody, and the harmony, growling for emphasis and loudly tapping his foot.

His improvisations often pleased him as much as they did his listeners, and he would laugh noisily when he had managed a particularly difficult bass run or a complicated rhythmic shift. As I wrote later:

> He conceived each new chorus as a new challenge, and at his most fluid and inventive moments his improvisations developed into a series of variations, rather than the repetition of similar musical ideas that is the usual form other guitarists used for long solos. He was so skilled that he could set a rhythm in triple meter—3/4 or 6/8—against the basic duple meter—4/4—of the piece, which is something most improvisers also can do, but Spence was the only one I ever heard who could play 4/4—in the lower strings—and 3/4 in the upper strings at the same time. With all of his inventiveness he also had an irresistible sense of Caribbean rhythm to everything he played.[3]

When Spence had played as much as he felt like, he sat back and listened to what he'd recorded, laughing and shouting back and forth with the people still clustered around the porch. Finally he put on his straw hat, picked up his guitar, and he and a crowd of young women walked off toward the beach. As they moved into the shadows of the trees I could hear the guitar as he began playing again.

The next Sunday, John Roberts and the two singers who had been practicing with him stood outside our house and announced they were ready to sing for us. They were self-conscious and nervous. I recognized the two men with Roberts as the two singers who had joined in his rhyming at the wake. The heavily built bass singer, H. Brown, who had been standing in the corner, was physically intimidating beside the slighter Roberts, but he had a quick smile and he had the young islander's

Joseph Spence, playing on the porch for neighbors. *Photo by Ann Charters.*

deference to his elders. The treble singer had been sitting down at the wake. His name he told us pleasantly was C. Wallace. I thought he was in his twenties, like the bass singer. He had the same sudden smile, though I was conscious that he was anxious that they would sing well for us. All three of them were in their good shirts, and they had put on dressier slacks, instead of their usual work trousers. Since it was Sunday, and we were concerned about disturbing the stillness of the settlement—even though no houses were close to us—I had set up the recorder in our simple kitchen. They grouped themselves in a half circle against the bare boards of the wall. In a moment, each with a hand cupping his ear, they were singing "Dig My Grave."

We sat transfixed. The insistent tone of their voices and the rhythmic tapping of their feet as they accented the song's basic pulse filled the spaces of the room, drawing a fuller resonance from the enclosing background of the wooden kitchen walls. They sang with eyes tightly shut, sitting stiffly upright on our battered chairs, their nervousness forgotten after the first few measures. Their voices rephrased the simple lines of the melody and tightened the rhythms with a subtle shifting of the accents. Unlike the familiar form of a "round"—the English song form that was closest to what they were performing—their voices entered at

Sloops at low tide, Mangrove Key Settlement. *Photo by Ann Charters.*

irregular intervals, continually anticipating or delaying the harmonic resolution. Their structuring of the song re-created it with a new intensity.

As I played the tape back, they leaned forward in their chairs, listeningly intently to what they had just sung, and the mood lightened. They had never heard their voices before, and they were clearly pleased at the sound they heard. They nodded to each other with self-conscious smiles, sat back in their chairs, and with a nod from John they were ready to sing again. The next song took them a step closer to the rhyming we'd heard at the wake. It was a simpler song, titled "Depend on Me," perhaps from a later century than "Dig My Grave." It began with a simple phrase by John's solo voice, "Oh, 'pend on me, and I'll 'pend on you," and after a handful of verses that stretched to include the rhythmic phrases and melodic elements of his rhyming style, he ended the song, nodding to the other two, his expression showing his own satisfaction. They were ready to begin rhyming.

For the rest of the afternoon John's voice became an insistent goad, prodding at the possibilities of the texts and rhythms of each new song, as he "rhymed" the song's story. After their rhyming songs they turned to a new group of songs I had known nothing about. The Andros singers like John, in their long nights on the schooners out on the sponge beds, had also created a body of ballads telling about their lives at sea. The ballads were about shipwrecks and drowning, about voyages in fierce storms, about the people left waiting on shore, about friends they knew and worked with. Each of the ballads had many verses, and the verses ended with a line sung in unison, like the ballads of England and Scotland that were the obvious models for the form. As John sang the verses, the other two accompanied him with humming voices, adding a harmonic texture. The ballads, unlike their English models, were fiercely rhythmic, and their feet tapped heavily on the boards of the floor, insistent on telling the story of the song.

As the afternoon ended we suddenly were conscious that the cramped room had become stuffy and hot. We were all perspiring, and stiff from holding ourselves still for so many hours. The men's voices were hoarse from the intensity of their singing, and their shirts clung to their chests. I looked over at Annie, and it was obvious in the slump of her shoulders that she was as emotionally depleted as I was. I was conscious that the singers had drawn us with them back into a moment of their lives on Andros that had almost been forgotten, and we each understood that in a few years it might not be possible to experience a moment like it again. They lingered with us on the porch, feeling the first stirring of the evening wind, laughing and nodding at each other. Slowly, almost as if they didn't want to leave the afternoon behind them, they nodded a last time, went down the steps, and walked away along the scuffed paths toward their houses.

Our life on Andros was so isolated that Nassau and the other islands had come to seem almost from some other time, but a rusted mail boat with space for passengers sailed from Nassau and passed the creek mouth once a week, anchoring offshore since it couldn't come in through the opening in the reef. A week later, in a rising wind, an overloaded dinghy carried us with our bags and the recording equipment out to the pitching deck of the mail boat. It was sailing to the south, to a settlement where we hoped to hire a sloop to take us farther south to the end of Andros. We had said goodbye to the people and the settlement, and we had assured them that we had decided that we couldn't journey this far and not go on. Somewhere along the island, beyond where the mail boat would take us, we might find Frederick McQueen, the singer whose voice still haunted the people who had heard him so many years before.

8 * Pretenders, Caressers, Lions, and a Mighty Sparrow

Trinidad's Sweet Calypso

At the end of a hazy, sun-tinged, Trinidadian day, the traffic was heavy heading south away from Port of Spain as people returned home from work. But we were going north, from the cane fields back to the capital, and we were moving steadily. Ahead of us, at the edge of the city, loomed the ragged mountains that had given the island its name. On August 1, 1498, as Columbus sailed toward the mist-shrouded shore from the north, on his third voyage, he could make out the summits of the three highest peaks and named the island for the Holy Trinity, La Trinità. I was wearily sprawled in the passenger seat beside the tour operator of Indian descent who had taken us—my photographer daughter Nora and me—down to see a little of the sugar cane harvest and the boiling of the pressed juice in a large, sooty "factory" close to the fields. We'd been in the cane fields since dawn, and Nora was napping behind us, her long legs stretched out on the car seat.

The narrow strip of mountains along the edge of the northern coast gives the island more than its name. The mountains define Trinidad. The name printed on the maps is "Northern Range," though "range" is too grand a word for the rough barrier of tree-covered slopes and narrow valleys that rises out of the island's rolling green plain that is the rest of the island. Without its mountains the island would be only a muddy, low stretch of land off the coast of Venezuela. The thirteen miles that separate Trinidad from the tangled mouths of the Orinoco River on the mainland of South America have widened the distance between the newer English roots of the island's culture, and the older Spanish world to the south. In its own idiosyncratic style Trinidad still clings to its old way of life as a colony of the wide flung British Empire, even though it is closer to Venezuela than it is to the smaller island of Tobago, which lies to the northeast, and has been linked with it in the Trinidad-Tobago Confederation since the islands were joined as the colony of Trinidad and Tobago in 1889.

In its isolation at the southern end of the chain of islands of the eastern Caribbean, with Trinidad's contacts with the Spanish culture of South America and its diffuse history, it could have been forgotten—another of the distant Caribbean islands with a sugar economy and its roots in slavery—without anything to make it unique. It is small enough to have been forgotten—the two islands together, Trinidad and Tobago have only about one and a third million people today—but from Trinidad have come two African-rooted musical styles that have journeyed everywhere in the world. It would be impossible to survey the music that has emerged from the African diaspora without experiencing Trinidad's irreverent, irrepressible Calypso singers and its noisy street orchestras—the steel bands.

In the modern world, which is often accused of imposing universal cultural values over even the most isolated of the world's societies, the music of the calypsonians and the "pans"—as Trinidadians call the steel bands—is as vital today as ever, even if it still sweeps everything before it only for the months of Trinidad's exuberant carnival. Although the musicians of both Trinidad and Tobago are continually tempted to Port of Spain for its rich musical life, at Carnival they are joined by thousands of visitors who swell the crowds. What the new arrivals find is a crowded, congested, rundown city of about seventy thousand people in the northwest corner of the island, with a dingy harbor area and for a beach only a muddy strip of red earth on a peninsula a few miles west of the city. The center of Port of Spain is a vast, open, grassy space, Queen's Park Savannah, always called simply the Savannah. Everything in Port of Spain is described by its relationship to the Savannah. "If you go by car you goin' by the Savannah." "Now you see where you got to when the Savannah's runnin' along beside you." When the steel bands surge through the streets for the judging of their Carnival competition Panorama, their last turn brings them to the grandstands that have been constructed for the week on the edge of the Savannah. In the weeks before Carnival, pavilions and stands selling beer and island food cover the southern edge of the Savannah in rows of small huts, looking like a bright, imaginary medieval village.

Close to the northern edge of the Savannah there are memorials to the Trinidadian's love of their music. At an intersection, where the wide street on one side of the Savannah meets the winding road going up into the hills, is a traffic roundabout with a tiny, lush park and a bright, red-bronze statue. The statue is life-size—a stocky man in a suit looking intently down the street. The statue is new, and it's hard to imagine that it might have been put up in some earlier moment of the island's history. The figure in the statue is the great calypso singer Slinger Francisco, much better known as the "Mighty Sparrow." For once a tribute has been paid in time. Sparrow moved to New York City many years ago but he is still calypso's reigning personality. He returns yearly at Carnival season, and his new recordings continually show up in the island's shops. There have already been more than a hundred albums in a musical career that remains unquenchably flamboyant and inventive.

A half mile along the edge of the Savannah to the west of Sparrow's statue, a few small blocks on the way to the St. Anne shopping district, stands another of the new statues. This figure is tall and lanky, dancing with one leg outthrust and his face broadly smiling. It is the other illustrious figure of modern calypso, Aldwyn Roberts, the enduring "Lord Kitchener," the beloved composer of so many of the "road marches" played by the steel bands. "Kitch" died in 2000, but his music is still a vivid presence in the Carnival season. A year after his death a sheet music collection of Carnival hits from 2001 appeared, titled *For Kitch*, and one of the songs, sung by calypso performer The Original Defosto Himself, was "Kitchener Say," with Kitch's voice from heaven telling the pan players that he would be back, "He say yes he coming for sure."

When I walked along the edge of the Savannah in the midst of Carnival fever in January, 2002, it felt as though the statues symbolized today's Trinidad, just as the Savannah, once a sugar plantation, symbolized Trindad's past. Land which once grew sugar is something the island shares with almost every island in the West Indies—but Trinidad can proudly claim calypso and the steel pans for itself.

Trinidad's history is an indelible part of Caribbean history, and there is little in the background to suggest that centuries later the Trinidadians would erect statues to singers descended from Caribbean slaves. In the summer of 1498, when Columbus first glimpsed its three peaks, there were only scattered bands of Arawak Indians living on Trinidad. To the north, on Tobago, there were Caribs. Columbus was again disappointed in his search for the empires of China. Instead he was met by the now depressingly familiar canoes filled with naked, sullenly curious Caribs, who paddled out close enough to stare at the Spaniards. Columbus, in a dispirited effort to convince the natives that he wasn't dangerous, presented a show of drum and pipe music, while some of his sailors danced on the deck. After another silence the Caribs fired a volley of arrows at the dancers and paddled back to the shore. Six years had passed since the first Spanish landings, and the natives had already learned what they could expect from the grim, bearded men in armor who came off the ships.

Calypsonians have always had a more realistic view of the history of their land, and the gruff modern singer Winston Bailey, known as "Shadow," expressed a personal view of Columbus and his voyages in his calypso "Columbus Lied."

Columbus was a mighty sailor, he sailed the open seas.
He went down in the Caribbean and he called it the West Indies.
He said he found a new world, and he expect me to believe.
But how could this world be new, when it's older than Adam and Eve?
(Chorus) Columbus lied, Columbus lied, Columbus lied,
   Columbus lied, lied, lied . . . [1]

The first brush with Columbus's small fleet did little more than open Trinidad to Spanish brutality, but the endless European religious and dynastic wars of the next three hundred years tugged back and forth at the Caribbean islands. When the British finally seized Trinidad in 1797, in the turmoil of the Napoleonic wars, it had been considered a French outpost for some time. At that moment in its chaotic history the island was almost empty. The native population had long been exterminated, and there were fewer than eighteen thousand new settlers. The largest group of Europeans was French, followed by the Spanish, and finally a small number of recent English settlers. The largest of the island's groups of people were the more than ten thousand slaves. Sugar was beginning to make its way on the island after the French had introduced the crop in Tobago in 1781. Within the next few decades the Trinidadian lowlands were cleared and thick stands of cane sprang up along the new mud roads. The new sugar entrepreneurs, however, were already facing a new English public mood that was clamoring for the end of slavery, and there was only a brief period when they could supply their impatient need for labor with Africans.

The streets of Port of Spain today reflect a much more complicated history than simply an account of the island's slavery would suggest. Following the abolition of slavery in the British colonies in the 1830s the plantation owners attempted to set up a so-called "apprentice" system, but in the stifling heat and mud of the cane fields they found it was impossible to keep African labor. Free at last to choose for themselves, the ex-slaves streamed out of the crude hovels beside the cane fields and crowded into the colony's small cities. The owners were forced to find other sources of labor, and the answer for Trinidad—and for many of the West Indies—was indentured workers imported from India. They worked under the terms of specific contracts, similar to the indenture contracts that were also common in North America. The term of indenture was usually several years, and in addition to their transportation to the new land, the workers were given a requisition of clothing, food, and some kind of shelter, similar to what had been provided for the slaves. The faces of the Indians add the other dimension to the crowds on Port of Spain's busy streets, and mingling in the smells from the

The Trinidad landscape. *Photograph by Nora Charters-Myers.*

small restaurants are the aromas of the herbs and the exotic ingredients of the Indian diet.

For the Indians who made the journey, their presence on the island is as much a matter of choice as it was dictated by their circumstances. The working conditions for the indentured workers were cruel and demanding and only a little better than slavery, but they had some legal rights, and they were paid a small salary, which they could save or send back to their families. If they chose to return to India at the end of their period of indenture they were guaranteed passage home. If they chose to stay they would have full rights in the new country. The terms of indenture were so attractive to many struggling people, however, that there was even a small influx of Africans into Trinidad. Yorubas emigrated from the Gold Coast, bringing their language and music with them. Of even more importance was their religion, including the Shango cults that continue to be an influence on island life today.

Within a few years it was the Indians who were sustaining the sugar industry. Between 1845 and 1917 a half million laborers came from India to the Caribbean. Almost a third of them, 143,000, came to Trinidad. The Africans—"Creoles" in the island's terminology—who had already dealt with three or four new languages, might have expected that they would have to learn still another vocabulary, but the two groups remained separated—the Indians in the south close to the fields, the Creoles in the towns and cities—until English at last emerged as the language most Trinidadians could understand.

In the early years, the colony was administered from London and the Indians continued to live in isolated communities in the countryside. The Creoles' derisive term for the Indians, which turns up in many early calypsos, was "Coolies," and it was assumed that the Creoles would dominate the government. In recent decades, with the growth of the oil industry and the steady drift of people into Port of Spain and other small cities, the two societies have become more nearly equal in political influence and the tensions have grown. Each of the groups now has about 40 percent of the population. It was the Indians who were working in the cane fields when we drove from Port of Spain to see the harvest. We could sense the edgy mood when we went to the cane fields with our Indian driver. For months in the winter and spring of 2002 it was impossible to form a government after the new election, because the voters had divided the seats equally in the island's parliament, and neither party would allow the other to select a prime minister. The turmoil became a persistent theme for the calypso singers during the Carnival competition. With today's new consciousness, however, their attacks weren't aimed at the Indians, but only at the politicians of each of the main parties, who were too stubborn and too suspicious of each other to yield to the common needs of the country.

Sometimes in the days when I was alone in Trinidad before Nora joined me, as I squeezed my way through Port of Spain's crowded streets in the din of the traffic and the deafening medley of songs from the record stalls, I thought with some irony of the difficulty I had experienced searching for the local musical traditions in other places I'd journeyed. Trinidadians—or "Trinibagonians," the more formal designation—claim with only a little exaggeration that the islands have only two seasons of the year, Carnival and Preparing for Carnival. I couldn't walk anywhere without being engulfed in the excitement.

Sometimes, in the noisy crowds along the streets, it felt as if Carnival had already begun. Most of the people in the city were planning to be out on the streets in one of the "bands." They are loosely organized groups of friends from the same neighborhood who decide on a costume, hire a group of musicians, and dance their way together through the tumult of Carnival day. It was expected that the mothers, wives, and daughters would sew the costumes, and the colors and emblems that the groups had selected hung in shop windows and on crude racks in the murky stalls of the old covered street market behind the city's newer shops. When I walked along the side streets I found large, weathered nineteenth-century buildings with worn, castle-like doors that opened from floor to the high ceilings out onto the sidewalk. Festoons of bright cloth streamed from their balconies. When I stepped inside to get out of the heat I found the aisles filled with women who had come to buy the materials for their costumes. The capacious shops were a warren of cramped aisles heaped with bolts of bright cloth—flowered, striped, patterned, woven, sequined—a mansion of Carnival finery. I had already passed other shops close by that sold beads, decorations, and arrays of colored feathers to embellish the costumes.

When I retreated to the street I walked past lines of sidewalk vendors who shouted and waved recorded cassettes of this year's Carnival calypsos. The competition for the awards as the best and the most popular new songs was as freighted with emotion this year as it was every year, though many of the people who crowded the streets during the celebrations would have had a difficult time remembering what song won the year before. If I tried to escape the congestion of the sidewalks by sneaking from one street to another through one of the new air-conditioned shopping arcades, the insistent rhythms of the songs eddying from the record kiosks inside the arcades rattled the shining glass of the display windows.

Nora and I found it impossible to escape Carnival even when we flagged down one of the old passenger cars that cruised the streets in place of city bus lines. The year's new calypsos had been a staple of daily radio for weeks, and most of the drivers had decided opinions about which of the songs they liked. The city had tried to insist three or four years before that the cars turn down the volume of their radios, since the passengers, sometimes five or six crammed into the back seat, often couldn't make themselves heard over the noise to tell the drivers where they wanted to get off. Even with the radio levels lower, we still ended some journeys with our ears ringing. When the calypso groups and the competition steel bands come up the street to the grandstand they will be playing one of the new songs, and the song that is played by the most bands will be declared the winner of the year's Road March Competition. In the interminable arguments with the other riders squeezed in around us, the drivers insisted that they could tell us which song it would be, and which artist would be the year's Calypso Monarch.

When I was first in the city, getting to know its streets, one of the addresses I had was a record shop that had been mentioned in the lyrics of one of 2001's most poignant calypsos, Denyse Plummer's "Heroes." In her song she described the sad fate of some of the legendary modern calypsonians, and lamented that their records "don't sell out by Crosby's." Crosby's was listed in the telephone directory in the St. Anne's shopping district, past Kitchener's statue on the road leading north toward the mountains away from the city. On my city map it looked close enough to walk there, along a busy thoroughfare named Tragere Road, but the sun made it a longer journey. There was no shade on the sidewalk, and every few minutes I had to retreat under an overhanging roof to get away from the blazing heat. Finally I spent a half an hour in a neighborhood ice cream parlor and shared its quiet afternoon with a table full of schoolchildren and two mothers with sleeping babies.

Once I'd found the shop, Crosby's didn't look much different than an ordinary music store anywhere in the Caribbean. It was larger than the shops I'd seen in the arcade downtown, but the only hint that it was something different was a back wall lined with the gaudy covers of the newest Carnival CDs, and a glass case beside the counter that was stacked with video cassettes of calypsonians and steel bands from least year's competitions. The shop also sold tickets for the concerts in the "tents," the word describing the array of artists who would be appearing, and also used for the theaters and outdoor stadiums where the calypso concerts are held. In a smaller space behind a counter were songbooks of winning calypsos, enthusiastically produced local histories of Carnival, and mimeographed pamphlets painstakingly listing every winner of every Carnival competition since the first prize was awarded to King Radio for his "leggo"—the old term for road march—"Tiger Tom Play Tiger Cat" in 1932. Immediately forgetting the wilting heat that waited for me outside, I began enthusiastically piling titles on the counter in front of me. If I wanted to know who won the Road March title in 1956 all I had to do was look in a blue covered mimeographed pamphlet written and published by Sookram Ali, "Ultimate Spectator." (The winner was the Mighty Sparrow, with his song "Jean and Dinah," about the situation for the women of the islands as the U.S. troops departed. The song also won him that year's title of Calypso Monarch.)

Sometimes when I had walked along the streets of a city like Port of Spain, or browsed in small shops like Crosby's, I had wondered if there were any books that already presented some of the artists or the music that I was trying to find. What if someone before me had found the people I was looking for, when it was still possible to sit down with them and let them tell their stories themselves? It always seemed that I had come just too late. At some point I had given up hope that I would ever find anything like this—and then I saw a book on the shelf at Crosby's!

The book was a paperback with a glossy cover that had been printed in Port of Spain in 1999. It was titled *Calypsonians from Then to Now*,

Part II, and it had been written by a man whose name I didn't know, Rudolph Ottley.[1] His book was a collection of his interviews with calypso singers, old and young; anyone who might have been appearing in the tents in the many years he was collecting material for the book. Ottley, whose serious, dark-faced portrait was on the back of the book, was obviously so close to the calypso world that the performers felt free to talk openly to him, and they also allowed him to quote from their lyrics. The interviews read as though Ottley had transcribed them without editorial revisions. He had also amplified many of the interviews with extended essays about the artists' careers and their compositions. Each of the interviews was illustrated with a bright, busy color photo he'd taken himself of the artist, usually when they were performing onstage.

After I had paged wonderingly through the book I stood quietly for a moment, thinking of what it would have meant if someone like Ottley had given us books like this for the southern blues artists. I thanked him silently for the book I had in my hands. A note on the back of the jacket for this book told me that it was only one of three he'd published. The first volume had begun the series of interviews with the male singers, and the second was devoted to a collection of interviews with the women artists. The pleasant, middle-aged Creole woman behind the counter shook her head regretfully when I asked excitedly about the other two. They had sold out of them, and she was certain they couldn't obtain any more copies. Disappointed, but still excited, I bundled up the books, the song collections, the mimeographed pamphlets, the CDs, and the videos I had bought in a plastic bag, and this time, as I went out onto the sidewalk and began walking back toward the Savannah it was several moments before I even noticed that the sun had been hovering over the street, waiting for me.

One of the calypsonians Ottley interviewed was Willard Courtney Harris, who is known in the tents as "Relator." Harris had a very personal response to the common attitudes toward the singers.

> I feel very uptight when people ask me apart from singing calypso what do you do? I get vex, mad, and crazy for that because if I were to show you my passport, places that I went, if I was sitting down in a government office here, I could never have seen these places and I am very grateful to be a part of the calypso art form that has afforded me to travel and see the world. I could never pay, I would always be thankful, I couldn't have afforded it if I had another job.[2]

Calypso today is an art form that takes its best-known performers around the world, and gives a singer like Relator an opportunity to feel

Cover of
*Calypsonians from
Then to Now,
Part I.*

himself part of the excitement, but calypso still struggles to find the kind of success that the Jamaicans had with reggae. What the calypso audience lacks in size, however, it makes up for in the enthusiasm of its fans and their dedication to everything that characterizes the music. Calypso is much older than other styles of African-influenced music, like reggae and the blues, and there is considerable controversy about the sources of early calypso, but this only heightens the interest of the true calypso enthusiast. Several histories have already been written about Trinidad's flamboyant song style, each of them drawing conclusions that emphasize the different pieces of what is a complicated musical puzzle.

At the heart of calypso is its social commentary, which is delivered in sly, colorfully rhymed and succinctly presented texts. It is sometimes suggested that what is most African about calypso is the *role* of the singers, which has some superficial resemblances to the social function of the griots, the praise singers of West Africa. The calypsonians, however, feel free to comment on scandal and corruption with an openness that no village griot would dare. Also, in the constrained atmosphere of most West African villages, the sexual casualness of a calypsonian like Lord Kitchener or the political irreverence of an artist like The Mighty Sparrow would put a local griot behind bars.

There were, however, moments when the calypsonians did their own praising. Between 1934 and 1937 the recording trips which the leading singers made to New York were financed by a Port of Spain businessman, a Portuguese retail merchant named Edwardo Sa Gomes (pronounced roughly "Saw Gums.") Sa Gomes was also the representative for an American record company, and he hoped to obtain recordings by local artists to sell in his "Six Palaces of Good Music" around Trinidad and Tobago. For the first trip in 1934 he arranged for The Roaring Lion (Hubert Raphael Charles), and Attila the Hun (Raymond Quevedo, who had been born in Venezuela), to record for Decca Records. On the recording trip the next year, in March 1935, Attila, Lord Beginner (Egbert Moore), and The Tiger (Neville Marcano), recording as the Keskidee Trio, composed songs which showered praise on their sponsor in the classic griot fashion. Their "Sa Gomes' Emporiums" was a shameless ladling of flattery that would have satisfied any African village gathering. Beginner opened with a low-key introduction that mentioned the location of the largest "emporium" and concluded with the line, "He sells the best records, is what we know."

With some of the swagger that gave the "wars" between the calypsonians their humorous bite, Tiger followed with:

> He's a gentleman of tenacity,
> He treat you with the greatest hospitality,
> He selling so cheap, he's ready to give,
> Just because he's loyal to where he live.

Atilla accepted the challenge to find even more extravagant phrases to praise their benefactor, and in the next verse he lauded the wonders of the flashlights for sale in the Emporiums.

> I'll tell you something you can't deny,
> With Sa Gomes' torch light, you can peep in the sky,
> You can examine all of the stars,
> And tell the difference between Jupiter and Mars . . .

The praises for Sa Gomes and his emporiums—"Unrivalled, unequalled, and unsurpassed"—reached their peak in a 1938 recording by

The Roaring Lion. In his boundless enthusiasm Lion managed to single out not only Gomes, but the names of some of the other artists on the records he offered for sale, as well as the name of the Zenith Radios that Sa Gomes represented in Trinidad.

At last, at last, we have found out a store
With prices to suit the rich and poor,
So let's join the chorus and sing,
Mister Sa Gomes the record king.

The pioneer of music in the West Indies
He maintains his supremacy with ease,
Unrivalled, unequalled, and unsurpassed,
Predominately he stands to the last.

Sa Gomes' Emporium, everyone knows,
There you can get your classic calypsos,
With Atilla and the Lion and Bing Crosby,
Ruth Etting and Morton Downey . . .

If you want to be feeling happy at home,
Especially when you are melancholy alone,
Take my advice, don't be a knave,
But tune in yourself a Zenith short wave . . .

Perhaps because there is no clearly documented path that leads back to the beginnings of calypso, many theories have been presented. One of the complicating factors in the story is that the common language and culture of Port of Spain's streets in the early 1800s was French. There are descriptions of calypso songs from the Carnival seasons as early as the 1830s, but the verses quoted don't fit any of the melodies that came to be used later. Some histories of calypso propose an even earlier beginning, in the 1790s, in a slave song said to be from West Africa called *gayap* or *gayup*. Freed slaves had settled on land outside of the small towns, and to help with the work of clearing, planting, and harvesting they would invite other freed farm workers, or even slaves from nearby plantations, for a day of work and celebration. At the end of the day there were exuberant comparisons of the amount of work the two groups, the hosts and their visitors, had managed to finish. This turned into a two-part call-and-response song.

If the freed laborers and slaves had completed the most work, they sang the first lines to celebrate their "victory," and then they continued, in the next lines, to humiliate the losers. The singing was led by a "chantuelle," the term which became later in English a "chant well."

The problem with crediting the gayap as the source of calypso is that the style of call and reponse is a communal performance, with the group responding to the lines of the chanteulle. In the classic calypso style of the 1930s—called *oratorical* calypso—the choruses follow the verses, similar to the refrain of a topical song in the English street ballad tradition.

It is probably hopeless to try to trace the early musical sources for the most widely used calypso melodies, but the style of the rhyming verses in oratorical calypso is documented as early as 1873. In his book *Black Music of Two Worlds* John Storm Roberts quotes an incident following a street argument between a well-known woman singer named Bodicea and another calypsonian over the theft of a body from a cemetery. The man is reported as replying to her taunts with a rhyming verse that was sung to a "declamatory tune sung most on one note," an indication that calypso was fully developed by the 1870s.[3]

It was shocking, it was shameful and bad to see
Carnival in the cemetery.
It couldn't happen in Grenada,
St. Kitts, Martinique, or Antigua.
When such lawlessness can prevail,
Tell me, what's the use of the Royal Jail?
Bodicea the jamette whom we all know
Is a real disgrace to we cariso . . .

("Jamette" is an old term that can mean someone of lower class, or even a prostitute.)

The thirteen miles that separate Trinidad from Venezuela have never been a cultural barrier, and Latin American dance pieces have also been proposed as the source of the minor key, eight or sixteen bar melodies that are characteristic of the oratorical style. At the end of the 1800s small Venezuelan-styled string bands were increasingly popular among Trinidad's polite society, and their dance numbers—*paseos* or *pastilles* as they are called locally—were heard everywhere on the island. Many of the older calypso recordings were listed as paseos in the company catalogues, to help the purchaser know what kind of dance rhythm they would find. As the string bands added other instruments—trumpets, flutes, and clarinets—they became one of the important orchestral accompaniment groups for the calypsonians.

Considering all of the sources that have been proposed as the source of the calypso style, what is obvious is that all of the earlier music and song—the West African gayap songs, with their call and response, the drumming of the island's Shango cults, the British topical ballad, the

French "cariso," and the Venezuelan paseo—found its way into the rich tapestry of calypso song that emerged. If you listen to collections of performances from the 1930s you will hear, in one song or another, the call and response and the clanging beats of the gayap, echoes of Shango drumming, the plucked melodic guitar of the paseo, the melodic forms of verse and chorus from the English broadside ballad traditions, and phrases and interjections that survive from the old Creole French. The African genius for adaptation has turned these disparate sources into a new musical form. What gives all of it its character as calypso is the rhyme, the social stance, that secures the place of the calypsonian in Trinidadian society. Calypso is a song like nothing else in the world of music.

If you begin at that moment in the 1930s, when calypso recording was in its classic period, and this time you go forward in time, instead of backward in search of calypso's past, you will discover that calypso has managed to make room for the Charleston beat, for swing, jazz, rock, disco, reggae, and rap. The bass player for the recordings of Wilmoth Houdini in the late 1920s was the New Orleans classic jazz musician Al Morgan, who went on to anchor the rhythm of the great swing orchestra of Cab Calloway. Calypso is a music that continually renewed itself, while still holding on to its basic form, which is a singer standing alone at a microphone reciting truths about the society in which both the singer and his audiences live their everyday lives.

In the years when the first recordings were made, calypso was still music from the streets—raw and bawdy. In his colorful, detailed story of calypso, *Rituals of Power and Rebellion*, the well-known calypsonian the Mighty Chalkdust (so named for his early career as a schoolteacher), who in everyday life is the educator and music historian Dr. Hollis Liverpool, quoted one early singer as saying he wouldn't be known as a calypsonian, since "A calypsonian was a dog."[4] Within a few years, however, calypso had begun to move indoors, and the new style of presentation became a tradition that continues in today's shows. In the first years the term given to the new calypso presentations was *tents*, even though the word now generally describes the performers appearing in the show, as well as the place where the show is presented. The early tents evolved from the enclosed spaces, the drum yards, where African dances were performed during Carnival. There is disagreement over who set up the first tent, but the name that occurs most often is Walter "Chieftain" Douglas, of the city of San Fernando, seventy-five miles south of Port of Spain, close to the cane fields. His first tent was a small space in a residential compound that he set up to be able to charge admission for the music. Douglas was an ex-soldier who had worked for a time for the railroad, and he used railway equipment to help set up his first tent. As "Chalkie"—the name by which Dr. Liverpool is universally known—described the new venue, "Previous to this, many persons collected money for singing in the yards, but Douglas 'put up the first real tent' when he borrowed tarpaulins from the Railway and used gas lamps instead of kerosene flambeaux."[5]

The "tent" was an enclosure of bamboo stalks and branches, with an improvised roof and bamboo benches. An early drawing of a tent in Dr. Liverpool's book shows the singer performing behind a waist-high barrier, and the barrier is described by some singers as being typical until the 1950s. Photographs of islands shows during the Second World War don't show any kind of barrier, however—though they do show that the audiences were segregated, with front seats reserved for white U.S. servicemen.

For Dr. Liverpool, the tents signaled a distinct change in the music itself, as the small entrance fees of a few pennies encouraged more middle-class audiences, which in turn brought in more artists who had larger social ambitions themselves. The changing audience brought about a new emphasis in the subjects of the songs. Instead of the street chants and boasts of the neighborhood marchers, the singers began to perform Trinidadian folk songs or ballads from the other islands, while at the same time their own calypsos turned to more topical commentary on everyday life in Trinidad. Finally, as the artists sensed a larger audience for their songs, they turned to commentary on events throughout the world.

By the mid-1930s, the years when Sa Gomes was sending the island's leading calypsonians to New York to sing the praises of his music emporiums, the tide of topical songs had swollen to a flood. In 1936 The Caresser (Rufus Callender) had an international success with "Edward VIII," about the abdication of the newly crowned king of England. Its sorrowing chorus, "It was love, love alone/ That caused King Edward to leave his throne," became a calypso anthem. Other singers didn't hesitate to deal with any subject that caught their attention, like "Graf Zeppelin," "G. Man Hoover," "Walter Winchell," or "The Gold in Africa" by The Tiger (Neville Marcano), which protested against Mussolini's invasion of Ethiopia. Most of the subjects, however, were out of the newspapers headlines of Trinidad and Tobago, "The Governor's Resignation," "We Mourn the Loss of Sir Murchison Fletcher," "Mr Nankivell's Speech," "Send Your Children to the Orphan Home," "Try a Screw to Get Through," which dealt with the problems of unemployment during the period. A number of calypsos commented on the labor turmoil of

1937 and the disappearance of popular leader Uriah Butler, including "The Strike" and "Where Was Butler?"

In the summer of 1958, in the little settlement of Fresh Creek on Andros Island in the Bahamas, it was a calypso by The Mighty Sparrow that helped us get through the long, still nights. The song "Dear Sparrow" was on the jukebox of a ramshackle, open-air bar run by a man from the settlement and Ann Danberg, the young woman with me, and I danced to it every night as we drank a beer and talked with the owner and his waitress. They were usually the only other people there. The song was a funny, wry complaint about a man whose wife has been unfaithful and writes him artless letters about her new baby, "that looks like your uncle Joe" and then mails them off to her "Dear Sparrow." The Mighty Sparrow was a fitting introduction to the art of the calypsonians, since he dominated the musical world of Trinidad for many years. The song, however, was not typical of his themes and preoccupations. In his long, successful, productive career Sparrow has continually protested against discrimination, economic inequality, and social injustice. In one of his many collections, a typical collection released in 2000 titled *Corruption*, he commented bitterly on the U.S. invasion of neighboring Grenada, attacked the African dictator Idi Amin, analyzed the acquittal of O. J. Simpson in his murder trial, and presented a moving tribute to Martin Luther King Jr. that Sparrow performed with a ringing rhythmic background—insisting through the bright sound of the horns, infectious conga rhythms, and the voices of the backup vocalists, "This we cannot abide / And segregation must be destroyed."

Although there were persistent complaints that Sparrow was born not in Trinidad or Tobago but in Grenada, in 1935, he was an immediate success in the calypso shows. His parents brought him to Trinidad when he was a year old, but the whispers continue that he can't be a "true" calypsonian. Between 1956 and 1992 Sparrow won the Carnival Monarch title eight times and the Road March award seven times. He finally retired from competition, though he continued to be a dominant presence in Carnival celebrations. The Trinidadian writer C. L. R. James described a moment in a Carnival tent when Sparrow sang a new calypso he'd written about Trinidad's break with the larger Federation of Caribbean nations. The Federation had collapsed after continual rancor between Jamaica and the other member countries.

> I was in the tent the night he returned and first sang it. When it became clear what he was saying, the audience froze. Trinidad had broken with the Federation. Nobody was saying anything and the people did not

Statue of
The Mighty
Sparrow, Port
of Spain.

know what to think, far less what to say. At the end of the first verse on
that first night Sparrow saw that something was wrong . . . But the people
of Trinidad and Tobago only wanted a lead. Sparrow defined their mood,
for henceforth he became increasingly bold and free. When he sang at
the Savannah he put all he had into it and the public made a great demonstration. They wanted, how they wanted, somebody to say something.
He attacked Jamaica and Jamaica deserved to be attacked. But Sparrow
said what people wanted to hear, "We failed miserably."[6]

When at last I came to a calypso tent in Port of Spain, it was at a heavily
advertised show presented on a side street close to the Savannah. The
"tent" was being presented in a spacious modern auditorium. The popular island term for calypso is the African word *Kaiso*, so for the night
the building was titled "Kaiso House," on the banners spread over the
marquee. The sidewalk outside was crowded with people who called
out greetings to each other as they waited for friends. Many of the men

were in light suits, with shirts and ties, and their wives were in bright dresses or fashionable pants suits. Alongside the curb were the usual city street vendors, with vivid painted wagons that they had wheeled through the night streets filled with nuts, sandwiches, beer, and bottled soft drinks. Even though I'd walked to the theater and gotten there early, when I went to look for my seat I found that the rows were already filling with some of the excited crowd I'd seen outside. The tickets to any of the concerts were expensive by island standards, but when I'd stopped at one of the small Indian ticket agencies on the main street I'd been told that many of the shows everywhere in the city were already sold out.

The half-lit auditorium was a typical high-ceilinged, unadorned community center, with red curtains hung at the back of the wide stage. The rows of seats were covered in the same dark red material. There was no curtain on the stage and as I found my seat I could see dance-band music stands set up along the back of the stage. The musicians were already there with their instrument cases open on the floor, warming up with scales and sorting through their stacks of music. Most of them were wearing matching shirts—black with white leaves and flowers— but three of them were in matching striped shirts obviously for another band. All of them had their shirt tails hanging loose over an assortment of dark slacks and tan chinos.

The orchestra had the typical calypso instrumentation: two saxophones, two trumpets, two keyboards, electric guitar, bass, a drummer, and two percussionists. The percussionists were lean, wiry men with their shirt sleeves rolled up to their shoulders and they were fussing over their congas and timbales. We stood for Trinidad's national anthem, then the orchestra members settled in their chairs for what they know from much experience would be a long, tiring night.

The audience around me seemed to be mostly groups of friends or young couples, all of them dressed in their best clothes for one of the year's biggest evenings. In the light reflected from the stage they seemed to be in their late twenties or early thirties. I could make out a few white faces in the rows behind me, and an older white news photographer was perched on the edge of a seat close to the stage, holding a box-shaped flash camera that looked like it had been used to photograph a generation of calypso shows. The other faces around me were Trinidadian Creole. I didn't see anyone I recognized as Indian.

I'd been to calypso concerts in Brooklyn, presented to an audience of Trinidadians whose homes were in the United States, but whose hearts were still with their life in Trinidad. The concerts had given me some idea of what I would be seeing, but this time I could feel a different tension close to the stage. In front of our seats in the darkness was a long table with small lamps and hard backed chairs set around it. Twelve judges would spend the night there scoring every song for the Carnival competition. After they had heard the songs in every tent they would have a rancorous meeting and finally decide which singers would go on to the semifinals that would take place as part of the Carnival weekend. The judges were a mix of men and women, wearing the same bright shirts or dresses as the people around them in the audience, but their expressions were guarded and self-conscious. Whatever else they were expecting from the long night, they weren't expecting to enjoy it. From their mood, as they spread their evaluation sheets on the table in the small rings of lights that had been set up for them, they could have been deciding on Trinidad's next constitution. Throughout the hours of the show most of the singers who were competing either tried to pretend the judges weren't there at the table staring up at them, or they climbed stiffly down to a cramped platform that had been set up at the edge of the stage and gave their performance for the expressionless faces a few feet away.

What does an audience hear in an evening with one of the calypso tents? The show's format never varies. An occasional guest star will be given an extra number, but all the other singers perform one song, their competition song, accompanied by the orchestra, whose members shuffle through the dog-eared arrangements on their music stands as each new act comes out from the wings. On one side of the stage there are three or four tireless backup singers, who manage to get through the entire night without using scores for the dozens of songs that they have to know. The entire evening has been planned and rehearsed for weeks, but it was still a long array of songs to remember. Usually two or three of the singers will be women, with the high voices that are one of the constant features of backup vocals everywhere in the Caribbean. The sound has sometimes been described as a lingering vestige of the shrill sound of women's voices that are characteristic of West African village singing. Sometimes the little group also includes a man, but it is the women's high voices that most often can be heard over the bright tone of the trumpets and saxophones. Since everyone who comes to a show has paid a lot of money for a ticket, and the evening out is one of the prized Carnival memories, each of the tents presents a long list of singers, some of them nervous beginners presenting their song for minimal pay, and the shows are expected to continue long into the night.

The musical directors of each tent have spent months sifting through the songs and the artists who have presented themselves at the offices, and although the format of the show is unchanging, the choice of singers is highly personal. Some of the directors choose younger artists,

In a Calypso tent, a performer onstage at the Calypso Revue, Port of Spain, 2002. *Revue photographs by Nora Charters-Myers.*

which means there's more *soca*, an uptempo, modern dance variety of calypso, and there's more sexual teasing between the singers and the audience. Calypso, however, is intensely conscious of its traditions, and each of the tents includes two or three veterans with each show, who are received with welcoming applause. The older women usually sweep onstage in long, full, brightly patterned robes, with matching turbans. The men, dressed in sober suits and ties, often with snap-brim fedoras that give them the look of insurance salesmen, stand almost without moving at the microphone, and with their barbed social commentary they remind the audience of calypso's role in Trinidadian life.

At Kaiso House, an hour of young stars with glittering costumes and perspiring stage acts was followed by a veteran performer, The Mighty Bomber. He was perhaps in his fifties, and clearly still trim, wearing a gray suit and a matching fedora. As he walked from the wings he came up to the microphone with a sly grin. He had beaten The Mighty Sparrow for the Calypso King crown in 1964, and with only a lift of a neatly jacketed shoulder or a thrust of his chin he drew more shouts of laughter from the audience than the hard-working acts that had preceded him. Everyone was brought back on stage for an encore by the tirelessly enthusiastic master of ceremonies, but the applause that brought him back for an added verse was noisy and sincere.

The format of the shows may be unchanging, but there's no way to know what the next calypso will have for its subject, or what kind of dancing or stage movements will go with it. What you can't see on a recording is that the artists have grown up with a long tradition of stage presentation. A veteran like The Mighty Bomber can win his laughs with minimal shrugs, but other singers create a flurry of dance and energetic movement. The singers who have picked up the tempos with *soca* rhythms burst out onto the stage in capes and tight sequined trousers. If they have long hair, at some point they bend down and sweep the stage with it. Women singers might appear in a motherly skirt or blouse, or they can present themselves in hot pants and a glittering bra. Denyse Plummer, who triumphed as Carnival Monarch in 2001, climaxed her performance at a Brooklyn Mother's Day show with an exultant dance that finished with her kicking her shoes off into the audience.

Whatever kind of costume the singer is wearing, however, or whatever energy they give to their stage act, what the audience is listening for is the message of their verses. Until I sat in the audience for a calypso tent I didn't understand why the shows were held in auditoriums or meetings halls—or even in the soccer stadiums where Port of Spain's biggest shows were presented. Nobody in the audience dances. Around me in the darkness I could see that people weren't even tapping their feet, despite the relentless swing of the congas and the timbales and the punchy ring of the saxes and trumpets. Some of the couples were leaning forward in their seats, listening so intently to the texts of the songs, waiting so patiently for a moment to laugh at an insinuation or nod at a clever rhyme, that dancing would only have gotten in the way of their enjoyment.

As the long night wore on, the mood at Kaiso House became so intense that it felt almost as though it had a physical presence. The first artist of the night, a serious performer in a white suit and a dark shirt, stared down defiantly at the judges' table and sang a series of verses about the island's political corruption. With his first lines the people around me leaned closer, and at a verse that named one of the government ministers and revealed a hidden overseas bank account there was an audible gasp and shouts of noisy encouragement.

In the column the next morning one of the newspapers that covered the shows, the *Express*, also responded to what I heard from the stage, even if the writer, Sean Douglas, went out of his way to praise a singer who didn't follow the pattern of social commentary.

Its stable of past Calypso Monarchs has traditionally made Kaiso House the tent to go to for "serious" social commentary, but for a moment on Wednesday night the tent took on a more musical flavor more typical of rival Calypso Spektakula.

Xtatik front man Roger George really lightened the program with his harmonious "More Love," his pleasant voice recalling the heartfelt sounds of soul and gospel and even Bajan music.

George gave a sweet delivery, his voice singing a calming message of light lyrics and deep melody.

It was a song that you could sit and listen to for its lyrical inspiration "Walk away from your anger. And you will feel better," or that you could dance to, for its musicality.

It was a wonderful enhancement to the tent, deserving its fourth highest billing, and we have hopes George's song will be accepted on the wider calypso/soca circuit.[7]

As the night went on, the procession of singers seemed unending, but the judges' attention was unwavering. Between each song I could see their heads bent over their sheets as their pens scribbled quick notes. The master of ceremonies, a tall, perpetually smiling man who hurried on and off the stage whenever there was a pause in the procession of artists, insisted on bringing each performer back, even if there hadn't been more than polite applause. A newcomer, a teenage girl in an elegant long white dress that looked as though she might have worn it for her high school graduation ceremony, sang an earnest song that tried to convince us of the importance of good money management. She was followed by a cheerful, stocky woman in an ordinary blouse and skirt who performed a startling, off-color calypso about the discomfort of wearing thong underwear, which was greeted with screams of laughter. In case we were missing the words, the backup singers waved a variety of underpants at us as they performed the chorus.

In the classic traditions of calypso rivalry, one of the veterans, The Mystic Prowler, who was the Calypso Monarch in 1998, answered a song by The Shadow, a feature of the show, that insisted it was the unemployed men whose wives "horned" them. As the *Express* noted, "Prowler gave an energetic, fun-filled performance, egged on by friend and songwriter Gregory 'GB' Ballantyne—'Tell Shadow to let the boy go and marry if he will; Let him work like soldier ants; Provide romance and finance; If she's the type she'll horn as well.'"

The backup singers at the Calypso Revue.

The night's first galvanizing moment was the appearance of one of the veteran women calypsonians, Singing Sandra, who had been only the second woman Calypso Monarch with her "Song of Hope" in 1999. She strode onto the stage in long robes, a majestic and strongly disapproving presence who made the broad stage suddenly seem considerably smaller. Two hand drummers slipped out of the wings to join the band's drummer and the two percussionists seated in front of the orchestra, backing her songs with an overpowering percussion section. Her song "National Pride" impatiently dismissed all the politicians and all the parties and issued a stern call for the people of the islands to stand up for something better. One of her scornful diatribes concerned the previous year's Independence Day concert, which had featured four artists from Jamaica. Had Trinidad now become a colony of Jamaica, and was the Road March prize be awarded to Jamaica's Shabba Ranks, and next would a statue of Bob Marley be erected in place of the statue of The Mighty Sparrow? Her scolding voice was fierce enough to cut through the pounding rhythm of the drums and around me people cheered and stamped. Kaiso House rocked with the response. People leaped to their feet as they applauded. This time the encores were genuine. She was brought back again and again in a wave of drum rhythms, and each time she challenged the audience with a new verse that showed us still another aspect of her displeasure.

By this time the show had already gone on for two and a half hours and we hadn't even come to the intermission. I was sweating in the steadily rising heat in the auditorium and my ears were protesting against the amplified roar of the orchestra. I decided this was as good a time as any to take a break. Around me people had been squeezing in and out of the rows since the beginning of the evening, but I hadn't wanted to miss any of the singers. Once in the lobby, with only a handful of people talking, I stretched my legs and shook my head to clear my ears, then I went out onto the sidewalk and bought a bottle of cold beer from a woman in flowered robes who was waiting on the sidewalk beside a much-used ice wagon. A half-dozen young men in wrinkled T-shirts or short-sleeved shirts and casual trousers were sprawled on the steps, talking and laughing in low voices and paying no attention to the excitement inside the auditorium. Back in the lobby I stood sipping my beer and listening to the applause and the laughter and the music, which sounded almost as loud as it had in the auditorium. I noticed that two young women in party skirts and blouses had spread out a handful of CDs and three or four books on a back counter. As I picked over what they were offering I suddenly noticed, to my pleased surprise, that one of the books was another of Rudolph Ottley's collections of interviews with today's calypsonians. It was his book focusing on the women performers, *Women in Calypso.* I hadn't found it when I'd seen the first of his books at Crosby's Music Store. As I was paying for my copy one of the women murmured shyly, "Would you like to meet the man who wrote the book?"

For a moment I wasn't sure I'd heard what she said. Would I like to meet Rudolph Ottley? Of course I would! She smiled and turned to say something to the young woman beside her, who hurried out the door and in a few moments came back across the lobby with one of the men I'd seen lounging on the steps outside when I went to buy a beer. Rudy Ottley turned out to be an affable, good-looking man in his forties who had been in the center of the group sitting out on the steps. It was too noisy for us to carry on much of a conversation. He had to lean close to tell me that he supplied the food and the drinks on sale inside the theater, so he had to watch everything until the show was over. The women selling the CDs and the books were working for him, as I understood immediately from their shy deference. Like the others in the group he was sitting with he was in a short-sleeved shirt and loose trousers, but his hair was carefully trimmed and he clearly was in charge of the modest food and drinks operation. From his appearance there was no way I could have guessed that he was the enthusiastic interviewer and writer who had produced the invaluable series of books. Yes, we certainly could talk, he agreed, but it would have to be some other time. He knew the hotel where I was staying. He was going to be there the next evening with another musical presentation, and we could talk when there wasn't as much noise. When I told him how excited I was by his books he tried not to seem too pleased. He made a despairing gesture with his hands.

"I have still two more I want to do." His voice was discouraged, but he brightened and signed the copy of the book with a flourish: "to someone else who wants to carry on the traditions." We would meet the next evening.

I found my seat again in the darkness. The show was going on with undiminished energy. A new announcer, a plump, exuberant woman named Rachel Price, in a gleaming tight dress and with a shining face and short, curled hair, came out to replace the lean, endlessly enthusiastic man who'd begun the show. She was well known to the audience and there was a noisy welcome. She favored us with a broad smile, turned her face into the spotlight so we could admire her profile, and told us grandly.

"That's right! You make your noise, because I'm wonderful!"

She also continued the argument that The Mystic Prowler had begun when he had insisted that women would "horn" even if their husbands were making good money. She protested with some conviction that "Women don't horn just so. If you treating them good and providing for them, they ain't leaving a good thing." Around me people shouted their agreement.

Another singer, Protector, continued the political lament with his "Somethin' Got To Happen," and a serious-faced artist who was using his own name, Horace Wright, presented a sensitive calypso titled "Lamentation." Finally at midnight there was an intermission. The second half of the show, with the two stars, Shadow and Black Stalin, was still to come, but I had seen them before and I knew their songs and I knew how entertaining they were on stage—and I had run down. There had already been so much music, so much shouting and applause. As

I was leaving I saw Rudy Ottley again, leaning back on the dusty steps with the gossiping group of men around him. I held up my hands in a gesture of defeat.

"It goes on too long," I called over to him.

He laughed and shrugged. "It's always this way." He nodded over his shoulder. "Shadow's staying out here too. It's too hot inside."

I turned and there was Shadow, the main star of the night's show, standing on the sidewalk, a thick, grizzled, friendly looking man in a dark jumpsuit. His hands were in his pockets, and he was standing under the streetlights talking cheerfully with a man who had a small stand selling crumpled bags of peanuts.

9 ✳ It Be Like Thunder if a Man Live Close

Nights in Trinidad's Pan Yards

The night had finally become cooler, as the winter nights always did in Trinidad. The wind was stirring and there was a subdued noise of swaying branches from the trees above the hotel's wide terrace. The hotel, on the outskirts of Port of Spain, was in a quiet neighborhood off of a winding road that rose into the mountains that close off the island's north coast from the cleared flatlands. The hotel's wide terrace felt the winds before the rest of the city. The modest bungalow neighborhoods close by were spread around the wide grassy stretch of the Savannah a half mile from the hotel's narrow entranceway, past quiet blocks of older houses enclosed with fences and gardens. The mild air was filled with the delicate scents of the flowers planted around the terrace and the stronger smells that drifted down from the bushy slopes behind it.

A small truck had just pulled into an entranceway across the courtyard, and two men in orange work overalls were wheeling large metal drums onto it. If it were anywhere else I'd have taken it for granted that they were emptying the trash from the media party that had been held in the courtyard two hours before—a promotion to help attract more visitors to the island. But this is Trinidad, and what they were loading were the bass instruments of the steel band that had been part of the show. After learning that the program was going to be the usual kind of presentation, with the usual speeches by people from the Chamber of Commerce, I had gone off to the lobby to talk with Rudoph Ottley, who had arranged for the appearance of the band and the two singers who had come along with them.

I had known about Rudy Ottley for two or three days, when I had found one of his invaluable books on modern calypso at the small music store in the St. Anne area of small businesses and shops not far from the other edge of the Savannah. By chance I'd met him at the calypso concert I'd attended the night before, setting up the refreshments and supervising the sales at the counter in the theater lobby. One of the young women who had a copy of his book on sale

Rudolph Ottley.

offered to introduce me, and he turned out to be one of a group of men sitting on the steps out in front of the auditorium. He was wearing a light shirt and loose pants—his work clothes—since he was responsible for carrying in the food and the drinks on sale at the show.

Rudy had dressed with considerably more style for the media gathering at the hotel, with the government people present. He was wearing well-cut slacks, a handsome reddish brown, collarless shirt, and he had on gold jewelry that gleamed against his dark skin. He was tall, well-built, a good looking man in his late forties, broad faced, with short trimmed hair that was graying at the temples. He was in different clothes from the night before, but he had the same quick smile and easy manner. He was still planning to do two more books, as he'd said the night before, but he had to fit the interviewing and the writing in and around a hectic schedule of jobs, appointments, committee meetings, and entangled responsibilities that involved what seemed like half the musicians in Port of Spain. The only free moment he had to turn to his books was the break in the middle of the year, when Carnival had ended and the frenzy hadn't begun to build for the next season. He told me seriously, "Calypso is my life," and any question I asked him about calypso was answered in an enthusiastic rush.

Rudy had left Trinidad for many years when he was studying, and he had lived and worked in Toronto.

"I loved Toronto! I had so many good friends! But those winters!" This time his laugh was loud enough to cause the conscientious clerk behind the hotel desk to look over at us with some concern. "Those winters just go on, after Trinidad, you know, they are so hard." It was marriage and in part his passion for calypso that brought him back. His steady joke is that to buy all the current records and books, "I spend every penny my wife makes," and this time his quick laughter has a rueful edge. He had brought with him a last copy of his first book, *Calypsonians from Then to Now, Part 1*. It had a wonderfully colorful, evocative cover that caught the spirit of the singers and their audiences, and among the interviews was a thirty-page conversation with Lord Kitchener that is essential to understanding today's calypso. The book was already a classic of modern calypso scholarship. I was conscious that in all the places I had traveled where there was a music that had grown out of a local culture it was the enthusiasm of people like Ottley that helped preserve and revitalize its traditions.

I wondered why his books only dealt with current calypsonians, and he answered with a touch of the skepticism of Lord Kitchener's attitude toward competition judging. "Most of them, those calypsonian from the old times, they have passed away, and I don't give belief to much that I read in the papers when the reporters write about them. It's the living interview that's interesting to me."

Ottley, however, because he is so close to the scene, is also seriously concerned with questions like authorship of the calypsos—which isn't an important consideration for the average record buyer. For the calypso purist this is such a divisive issue that I had noticed in his book on the woman singers, which I'd bought the night before at the "tent" concert, that the troubling issue of composition had come up and up again. What was this about? His answer was quick.

> It's about writing your own calypso. If you don't write what you sing [he put his hand on his heart] you don't feel it here. They are good singers, and we say—"They're calypso singers"—but they're not calypsonians. They get their songs from someone else and the songs don't say what they feel themselves. That makes a difference.

He nodded vigorously, assuring me, "The audience can feel it."

At the same time that we were sitting in the hotel lobby talking, Rudy was listening with half his attention to what was happening on the terrace, with its crowd of formally dressed media people helping themselves to the canapés and free drinks. He stood up abruptly and waved apologetically. The next speaker was one of the government ministers and Rudy was expected to listen. Nodding and smiling to friends, he made his way back through the crowd and squeezed onto a wooden bench beside two of his musicians.

I left the crowd to walk a little in the quiet streets, and when I returned an hour later Rudy was still sitting on his bench—the usual booking agent's protracted wait for his artists to get packed up and the people who hired them to come and either nod in pleased satisfaction or complain with sour looks. His long legs were stretched out in front of him, a foot moving with what had to be some impatience as a stream of people held out papers to be signed. At the same time he was calling out a steady stream of instructions to the men who were putting the smaller steel pans back into their instrument cases.

"Your work doesn't get finished," I said, laughing, as I sat beside him for a moment.

He looked up from a clipboard that had been thrust at him, smiled his relaxed smile, and shrugged.

"It's just what I told you. It's my life. Calypso is what I do."

Of everything that the gangling modern giant of calypso, Lord Kitchener, accomplished in his long career, when he talked to Rudy Ottley it was his contribution to the development of the other great Trinidadian musical style, the steel band orchestras—the pans—that he was most proud of.

> As a matter of fact I was living in the same yard where the Renegades [one of first steel bands] started. In those days they were called Bar 20 and I lived right in the yard with the boys beating the tins. So I got the inspiration for composing steel band music through that because I grew up in a pan yard. When I came to Port of Spain I live right in La Cou Harp in Renegades pan yard, right there, and every night is ting le tang ting le tang. I being a musician was able to improvise on the two notes. The first pan calypso was composed by me: "The Beat Of The Steel Band," was composed in 1944.[1]

What is so startling in Kitchener's memories of those early days is that sixty years ago the instruments could only play two notes. Among Trinidad musicians it is a matter of considerable satisfaction that the pans were the only genuinely new musical instrument developed in the twentieth century. The pan yards—the rehearsal locations of the steel bands—had brought me to Trinidad as much as the calypso tents. As the pans themselves developed—seemingly almost daily—from clanging

Statue of Lord Kitchener,
Port of Spain, Trinidad.

one and two note noisemakers for a neighborhood carnival procession to the subtly tuned orchestras of hundreds of players taking their glistening instruments on world tours, the whole pace of change has been so rapid that the players themselves have difficulty keeping up. What was just as exciting was the new music that was being created for the orchestras to play.

I had wondered how I would find where the bands were rehearsing, but for the Carnival season, the "pans," like the Calypso tents, were harder to escape than they were to find. It seemed simplest to begin asking at the hotel. In a quiet moment at the reception desk I began talking to one of the young hotel clerks about the pans. He was tall and still gawky, dark skinned, with an engaging laugh. He was wearing the obligatory shirt and tie, and his hair was properly trimmed for his job, but he still seemed uncomfortable dressed so formally. He was probably in his early 20s, somewhere on that inevitable journey from schoolboy to sober family man. The women working with him behind the desk and in the hotel office were all older and they cheerfully took turns mothering him. The laughter and teasing had no sexual overtones—he was clearly a solid, nice boy, and they were enjoying his engaging pleasantness. When I asked about the pan yards he glanced around, obviously uncomfortable at talking about something like Carnival music while he was at his job, then he rummaged behind the counter for a piece of paper, and in neat school handwriting he wrote down three names,

Star Lift
Phase II
The Invaders

"These are the best." He nodded with such conviction that I was sure these *were* the best. He also seemed convinced that I would know where to find them. The steel bands are so revered in Port of Spain that of course I would know where to look for them. When he saw my blank look he took my map of the city, with a little embarrassment and surprise, and bent over it, fingers tracing the streets.

"The three of them, the yards you know, they're very close. One yard isn't a long way from the other."

But would there be somebody practising?

I could see from his sudden, half smile that he had never been aware that there were people who understood so little about something so important.

"Every night to Carnival. Sometimes they go to two in the morning."

Something proprietary in his tone made me realize that he probably knew all about the rehearsals because he'd played in one of the bands himself.

"Do you play?"

His smile was broader. "Two years. I was a member of Star Lift."

"But you went to practice every night?"

"Oh, yes. Every night. But you do it, you know—if you can find a way."

One of the women interrupted with a noisy laugh. "If you unemployed!"

The young man looked down at the counter sheepishly. "That's right. Just at that time I didn't have a job."

For a moment he was only a schoolboy in a neatly ironed tan shirt that his mother had probably laid out for him. I tried to cheer him up.

"But you have to audition to be in one of the bands!"

He shrugged modestly. "Anybody can play. You could play if you wanted. No," he corrected himself. "Carnival too close now. You wouldn't have the time it needs to learn so many notes."

I couldn't believe he really meant "anybody."

The women in the neat white blouses and dark skirts that seemed to be the office uniform had slowly converged on the counter and they were pretending to sort through loose piles of papers while they listened. They all nodded in agreement with what he had said. Encouraged, he went on.

"If you come to the yard and you come a few times and they see you, they ask you if you want to play. All you must do is bring your sticks and let them see that you have them. Then they give you a pan to play."

"Just bring your sticks?"

He nodded decidedly. "That's all you need to do."

I thanked him and picked the list of names and the map he'd marked off the counter. I considered telling him that I didn't own any sticks, but I wasn't certain that this was something he could take in with any seriousness.

It isn't only the pans themselves that developed and changed in the last sixty years; the attitude toward them in Trinidad and Tobago has changed as well. Every schoolchild on the islands has some experience playing the pans—which is why the young man at the hotel expected that I would still have my old sticks. But the pans came out of the ragged stick fighter gangs of Port of Spain's slums, and in the first years the bands spent as much time battling each other as they did parading with their crude instruments. Just as today, when the Panorama competition for the steel bands is one of the features of Carnival, pans have always been associated with the yearly celebration. The French, who had controlled the island until 1791, had accepted the African drums as part of the slave's culture—perhaps because on the small holdings of tobacco and cacao there were relatively few slaves. With the flood of slaves that were imported to expand the sugar plantings after the British seized control, there were not only more people of African ancestry—also in the cargoes were British colonial attitudes, which everywhere were less sympathetic to native cultures.

Carnival had begun as a restrained and very decorous family celebration among the French colonists, usually friendly visits between the isolated plantations. By the time slavery was abolished in 1834, however, Carnival had become a chaotic street celebration on the streets of Port of Spain. For people in the slums, the centerpiece of the celebrations were the pitched battles between gangs armed with long staves, the "stick fighters." Stick fighting survived in many areas of the Caribbean, and in its ritual forms is still one of the haunting street arts of northeastern Brazil. The British authorities may have tolerated it for so long because it had many similarities to the old English quarter-stave exercises, which were part of the rural culture in England. To the Africans, however, stick fighting was bound into the worship of the warrior god Ogon, which had been reinforced by the arrival of Yoruba contract workers from Africa, who established the island's Shango cults. Drumming was an essential part of their rituals, since it was the drums that called forth the spirits, and without the drums there could be no worship.

Carnivals, however genteel their origins, quickly get out of hand. So many people began wearing masks on Carnival day—the source of the term "mas," one of the words used today for the celebration—that the police had continual difficulties maintaining any kind of control on Port of Spain's jammed streets. The drumming continued for half a century, but by 1884 the turmoil had grown to such disturbing proportions that the colonial administrators abruptly banned the use of all drums with "heads of skin." Carnival obviously couldn't be celebrated without the rhythms of the drums, and the street musicians responded by creating rhythm bands out of hollow stalks of dried bamboo that they pounded on the pavement. The bamboo percussion bands had already made their appearance in Venezuela, and they made the short journey between the two countries without difficulty. In his colorful history of the steel bands *Ring of Steel*, Guyanian Cy Grant emphasized that the new percussion groups again reflected the African's stubborn insistence on preserving whatever elements they could of their traditional cultures.

> To replace the drum, another old African tradition was resurrected, the tamboo bamboo band (tamboo from the French word *tambour* for drum). In this, hollow tubes were cut in lengths to produce different musical tones when struck . . . There were three types of bamboo instrument. The *bass booms*, made from the stoutest bamboo were stamped vertically on the ground. The *foule* or *fuller* was made from shorter, narrower stalks, and could be hit together, end on, or on the ground. The *cutter* was beaten with a stick or struck on the ground.[2]

Grant noted that the terms *foule* and *cutter* were also the names of the Shango ritual drums, and the Shango rhythms soon blended with the other rhythms of the Carnival streets.

When Theodore Perry and a group of technicians for Victor Records arrived in Port of Spain in August 1914, they informed the interviewer for the *Port of Spain Gazette* that they had made their special trip "for the purpose of recording a complete repertoire of Trinidadian music."[3] In the weeks that they stayed on the island they largely succeeded with their ambitious program, and thanks to their industry—and curiosity—we have the only recordings made of the original tamboo bamboo music.

In the catalogue listing the term that was used for it was the Creole word *Kalendas*, a general term in the Caribbean for any kind of African-influenced music. The engineers recorded two titles, "Bagai sala que pocery moin" and "Ou belle Philomem (e)" The singer with the group was Jules Sims, and the acoustic discs were released under the heading "Native Trinidad Kalendas."

The Victor engineers should be awarded some sort of posthumous medal for their efforts in Port of Spain's heat and humidity. The recording of the bamboo band captured a musical style that is perhaps as close to African roots as anything that could be found in the Caribbean. The chantuelle, Sims, sang a representative African chant melody, which was answered by the responses of the chorus, which, as would be the practice in West Africa, was dominated by the high, piercing women's voices. A clanging tone, again typical of African drum orchestras, set the beat. For the recording it was probably a spoon beating on a Dutch gin flask. The basic rhythm was a steady 4/4, with the strong accents on the first and third beats of the measure. Over the strong thump of a heavy bamboo stalk there was a thicket of cross accents and syncopations played on different lengths of bamboo—the *foules* and the *cutters*. The singing still retained the character of a free chant, floating over the rhythm as if independent of the group's pulse—a level of polyrhythmic complexity that was one of the first musical elements to be lost as the memories of Africa faded in the new environment.

In the heyday of calypso recordings twenty years later, there were occasional efforts to revive the sound of the tamboo bamboo bands, and artists mentioned their music in many songs. There were now many different styles of Carnival music, but the bamboo bands still could be heard on the street, celebrating the fighting prowess of their neighborhood's stick fighter. In "Ancient Carnival," by the Roaring Lion, he complained that the violence of Carnival could be "Too much for me bamboo band." Both his song "Man, Man, Man Peter" and the Growler's "In The Morning," describe the ravages inflicted on his opponents by a stick fighter named Peter Agent, and Lord Invader's "Ten Thousand to Bar Me One" is a boast by fighter King Dewars that to stop him it will take "ten thousand" men. Attila the Hun tried to re-create the old style in the recording studio, using a tamboo bamboo band for his recording "Fire Brigade," which referred to the turn of the century, when the smartly uniformed Fire Brigades were widely admired, and performed a useful service by watering the streets in the summers to keep the dust down. Attila's band caught some of the feel of the old 1914 recording, but twenty years is a long time for street music. The rhythms had been smoothed out, and the voices stayed closer to the pulse of the band. He titled his song

"Kalendar," a new spelling of the old word, and the enthusiasm of the performance made it clear that the sound of the bamboo bands was still alive on the Carnival streets.

The Port of Spain telephone directory listed another music store besides Crosby's, where I had found the Carnival song collections and Rudy Ottley's book, and I decided I might find something new there. I found the address—on a side street up the hill from the downtown area—and took a cruising taxi van down to the main square. The other passengers made room for me to squeeze in, and in a moment the talk picked up again as everyone tried to make themselves heard over the newest selection of Carnival calypsos. Close to the main square there were two shopping areas—one an old-fashioned warren of narrow aisles and small booths crowded with bolts of cheap cloth, plastic purses, shoes, hair ornaments, and a variety of tourist goods. The aisles were shaded from the sun, but it still was hot and muggy, and I never saw more than a handful of customers. Not far from it a modern mall filled the center of a city block. It rang with music and its lavish shops were filled with the newest bathing suits and colorful Carnival costumes for women too busy to make their own. The mall was also air conditioned, and it always had people in it, even if they were only using it as a comfortable passageway to walk from one street to another.

I usually found something to eat when I was downtown. The hotel was pleasant and there were two restaurants, but I never felt I was part of the downtown workday if I was sitting out on the hotel verandah. As I looked for the music store I found an Indian restaurant serving mixed beans, spiced meat, and rice, and I took the plate outside and sat at a sidewalk table under a tree. People hurried past me, many of them in their office clothes, and from the stalls of the street merchants in the next block there was the same blare of the new Carnival calypsos that I heard in the taxi vans. Carnival was as strong a presence in the Port of Spain streets as the sun and the winds off the ocean.

The music store was on a narrow street of one-story stucco buildings, most of them decorated with shops signs and advertisements. Once inside the door I found myself in a low-ceilinged room that was crowded with customers, all of them speaking loudly, and its walls lined with battered wooden shelves, all of them empty. There was no air conditioning and the harassed sales people were in shirt sleeves, their faces glistening with perspiration. On the counters, or set back against the walls were the gleaming shapes of steel pans.

The atmosphere inside the shop was as loud and as confrontational as the feeling inside Crosby's had been comfortable and polite. Angry men, some of them with their young sons, were confronting the sales people, demanding to buy pans for Carnival. The shop's employees were trying to explain to them, with mounting impatience, that they should have had the good sense to order their pans months ago, the way all their regular customers did. There was agitated pointing at the pans still in the shop.

"No, no, no"—the sales person was equally agitated—"That man who have that pan, he come here two months ago, he paid already. How can I sell you that man's pan?"

One customer protested that he would pay two times what the pan cost so his boy could have an instrument for *mas*.

"You should tell your boy to get him a hammer and beat out his own pan," the salesman retorted.

I stayed a few moments longer, but there was no way I could talk to anyone in the confusion. It was obvious that the pans still play as emotional a role in the Carnival days as in their crude beginnings only half a century ago. I could still hear voices arguing loudly as I slipped out the door and looked for a van to take me somewhere out of the heat.

It was the old problem of Carnival violence that led to the creation of today's pan orchestras. The street fighting between the neighborhoods that led to the silencing of the drum orchestras now began to affect the new tamboo bamboo bands. The police still found themselves confronting drunken groups streaming down from the hill districts in a crowd around their chanteulle and stick fighter, on the prowl for other groups who had also descended on the city's center. Finally in the 1930s, with unemployment and labor agitation adding to the unstable mix, the colonial authorities began passing restrictions on the bamboo bands. It was this new attempt at control that led to the pans. Just as had happened with the banning of the drum orchestras, the street groups insisted that without their instruments to call forth the gods there could be no Carnival. Stubbornly refusing to back away, the musicians began beating on pieces of metal. Anything that made a clanging sound was good enough—from biscuit tins and paint cans to buckets, hubcaps, and tire irons. For a time the new bands called themselves "iron bands" or "tin biscuit bands," depending on what the musicians had picked up to beat on. In their determined defiance to the new regulations the musicians even created names for their improvised instruments, inventing half-serious titles like "cuff boom," "dudup," and "ping pong," names that were carried over to the early pans.

The new bands were soon so popular that people in some neighborhoods complained that if they didn't tie down the lids of their garbage cans the lids would go dancing down the street as part of an orchestra.

Part of the legend of the pans is the belief that it was the U.S. Navy that inspired the development of the first instruments by obligingly leaving thousands of empty oil drums behind when it closed its base on the island after the Second World War. The Americans, as allies of the British, had been a generally accepted, if upsetting part of island life until their departure in 1962. Trinidad, however, had been an oil producer for several decades, and the island had a useful supply of old oil drums. Up until that time no one had thought of anything to do with them.

The pans couldn't have developed without the series of technical innovations that were discovered by the "tuners," as the workers with the pans were termed. One of the most gifted of the tuners, Spree Simon, who is often called the "father" of the pans, found that if he hollowed out smaller separate sections of the metal head of an oil drum, then each different section would have a different pitch. He first made his discovery when he was trying to hammer out a paint can he'd lent to a friend, who played it until it was beaten out of shape. As Spree hammered out the can he found that he had two different tones on either side, and that the pitch of each note would depend on the size of the indentation that was pounded into the metal. The oil-drum tops were not only wider than most of the circular metal pieces the tuners had to work with, they were made of steel, which had a brighter tone, and once shaped they held their note longer.

The tops the tuners used were the large fifty-five gallon size, which made them even more useful, since there was enough area for many notes. The tuners found that it was difficult to control what they were doing with the tops of the oil drums in their original state, so their first step was to take a five-pound sledgehammer and beat the metal down until it was a concave surface four or five inches below the metal rim. Then began the work of "burning"—heating and hammering and shaping and rubbing the top of the pan into protruding blisters of different sizes for each note of the scale. It was a laborious, exasperating job to sit in a littered yard in the Trinidad heat and hammer a musical instrument out of a steel drum lid, creating true pitches for a tempered scale, and arranging them on the surface of the metal so they could be comfortably reached with quick hand movements. Then the same system of protruding bulges, identical to the prototype instrument, had to be beaten into an entire set of oil-drum tops to create enough instruments for an orchestra. The swelling assortment of instruments that had to be "burned" for the first bands were created with an obsessive labor of love.

The tuners who spent most of their time sweating over the first instruments became as well known as the players, and following the title of a

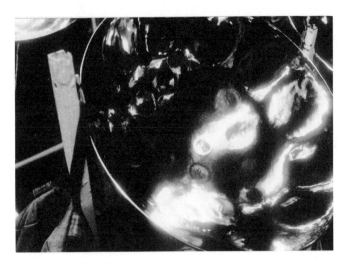

In the Pan Yards. *Photograph by Nora Charters-Myers.*

song performed by a band today the credits generally list the names of the leader, the composer, the tuner, and the arranger. In the first years that pans were being constructed one by one in the tuner's yard, there was no uniformity in the arrangement of the tones, and there are still pans hammered out in different parts of the island with different systems of notes. Originally the tuners worked only with their own band in their own neighborhood, and the bands still had more of the casual style and rumble of a street gang than a musical ensemble. Today most of the tuners work with several bands at the same time. They spend long hours reshaping the tops of the pans as the players pound them in the hours of rehearsal that go into a pan performance. As Carnival comes closer, it's not difficult to pick out the tuners in the yards, with their tired, worried expressions and the small hammers stuck in a pocket of their jeans.

By 1946 the pans had developed to the point that Spree Simon's John John Steel Band could play popular selections for the island's colonial governor, including pieces like "Ave Maria" and "God Save the King." Only a few years later the much-expanded band, performing on what had grown into an impressive variety of pans, was brought to England in 1951 as part of the Festival of Britain, and then went on to tour Europe. Spree Simon was one of the members of the touring group. There were now several families of pans, and they had been given names that suggested a more serious attitude toward the music. The "ping pongs" had become "tenor pans" and the "tune booms" had become "cello pans."

"Booms"—the bass instrument made from an entire oil barrel—were still "booms."

Before the clanging sound of the street bands could be used for classical compositions, however, there had to be another innovation. Another pioneering tuner, Ellie Mannette with the Invaders, found that if he covered the tips of his sticks with rubber padding the tone was much softer and muted. With this mellower tone and with the faster hand movements that the rubber tipped sticks made possible, a performer with only a little practice could play sustained tones that had a new haunting sweetness. Suddenly the pans did more than clang and clatter, with a noisy stick pounding on a metal drum top, now they could sing with the soft, caressing tone that has seduced succeeding generations of pan players and their audiences ever since.

The busy streets of downtown Port of Spain are on flat land that lies beside the harbor, but hemming in the old colonial area are sharply sloping hills that begin at the end of the crowded business district. The Laventille Hills were built up with twisting streets and small bungalows crammed tightly together behind walls and fences. It was in this area where the African contract workers settled after they finished their years in the cane fields, and where the street gangs and the tamboo bamboo bands flourished. Every few blocks there are small grocery stores and the ever present Chinese restaurants—mostly a newly painted outdoor table and a counter behind a wire barrier where people wait for the dinner to be passed over in paper bags. In the 1940s and 1950s the social life of the neighborhoods centered around popular bars and pool halls. The streets were poor, and every section of the area, like Belmont, East Dry River, or Watertown, had its own band, its own stick fighters, and its own chantuelle. It was on these hilly streets, back in the crowded yards, where Spree Simon and the other tuners spent their days "burning" their pans.

The pans still were tied in people's minds with the violence of the stick fighting days, but there was a strenuous effort on the part of local cultural groups to bring the bands into the broader stream of Trinidadian life. Following the success of the large orchestra that traveled to Britain, the bands were invited the next year to participate in the Trinidad and Tobago semi-annual music festival. Already in the late 1940s there had been a rising interest in the pans by young "Trinibagonian" college students, and they insisted that the pans had a place in the island's musical culture. When the new "pannists" were questioned, as described in *Rituals of Power and Rebellion*, they said they "couldn't afford pianos and other expensive European instruments even though they were not

In the Pan Yards. *Photograph by Nora Charters-Myers.*

as poor as the majority of the people in the city and better off than most . . . Although they had to hide the pans from their parents, they were astounded and captivated by its unique sound." Women were also excited by the new instruments, and in the early 1950s a school teacher named Hazel Henley organized an all women's band, the Girl Pat Steel Orchestra, and they soon were joined by a second women's band, the White Stars.

At the same time, the old Carnival habits died hard. The neighborhood gangs still swept down from the hills, and mingling with each noisily drunken procession were the men with their long fighting sticks. As novelist Earl Lovelace wrote in *The Dragon Can't Dance,*

> These were the days when every district around Port-of-Spain was its own island and the steel band within its boundaries was its army, providing warriors to uphold its sovereignty. Those were the war days when every street corner was a garrison, and to be safe, if you came from Belmont, you didn't let night catch you in St.James; if your home was Gonzalez Place, you didn't go up Laventville, and if you lived in Morant, you passed San Juan straight.

There were continuous clashes in the city streets all through these years, and the resigned constabulary spent much of its time trying to keep the bands separate. The Carnival in 1950 was long known for a street battle between followers of John John's band Tokyo and the Invaders that continued for several hours before the officers managed to break it up.

"The Beat of the Steel Band," the calypso that Lord Kitchener wrote in the early years of the band's popularity, captures some of the spirit of these tumultuous processions, and it also emphasizes how personal it all was—since everybody in the small city seemed to know everybody else.

> Port of Spain nearly catch afire
> When the bands were crossing the Dry River
> Zigilee, master of the Ping Pong
> Had people jumping wild in the town.
>
> Bitterman, Pops and Battersby
> Were chopping with a semi-tone melody
> When they start that contrary beat
> They had people jumping wild in the street.
>
> Well, the boom was beaten by Ossie
> A foreman boomer from Bar 20.
> The vibration near break down a wall
> An American say, "Joe, don't stop at all!"[4]

In another of Kitchener's calypsos—after he had decided to give up competing—he describes what he feels when he hears the pans. "On the road" means to be out on the streets, and "to wine" is the modern expression for grinding your hips. Every season, in the weeks leading up to Carnival, there are pious newspaper editorials complaining that young girls "whose mothers and father certainly know better" are "wining" all over town.

> For this year Carnival
> I already makeup meh mind
> Ah go enjoy meh self and stop worrying . . .
> I shall be out on the road and forget everything
> I only just waiting to hear the beat of pan
> And no one could stop me from jumping inside a band
> Ah going to wine like ah crazy
> And just ignore everybody.
> Ah go play med mas
> And smoke up meh grass.[5]

It was already cooler on the streets when I looked at the note with the names of the bands that the young clerk at the hotel had given me and decided to walk to one of the pan yards he had listed. On the map it was easy to find. It was on Tragere Road, only a few blocks from the dancing statue of Lord Kitchener north of the Savannah. The Savannah, as I circled it on its wide sidewalk, lay heavy in shadows, and its broad stretches of grass were empty. When I came to the other side of it I found myself in solitary streets lined with modest bungalows, one-story, light-colored stucco or frame houses surrounded by bits of garden, set off behind low walls at the edge of the sidewalk. There was the familiar delicate, continually changing smell of flowers from behind the hedges, and over the hum of the air conditioners I could hear the murmur of television sets and radios. To reach Tragere Road I had to skirt the Port of Spain cricket grounds; a black hulking shape of metal fences and enclosed grandstands that loomed above me as I made my way uncomfortably along the shadowed rough sidewalk that followed its back wall. For a moment I was conscious that I was the only person out walking on the still streets.

But "still" is not a word I would use for the nights before Carnival in Port of Spain. In the unlit spaces behind the cricket grounds I lost the faint, humming sound of the air conditioners and the muffled television voices, but a new sound swelled in the darkness around me while I was still on the other side of the pavilion. As I turned the corner of the road, the rush of noise engulfed me. I had found the pan yard.

The yard was on the other side of Tragere Road, a broad street lined with businesses, and it was about one hundred meters from where I was standing. It was the practice yard of the famed Invaders, and the scene at the fenced-in enclosure was unforgettable. The space, about the size of a small parking lot, was brightly lit, and a smaller area close to the road was crowded with "limers," the crowd that comes by to listen and have a drink. They were standing along the cyclone fence that separated the yard from the sidewalk, or gathered in noisy groups inside the fence. The space was, literally, a yard. It had been paved with cement, but there was only a high, partial roof along one side of the space, with a toilet and rooms for the players to change out of sweaty clothes or leave any rain jackets they'd brought with them.

The small area had been left clear inside the metal fence for unsteady wooden benches and a wooden stand that sold cold beer and soft drinks. But the rest of the space was filled with gleaming rows of pans. There were pans of all sizes, the tenor pans lined up together in the center front, the deeper-toned pans behind them. The bare cement had a series of much used wooden tiers that extended along one wall, then continued at the back of the yard on the other side of the band. The large bass pans were set up on the highest tier—one player at each set of brightly painted drums. All of the musicians on the high tiers were women, each of them responsible for four of the "boom basses," which were full-sized oil drums. There were probably about eighty performers at the rehearsal, with another twenty-five of us standing inside the fence listening. I had never heard anything like the sound they were creating. After the small pan concerts I'd heard, and after the hours I'd spent in the recording studio with musicians who were playing the pans, I thought I had experienced pan music, but after five minutes of watching the serious-faced, intent concentration of the Invaders' musicians and listening to the intricacy and the musicality of their arrangements I became a pan enthusiast for life.

Ecstatic poems and songs have been written about the pans, and the musicians—the "pan men"—have been eulogized in fervent testimonials, but what excited me was the every day ordinariness of the people sweating under the bright lights of the crowded yard. Many of the "pan men" were women, and there were clusters of tired but enthusiastic high school students. Scattered through the rows of players were the scratchy, bearded faces of older white men, and the shiny, sweaty faces of young white women. In some sections of the arrangements the pans were gently stroked, but mostly they were pounded with ringing energy. Music was again demonstrating that it could reach across any boundaries of race or age. During a short break, while there was a discussion between the arranger and the tenor players about the phrasing of the melody, one of the graying white men, in a sweat-soaked school T-shirt, faded jeans, and running shoes clambered out of his line of shining pans. He shrugged with a weary lift of his shoulders.

"Time for a beer. Time for a pee."

When the music resumed, I moved closer so I could watch two of the young, serious-faced Creole women playing the bass pans on the wooden tier against the side wall. Their space was so cramped that they had to play with their backs to the other musicians. They stood a few feet above them, staring at the white painted cement wall. Even though they couldn't see the others there were no hesitations in their playing, no break in their concentration. Elaborate phrases, endings of sections, long melodies, abrupt introductions were practiced over and over, but the women seemed able to follow the directions by staring at the wall. The musical director, a gray-haired man dressed, like most of his musicians, in a wrinkled shirt, baggy trousers, and running shoes, hovered in front of the row of tenor pans, listening with sober intentness. Time

At the Pan Yards. *Photograph by Nora Charters-Myers.*

and time again he banged with a long stick, his "baton," on the side of one of the pans to stop the music. He clanged out the phrasing he wanted, or demonstrated the crescendo on the pan's metal side, and everyone picked up their sticks and began again. Whatever tiredness or impatience they felt at the continual stops, at the incessant corrections, were forgotten in the clamor of the music when they picked up the arrangement again.

The arrangement was a ringing succession of rhythmic changes and snatches of melody that swelled out of the torrent of sound, but I found myself watching the players as closely as I was listening to what they were playing. A pan orchestra is a complicated choreography of movement. The hands of the players bent over the small pans are almost hidden inside the rim of their instrument, and they seem to be kneading some kind of dough with persistent, fussy movement. The performers on the bass pans, in an energetic contrast, must swing their long sticks from one pan to another to play each note, sometimes pivoting 180 degrees to reach the next thundering tone. Slim arms and muscled shoulders move in flowing rhythms with the grace of a length of cloth fluttering in the wind. The eddying sweep of outstretched hands clutching stubby sticks or the shift of moving feet—each group of pans with its own gesturing rhythms—is like the swirling surface of the sea as it streams around a stone in its path.

Most of the musicians dance as they play, since all of them stand over their instruments, and the unsteady, wheeled platforms where the pans are mounted sway with the joyous rhythms of sandals and running shoes. Since they will perform the same repertoire of compositions over and over as their pans are pushed along the street and there will be thousands of spectators shouting and waving as they compete, each of the players create their own movements, in their own cramped space. As they wearily pick up their sticks to rehearse a section or phrase again with the clang of the director's baton, the free, exultant flow of movement begins with it.

When I returned to the pan yards two nights later it was with Nora, who had photographed in the cane fields at dawn with me, and she'd brought her camera to the pan yards. How would the Invaders sound to someone who had never heard the pans before? This time the crowd of limers inside the fence was larger, and even more of the musicians had turned up for the rehearsal. A clatter of the director's stick released the same roar of sound, the same intense concentration on the faces of the musicians as they swayed and danced, swinging their arms to reach the notes on the bass pans or with their heads bent over their small melody pans. If they made it to the finals of Panorama on the Savannah there would be costumes and decorations for the racks holding the pans, but in the yard there were only unironed T-shirts or loosely buttoned short-sleeve shirts hanging outside faded jeans or wrinkled shorts. Nora, in her own jeans and T-shirt, and her surprised laughter at the energy and surge of the music, could have passed for a band member herself.

As I followed the shifts and changes in the flow of sound I found myself wondering if the bands presented such ambitious arrangements because they were reluctant to relinquish any elements of their complicated cultural heritage. Certainly the reality that the arrangements of their three competition pieces would count for 40 percent of their score in the Carnival competition had an obvious effect on the mood of the rehearsal, but I was also conscious that each element in the music represented the complexity of the interaction between the two musical cultures, European and African. In the music of the pan orchestras the acculturation has enriched both cultures. I also realized, as I stood at the edge of the section of cello pans, that the piece they were playing was as complicated as a movement of a symphony by Haydn, but they would have to perform it from memory as they were being pushed along a jammed street in a Carnival crowd. I could understand why they went over and over arrangements, why they would accept—with tired patience—the stops and starts and the insistent clangs of the director's baton which signaled that once more they had to go back and begin again.

Finally there was a signal for a break. Stretching stiff arms and wiping the perspiration from their faces, the musicians straggled off to the stand that was selling beer and soft drinks, or they joined the lines that were forming outside at the toilets. Our ears still ringing, Nora and I decided to go on to the next pan yard, the Star Lift yard, which according to our map was farther along Tragere Road, a short way beyond Kitchener's dancing statue. After the roar of the music, the road noises—cars passing, gangs of men outside of the bars shouting loudly at each other and at passing friends, the busy sounds of jukeboxes—seemed almost lulling, like the lapping rhythms of a quiet sea.

We found the Star Lift yard in a shadowy street, and went through the entrance into a wide field, with dangling rows of electric lights above the rows of pans. The yard was crowded with people who looked like the musicians we had seen a few blocks away, but they were standing along the paths beside the pans, talking and stretching their arms. There was a line at the stand selling drinks. We'd come just as they'd taken a break from the rehearsal and the sounds around us were laughter and voices calling to friends. The mood of the yard was more subdued. The Invader yard had been brightly lit, but this one was almost in darkness. The only lights were the strings of bulbs reflected in the gleaming mirrored surfaces of the pans.

"Oh, look at the stars!"

Nora was standing a few yards away from the last row of instruments, looking up into the night sky. The lights of the city were dim here, and above us was a weave of stars.

"I didn't know there were so many stars!"

We could tell, after a few moments, that it was going to be some time before the musicians went back to their pans, and it was getting late. The Phase II yard was not far. Our map placed it only a few blocks away, on a long, curving side street off Tragere Road. It turned out to be a street of tidy bungalows. An occasional car passed us as we walked, but it didn't seem possible that there could be a pan yard in the middle of this quiet neighborhood. Then after we'd walked two or three blocks more we began to hear the sound of pans in the distance, and after another block we could see the glaring lights over the roofs. We had only to follow the sound and the gleam of the lights to find the yard. The yard was a graveled field at the end of a narrow road that led between two houses,

At the Pan Yards. *Photograph by Nora Charters-Myers.*

and we could see immediately that it was larger than the Invaders' yard. The gleaming platforms of pans seemed to stretch to the limits of the strings of overhead lights.

There was the usual small crowd of twenty or thirty limers sitting on folding chairs or standing closer to the band. There was even a modest grandstand that had been erected for visitors beside the customary stand-up bar, but there had been a rain shower earlier, and the wooden planks of the grandstand were too wet to sit on. The bar had a long, open window above a slim counter, partially protected with a metal grating, and beer and soft drinks in a much-used, ice-filled cooler. The rows of the pans were familiar, but I felt a different mood in the crowd of visitors. Phase II had won Panorama two years in a row, 1987 and 1988, each time with one of Denyse Plummer's songs, and even though it had been some years before, the visitors were listening with the serious attention that is given to a winner. The limit of the number of musicians for the competition is 110, and it looked as if at least 100 of the band members were there for the rehearsal.

What I found irresistible was the space of the yard. Unlike the Invaders' yard, Phase II's ground was like the Star Lift yard we'd just seen, only it was even larger, and there were more rows of lights over the instruments. There was enough space for us to circle the entire band

and listen to each section of the pans. I could stand by the bass pans, lean closer to the cello pans, watch the flying sticks of the lines of players with the tenor pans. And for the first time I could get close to the "engine room."

At the heart of every competition steel band is a percussion group mounted on a high platform in the center of the array of pans. The energy and drive for the arrangement comes from the percussionists—which is why it's called the engine room. It is the distinctively African element that identifies the source of the steel bands' music—as though the old tamboo bamboo and tin biscuit bands still had their place in the spirit and thrust of the percussion. Phase II had a percussion group of twelve men playing a variety of instruments that included a dance band drum kit, with its conventional bass drum, snare drum, and cymbals. The drum kit was augmented with conga drums, scrapers, small gleaming metal discs, and a variety of brake drums and metal beaters. An old man, gray haired and with spindly arms, was using an iron spike to strike a much handled brake drum with a hole broken in the middle for him to reach his fingers through. I sensed from his fingers' complicated movements as he damped the sound, and the determined set of his outthrust jaw, that he had been playing that brake drum all of his life.

I could hear the same irresistible surge of rhythm in the relentless pounding of the percussion section that I had encountered everywhere in West Africa. Above the rich texture of sound there was the same fierce clarity to the beat. In every drum orchestra I'd heard there had been some kind of high, ringing metal chime that kept the basic pulse over the shifting rhythms of the heavier drums. Crouching beside the old man with his brake drum was a sweat soaked, thick shouldered young man clanging out the raw pulse of the rhythm on a set of matched metal discs the size of a cooking pot lid, but cast out of shiny chromed steel. Somehow above the surging beat of the engine room's drums and the flooding ring of the pans his insistent rhythm centered the pulse of the arrangement.

For an hour the band obsessively repeated individual sections of their competition piece. Again and again the leader, a blocky, older, light-skinned man, clattered his stick on the closest pan to stop what they were doing. He was continually searching for more subtlety in the phrasing, for a smoother rise in their long crescendos, a more flamboyant crash of sound when they broke into a new section. Each time the music stopped it seemed that the men in the engine room could never build up to the same muscular intensity, but at the insistent count to start again, all twelve of the percussionists instantly picked up their clamoring beat. The wiry man sitting at the drum kit would listen to the new phrasing, his chest heaving, then with the new count his sticks would slash down on the snare drum and cymbal and his foot would pump out the beat on the bass drum pedal.

Nora and I had moved back to the grandstand to rest our ears for a moment, standing close to the shed with its wire mesh screen, where the two young men were selling beer and cold drinks. Nora cried suddenly, "There's Denyse!"

It was Denyse Plummer, the singer who had won the title of Calypso Monarch the year before with her song "Heroes," with its moving text about the old singers, many sick or dead, who were being forgotten, and whose CDs "don't sell out by Crosby 's." She was only the third woman to win the competition. We had heard her for two exciting, high-energy songs in her performance "tent" the night before. She was standing with two or three friends a few feet from us. She was still in her stage costume—dark pants and a sequined top, her tousled black hair woven with colored ribbons. When the orchestra leader glanced back and saw her, he led a pleased welcome from the players. She waved with cheerful friendliness—two Carnival champions meeting in the shadows of the yard—and the pan players responded with wagging sticks. As the rehearsal picked up again it felt as though there were a new swagger to the rhythms. Denyse listened while she talked, nodding to herself at some of the music's changes.

It was late when we left the yard, and we were too far away to walk back to the hotel. At night almost any car in Port of Spain might be working as a taxi—or it could just be someone out driving, looking for people alone on the street. A new-model car finally slowed down for our wave, and when we looked in the window we were uncertain abut getting in, since the driver was in slacks and an undershirt. Smiling broadly, he quickly assured us that he usually drove a van in the daytime. He had taken his car out again to get himself something to drink and when he saw us he decided a last fare would wind up his day. After the hours at the rehearsals Nora and I were hungry. Did he know anywhere where we could get something to eat? We knew that downtown in the city it was dark—what did he suggest at this hour? He grinned, nodded, and turned the car the other way. There was another part of the city, up in the suburbs at the base of the hills, that we knew nothing about. Suddenly we left the old Port of Spain behind and we could have been in a busy shopping center outside of San Diego. There were new, crowded fast food restaurants and busy bars. On the way, we stopped at an all-night gasoline station, with what seemed like half the cars in the city lined up at the pumps. Inside there was a busy convenience store that sold everything from groceries and liquor to work gloves and car parts.

When we'd gotten a sandwich and the driver had picked up the bottle of Puncheon Rum—75 percent alcohol—that he'd come out for, he drove us back through the deserted streets to the hotel.

"What were you doing out on the street so late like that?" he asked. "It not be too good to be out in the dark." I told him we'd been at the pan yards. He laughed and slapped the steering wheel.

"I love the sound of those pans, oh I love them. Come *mas* I be out there wining with my friends and we be having a so good time. That music a man can move his feet to. But I don't want my house to be too close to the yards. No, no. Those pans, I tell you, they be so sweet, but it be like thunder if a man live close."

I didn't choose the battered taxi that slowed down on a dark corner in Kingston, Jamaica's unkempt capital city, because it looked less battered than any of the others that were cruising with little optimism through the shadowy streets, searching for passengers like me. I couldn't even see enough under the dim streetlamps to tell if the seats were torn and broken, as they were in some of the cabs. The driver looked younger than most of the others, and his anxious face had a hopeful expression, and that was enough for me to hold up my hand for him to stop. I thought also that since he was young he might know something about what I was looking for. In the nights I'd already spent in Kingston I had been trying to find some place that played reggae. This was the 1970s, reggae music at that moment was one of the world's most popular new styles, and it had come from Kingston. But how could I find it?

I had the address of a dance hall on the edge of Trenchtown, the poor, uneasy Kingston slum that had seen the emergence of reggae, and the city's most-read newspaper, the *Gleaner*, had announced there was going to be a dance. Could the taxi driver find it for me? His expression darkened in a worried flush, then he nodded emphatically. He knew where it was. He would find it but he'd wait for me outside. It wasn't a place somebody like me would want to stay for long. With a lurch he pulled away from the curb and in the middle of the street we struck the first of the Kingston potholes. There was a ringing metallic clang, the cab slewed into the next lane of traffic, and my head grazed the roof of the space above me. A new pothole, and there was a repeat of the clanging noise and this time the cab slid back toward the curb. As I pried myself off the broken door where the heaving had thrown me, I realized that the cab had no springs and no shock absorbers. Its undersides had been forced to deal with too many potholes. I leaned forward on the sagging springs of the seat to shout to the driver that I wanted to get out and find another cab, but in the half-light of another streetlamp as we lurched past I could see from his desperate expression that he needed me as a passenger. Any passenger would do, but if he didn't have some kind of paying fare he was in for an empty night. To prevent me from saying anything he began driving faster, jerking the wheel to avoid the worst of the breaks in the pavement. I leaned back uneasily—the seat seemed to be intact—and finally decided to accept whatever might happen. Kingston was a new town, and for a while I would have to take everything as I found it.

The man in London who had sent me to Kingston had been disarmingly vague about what he wanted me to do there. His name was Rod Buckle, a rotund, bearded man with glasses and a cheerful attitude, who was the managing director of the English division of Sonet, the Swedish record company I'd been associated with for several years.

"Look around, get the feel of the place. We're interested in doing deals with anybody who has something to sell. I send them nice letters offering them all the usual nice things and the bastards never get back to me."

We were sitting in Buckle's upstairs office on a once elegant side street of fading brick and stone mansions close to Notting Hill Gate. We had worked together since he'd set up the first Sonet office in Soho in 1971, and I was used to the optimistic imprecision of his suggestions. Looking around and getting the feel of a place was what I did anyway.

"You never know how long one of these booms is going to last and we've had—I don't know—three or four years of reggae? It's a long time for one of these things to go on. Maybe it's not going to go away?"

Buckle pushed himself back in his swivel chair and turned it around so he could look at the line of converted mansions on the other side of the street. He was drumming on one arm of the chair with his fingers. I knew him well enough to know that as far as he was concerned we'd talked enough about what he wanted me to do. He tapped the arm of the chair decisively, still looking out of the window.

"I had a bit of good fortune. The copyright people let me register the name *Red Stripe* for anything we put out. It has a nice Jamaica feel to it. It's their most popular beer."

Since the idea had come to Buckle late and reggae had already turned into the jungle of hasty contracts and impatient lawyers that quickly grows up around any popular music that begins to get some attention, he had only come up with an airplane ticket. I was excited by the new sound, and I had planned to journey to Jamaica myself, so I took care of the accommodations. The tourist facilities were clustered on the north coast of the island, but I wanted to be in Kingston, on the island's south coast. Kingston was the birthplace of reggae, and it was also in Kingston's minimal recording studios and noisy dance halls where the styles that led up to reggae, ska and rock steady, had taken shape in the stream of popular 45 rpm dance singles put out for the local audiences by ambitious producers. Kingston had the usual assortment of international hotels—reassuring to most business travelers since they offer virtually identical meals and services everywhere in the world—but not what I was looking for. A tourist office listing for a guesthouse close to the center of the city looked possible, and the English voice on the other end of the line seemed reassuringly friendly, so I took the room over the telephone without bothering to look at it first.

Jamaica is poor, and in the 1970s, only a few years after it had had gained its independence from Great Britain, it was growing steadily poorer. After some hapless circling through narrow streets of small wooden and stucco houses the tourist office's driver finally found the address we were looking for on a back street. The guesthouse was a one-story building behind a fringe of dispirited palm trees, its dark green painted front hung with dusty vines. There was a row of windows facing the street, and behind them, when I went inside, was a dimly lit bar with a handful of people whom I recognized as the bar's old colonial "regulars" slouched on worn stools staring down into their glasses. They were as typical of bar regulars everywhere in the world as the large hotels downtown were typical of their counterparts in dozens of other cities. Pasty white faces that hadn't been outside in the sun for years lifted a moment to stare at me, then turned to consider their glasses again. The room that I'd rented over the telephone was in an elemental wooden building on the other side of a small courtyard crowded with a variety of leafy plants and elbowing trees. To show me the door the English woman in a busy print dress who was renting the room had to bend under a looping vine. She was determined to please and stayed discreetly by the door while I looked inside. There was a large creaking bed, a splotchy mirror over a stained washstand and a scarred chair. The walls, made out of pine boards, had been painted a drab gray-blue, and as if even that much had been considered too decorative they were otherwise completely bare. The room was dark and stuffy, but perhaps because it was so unwelcoming I didn't notice the usual collection of insects, and it was as cheap as it deserved. I stayed.

After some uncertain lurching through side streets on the edge of Trenchtown my dance hall taxi driver pulled up at a vaguely white, box-shaped building that looked like a school. At least we hadn't experienced a power failure, which was happening in Kingston with dispiriting regularity, but the glow from the one light on the street was distant and dim. I spent a minute insisting that the driver go on without me. No, I didn't want him to wait. I could hear music through the dark door, and I was going to stay. I also couldn't face another clanking journey over the potholes, which he probably suspected. He finally rattled away from the curb, his expression disconsolate, to go back to the lights and the lines of unsteady cabs cruising the empty streets.

My problem in the casual Trenchtown dance halls, and in the corner bars with jukeboxes, was simple. It was Kool and the Gang. They were an American soul group who were riding a series of hits in the United States. I had just seen them in a Mardi Gras parade they'd helped sponsor in their old neighborhood in New Orleans. They stood up on a carnival float, grandly throwing beads to the crowds, hugely pleased with their success and enjoying their flurry of fame in front of their families and friends.

In Jamaica their song "Ladies Night" was having the same effect as a Caribbean storm. It was washing over everything, and there was no way to get away from it. Most of the jukeboxes I'd listened to when I glanced into one of the Trenchtown bars were playing "Ladies Night," and if it wasn't playing their hit, it was another Kool and the Gang song that filled the air. What I was hoping to find in the dance hall was the reggae sound that at that moment I was hearing everywhere in the United States and Europe. I had some faint expectations, from the sounds I was hearing through the door of the dance hall, that there might be a band, but I always had to accept the reality that Jamaica *is* poor. The best I could expect from a Trenchtown dance was a sound system—one of Jamaica's complicated systems of turntables, microphones, and scuffed loud speakers patched together with tape and wire by an energetic deejay. The deejay's irrepressible toasts and brags were the beginnings of what was to grow into rap a few years later in the school yards of New York City's Bronx neighborhoods.

At least the dance was where *The Gleaner* had said it would be—but there was the familiar problem with starting on time. Even if all we were getting was a sound system, the deejay, a short, thin man with a heavy beard and his dreadlocks caught up under one of the ubiquitous green, yellow, and red knitted hats, wasn't going to start the dance any sooner than he liked. There were perhaps fifty people when I came into the long, shadowy room. The noise I'd heard in the street grew to a deafening thud once I was inside. Even though nothing had officially started, some people were dancing anyway, with a loose swing of arms and hands, their feet mostly close together, their bodies swaying with the rhythms from their waists up. The men were in tight shirts, the long sleeves buttoned at the wrist. The women were in dresses with loose, swinging skirts. The music was Kool and the Gang. To save himself trouble the DJ had put on the entire album, and then when it was finished I realized with a sinking despair that once he'd talked us up with a little of the neighborhood's patois, he was going to play the entire album again.

An hour later the deejay turned up the volume of the speakers a little, and we finally had some different records. What we got to hear was a series of American soul hits. This didn't seem to concern the dancers. There were perhaps one hundred and fifty of us now, and there was a loose, strutty feel to the dancing. If the couples filling the floor had any feeling that they were missing their island's own sounds, their own music, I didn't see any sign of it on their perspiring faces as they created free shapes in the air with their hands and fingers.

In my first days in the gray room behind the garden I spent time just getting used to Kingston. In a familiar city, you know, without being conscious of it, about the conditions that shaped it. I had to know something about Kingston—about the conditions that had shaped it—about the conditions of history that had shaped Jamaica itself, if I wanted to find its music.

The size of the island was difficult to grasp. It seemed larger than it is. It is large by the standards of other British islands in the Caribbean, but if you look at it on a map you see that Cuba, only 90 miles to the north, is many times its size. Jamaica is the third largest of the Caribbean islands—after Cuba and Hispaniola, which is split between Haiti and the Dominican Republic—but it is only 146 miles long and 35 miles wide. Its population also seems larger, but in 1990 Jamaica had less than two and a half million people, fewer than the borough of Brooklyn in New York City. When I took busses away from Kingston, back into the country to Spanish Town, the capital city when Jamaica was a Spanish colony, or toward the villages on the east coast, I seemed to be traveling in an unending green countryside that stretched beyond every turn of the narrow road ahead of the bus's windshield. Over the trees I always seemed to glimpse the lumbering shapes of Jamaica's mountains.

Jamaica's complicated, often violent history begins early. Columbus sighted it on his second voyage in 1494, and the Spaniards set upon the natives with their customary ferocity. The Arawak Indians who were living in scattered bands on the island were enslaved, and there was a half-hearted attempt to colonize the land. There was little gold, and since that was the only thing the Spaniards were interested in, the island was given scant attention. At its most developed period it still had only a fringe of Spanish settlers and their domestic slaves. The single important crop was tobacco, grown on haphazardly cultivated plots of land. There was a long period of confusion as the island was fought over and bargained

Street vendors on Queen Street, Kingston.

back and forth with the other Caribbean islands in wars that were decided thousands of miles away in the capitals of Europe. Finally, in 1655, the English landed with a small army and seized control. The English offered the scattered groups of Spanish settlers the right to retain ownership of their slaves if they would stay under English rule, but the Spanish left perfunctorily; and, in a move that was to cause great difficulties for the new English governors, they freed their slaves, almost fifteen hundred men, women, and children, who fled to the mountains.

The freed slaves built crude settlement in the slopes and valleys of the mountain forests, and welcomed escaped slaves from the new English plantations. The Spanish word for runaways was *cimarrones*, which in English became *Maroons*. Many of the Maroons had grown up in warrior societies in Africa, and in the mountains they went back to raiding isolated farms. If any English soldiers strayed out of their encampments they could expect to be quickly and brutally killed. The Maroons harrassed the English colonists for more than forty years from their hidden villages in the mountain forests. An uneasy period of peace ended with the first Maroon War in 1728, a violent struggle that continued for twelve years before the English finally gave up and left the Maroons in their villages, with the condition that in the future they might join the English in putting down slave rebellions. After a period of relative calm, the English attacked the Maroons again in 1795. This time they tricked the Maroon leaders with a ruse that led to their imprisonment, then brought in hunting dogs trained in Cuba to fight slaves and offered the surviving Maroons a peace treaty, which the Maroons accepted only to be tricked again and exiled from their homes in Jamaica. It was years before they were able to return to their villages.

The mountains have played a continuous role in Jamaican life. The Blue Mountains begin north of the plateau area above Kingston, but most of the Maroon settlements were on the north slopes of the mountains, where it was even harder for the English to get at them. The vast sugar plantations on the surrounding lowlands were poorly managed and isolated. Only a handful of the plantation owners chose to leave the comforts of London for the diseases and dangers of the island. There were continuous violent slave rebellions, and escaped slaves quickly found their way to the mountain hideaways. Some Rastafarians, like the slaves, have fled to the mountains today, to escape what they consider the government's repressive policies on the use of marijuana and toward their religion. Often photos of the Rastas and their families show them settled in mountain clearings and washing their laughing children in the streams.

As I slowly found my way through Kingston's jammed streets and litter-strewn squares around Trenchtown I was only cursorily of interest to the lines of women squatting along the curbs—the higglers—with their small stocks of fruit and canned sausage, matches and body oils set up on boxes in front of them. I obviously wasn't going to buy anything. There was more curiosity at the guesthouse. The first two or three mornings the woman who had rented the room to me somehow managed to be at the bar when I went out for breakfast. She was English, probably in her fifties, with dyed dark hair that she wore tied with a band, and a series of blouses that all looked as though she'd brought them with her when she'd emigrated to Jamaica as a young woman.

"You're off again," she would say.

"People to see," I usually answered.

"Someone I know?" she would ask, in a half-joking tone.

After the third encounter I explained pleasantly that I was looking for some of the record company executives who were behind the new reggae sales boom. Most of them, I had found, were out of the country, along with most of the musicians, but I still had a number of meetings. She nodded, apparently smiling with some relief that I didn't seem to be involved with drugs or political agitation, the two troublesome areas for the Jamaican government. It was necessary for her to pass on the information to her regular customers, and for the next few days I found the man who looked the most typically British of the bar regulars waiting for me. He was tall and thin, with lank hair, and he wore the same clothes everyday—cricketer's flannels and a white cricketer's shirt with the collar turned up. Both the shirt and the flannels had seen enough hard use to fit into the ambience of the fading barroom.

"Off to see the nignogs now, are we?" was his standard question as he turned to stare at me with as much hostility as he could manage, swiveling on his bar stool so he could plant his feet firmly in their worn sandals.

"Here! We won't have any of that," the woman running the house would announce in a sharply disapproving tone, and as I went out into the heat of the street I was aware that each of them was acting out some kind of personal scenario that helped them start their day.

Reggae had become a serious business in Jamaica, and I found that the people involved were elusive and rushed. After a moment as I sat talking in the office of the well-known producer Joe Gibbs, who ran one of the many recording and sales operations for the local artists, he held up his hands in an expressive shrug.

"Everybody come to me now. I mean everybody. But already I have so many contracts I can't do more."

Gibbs was solidly built and dark-skinned, and since he was running a business that had suddenly moved into the mainstream he was wearing a new shirt and tie and a light jacket. He was sitting in his large office behind a desk that was even more cluttered than Buckle's.

"Why you don't come three years ago? Four years ago? Jamaica's on the map now and before that nobody knew if we were even on this planet." He looked at me and sighed. "You want to make a deal with someone, you come to me and I tell you if this man's ok. But why you don't come three years ago?"

He held up his hands again and his expression was suddenly serious. "I can tell you that in Jamaica it isn't what it used to be. Before we had singles selling maybe 50,000 to 100,000, now a normal good single is 20,000 to 30,000, and the cost we pay for doing anything goes up every day. The business is at the stage now where we must have honesty and realism."

I thanked Gibbs and left him staring unhappily at the scattered papers in front of him.

His office was above his store, one of the largest of the Kingston record shops, and on market days it was jammed with people waiting to hear new releases. No one would think of buying something they hadn't heard, and the clerks behind the counter stood with four or five 45 rpm singles between their outstretched fingers. When they could make out what someone was shouting at them from the crowd it was almost invariably one of the new singles they were holding. There were two turntables in the middle of the counter, and before the voice in the crowd had finished shouting out the request the record was usually on one of the turntables. Half a chorus was enough—maybe an entire chorus if the buyer's face still showed some perplexity—but that was the end. There was a new shout—someone wanting to hear a different song. Gibbs had gotten his start producing local dance hall singles, and if he wanted to know what was selling in Kingston on that day he only had to call down to his clerks and ask them what they were holding between their fingers.

One of the intriguing things about reggae was that it didn't sound like traditional Jamaican music. It was, as one of the new groups, the Wailin' Wailers, sang in one of their most successful albums, a "new bag." The musicologist John Storm Roberts spent considerable time in the Jamaican mountains, recording singers and musicians who still carried on the old traditions, and he found fewer traces of a survival of African music than he'd encountered on other islands. Much of what he recorded showed obvious African vocalisms and rhythmic accents, but the songs themselves came from sturdy English folk backgrounds, and the sound had an infectious, loose-limbed dance beat, with the relaxed cheerfulness of a gathering of friends with a bottle to pass around. The music had the island name *mento*.[1]

There were much closer links to Africa in the drumming of the island's religious sects. Most of the Jamaican people belong to either the Baptist or Pentacostal churches, but there is also a strong following of the Pocomania and Cumina cults, which base their message on spirit possession. In the 1950s there was considerable documentary recording of Jamaican drumming by the musicologist George Simpson, and the relationship to Africa was immediately clear in the rhythmic structure of the drum music he recorded. The Rastas also emphasize drumming. At Rasta gatherings, called *grounations*, there is continual drumming and chanting. The musicians perform on three matched drums: the *bass*, the *funde*, and the *repeater*, and their music is known as *nyahbingi*. The essence of the drumming that became part of the reggae style of the 1970s was the tone of the drums—the deep, resonant sound of hands on vibrating skin heads. It became an element of reggae's rich tonal texture. In all of the drumming there is the characteristic polymetric, polyrhythmic profusion of accents that have marked African music everywhere in the new hemisphere. If the more overt African memories had faded in the mountains—because of their isolation, Roberts suggested—they had continued to find a voice in the religious services of Jamaica's cities.

Until independence in 1963, if Jamaican popular music strayed from American sources it usually imitated Trinidadian calypso. It was in the first years of independence, when there was still optimism that there would be an economic upswing with the new government, that a new music scene emerged in Kingston. I could see some of the old optimism still asserting itself in the people crowding into Joe Gibbs's record shop, and there was a mood of professional upbeat enthusiasm on the radio and television.

Ska was the first of the new Jamaican styles to catch on in the dance halls, and then with Jamaican immigrants in England. It was an up-tempo dance music—as close as Jamaica came to mainstream American rhythm and blues, with horn sections, jazz-influenced instrumental solos, and vocals performed by a solo singer in the American style or by one of the popular vocal trios. Ska looked forward to the reggae styles of the next decade with its heavy emphasis on the afterbeat and its thick bass tone, and it looked back to the more innocent rhythms of mento with its regularly accented pulse. Over all of this was laid a texture of jazz instrumental solos, horn section arrangements, and soul effects borrowed from American recordings. Ska's reign in the dance halls was short. Since the Kingston scene was tied so closely to the singles that were produced for the dance hall crowds, the styles changed with the mood of the young dancers, who were also listening to American soul hits and to the popular calypsonians. Nothing lasted long on the local market.

Ska dominated the dance halls in the early 1960s, though in West Kingston, which was the Trenchtown area, a style called "rude boy" briefly emerged from about 1965 to 1967. The rude boy singles emphasized the electric bass, which had replaced the stand-up acoustic bass only a few years earlier, and the songs took up the theme of the unemployed ghetto men—the rude boys who had been forced out of the rural villages by the economic difficulties and were without work or hope in the streets of Trenchtown or the city's other poor neighborhoods. What is usually considered the first Rude Boy song, "Hooligan," recorded in

1965, was performed by the Wailin' Wailers, with the lead vocal by a very young Bob Marley and the harmonies by Peter Tosh and Bunny Wailer. In 1971 the Jamaican-produced film *The Harder They Come*, which featured the singer Jimmy Cliff, brilliantly captured the tense and angry world of the rude boys, and it was the first product of the new Jamaican consciousness to achieve international success.

In late 1966 a new dance rhythm called rock steady edged out ska. One of the accounts of its beginnings is that a singer named Hopeton Lewis was having trouble working in the lyrics to a song called "Take It Easy" at the band's fast ska tempo. He asked them to slow the song down, and as they listened to the playback the pianist commented that the new rhythm was "rock steady." The term quickly spread among the musicians. The slower tempos, the emphasis on the vocals, and the stronger melodic role of the electric bass were all to be part of the reggae style that emerged two years later.

The reign of rock steady in the dance halls was even shorter than that of ska. By the summer of 1968 it was over. The same year a vocal trio called the Maytals, with lead singer Toots Hibbert, recorded the first song with the word *reggae* in the title, "Do the Reggay," which described reggae as a new kind of dance. In its early years reggae absorbed a kaleidoscope of strong influences—each of them a factor in the creation of what became known as roots reggae. In the Mid-1970s the most crucial influence was certainly the Rastafarian faith. Although the new religion had none of the distinguishing characteristics of the African religious cults that flourished in the other Caribbean islands, the core Rasta beliefs—the allegiance to the spirit of Haile Selassie and the belief in the Ethiopian Empire as their spiritual homeland—had more consequential African roots.

The Rastafarian faith is still a religion without priests, and it has not yet cohered around a clearly defined set of beliefs that every adherent would accept. In Jamaica there were several forms of the faith known as the Twelve Tribes Of Israel, a sect popular with upscale Kingston believers, that attracted many of the musicians, including Bob Marley. Some Rastas continued to lead ordinary lives and went on with their everyday jobs; others retreated to the mountains to live in idealistic communes. Most of the musicians believed in letting their hair grow in luxurious dread locks and in the spiritual benefits of "herb," the marijuana that became one of the most obvious attractions of reggae music in its period of worldwide popularity with young audiences.

The roots reggae that emerged in the mid-1970s was shaped by the themes that reflected its Trenchtown rude boy antecedents in its descriptions of the life of the Kingston ghetto. The song "No Woman No Cry," composed by Vincent Ford and popularized by the Wailers, includes a touching description of a night gathering in Trenchtown.

> I remember when we used to sit
> in the government yard in Trenchtown.
> And then Georgie would make the fire light,
> Log wood burnin' through the night.
> Then we would cook corn meal porridge
> Of which I'll share with you.

Much of what we know as classic *slow beat* reggae was developed by a Kingston producer named Lee "Scratch" Perry, a nervously thin, bearded man who was often photographed in a cloud of smoke from his spliff, as a marijuana cigarette is called in the Jamaican slums. It was their work with Perry as their producer from the summer of 1970 to 1972 that shaped the Wailers' final style, and Bob Marley's singing also changed so that his phrasing and intonation were closer to Perry's. For some months Marley lived in the front room of Perry's house in Washington Gardens, and worked with him in the studio. A singer named Max Romeo, one of the many hopeful artists floating in the chaotic world of the Kingston dance halls and impromptu recording sessions, described the ambience of Perry's studio, the "Black Ark."

> Black Ark is a studio you walk in it was like somebody's study. It doesn't look nothing like a studio until you hear it. No one know what technique Perry used. Because he used those small track tape, and he seemed to get sixteen tracks stuffed into that four-track. It was a marvel—until today no one knows how he did it. The vibe of the Black Ark was like all these people gather around. It start like ten o'clock. Guys start gathering. There's a kerosene pan on the fire bubbling some dumpling, some jelly roll, some ackee and ting. Everyone throw in something to what we need. There might be a guy outside with his guitar, chantin', and Scratch is tunin' to him. Then Scratch jus' go out and say, "Let's go inside there and find riddim."[2]

Reggae, like calypso, is one of the musical styles of the African dispersion that has only tenuous links to its African backgrounds, and it is also interesting that its stylistic links to the music it borrowed the most from—black American soul—are even more thinly stretched. Reggae is a uniquely Jamaican musical style. It is connected by loose ties to Africa through its rhythmic texturing, but the rhythms themselves are not characteristically African. Although thousands of reggae songs were recorded, the style quickly settled into a series of musical trademarks that immediately identified the music as reggae. The beat of reggae was slow—slower than almost any other of the African-influenced forms—and the rhythm was carried by the bass. On recordings the bass was placed close to the front of the mix, and the tone was thickened with electronic equalization. The reggae dance beat was also less insistent. It didn't drive a crowd of dancers in the way that the beat in rock or swing does. The rhythm was a repetitive interplay between the bass, which entered on the first beat of the measure, and the drum, guitar, and keyboards that followed with the heavy afterbeat. As the reggae musicians shifted the first beat to the bass, it was used in a variety of patterns, but almost always invariably with the bass note left alone in the space. The pulse of slow beat reggae had a sustained rocking rhythm, like someone slowly moving their head from side to side, their hands following the beat in a pantomime of the rhythms. Unlike nearly every other Caribbean style, the drums have a minor role in the reggae rhythms. On some singles from the Kingston studios the drums are mixed so far back in the sound texture that it's almost impossible to hear them.

Nine years after Jamaica had become independent, in 1972, there were changes in both Jamaica's political climate and in Jamaica's music. The tall, charismatic Democratic Socialist Michael Manley was elected prime minister, and for many people in impoverished areas like Trenchtown, Jones Town, and Denham Town it seemed that a new period in the nation's life was about to begin. Finally the descendants of Jamaica's slaves could expect the long promised justice. The same year, the Wailers found themselves out of money in a cheap bed-sit in England. They had left Jamaica on a tour with soul singer Johnny Nash to promote their own single "Reggae on Broadway" for CBS Records. The tour had collapsed and they were about to give up and return home. A man who had been hanging around the band offered to try to get them a record deal, even though they were under contract to a small label back home in Kingston. In London the man contacted a white, Jamaican-born record company executive named Chris Blackwell, who owned Island Records, one of the most successful of the new rock labels. Despite the potential legal problems of their existing contract Blackwell offered the group a recording deal and a substantial enough advance to produce an album. When the Wailers returned to Kingston it was to create the music that would play a major role in the world's emerging alternative music scene.

Could Marley and the Wailers have created their music without Blackwell? Popular music isn't like traditional music—growing out of

The Tuff Gong recording studio, where Bob Marley and members of his band were attacked and wounded by still-unidentified assailants.

circumstances of culture and heritage. In the world of popular music decisions are made, money is spent, and for someone who is ambitious and talented, as Marley was, the door is left standing open. It's up to the artist to decide whether to walk through it. Blackwell had already introduced a major reggae artist, Jimmy Cliff, and the album on his Island label of the singles from the film *The Harder They Come*, including Cliff's single of the title song, had been a major international success. Cliff, however, decided to sign a contract with EMI, and Blackwell, who had begun the reggae boom, was left without a major artist to promote. When Marley, Tosh, and Bunny Wailer stopped by his office they presented a possible solution to Blackwell's dilemma. Blackwell later said about Cliff and the Wailers, "I was upset about that, because I knew the way to break him [Cliff] was through the rebel character he portrayed in the film. But when the three Wailers walked into the office, here was the real thing."[3]

There is a calculated finesse in Blackwell's characterization of the Wailers as the "real thing." In his early years working with Kingston's busy recording producers he had already licensed some of their releases for his own label. The Wailers had been making local singles, some of them minor hits, for ten years, mixing their own compositions with everything from soul songs to the Beatles and Bob Dylan. The Kingston dance halls and the local sound-system deejays were satisfied with singles, and that is what the Wailers had been producing. What Blackwell needed was an album.

With the money from their Island advance, and the income from a single they had produced for the local market on their own Tuff Gong label, the Wailin' Wailers spent a year in Kingston producing the tracks for their album. What they delivered to Blackwell were eleven tracks produced with their usual musicality, and with considerably more care in rehearsal and production than was customary in the distinctly druggy Kingston scene. Blackwell felt that although there was promise in what they had created, it needed more of what he called a " . . . drifting, hypnotic feel."[4] The essence of the album was in the tapes, in the arrangements and the songs the Wailers had created, but the instrumental work was ragged and the sound was thin. Marley played some of the guitar rhythm, and at that point he wasn't much of a band instrumentalist. Blackwell turned the tapes over to two American musicians who were working with Island in London, John Bundrick, who had played keyboards with Johnny Nash and knew the Wailers from the English tour, and Wayne Perkins, a guitarist from the famed Mussel Shoals studios in Alabama.

Working with Blackwell, Bundrick and Perkins did considerable remedial work on the tapes—covering up weak guitar lines with overdubs, strengthening bass lines, replacing or adding additional backup vocals. Then they mixed in effects from the current psychedelic trends to create the "drifting, hypnotic feel" Blackwell was looking for. Two of the tracks—both love songs—were dropped, and the remaining nine titles were remixed and packaged as *Catch a Fire*. Initially the album was released in an unwieldy package that simulated a cigarette lighter. It was hard to open the album, and after a little use the top of the jacket usually fell off. The packaging was the only ingredient in the promotion that didn't work, and the album was soon repackaged. In a less than subtle depiction of the album's "hypnotic" feel, Marley was photographed smoking spliffs in all settings. In its promotion campaign Island presented the band as a self-contained "rebel" group like a rock band, instead of what it was, a vocal trio with a backup band, like the American soul artists they were assiduously emulating. At every opportunity the photographers showed them, like Marley, in a rough setting in a cloud of smoke.

Even with the notice of the rock press and the group's tireless touring there was still a long period before there were returns on all the effort, but Marley himself never hesitated. The door had been opened for him, and without hesitation he strode through it.

"When it gets close like that I begin to feel a little frightened."

I usually ate breakfast in a cramped, white painted coffee shop on one of the main streets close to the guesthouse, and as I walked through the bar on the way from my stuffy garden room to the street I found the woman who had rented me the room was somberly turning over the pages of the *Gleaner*. This morning she was still in a house dress, pulled close over her nightgown, and her hair was loose of its customary cloth band.

"What do you think you're going to do about it?" the bar regular in the shabby white cricket costume insisted. He was trying to upset her, but in the tone of his jeering I could also sense his own concern. I leaned over her shoulder to look at the newspaper. There had been another shootout on the street between police and three men in an automobile. The men were dead and one of the policemen had been shot. Violence was so endemic in the poorer neighborhoods like Trenchtown that it often stayed on the back pages of the paper, but this had occurred in our neighborhood, at an intersection a few blocks away. The police had set up a road block to check for drugs, and the car had tried to run the barrier. The police hadn't found any drugs, and there was no clear explanation why they had started shooting, but the violence had come closer to us.

"We'll have those street hoodlums crawling in the window before the police come around to see what the trouble is. I know what the trouble is," he smirked at her, "and so do you. No one is in charge. Not the way we used to be. No one has the spunk to speak up and say what needs to be done and take charge to do it. You know that's it as well as I know it myself."

With his smirk still firmly in place he turned to me.

"The nignogs again, even on a morning like this?" he asked me with the pretence of a pleasant smile.

The woman was still leaning over the bar, staring at the newspaper, and for once she said nothing.

I was still new to Kingston, and I wasn't always able to read the expressions of the men leaning against the crumbling walls who stared up at me as I waited for a bus, or turned down a different back street around the city's dirty square. I didn't know how nervous I should be at the occasional shouts that followed me when I was walking in the poor neighborhoods. I was more and more aware now that there was a constant level of tension everywhere I went. In some parts of the city there was no water between 8 a.m. and 6 p.m., because of a drought and the government's lack of money to pay for oil for the pumps. The tourist hotels strung along the north coast had all the food they wanted, but in other parts of the island there was a shortage of most staples, even rice, and the newspapers somberly reported increasing resentment at the tourists' privileges.

I wasn't surprised that there had been a shooting close to the guesthouse. Sometimes at night, in Kingston's muffled darkness, I would walk a few blocks to a garage where several men had set up tables and crude benches. They cooked jerk chicken and jerk pig over low fires on the ground in front of the garage's open doors. By the time I got there they usually had finished with the early cooking and their charred product was laid out on a smoke blackened grill over a darkening bed of coals. They kept the meat covered with pieces of corrugated iron that one of the boys who helped them would lift with a stick when you wanted to buy something. It was rough food and I could taste the raw pepper burning my throat as I ate their chicken, but there was beer on another table, and I got everything down with a warm bottle of Red Stripe.

The night scene, with the low fire and the figures moving back and forth in front of the glowing coals, the laughing voices, the abrupt swearing when a piece of chicken fell into the fire, could have been a gentle description out of one of the Wailers' songs, but I could sense a level of tension behind everything that was said or done. Men stumbled out of the darkness, drunk enough to demand food, even if all they could find in their pockets were a few Jamaican shillings. A car would stop with rude boys, and they would saunter over to the fires, leaving car doors open with someone sitting in the shadows behind the steering wheel. They would point to what they wanted, not bothering to speak. A few bills would be dropped onto the ground as they turned to leave.

Every night when I came toward the crowd, or left the fires and their clustered figures behind me to walk back to my room with my wrapped pieces of chicken, I was beset by boys, teenagers, young men. They were selling marijuana, and every time one of them approached me I could feel the same contradictions of fear and insolence. They were dressed in crumpled T-shirts and dark trousers, most of them with hair that was left long, but cut before it got to the length of Rasta dreadlocks. It was almost as though I were being tracked by moths. One of them would flutter out of the darkness close to me, I would hear a whispered "Smoke," and then he would flutter back into the shadows. It was only after I had been approached several times without reacting that they would come to a silent decision that I wasn't a police informer. If I said something and they heard my accent, their shoulders lifted and they almost let themselves smile. They were certain that no American would be working with the Jamaican police. They would flutter closer and stay long enough to come out with whole sentences.

"I got good smoke."

"You try me, I got smoke no mon don' believe."

"You go high with my smoke, mon, you go so high they come get you with a airplane."

A tightly bound ball of marijuana about the size of an American base-ball or a British cricket ball cost five U.S. dollars. Anything I did, any movement that was unexpected, scattered the dealers like sparrows. What I felt so strongly in them now was the fear that they would be caught, and I began to smell the fear as soon as I was within a block of the garage and its smoky fires. For the first time I began to be uneasy as I walked through the dark streets, since what I could feel in the shadows beside me now was the edge of my own fear.

An advertisement in the *Gleaner*, which I had taken to reading over the sweet tea I drank to finish breakfast, announced in large type that finally I would have a chance to hear some Jamaican reggae in Jamaica. There would be an important concert with the dub poet Linton Kwesi Johnson, a new group, Black Uhuru, and the original member of the Wailers who had been most involved in Kingston's political turbulence, Peter Tosh. The supporting musicians would include the superb rhythm section of the bass player Robbie Shakespeare and the drummer Sly Dunbar.

What kind of excitement would I find in the outdoor area when I found my seat in the hustle of the crowd around me? I had been listen-ing to reggae club bands in Europe and England, and I had seen Jimmy Cliff in an ecstatic concert. Cliff, tall and imperious, a hard rude boy in the middle of the large group of sweating musicians who backed him, had filled a rapturous concert hall with an enthusiastic audience that had seen him in the film *The Harder They Come*. The first concert I'd seen with Marley had been on an amusement park stage and he'd had to work harder. There were only a few hundred of us standing on the wet concrete in the audience. Two of the original Wailers, Bunny Wailer and Peter Tosh, had left the group, partly because of Island's relentless promotion of Marley, but the vocal harmonies were sung by the vivid "I Three," the women's trio that included Marley's wife, Rita, who filled their side of the stage with the flowing movements of their long, brightly colored skirts and loose blouses. The music was as fresh and spontaneous as if they had only decided what they intended to play as they were coming onto the stage. What I found unforgettable were the moments when Marley handed off his guitar and spun across the stage in flapping, spinning moments of dancing that gave him the look of a stranded stork.

Before their second concert at the amusement park there were increas-ing problems for the groups coming to perform because of new marijuana laws. Paul McCartney, appearing with his new group Wings, had been arrested for possession not long before the Wailers returned to the same stage. Probably because of the intense media disapproval following McCartney's arrest, the police left the Wailers in peace. Backstage, the band waited to go on in a cloud of marijuana smoke, most of them smoking spliffs the size of a cigar. In the months before their new tour Eric Clapton had taken his version of Marley's song "I Shot the Sheriff" to the top of the sales charts in both Europe and the United States, and this time hundreds of people had called our company's office, begging for tickets. When the Wailers finally eased on stage the clamoring, overflow crowd was hanging from trees and blocking the park's Ferris wheel that hung silently beside the stage as they performed.

I had been looking for some of this excitement as I listened to the jukeboxes in Trenchtown bars or went by whatever dance halls were open. What I learned in the hours I sat in the night air at the Kingston concert was that the merchandising of popular music plays a very complicated role in every society. More than the music, what I learned about was Jamaica, and its struggle to find some way out of its dilemmas. In Jamaica today the annual festival, the colorful and crowded Sun Splash Reggae Festival, attracts large crowds but is held on the north coast, where the tourists congregate in the beach hotels. The mood is closer to a mainland rock festival, and the artists, new stars like Beenie Man and Jean Paul, and names like Buju Banton, Bounty Killer, Sugar Minott, Cutty Ranks, Bob Marley's son Ziggy, Yellow Man, and Ken Boothe play mostly uptempo music that goes by the name of *ragga* or *dance hall*. The rhythms are generally faster than those of the classic bands of the 1970s, and the energy of their shows suits the mood of the new dance crowd. There was another feeling in the air at this concert in Kingston a decade before.

The Gleaner had written glowingly about the musicians coming back to the islands from their international tours to perform in front of their own audience, and as the stage was being set up I could see that these musicians weren't spending their lives in Jamaica. The broad stage gleamed with the chromium of guitar stands and the shining polish of drums and a thicket of microphones. There wasn't enough money in all of the Kingston dance halls to pay for equipment on this level. The technicians were in uniforms and the scene was noisy but contained. The tickets were expensive—too expensive for a Trenchtown crowd. The front rows of seats were filled with middle-class Creole Jamaicans, many of them in family groups. There were rows of young women in light colored party dresses and carefully arranged hair. The mood was more like a school graduation than a reggae concert. The dividing line between the families in the front rows with their attractive daughters was the social gap I had observed everywhere in the Caribbean. The families in the front were light skinned, while the crowds I had seen around Kingston's downtown square and on the streets of the city's poorer neighborhoods were darker. Everywhere in the Caribbean, Creole cultures have maintained their social advantage through all of the twentieth century's upheavals.

Sitting around me on our rows of tightly packed folding chairs were younger men without families, most of them with neat hair cuts who looked like they had comfortable office jobs. Their skin was also lighter. They dressed in short-sleeved shirts and neatly pressed trousers and were laughing quietly among themselves, occasionally standing up to call to one of the pretty women in the front section of seats. The air was heavy and warm, and in the darkness above us I could see a faint haze gathering.

Even if the mood wasn't like any rock concert I'd ever attended, there was just as long a delay for the musicians to come on to the stage to check the instruments, and we had an hour to listen to loudspeakers drowning us in the usual pre-concert warm-up set. It was Kool and the Gang again. We listened to them sing "Ladies Night" three or four times in the middle of a set of their other hits. The young women in the front seats sang along to each other, smiling bright smiles and stopping every few moments to shake their heads in their pleasure at their own prettiness.

The sound of the backup group on the stage was skillfully miked, and when they finally began to work tentatively with the instruments I could hear the warm tone of Robbie's bass, and the sharp ping of Sly's cymbals. The members of the band were wearing the street costume of knit caps and T-shirts, bell-bottom trousers, and what the island-ers call trainers—running shoes in American terminology—but all of the clothes were colorfully expensive. Robbie stood impassively with his bass, looking out at the audience through carefully fitted dark glasses. This was reggae on the international level—it was as slickly presented and as polished as Kool and the Gang—and I was conscious that this Jamaican audience wanted to hear it just that way.

Linton Kwesi Johnson—slight and intense, in a dark, long sleeve knit shirt, and his eyes hidden behind dark glasses—recited his revolutionary poetry in a sing-song flow to the group's chugging rhythms. The band produced a classic reggae sound—gnarled and heavy on the lower end, with a flurry of sharp accents on the smaller drums and the offbeat kick of Sly's bass drum. There wasn't much excitement from the audience, and I was conscious that the style of Johnson's poems was much more suited to a British rock audience, white and disaffected, than it was to this middle-class Jamaican audience. As Johnson recited lines about police brutality in English cities and the injustice of the social system that left him feeling like an outsider in the land of his language and culture, the pretty young women who had been singing along with Kool and the Gang leaned across each other to talk excitedly about something else that seemed, from their expressions, to be much more interesting.

The musicianship of the group was also on an international level. These were the early years of *dubbing*—the studio technique which had been developed by several of the most adventurous producers. In their dubs, instruments in the original accompaniment tracks, even the vocal leads, were phased in and out of the mix, and repeats and echoes were added to the words and the rhythm. The purpose of dubbing, whether the producers were entirely candid about it or not, was to reproduce the effect of listening to one of the records after smoking a lot of marijuana. It became a musical form in itself, and many of the new releases at the time had a dub version to go with the standard version. Popular dubbers like King Tubby had a long line of producers waiting for them to turn to their masters. Dubbing was certainly one of the cornerstones of the rap sampling and mixing that emerged in the Bronx a decade later. What fascinated me as I listened to these musicians on the night stage was that they had worked out ways to play as if a dubber were turning the sound knobs for the microphones. The sound engineers were adding some of their own effects, but I could see Sly holding up his sticks and only playing a tom-tom at irregular intervals. Robbie would drop out on his bass line, then after a pause pick it up again. The guitarist worked with his tone control so that the offbeats abruptly became thin and brittle, then fattened out to a thick, thudding, echoing sound. The musicians had done it so often that they worked against each other's ideas in a complex and effective interplay.

Black Uhuru, who followed Johnson, was a new group—this was its first big Kingston concert. The group was composed of two tall, skinny men with dreads, Ducky Simpson and Michael Rose, and Puma Jones, an equally skinny American woman in bright layers of skirts and bandannas. With the first notes they began dancing, and the pretty young women in the front rows looked more interested. Jones swirled and spun in her sweeping skirts and the men bent from the waist in the kind of loose armed dancing I had seen Marley do on the amusement park stage. The sound system wasn't good enough for anyone to follow all of the words they were singing, but their songs were part of the classic reggae vocabulary. They were much more enthusiastically applauded than the poet, even though I could hear enough of what they were singing to realize they were also attacking the attitudes and styles of the audience in the front rows.

When I had listened to Marley's songs in California apartments or watched reggae artists perform in European concert halls I hadn't understood the realities of their world. The words they were singing—about Babylon and injustice and herb—were about these people sitting in front of them. To Jamaicans who could afford to come to the concert, the reggae attitudes were disturbing and dangerous. The romance that European and American audiences found in dreadlocks and marijuana was a difficult social problem for middle- and upper-class Jamaicans. Rastas were in open conflict with the government. Manley's social policies, which artists like Marley supported, seemed to them to be leading the country into an alliance with Castro's communist Cuba, and they considered the drugs as an illegal business that was leading to violence and corruption. It was cheerfully uncomplicated for outsiders to stand in a concert audience somewhere else and wave a toke and sing along with songs asking for some kind of social upheaval. They didn't live in Jamaica, with its poverty, its seething social unrest, and its inexperienced and indecisive government.

While I had a chance—before Peter Tosh came on stage—I went to the back of the seats and moved through the crowd. It was cooler now, and the haze had lifted. It was a pleasant, soft tropical night. I was used to concert crowds, and I kept smelling the air, wondering why I wasn't smelling marijuana. Finally I caught a faint scent of herb from some seats close to the back. I edged through the crowd and found I was standing behind three young white American teenagers, well dressed and hair properly trimmed, who were trying to hide a small spliff under the seats. When a Jamaican close to me—one of the office workers in shirt sleeves and neat slacks—noticed that I'd also smelled the marijuana he laughed and leaned close.

"Them boys from the U.S. Embassy. Nobody goin' say nothing to them." And he laughed again and shook his head.

I went from one edge of the crowd to the other. I didn't smell marijuana again. There was as little dancing—nothing like the acres of pumping dancers I was used to in the concerts outside of the country. I finally noticed one person who was dancing, a young, muscular white man with short, curly black hair who was wearing a track suit from a Brussels athletic club.

It was when Tosh was performing that I could finally sense the audience's mood clearly. He had taken strong revolutionary stands with his music, and he was identified with the country's problems with drugs. As if he wanted to provoke us he sat at the front of the stage for the first two numbers, his head turned away so that what we saw was his thoughtful profile. He was wearing a shining shirt, a bright scarf knotted around his neck, and his lanky, tall body was motionless. When he did get to his feet and go to the microphone, one his first numbers was the anthem he'd written with Marley, "Get Up, Stand Up," with its chorus, "Get up, stand up, stand up for your rights." He gestured for the audience to get on their feet, as he had done at hundreds of concerts around the world. After he'd motioned several times, a handful of the nicely dressed young women stood up, giggling with embarrassment, their carefully arranged hair softly gleaming in the reflection from the stage lights. After a moment, looking uncomfortably around them, they sat down again. The rest of the audience sat unmoving, watching Tosh pace the stage as he glared at them. What I was experiencing was not just an outdoor concert on a hazy Kingston night, I was seeing clearly the gulf between the privileged social classes that had helped bring the country to its uneasy situation and the Jamaican working people who were paying the price.

The streets around the guesthouse seemed quieter the next morning. Quieter—or more watchful. I was conscious now that there were police on the streets, that knots of young men milled in uneasy groups on the corners, their heads covered with dirty knit caps. In their tattered shirts and trousers they looked as if they were sleeping on the beach. Sometimes an old car would burst out of a dirt alleyway and skid down the street, while people along the sidewalk stared at the pavement in front of them as they walked, making certain they were seeing nothing. I was also aware that the people I ate breakfast with in the little coffee shop were like the nicely dressed young women I had seen at the concert, and often I caught them stiffly looking over their shoulders at the shifting groups of men on the streets outside the windows of our air-conditioned shop. I was beginning to see Kingston with new eyes.

One of the artists I had been most drawn to, in the lesser-known world of Kingston's local musicians, was an instrumentalist who had opened up new dimensions in dub music and in his own production work with other artists. To reggae aficionados he was almost as legendary as the major reggae artists. With Marley or Tosh, Bunny Wailer, Burning Spear, Toots and the Maytals, Jimmy Cliff, we were in the familiar world of stadium concerts and aggressively advertised tours handled by professional promotion teams. Their record labels were pushing their releases everywhere they could find space in the world's record shops. With the Kingston artists we were still in the world of singles and dance halls and deejays, with all the economic uncertainties that bedevil the alternative artist. The musician's name was Horace Swaby, and he had made his record debut with a locally produced single in 1969 titled "Iggy Iggy." He had taken the name Augustus Pablo and he had lifted the melodica, his simple plastic child's instrument, into the reggae mainstream.

Pablo had his own record shop in the east part of Kingston, on a street called Linster Close on the other side of the harbor from Trenchtown. The man who told me about it drew a cross for me on my much creased city map. I had to try two or three clattery local buses to find the neighborhood, and I found myself on a long, broad street with the bare fronts of shops lining one side. Across the street from the shops was a public building with a revolutionary mural in the Mexican style crudely painted on the empty wall. I had expected something like the noise and the crowds of Joe Gibbs's shop by the square, but despite his fame outside of Jamaica, Pablo's little shop had only two or three young men hanging around the door, baggy caps knitted in Rasta colors covering their dreadlocks, their clothes looking as if they had found them in one of the little charity shops run by the churches. Jamaica's poverty seemed to brush against anyone who wasn't part of the privileged audience I had seen the night before.

The shop had two wooden counters, one at each end of the room, with a thinly stocked rack of LPs and singles against the long wall. A spindly teenage boy was stacking singles at one end of the store, watching me out of the corner of his eye. Leaning on the other counter on his elbows, his face expressionless, was Augustus Pablo. He had pulled a bulky knitted cap over his locks, and he was dressed in a much-washed shirt and trousers. Two or three of the men from the sidewalk followed me inside, but with a nod he motioned for them to go outside again. Unlike any other record shop I'd ever been in, it was completely still. Even an unprepossessing outdoor rack of on-sale LPs close to the place where I ate breakfast had more customers than Pablo's small space. I said the expected things, that I knew his records, that I liked his music, that I had been sent to his shop by one of the producers I'd met. I said all of this with the usual enthusiasm, and I waited.

He didn't move. I could see that he was thinking about what I'd told him, and he was considering whether it was of any consequence to him. After a moment he nodded politely, but he said nothing. I waited uncomfortably to see if he might reconsider. He didn't say anything. He was tall and thin, with bony shoulders and long, expressive fingers. I could see that much even as he continued leaning over the counter. His skin was the color of sand. His face was long and sharply profiled, with a decisive nose and chin. He could almost have been a Bedouin, a Berber from the North African desert tribes. His softly expressive eyes, as he watched me moving along the record racks set up against the back wall, were the only sign that he was aware of me. The things I had said were obviously of no importance to him. I felt as though I had ventured too close to a shy antelope that would rise up on its long legs and sprint through the door if I came a step closer.

Did he have any new singles?

That was a question that came into the framework of what he did in his shop. He turned and rummaged on the shelves. He pulled a single out of a cardboard box, searched through a drawer for a rubber stamp and a pad, and he bent carefully over the single—which I could see had a blank label—and printed the title in the space with the rubber stamp. He pushed it across the counter to me with a diffident shrug.

Could I hear it?

He shrugged again and put it on the shop's worn turntable. The music was one of his dub instrumentals, built in intricate bits of sound on the tracks of the studio tape recorder. There was a melodica like the instrument he was playing on the single on an empty shelf behind him. It was an ordinary toy instrument for children, made of bright plastic, about a foot long. It had a straight, flat horn shape, with a mouthpiece that required nothing more than blowing into it. Along the side of the horn was a row of plastic keys, like an octave of a piano, that played a simple scale. This is what Pablo used to create the effects in his arrangements. In the studio he added echo and repeated tones to the "Eastern" modal melodies he improvised, and the gentle, innocent tone of the plastic toy was made to float over the thick texture of the rhythm. He also played studio keyboard instruments—pianos or a keyboard called a clavinet with a dark, growly sound, and he used the same dub techniques with their melodies. Sometimes as I listened his instrumental lines seemed like colors themselves—dark mauves, or wine scarlet, or rich earth browns. With Pablo's music I seemed always to go down into the earth, and not away from it.

The sound of music attracted new faces to the door of the shop, men in dreadlocks and dirty T-shirts, but again Pablo nodded for them to go away. It was obvious as I stood listening why there was nothing that he felt he needed to say to me. It was all there in his music.

I bought the new single and another that he put on the counter beside it with a questioning look. As I was paying he seemed to feel that we had passed some kind of barrier and he began to talk a little in a soft voice. It was hard to sell the singles now. It wasn't the way it had been three or four years ago when all of the deejays came to buy for the dances. "I know what they listenin' to now. Not the same."

I could feel that even if it wasn't "the same," Pablo would go on making the music he heard inside himself. The ordinary annoyances of the

Augustus Pablo.

music industry somehow ended outside the door of his struggling shop. He only shrugged when I asked him if I could take a picture. Again, he leaned on his counter on his elbows, his long fingers gently laced, his eyes looking off at something in the distance that he could see but that wasn't visible to me, even though I was standing in front of him.

It had taken me so long to find Pablo's shop that it was late afternoon when I came out on the street again. I was hungry and I began drifting toward the west side of the city, toward Trenchtown, looking for something to eat. This time I was conscious of the ragged lines of men sitting on the curbs with bottles who shouted after me as I walked past.

On one corner the boys who were clustered against the wall in their bright basketball shirts and thick, bunched hair turned as I came closer, and two or three of them took a step toward me. I crossed the street to a spattering of laughter. I found an Indian restaurant close to the square, and at that moment I needed the reassuring richness of curry and rice. It was crowded inside, with a dozen Indian couples and several Jamaicans who looked like they worked on the docks. There was beer on the tables and a noisily cheerful mood as I waited for the overworked, small waitress in a wilted sari to get around to me.

When I came outside again the city was almost dark. I could see the last fading splash of a sunset over the dark bunched leaves of the trees on the Trenchtown streets. There seemed to be more people out on the pavements now, and more people watching me. I began walking back to where I thought I might find a bus; then, with a barely audible sigh, like an exhaled breath, the city's power failed, and I was left in the street in the darkness. As I tried to keep moving, groping along the fronts of the shops and the small houses I felt a surge of the same fear that I had sensed in the boys hoping to sell me marijuana. I stopped in the darkness and slid a few steps to the wall of a house and stood waiting for enough light so I could find my way back to the bus line. It was time to leave Jamaica.

11 ✳ To Feel the Spirit

Gospel Song in the Great Churches of Harlem

I think of New York as a city of statues, monuments, and memorials. Monuments to wars, statues to figures out of New York's history, memorials to old triumphs and commemorations. Some are new, most are old—left now in places where their significance has long been forgotten, statues left stranded in city parks, bronze busts in neighborhoods where their only role is that of a pigeon roost. At the moment of their unveiling they had some meaning for the crowds that gathered for the speeches and the music, but with time's inevitable drift, the statues and plaques, the larger-than-life busts, were left behind, their significance forgotten. The people who knew those faces, or felt some identity with these heroic figures, the people who could imagine the person within what was now only a bronze bust—they moved away from their old neighborhood to other New York streets where the statues and their bronze messages belonged to someone else. Of the statues in the city that I pass as I walk today, the only one that feels like *its* neighborhood is the shining, new figure of Adam Clayton Powell Jr. at the corner of 125th Street and the broad avenue newly named for him, in the heart of the new Harlem.

The sculpted metal shows a man striding upward against the wind, his coat flying in the gusts, and his face lit with determination. Whatever last photos the media delighted to print of him with a drink in one hand and an attractive woman nearby as he carried on his congressional duties from exile in the Florida Keys— this was who he was when he was a young leader in the struggles of Harlem's great churches to bring their people through the Depressions, the wars, and the racism they confronted every day of their lives. Powell, in his strident pose, is clearly at home on 125th Street.

Harlem has changed in many ways since I first took the A train up to 125th Street in 1958. The long slide into discouraged poverty that left its shops struggling to survive in a racially deprived economy, that left many of Harlem's young men and women in deteriorating

Statue of Adam Clayton Powell Jr. at Adam Clayton
Powell Jr. Blvd. and 125th St., Harlem.

apartments facing unemployment or a meaningless job, finally was
brought to halt, and in the next decades, after a prolonged struggle, it
was turned around. Nearly half a century later, Harlem's musical show-
place, the Apollo Theatre, has a new interior and a renovated building
front. A block away across the street is the newly expanded and vital
art museum, the Studio Museum of Harlem, with its presentation of
the work of Harlem's African American artists and their artistic roots
and influences. In the other direction from the Apollo, at the corner of
125th Street and Adam Clayton Powell Jr. Boulevard, is the tall, asser-
tive, modern government office building that has brought jobs to the
neighborhood, and with the jobs the sense that Harlem hasn't been
forgotten.

Often in the early 1960s, when I journeyed up to Harlem to meet a musician for a rehearsal or to spend an afternoon on 135th Street at the Schomburg Collection, the center for research into black culture, I had the uncomfortable sense that in the middle of this jammed city it would be possible to set up small truck farms on some of the battered blocks. So many buildings had been torn down and there had been so little re-building that blocks of empty space were all that was left. Only the soil would have to be reworked, since under the rubble was a dead earth of glass shards and crushed brick and plaster.

On many corners, behind clumsily bound lengths of chicken wire or sections of old cyclone fencing, farming, at least on a neighborhood scale, had already begun. People living in the nearby buildings had hope-fully planted community gardens, marking out the beds of flowers and vegetables with pieces of broken brick and decorating the fences with dented metal hub caps or old lengths of chain. On many of the lots there were weathered American flags hanging from the fences. In some sec-tions Harlem had been forced to accept the city's misconceived efforts to move people out of their homes. The city's large scale programs were meaningless to the struggling families who were dealing with the every-day reality that the buildings where they were living desperately needed repairs or were suffering from terminal landlord neglect. Most of the newly constructed housing projects that replaced entire blocks of once imposing town houses and apartment buildings with ungainly clumps of drab buildings in an effort to eliminate poverty were as dismally unsuc-cessful in Harlem as they were everywhere else in the United States.

Through all of the changes, though, there was still enough of the old Harlem, with its rows of once elegant apartments and town houses, to preserve its identity. It is this sense of identity, of a section of a city find-ing itself, that has been revitalized, and now, as you leave the streaming traffic along the main avenues and walk into the quieter side streets, you see that many of the old homes that managed to endure through the years of renewal have begun a new cycle of restoration. Along 125th Street there are new stores, a bustle of shoppers. There is a heady sense on block after block that a new cycle of growth and change in Harlem has begun.

In other ways, however, Harlem hasn't changed at all. On Sunday mornings along the busy avenues or on the quiet side streets, the side-walks are busy with chatting groups of women wearing bright, fash-ionable ensembles crowned with extravagant hats. On other corners there are women in white dresses, white stockings, and white shoes, talking as busily. Young men dawdle on building steps in newly ironed shirts and ties, gesturing with their prayer books. Families wait to cross a street, holding respectfully subdued children by the hand, the little girls in starched dresses and shiny shoes, their brothers in pressed slacks, dress shirts, and carefully knotted neckties. On Sunday mornings in Harlem it feels as though everyone still goes to church, in the same way that this outpouring of faith continues to be one of the unifying strengths in communities in every part of black America.

Although to someone not familiar with the streets the crowds on the church steps might look as though they were made up of families who shared their religious beliefs, the churches present a diverse assembly of faiths and denominations. Perhaps the best-known, the Abyssinian Baptist Church, on 138th Street, is a solidly impressive neo-gothic gray stone structure in the middle of a crowded block of older apartment buildings. On Sunday mornings a continual stream of limousines brings the members of the congregation, and the worshippers pausing for a moment on the steps have a style of dress and an ease with one another that comes from decades of economic security and a life-long association with their church. When its new building opened its doors in 1923 its pastor was the powerful Adam Clayton Powell Sr., who had led the church to Harlem from its old building on West 40th Street, behind what is now the Port Authority Terminal Building. His son, Adam Clayton Powell, Jr., carried on his father's defiant struggle against racial discrimination, and it was from the pulpit of Abyssinian Baptist that he took the first steps that ultimately led to his long years of service in the U.S. House of Representatives.

For many years the Harlem churches were isolated in their Upper Manhattan neighborhoods, but now Sundays take on a different look. This is the only time of the week when I see many white faces anywhere in Harlem except along 125th Street. On Sunday mornings, streams of tourists collect to wait for the services. At the corner of Adam Clayton Powell Boulevard and 138th Street, half a block from the Abyssinian Baptist Church, vendors sell soft drinks and donuts. Along the sidewalk leading to the church steps there are exhibits of African artifacts for sale. The line of tourists, waiting outside until all of the church's congregation have found seats, is often four abreast and stretches for a block and a half down the boulevard and around the corner of 137th Street. Harlem's churches have become an international tourist attraction. Often included in the announcements are names of the countries represented by the visitors, and guests are sometimes asked to stand and be acknowledged by the congregation.

Abyssinian Baptist has an opulent interior, as light-filled as the gray stone of its outer façade is somber and withdrawn. The interior is a contrast of white marble and red plush, with a semi-circular balcony supported by round pillars carved in a Romanesque style and a wall of stained glass that turns the sun into a kaleidoscope of color. The pastor was comfortably at ease as he read the weekly announcements and made an emotional request for people to attend a demonstration the next Saturday to protest the shooting death of a young man on the eve of his wedding the week before. The church is considered to be the largest Protestant organization in the United States, and its pastor, Dr. Calvin O. Butts III, a slim, serious, black-robed figure, is a community leader who has had an impact on national as well as city issues. As he ended the announcements he nodded toward the balcony and informed the congregation that among the guests that day was a group of Russian engineers, who had made the trip from their research station in Siberia.

On Sundays when the weather is good, the line of tourists hoping to find a place in the balcony of Abyssinian Baptist is too long for everyone to find a seat, and many turn and walk half a block east on 137th Street to the "Mother Church," an African Methodist Episcopal Zion Church, the oldest African American congregation in the United States. A simple sign indicating that this *is* the Mother Church hangs over the sidewalk, and a small announcement board wired to the iron fence beside the entrance lists the names of the church's most illustrious members: Harriet Tubman, Sojourner Truth, and Frederick Douglass. For many years it was known as "The Freedom Church," since the three members were leading figures in the struggle for racial equality, and it was a poorly kept secret that the church functioned as a station on the Underground Railway.

The church is smaller than its neighbor, Abyssinian Baptist, and its stone façade has an architectural kinship to the London churches going back to seventeenth-century Tudor architecture. It was built about the same time as the edifice on 138th Street, and its interior has also absorbed much of the character of England's Victorian cathedrals. Rich, dark woods contrast with white walls, and the stained glass echoes the designs of the same era. When I arrived there the church was less crowded than the Abyssinian Baptist, and the clusters of worshippers in suits and ties, the women in tailored clothes and elaborate hats, were seated between tourist couples in sweatshirts and blue jeans. The tourists were welcomed as a part of a long invocation by a woman in a white robe who addressed the congregation from the pulpit.

It would be almost impossible to count the churches of Harlem. Alongside the dozens of established churches, old brownstone houses on many of the sidestreets have been converted to Baptist congregations, where each of the small congregations is the fulfillment of the dreams and ambitions of an individual pastor. In the sections of Harlem closer to the East River there are still storefront churches, often with a gust of singing coming through the doors to the sidewalk during evening ser-

The African Methodist Episcopal Zion Church—the
Mother Church—137th St., New York City.

vices. There is a modern, bustling religious bookstore on 116th Street
between Fifth Avenue and Lenox Avenue, Zoe Christian Bookstore, and
within two hundred yards of its doors there are four large churches. On
a Saturday afternoon in December it was crowded with listeners for a
record release party featuring a singer from one of the nearby congregations, Lester Robinson, who stood on a square carpeted stage at the rear
of the store and performed songs from his forthcoming CD. In all the
years I have known Harlem I've never seen a club presenting a blues
singer, unless it was a lounge-blues performer like Jimmy Witherspoon,
but on Sunday morning Harlem's hundreds of churches stir with the
songs of faith and worship.

Someone who doesn't know the churches probably has the impression that in each of them they'll hear the rhythmic, fervent singing that
is the widespread perception of Harlem's gospel music, but each of

the denominations has its own form of services. At the Salem United Methodist Church, only a few blocks south of Abyssinian Baptist and the Mother Church, at Adam Clayton Powell Jr. Boulevard and 129th Street, the choir sings with the careful diction and the carefully rehearsed ecclesiastical harmonies of the choirs in the Episcopal churches where I grew up in Pittsburgh. An experienced, encouraging pianist assists the nervous singing of four girls about twelve and thirteen in blue robes who are performing their first songs for the congregation. Closer to 125th Street on the same side of the boulevard, the Shiloh Baptist Church has a louder, more emotional service, led by the choir, in the Baptist style that has become a trademark of the gospel sound, and its balcony is filled with tourists.

Most of the tourists who waited in line for the service at the Abyssinian Baptist Church the Sunday after the New Year certainly expected they would hear gospel music, but as the sunlight streamed down into the rotunda through jeweled windows, the congregation and the visitors listened raptly to a performance of Handel's *Messiah* by a small orchestra, including several young white musicians who might have been music students, the church's choir, and professional soloists. It was performed as originally scored, with the arias sung in a high baroque style to considerable applause.

In Harlem, as in the churches in every city, it is the apostolic congregations, the Holiness churches, where the music stirs the worshippers to shouts of exultation. Across 125th Street, still on Adam Clayton Powell Jr. Boulevard, is the large, modern Greater Refuge Temple, with its pastor, Bishop William L. Bonner, who has led the church since 1961. Bishop Bonner was the driving force behind the rebuilding program that created the modern temple building which opened in 1966. Thirty years of his sermons, titled *The Hour of Truth*, can be purchased on tape or CD in the Temple's bookstore, the Last Word Bible and Book Store, in the W. L. Bonner Youth Enrichment Center on 124th Street, around the corner from the Temple. Churches in Harlem are wedded to the community with bonds of more than worship and faith—there is a strong commitment to the community and its needs.

The large choir in the Greater Refuge Temple fills rows of seats behind the pulpit, and among the singers in the front rows are fervent soloists, both men and women, whose voices become the impassioned "call" of the call and response singing, responding to the surging "response" of the choir. The congregation spends much of the service on its feet, many with tambourines they have brought with them in purses or in cloth bags. There are the usual rows of tourists against the back of the church, but the seats in front of them are filled with worshippers. On a Sunday morning after the New Year the message of the singers and of Bishop Bonner's greeting was that the New Year should tell us to celebrate. "We have come to another year. We have come through the year that passed! We are still here!" The service was a joyous celebration. At one moment, as the choir swayed in swells of song, one of the men in the choir's front row stepped forward and began dancing exultantly, responding to the message of the song.

The streets are quiet on Sundays, except for the people streaming into the churches for the 11 A.M. services. 125th Street resumes its tempo of shopping in the afternoons, when the church services are over, but the traffic is lighter. There is none of the clogged impatience of the weekdays. The community catches up with its social life. A few blocks south of the celebrated churches, Abyssinian Baptist and the Mother church, there is a storefront at 2236 Adam Clayton Powell Jr. Boulevard, its window filled with jazz CDs, jazz magazines, jazz posters, and jazz memorabilia. It is a small, idealistic venture named Big Apple Jazz that presents a variety of jazz groups playing for contributions to the kitty in its back room every afternoon and evening. The shop sells books, postcards, and CDs, as well as coffee and something to eat while you listen. The shop also has a unique view of Harlem's churches.

The man behind the counter was in his thirties, friendly and tousled, a jazz fan who freely admitted that for the owner the shop was more of a crusade than a business venture.

"Do the church members like the tourists?," I asked him.

"Some people, I know, some of the people in the congregation, they're not very comfortable with it, but as long as the people who come respect what's happening then they don't mind. Just so people don't get up and leave when a prayer's going on! But I know the churches like it because it means some money, and they all need money. The Temple across the street," he gestured toward the window, "they come here and they talk about how they have to have a new roof. You see how big that building is! What's a new roof going to cost? They talk to me because they'd like some of my jazz musicians to play for services, but how would that help, even if I could get somebody to try it? But the churches like people to come—just some Sundays they have so many they don't know where to put them."

I often sat close to children in the congregations, sitting patiently beside their parents in their best clothes, and although there were sleepy nods of the head as the sermons went on, I didn't think they found the hours to be unpleasant.

"You didn't mind going to church, even spending the whole day there because you'd meet everybody you know. Everybody was going to spend the day in church, just like you were."

Doctor Robert Stephens, a professor of World Music at the University of Connecticut, leaned back in the chair of his crowded office. He is an enthusiastic, engaging, solidly built man in his fifties, who grew up in Savannah, Georgia, the grandson of the Reverend R. J. Dinkins, the minister of Savannah's Tremont Temple. The church Sundays were part of his life.

"At 6 a.m., we would all get up and my mother would prepare breakfast and we would have family prayers and everybody would have to recite a Bible verse. And everybody does it! That's a part of the tradition, that long prayer on Sunday morning and then everybody recites a Bible verse. If you're really young you might get away with something like 'Jesus wept,' which is about as short as you can get, but after that you've got to come up with something with a little more substance."

For Dr. Stephens, growing up in a southern city fifty years ago, it was the omnipresent reality of segregation that sharpened his response to his family's church Sundays, and his memories of those years confirm the emotional strength of the black church bringing comfort in a situation in which he and the others in the congregation felt they had no strength at all.

"Now the church—you know, we typically think of a structure or an institution, like the church, we think of it as a religious institution. But within our community it was a religious institution and it was also a social institution. It did more than just address our religious needs, it also addressed our other needs as well, and that was because, you know, the only other place where blacks had any control over their lives at that time, and it wasn't much, was school, because the schools were segregated. Every other aspect of your life was controlled."

For someone like him, then just a boy, the slights and the humiliations he barely understood framed his life, and strengthened his relationship to his church.

"One of the things that used to infuriate me to no end was my grandmother, who believed in those twenty-five-cents-a-week insurance policies. And these white guys would come every week to collect this money, and they would call her by her first name. But they would call her by her first name in such a way that you could feel it was demeaning. So when I say that the church was the only place that we had control of our lives—these other things you could not control. We were taught we had to believe and act in a certain way. If I saw you walking along the sidewalk with your wife, we were taught and we were conditioned—we immediately got off the sidewalk and waited until you and your wife passed. And whatever you do, don't look a white woman in the eye. Never look her in the eye! There were so many things in our lives that were so controlling, so when you got to church you tossed those things away. When the women get up and talk—and it's true with the men, too—that's the one time they can really get in touch with any sort of feelings they have of who they are. That's why religion was so important in the black community."

As he sat in his office, the door open for any students with a situation that needed his help, it was still possible to glimpse in his friendly face the boy that he'd been on Savannah Sunday mornings. Did he think of Sunday as a difficult day—with its hours of church and its morning prayers?

"I went astray, of course." He shook his head at the memory, and it was clear he didn't go very *far* astray. "I mean you talked a lot and you met everybody and of course there were girls and you'd see the girls and you'd talk, and you formed friendships and alliances, and your families, they did the same thing. That was something very positive and affirming. It wasn't, you know, like our family goes to church and that family goes. Everybody went! And if you didn't go, they would talk about you! They want to know what's going on. Why is this person not here? Everything just closed down for that particular moment because it was such a crucial thing in our lives."

Did the aura of well-dressed prosperity I had experienced in some of Harlem churches also carry over to the Savannah church of his childhood—for his own family of five children, with his hard-working father, a laborer, at its head? He shrugged.

"You know, there was a different sensibility about those kinds of material things. To be sure, we wanted to look good. Everybody wants that, and you do your best. In my family there were four boys and one girl, and we were all about the same size. The little monies that I would make when I began playing with that little band—I would have to come home and bring a portion of that home with me. My youngest brother used to wait tables at the Boar's Head, that was a famous restaurant there, he would have to bring money home, and those collected funds were sometimes used to buy things. But you know, we all wore the same shoes and sometimes the shoes would wear out and you would cut out a piece of cardboard and you put the cardboard in the shoes until you got them fixed. The point is, sometimes you didn't look that great, but people didn't—not in church—they didn't rag on you about it."

In the introduction to their 1867 collection *Slave Songs of the United States*, one of the three young editors wrote, "I never heard a secular song among the Port Royal freemen, and never saw a musical instrument among them . . . We have succeeded in obtaining only a few songs of this character."[1] A large majority of the songs that the editors included in their collection were the sacred songs that were soon to become known as spirituals. Although the editors felt that they had to apologize for this imbalance, a modern commentator, Lawrence Levine, in an article titled "Slave Songs and Slave Consciousness" suggested that the young Sea Island song collectors got their proportions about right.[2]

> It is possible that we have a greater number of religious [than] nonreligious songs because slaves were more willing to sing these ostensibly innocent songs to white collectors who in turn were more anxious to record them, since they fit easily with their positive and negative images of the Negro. But I would argue that the vast preponderance of spiritual over any other sort of slave music, rather than being the result of accident or error, is instead an accurate reflection of slave culture during the antebellum period. Whatever songs the slaves may have sung before their wholesale conversions to Christianity in the late eighteenth and early nineteenth centuries, by the latter century spirituals were quantitatively and qualitatively their most significant musical creation. In this form of expression slaves found a medium which resembled in many important ways the worldviews they had brought with them from Africa, and afforded them the possibility of both adapting to and transcending their situation.[3]

What Levine also noted about the Sea Island songs was that "sacred songs" and melodies strayed over their boundaries and were put to a wide variety of uses in slave society, and he cited one of the editors of *Slave Songs*, Lucy McKim.

> It is significant that the most common form of slave music we know of is the sacred song. I use the term "sacred" not in its present usage as something antithetical to the secular world; neither the slaves nor their African forbearers ever drew modernity's clear line between the sacred and the secular. The usage to which the spirituals were put is an unmistakable indication of this. They were not sung solely or even primarily in churches or praise houses, but were used as rowing songs, field songs, work songs, and social songs. On the Sea Islands during the Civil War, Lucy McKim heard the spiritual "Poor Rosy" sung in a wide variety of context and tempo.
>
> "On the waters, the oars dip 'Poor Rosy' to an even andante; a stout boy and girl at the hominy-mill will make the same 'Poor Rosy' fly, to

keep up with the whirling stone; and in the evening, after the day's work is done, 'Heab'n shall-a be my home' (the final line of each stanza) peals up slowly and mournfully from the distant quarters."[4]

The religious festivals of the American frontier, the camp meetings, are now largely forgotten, but they played a decisive role in shaping the first black religious song. As James H. Smylie described their beginnings:

> In the start, Baptists, Methodists, and Presbyterians united to hold camp meetings, but as time went on the Methodists and Baptists accepted camp meetings more readily than the Presbyterians. The meetings became known for providing social contacts for the lonely frontiersmen. They were also marked by fervent preaching, praying, and singing, which often lasted for days. There was criticism of the "nervous" behaviour caused by the religious excitement. At a meeting at Cane Ridge, Ky., in 1801, attended by an estimated 10,000 to 25,000 people, observers noted such manifestations as jerking, rolling, dancing, running, singing, laughing, and barking..
>
> For the sake of decency and order, some patterns and procedures began to emerge to organize the activity of the thousands of persons who attended. For example, encampments of tents and other facilities were arranged in rectangular, horseshoe or circular shapes, enclosing the open-air auditorium. Within the outdoor auditorium were places for pulpits, benches, and "anxious seats" for those particularly concerned about their religious condition. Often, out of these meetings, religious classes and societies were organized, and these sometimes provided the only means of moral discipline found in an otherwise unruly West.[5]

If any one event could be singled out as the source for the slave spiritual it would be the camp meeting. As the meetings grew in popularity, families came from hundreds of miles around to the great outdoor assemblies. The light from hundreds of campfires and the torches illuminating the crude stages erected for the preaching could be seen from miles away across the cleared fields. The worshippers brought everyone from their households with them, including their slaves, and the camp meetings tolerated the presence of free black families who also were crowding into the new lands. The families traveled in wagons, usually drawn by oxen, plodding at a pace so slow that most people left the wagons and strolled alongside. The meetings lasted for days, and the wagons were filled with clothing and provisions. At the site of the meeting the women slept inside the wagons, sheltered behind canvas curtains, while the men rolled up in blankets under the wagons or in small shelters that they built close by.

Among slave holders there was a long, divisive debate on the duty of the masters to allow their slaves to participate in religious services. The masters were satisfied that they could find justification for slavery in the Bible, but there was also the uneasy consideration that if their Christian faith permitted them to have power over the lives of other men and women, then it was their duty to bring these "less fortunates" into the shelter of the tent of Christian faith. This was a troublesome area of debate throughout the centuries of slavery in the United States. If the slaves also were baptized as Christians did this alter the master's relationship to them? What would be the effect of the continued cries for freedom in the Biblical stories of the deliverance of the Jews from their bondage in Egypt?

Every slave owner dealt with the problem in his or her own way. The only thing that they agreed on with any consistency was that the slaves should never be educated enough so they could read the biblical texts themselves. On some plantations slaves were excluded from the worship of the owner's family and there was a separate service for the slaves in a large cabin, where a white minister led the prayers and directed the singing. The most common solution to the problem was to permit the house slaves to be present in the plantation's chapel, but strictly segregated in a section of crude benches at the back of the small structure, or along the walls. The music the slaves heard was psalmody—"lining out"—a line of a psalm chanted by the priest and repeated by the family. Hymns were simple, sung in unison, and the emphasis was on the commonplace words intoning the promises of salvation and the lifting of the burden of sin. In some parts of the South there were itinerant musicians who conducted singing "music schools" and taught elemental note reading and singing in harmony. The kind of basic chord patterns which much later were termed the "barber shop harmonies" of the first arranged spirituals had their roots in these simple learning sessions.

The fervid music of the camp meetings burst the bonds of these formal restraints. To reach a vast crowd of strangers who came from myriad national backgrounds the songs had to be simple and immediately memorable. The melodies were often borrowed from well-known popular songs, and their new texts emphasized the familiar themes of Christ's love and the hope of salvation. To inspire the streams of people gathered in the fields under the billowing tents or around the rough platforms and lecterns, the songs generally took two forms. One was the familiar form of a song with verse and chorus. The preacher himself—or a song leader working with him—sang the verses, often from a printed song sheet, then led the worshippers in the chorus. The other form of song that swept across the massed worshippers was the equally well-known call and response. The song leader sang a single line of the text, and the worshippers answered with a short, unvarying musical phrase that was repeated as long as the song leader could find new phrases to embellish his text. For the Africans scattered through the crowds of the camp meetings the call and response was a song form that they knew well. These responsive styles were spread throughout the tribes of West Africa. As they added their voices to the responses they were returning to a vivid memory of their own past.

The publication of *Slave Songs of the United States* in 1867, the appearance in a Philadelphia magazine four years earlier of the first article on slave music, written by one of the book's editors, Lucy McKim, the closely observed descriptions of singing on a slave plantation by Fanny Kemble in her book finally published in 1863—all of this was evidence of a widespread interest in the forms of African American music that had emerged in the years of slavery. But it was in October 1871, when a tired, shabby, frightened group of African American students from a struggling missionary college in Nashville sang for the first time before a poorly attended white prayer meeting in a church in Cincinnati that the sacred songs of the slaves burst into the public consciousness. Eighteen chaotic and bewildering months later the little group, with the new name The Fisk Jubilee Singers, would appear in a London mansion as honored guests before an excited crowd of English nobility to sing a private recital for Queen Victoria.

In his moving book *Dark Midnight When I Rise* Andrew Ward has told the story of the Fisk Jubilee Singers, and at the same time he has drawn a complex, multi-faceted picture of the Anglo-American world that wept and cheered the singers at their concerts and then refused to share a dining room or the seats of a railroad car with them or let them find a bed in a poor rooming house in their endless travels.[6] The career of the singers was so well documented at the time in newspaper pieces, articles, and in their own memoirs, that virtually everything is known about the group's travails as well as their astonishing success, but there is still something particularly effecting in the story of their first months of singing together, when they sang shyly for each other in their dormitory rooms.

As Ward makes clear, the members of the first group of singers had come to Fisk University from small towns and farms scattered across the South, and they were young and homesick. The school was only one of many educational institutions that had been established by northern Methodist churches to provide some education for the newly freed slaves, and the funds were stretched pitifully thin. At that point in the school's struggle to survive, Fisk was occupying provisional quarters in an abandoned hospital on a low-lying stretch of poor land outside of Nashville. Often there wasn't enough food for the students or their teachers, and in the winter months they had to wear double layers of clothing to keep warm. Everyone lived with an uneasy despair at the prospect that the school might be forced to close at any moment.

In their bare rooms a few of the women students found that they shared a store of religious songs from their own memories of slavery; three of the singers who left on the first tour were ex-slaves. They also were familiar with songs that they had sung in their churches as children. In the beginning, though, they had to find ways to sing the songs together, since every congregation or praise house gathering sang them in their own way. The students hadn't realized that there were so many uniquely individual ways to sing their much-loved songs. But as they persevered they found that as they shared ways to sing the hymns together they also learned new songs in the exchanges. One of the singers, Ella Sheppard, remembered that they sat on the floor, since they didn't have chairs in their rooms, singing "softly, learning from each other."[7]

Still without any thought of performing in public they decided to sing for the school's president Adam Knight Spence, who wrote, "In the summer of 1871, when Fisk University was still in the old hospital buildings, one day there came into my room a few students with some air of mystery. The door was shut and locked, the window curtains were drawn, and, as if it were something they were ashamed of, they sang some of the old time religious slave songs now known as Jubilee songs."[8]

The students began to rehearse daily with the school's treasurer George L. White. He drilled them tirelessly, using his violin to correct pitches, correcting pronunciation and training them to breathe as a choir. Since they did so much of their singing in their rooms or in White's study they became skilled in singing in a pianissimo that was almost a whisper but still had the intensity of their full voices. As White told them, "If a tiger should step behind you, you would not hear the fall of his foot, yet all the strength of the tiger would be in that tread."[9] As Andrew Ward concluded, "The result was a sweet, coherent, monolithic sound that rose and soared and faded like a passing breeze."[10] Within a few months their pianissimo choruses were to move audiences of thousands to tears.

White has sometimes been criticized for his "refinement" of the songs the students brought to him, but that kind of judgement fails to consider the situation they faced as the first African Americans that many of their audiences had ever seen. In some towns people followed them down the streets, pointing and calling out to them. The bloodiest war in America's history had just been fought, in part to bring them their freedom, and they were watched and their habits studied as if they were from a different universe. Both in their manner and their singing they had to prove over and over again to their audiences that as a race they were worthy of the sacrifice that had been made. It was their singing that opened doors, but it was their carefully respectful personal bearing that opened their audience's hearts.

As the original Jubilee Singers traveled on their exhausting tours, they sold thousands of copies of a songbook with their melodies to help meet the expenses of their travel and lodging. The example of the books, and the effect of the groups' performances—as well as the interest in singing groups from other black institutions like Tuskegee and Hampton who hurried to follow their success—led other collectors to continue in the path of the editors of *Slave Songs of the United States* and search out any spirituals and songs that lingered from the years of slavery. The excitement was like the enthusiastic efforts by young white musicians and researchers to trace the surviving rural blues artists a hundred years later. As the new group of collectors quickly learned, there was still a rich culture of song to be harvested. In her conscientious work for her own book *Slave Songs of the Georgia Sea Islands* Lydia Parrish listed many of the collections that were the result of this determined effort to preserve these fading traditions.[11]

Jubilee Songs as Sung by the Jubilee Singers of Fisk University, Theo. F. Seward, New York: 1872.

Spiritualles. Sung by the Carolina Singers (Fairfield Normal Institute): 1872–73.

Cabin and Plantation Songs, Thomas P. Fenner, New York: 1874.

Old Plantation Hymns, W. E. Barton, Boston: 1899.

Southern Thoughts for Northern Thinkers, Jeanette Robinson Murphy, New York: 1904.

Calhoun Plantation Songs, Emily Hallowell, Boston: 1907.

Negro Folk Songs, Hampton Series, Natalie Curtis-Burlin, New York: 1918–19.

Negro Folk Rhymes, Thomas W. Talley, New York: 1922.

St. Helena Island Spirituals, N. G. J. Ballanta, New York: 1925.

Befo' de War Spirituals, Edward Avery McIllhenny, Boston: 1933.

Negro Spirituals and Work Songs, John Work, NewYork: 1940.

The sustained interest in the spirituals led to a reaction by some writers, who questioned the role of the slave singers in the creation of this great body of song. In their articles they pointed out that the obvious sources for many of the melodies were to be found in the frontier hymns and the camp meeting songs of the white settlers, and that the new hymns were a shared endeavor. This research culminated in the book *White Spirituals in Southern Uplands*, by George Pullen Jackson, which documented the extent of the borrowings in the spirituals from the standard white hymns and biblical verses popular during this period.[12] Jackson had done his work with considerable care, but as an article on the spiritual in the *Grove Dictionary of Music and Musicians* points out " . . . priority of publication is hardly proof of origin where folk music is concerned, especially when one body of music in question is that of a group whose illiteracy was enforced by law."[13] What is perhaps more important is that Jackson didn't fully emphasize the crucial importance of the *way* that the spirituals were sung. It was in the rhythmic shifts, the shadings of tonal emphasis that the African presence melded with the literalism of the commonplace texts. It was as voices lifted in song that the words and music, the exhortations and pleas of the spirituals, gave meaning to the first stirrings of a new African American consciousness.

The music, as well as the transcendent experience of the African American church, its sacred songs, spirituals, and sermons, was spread through early recordings before either jazz or blues made its appearance on records. Although it is customary to think of the 1920s as the "Jazz Age," a glance at the catalogs of the companies selling what was called "race music" makes it clear that sacred artists had as strong a hold as the secular performers on the black audience. The first sermon was recorded by Calvin P. Dixon, "The Black Billy Sunday," in 1925. The recordings of the Atlanta minister Reverend J. M. Gates, whose career began only a short time later, were such a major commercial success that other companies quickly searched for their own sacred artists. Gates's steady output was soon joined by the recordings of ministers like Reverend A. W. Nix and Reverend Edward Dickinson. By the late 1920s the releases by the guitar evangelist Blind Willie Johnson were outselling the new recordings by the blues singer Bessie Smith. The haunted gospel performances of the pianist and singer Arizona Dranes foreshadowed so much that would be "new" in religious song many decades later, and gospel quartets emerging from the small steel mill town of Bessemer, Alabama, renewed the spiritual tradition that had its roots in the singing of the Fisk Jubilee singers.

The popularity of the recordings also was the result of a basic change in the style of sacred black music. The slow tempos of the older spirituals had given way to the music of the new churches, the Pentecostal congregations, with a more emotional style that was rhythmically closer to African musical roots. For the white Pentecostal congregations that also developed their music during these years, the new songs marked a return to the emotionalism of the camp meetings. The Pentecostal movement, or Holiness churches, as they are sometimes called, emerged from a "sanctified moment," a deeply influential revival meeting in Los Angeles, the Azuza Street Revival, which continued from 1906 to 1909. Already in 1907 a group inspired by the new message established a Pentecostal congregation in Detroit, and in 1921 the *Gospel Pearls* hymnal collected examples of the new gospel idiom.

To lend the new recordings some of the excitement of the church meetings, the preachers were recorded with their "congregations," though in practice this generally meant only a handful of voices shouting comments and responses in the recording studio. The men and women who assisted on many of Gates's releases became so familiar that their names were included on the record labels. Gates also recorded hymns, but it was his sermons that attracted his large audiences. His preaching moved with determined energy, and an electrifying emotional quality. Gates remains, despite all the years of documentary recording that have followed him, the best representative of the sermons typical of southern churches during this period. Many of the rural artists whose sermons were documented by the field collectors for the Library of Congress a decade later had clearly been influenced by Gates's recordings, and he continued to leave his imprint on the recorded sermon long after his death. In a company catalogue photo of him in the pulpit he is a strong, dark skinned, burly man, his immense energy clearly evident even through the grainy quality of the catalog reproduction.

In the 1930s the now widely differing strands of black worship in song were drawn together by the pioneering work of a successful blues artist turned sacred song writer named Thomas A. Dorsey, who had worked as a duo for several years as pianist and song writer with guitarist Hudson Whittaker, known as "Tampa Red." Their recordings were released under the name "Tampa Red and Georgia Tom." Dorsey had already begun to write sacred material when he was performing as a blues artist, and in 1932 he was to create one of the classic gospel hymns, "Take My Hand Precious Lord." The song was an inspired arrangement that Dorsey had stitched together from two well-known hymns by Richard Allen, a widely influential ante-bellum Philadelphia African American preacher and composer of sacred songs.

What was even more important among Dorsey's many innovations was his founding, with artist Sallie Martin, of the Gospel Singers Convention at the Pilgrim Baptist Church in Chicago in 1932. It became a yearly event, led by Dorsey, and it brought singers and musicians from everywhere in the United States to Chicago. The conventions gave to the performers of sacred music a consciousness of the importance of their music to the African American community. Sparked by the new vitality of the sanctified churches, the emergence of vivid artists like Sister Rosetta Tharpe and Clara Ward and the cautious acceptance by the mainstream white audience of unaccompanied gospel quartets like the Dixie Humming Birds and the Delta Rhythm Boys, gospel music flourished in the years after the Second World War as one of the most vital expressions of the African American community.

The music of the African American churches continues as one of the strongest expressions of the African consciousness in the black community, even though the interest of white America remains fixed on the blues, and on the blues' celebration of the joys and the despairs of sex. There is a proud consciousness of the great gospel tradition. In the 1940s acapella vocal groups like the Delta Rhythm Boys were part of the regular guest fare on national radio programs. Through radio and recordings a great artist like Mahalia Jackson was able to reach out to an audience that was larger than anything she might have known if she had continued to sing only in local congregations. Other younger singers, like Aretha Franklin, the daughter of the famed Detroit minister Reverend C. L. Franklin, brought their gospel style to the popular music world. Aretha, at the height of her success, recorded a double album of gospel songs titled *Amazing Grace* with the pianist and arranger Reverend James Cleveland as a loving gesture to her own musical roots.

Of the many veteran small vocal ensembles, most, like the Swan Silvertones, the Pilgrim Travelers, or the Five Blind Boys of Alabama, were conscious descendents of the old Fisk Jubilee Quartet. Women's groups like the Sallie Martin Singers or the Original Gospel Harmonettes, spent much of their careers outside the spotlight of the music world's awards and ceremonies, though the distinctive and exciting group the Soul Stirrers became better known because of their young lead singer, Sam Cooke, who left them for a meteoric career in soul music. In the new consciousness of the 1960s there was room for a gospel hit that crossed musical lines. The song "Oh Happy Day" by a California choir, the Edwin Hawkins Singers, sold more than seven million copies. But gospel music, even in a society like the United States that is still strongly religious, continues to lead its own life within its own congregations, as an expression of its believers' faith.

In the 1970s and 1980s the "crown prince" of the new generation of gospel musicians was James Cleveland, the pianist, singer, and composer who had worked with Aretha Franklin in her tribute to her gospel roots. His contribution to the gospel song vocabulary was his development of a more complex musical extension of the churches' spiritual experience. Working with large choruses, he created arrangements that achieved in music the moment of spiritual transcendence that is the climax of the sermon-led worship in the church, and at the same time he drew into the arrangements the moments of spoken exhortation and prayer that are also an essential element in the church experience. His own term for the idiom he made his own was "sermonettes." A characteristic of his performances were the pauses when he spoke quietly, sharing with his listeners his thoughts on the message of the song's text, then turned to draw on the massed power of the choir as it responded in soaring exultation.

Cleveland began his career singing as a boy in one of Thomas A. Dorsey's choirs, and he never deviated from his dedication to traditional styles, though he performed with many groups and made hundreds of recordings. His album *This Sunday in Person*, recorded at the First Baptist Church in Nutley, New Jersey, was the first "live" gospel album. A follow-up live album, *Peace Be Still*, recorded with his Angelic Choir in 1962, ultimately sold more than 800,000 copies for the small New York label Savoy Records, which had only minimal national distribution. Like Dorsey, Cleveland instituted an important series of "Gospel Workshops in America" in Detroit in 1968. For the first of the workshops Cleveland drew three thousand singers, instrumentalists, and musical directors to sessions of discussion and song. By his death in 1991 Cleveland had influenced an entire generation of gospel musicians, as a choir director, as a composer and singer, and—not least—as a brilliant gospel pianist. He was active in many churches, and his Los Angeles congregation, the Cornerstone Baptist Church, began with one hundred members and had over seven thousand worshippers in 1990. His Gospel Music Workshop grew to be the world's largest organization dedicated to gospel music, with more than twenty thousand members. His recordings were honored with four Grammy awards, and he was such a dominant figure in the gospel community that shortly after his death he was awarded a fifth Grammy, presented posthumously. He was also filmed with many of his choirs, and he was a dominating presence, both at the keyboard and as musical director. He led his singers with a minimum of gestures. It was his concentration as he listened and responded to their voices that inspired his singers to their finest efforts.

Despite his transcendent abilities, as well as the far-reaching influence of his musical innovations, I never saw Cleveland's name included in the occasional well-publicized lists of influential African American musicians. Cleveland's name still was largely known only within the gospel world. Once, after I'd been listening for several days to his recordings I met Robert Stephens again, and I talked at an enthusiastic length about Cleveland and his achievement. I finally said despairingly, "Everything I've been listening to tells me James Cleveland is one of the geniuses of contemporary American music! Why don't I hear people saying this?"

Stephens looked thoughtful, then he shrugged, and smiled wryly, "Everybody knows it!"

With its lavish banquet of gospel sounds, Harlem offers a glimpse into the emotional fervor of the camp meetings, but in a richly elegant setting that seems centuries away from the old circles of wagons and the voices lifted in the firelight. With the "shout bands" of the United House of Prayer, Harlem's gospel music returns to its mission of moving the earth with song.

Over the entrance to the church on Frederick Douglas Boulevard the letters read "The United House of Prayer for All People." Upstairs, in the two-story, blocky building, on the corner of 125th Street across from the newly renovated Apollo Theater, the elevator opens into a large lobby, and from the lobby a set of sober double doors lead into the church itself. The interior is breathtakingly modern: severe, sumptuous, tasteful, and much larger than suggested by the brick facade of the building. The overhead wooden beams lead to a glass panel that opens up to the sky three stories above the rows of pews. The color scheme of the paneled walls is an elegant, muted contrast of grays and tans on the large paneled walls, and there are photographic portraits of the church's founders discreetly mounted behind the altar.

The elegant premises are a mark of the churches established by one of America's most successful evangelists, Bishop C. M. "Daddy" Grace. Grace came to the United States as a nineteen-year-old immigrant from the Cape Verde Islands in 1903, and after some years in New Bedford, Massachusetts, he built the first House of Prayer by hand in West Wareham, Massachusetts, in 1919. The Pentacostal denomination he founded has continued to grow since his death in 1960, and it now has more than three and a half million members, with its largest congregation in Charlotte, North Carolina, and its headquarters in Washington. Grace created a series of commercial products, including soaps and lotions, as well as tea and coffee, which were sold successfully through his churches, and with skillful investments the House of Prayer today continues its work as a solidly established evangelical ministry. The church of the New York congregation is a Harlem landmark.

As my wife Annie and I walked from the subway stop a block away,

The United House of Prayer for All People, from the window of Manna's Soul Food Cafeteria, Harlem.

we could see that with less congestion in the streets on a Sunday morning it was possible for cars to stop at the curb by the downstairs entrance to the House of Prayer. Families stepped slowly from open car doors, careful not to muss dresses and suits. Serious-faced children stood silently waiting as their parents gathered prayer books and walked respectfully with them into the building, holding on to their hands. As we followed the family groups to the stairs I stopped at a small stand in the corridor selling religious items and asked the woman behind the counter if the House of Prayer was a Holiness or Pentecostal congregation.

Her smile was immediate and welcoming. "They're just the same. One's the same as the other."

The wide, white rows of benches filled slowly, as well-dressed men and women paused at the door to look for friends and stop by family groups to exchange quiet greetings. The mood in the church as we sat waiting for the service to begin had no suggestion of the ecstatic fervor of a Holiness congregation. Filling the benches around us was a gathering crowd of worshippers with the look of any prosperous group in America—solidly middle class, tastefully and expensively dressed. Families occupied the rows with children in sober suits and dresses, there were whispered greetings and handshakes over the backs of the benches. A woman sitting a few rows in front of us slipped off her fur trimmed coat, unzipped her large hand bag, and took out a tambourine. As a gray-haired pianist softly sketched gospel chords on the grand piano beside the altar area, the deacon stood a few feet from the piano stroking a washboard with a bent coat hanger in time with the muted chording. Across the aisle, in an area in front of the seats there was a gleam of brass and silver. Three or four young men in neatly ironed shirts and dark neck ties were sitting with the rest of the instruments of one of the church's three "shout bands," the Sons of Thunder, the thunderous shouting of massed trombones that is one of the most distinctive expressions of worship in the House of Prayer congregations.

In some modern African American churches the services have muted their fiery tone, but the House of Prayer was founded as an evangelist mission, and the old fires still burn in the hearts of the church's worshippers. As the serious, gray-haired minister stood and walked to the pulpit, he stood for a moment looking out over us, his expression at once concerned and welcoming. He began his sermon simply by reading the church announcements—meetings to be held, members of the congregation who were ill, congratulations on new babies and weddings, condolences for recent deaths. Then he laid the paper on the pulpit, put his hands on his arms under the sleeves of his black robe and began talking quietly about a church meeting he'd just attended in Los Angeles, and about what it had meant to his own feelings about the spirit of God. And with this as his theme his voice took on a new resonance. He drew his hands from his sleeves to gesture to members sitting in front of him. His voice rose and fell in a rhythmic cadence, and a tide of emotion began to build in the church in a slowly gathering wave. With his voice rising and his foot striking the pulpit he began marking his own rhythmic cadence with a forced "WHA!" of his breath.

Already people had begun to rise in their seats to join him in the cadence. Hands were thrust in the air. Two well-dressed women, their faces creased with concentration, stumbled into the aisle and began dancing compulsively, watched solicitously by the young women in white dresses who had helped us to our seats and then hovered at the head of the aisle to assist the worshippers. The young men from the shout band, a dozen of them in their dark trousers, white shirts, and neat ties, had slipped in from a side door and were gathered in the rows close to the pulpit. The sermon reached its climax—the air was laden with the spirit that the fiery repetitions and exhortations had delivered into our presence—there was a breathless moment of silence. Then the musicians of the shout band leaped to their feet, lifting their instruments—a dozen trombones, a sousaphone, tambourines, a drum—and the echoing space burst with their blaring, massed wall of sound.

The noise of the trombones was, as their name proclaimed, a sound of thunder. Below the shining brass slides we could see a young boy backed against their legs, joyfully playing his own instrument, a small slide trumpet. One of the trombone players, a handsome young man in his twenties, tall and muscular, spun up the aisle in a joyous dance, his eyes glistening as he played a series of short phrases over and over in a brassy cry of exultation. In their rows of seats other musicians were jumping up and down, their faces, like his, radiant with the joy of their belief. The intense communication of the service and the brass shouts of the band had swept the congregation up into a living testimony to the continuing power of gospel song. Along with everyone around us in the luminous spaces of the church, we joined our clapping hands to the tumult of sound.

Thirty years before, when I had stood perspiring and half-deafened in the midst of a procession of Fula musicians in The Gambia, I thought of the word "din" that African travelers had used to describe the musical experience. In the cascade of sound in the House of Prayer the word that came to me was "exultation." What I was hearing in this sophisticated setting above a modern Harlem avenue was that memory of Africa's musical roots that I had heard so many times before—the texturing of the rhythms in the drums and tambourines of the young musicians, the roar of the melodies in the irresistible thrust of the tone of their trombones. It was a musical language so deeply ingrained in the cultural heritage of the families filling the church around me that it would never lose its power or its grace.

12 ✳ A Prince of Zydeco

Louisiana's Zydeco Blues and
Good Rockin' Dopsie

In the darkness the flat, featureless land on either side of the straight road could have been covered with pieces of board, stretching out until their length was lost in the shadows. Sometimes the van slipped past a house, but if there was a light still burning it was only a dim lamp left on over a porch or in the back by a shed. It was too late for anyone to be up and too early for people who had to get to work. At the occasional roadside stops there were lines of idling trucks with their yellow running lights outlining the bulky shapes of trailer rigs and drivers' cabs. Inside the low-ceilinged coffee shops I glimpsed the wrinkled backs of work shirts, the heavy-shouldered drivers wearing them leaning along counters covered with dirty dinner plates, crumpled napkins, and coffee cups. It was too late for us to stop. The van kept up its steady pace, the heater holding off the night chill of the East Texas fields. The men in the seats behind us were sprawled against each other in heavy, restless sleep, their ornate shirts creased, their buckled shoes pushed off.

Good Rockin' Dopsie (the name, despite the spelling is pronounced DOOP-sie), the man who was driving, talked in a slow, steady monologue. The van was lettered with his name and the men sleeping on the seats behind us were his band. Now, in 1979, he didn't need to spend the long hours behind the wheel of his van, but as he had done so many times before, he was driving his musicians back from a dance. He didn't have to be up the next morning for his day job—he stopped doing construction work three or four years ago when the dance jobs started paying better—but some of the men in his Cajun Twisters did have to get up, and he was bringing them back home to Lafayette so they could get two or three hours sleep in their beds. They'd be a little red eyed for their jobs, and there would be a next morning headache to remind them of everything they'd had to drink the night before, but they'd get through their day's work—just as they had done so many times before.

Dopsie didn't usually push himself this hard, but the Twisters had played a high school gym dance in Lafayette on Thursday night, then they'd driven over to Houston for a weekend of dance jobs. On Friday they played a long night under the strings of dangling, half-lit, colored bulbs that twined over the bandstand at Fort Spriggs, a shadowy, barn-sized dance hall for people from Louisiana looking for a little of their own music. The next day drifted past in visits with friends and relatives, cheerful, busy families with wriggling children scattered over the floor, staring up wide-eyed and open-mouthed at the loud talking, flamboyantly dressed musicians. The people the band members stopped by to see worked modest jobs or ran little businesses and they had made decent lives for themselves in neighborhoods of small frame houses out in the countryside beyond Houston's cramped ghetto.

Dopsie and the band tried to squeeze in a little sleep along with the laughter and the greetings, then there was another noisy dance in a smaller club. Finally, with the job over, the amplifiers tiredly heaved off the bandstand and the instruments shoved on top of them in the back of the van, Dopsie began the drive back over the empty night distances of the East Texas flatlands. The only markers I could see to measure the miles we were driving were the flares of the gas burning off on distant wells—fluttering, yellow-white torches in the darkness. For the first night hours they slid steadily past us with the measured pace of a stick floating on a river. But it had been a long weekend. Dopsie was tired. I finally felt his foot lighten up on the gas pedal, and he pulled over on the crushed shell slope of the road's shoulder.

"Could you take it for a little?" His voice was scraped dry as river sand after all the singing, but I could hear his apologetic tone.

"You know I didn't want you to have to do some driving, but, oh man, I got to rest and I still got to get those boys back. They got their jobs."

Again the flaring of the gas burn-offs in the distance, sliding slowly past the van, the interstate empty of everything except for the occasional rig eating up miles toward Houston or back toward New Orleans, sometimes a solitary van like Dopsie's. He couldn't keep himself going with music on the radio, since it would keep the others in the band awake. The only thing he could do to keep himself awake was talk. Now he tried to sleep a little, his head against the door panel, and for a time all I heard was the swish of the tires and fitful snoring from the figures slumped against each other in the dark shadows of the back seats. After a half hour I heard Dopsie's voice again.

"Wouldn't you know I'd be too tired to sleep. But I don't want to drive just yet. You keep going." And he picked up the story he had been telling me with a hoarse voice that didn't have much more sound left to it than the breathy swish of the tires.

The complicated patterns of the music that has emerged in the African diaspora often seem as though they were created out of an inevitable process that is tantalizingly lost somewhere in the past. With Dopsie's music, however, the unique musical style of the black culture of southwest Louisiana known as zydeco, it's possible to go back to the moment when the two cultures, the white, French-speaking Cajuns and their black Creole neighbors, exchanged musical languages. Perhaps the cross fertilization is closer here than in any of the other styles that have emerged in the scattering of the African peoples. Once the musical exchange had begun, it was musicians like Dopsie, driving their vans out of the little towns like Opelousas or Eunice, the small cities like Lafayette or Lake Charles, setting up their amplifiers and microphones on cramped stages in country dance halls who kept their music alive. It was bands like the Twisters who carried zydeco out across the empty spaces of western Louisiana, and over into Texas on Interstate 10, a highway that Dopsie had driven so often he felt he could almost—but not quite—drive it in his sleep.

Zydeco at first was a style that only a handful of bands like Dopsie and his Twisters played in the battered, boomy dance halls. Now dozens of other bands carry the music—one of the newest of the African American idioms—out into the Louisiana countryside and beyond that to most of the world. If nothing else about the new style, the name, at least, is more or less standardized. In most writing about it it's called "zydeco." This doesn't mean that everyone goes along with this way of spelling it. One of the first singles done in the new style was recorded in the late 1940s by Houston's resident blues man Lightnin' Hopkins, who heard the first bands in the nearby "Frenchtown" section of the city. On the label the name was spelled "Zolo Go." To suggest the tone of the new style Lightnin' played the accompaniment on an organ, which had some of the feel of a zydeco accordion. Occasionally the local print shop Dopsie used for the dance posters he handed out to the clubs where he was playing came up with "zordico." Other variants of the spelling were *zarico, zadacoe, zodogo, zottico,* and *zadico,* and they still stubbornly turn up on occasional local advertisements or posters. What is surprising about the variety of the spellings is not that there is some disagreement. What is the surprise is that the sound of all of the words is so similar. All of them begin with a "z" and end with some variant of daco, deco, or dico.

Although the root source of the word is no mystery, what is contained in the word is helpful in understanding the music itself. In the simplest terms, "zydeco" is a short, slangy way of saying the beginning of the Cajun French phrase "Les haricots sont pas salé," which means "the beans

Rockin' Dopsie, 1985.

aren't salty." Spoken quickly, the first two words come out something like "lezarico," which can be further squeezed down to "zarico," which then turned into zydeco. Haricots are snap beans—everyday food in western Louisiana—and what the expression is saying is that whoever was cooking them didn't have enough money to add salt pork to the pot, which would have given them a salty taste. The term began to turn up in songs recorded in western Louisiana after the Second World War, first as a term for the kind of fast dance that was done to a brisk, single chord melody that turns up on records with dozens of different names. The title of the song finally came to stand for the whole dance style. The use of a French word for the music emphasizes that the style comes out of the southwest Louisiana French-speaking culture, and the complaint about the taste of snap beans is a reminder that zydeco is poor people's music.

What zydeco *is* as a musical style is a more complicated Louisiana problem. The night I was driving the Twisters' van, the band had started the dance in the Houston club with a few numbers by the band members themselves. Their job was to warm up the crowd before the night's star, Good Rockin' Dopsie, made his appearance. They churned through a set of current R & B hits, with the backup guitarist doing the singing. When Dopsie came up on the bandstand to loud shouts and applause with his gold, two-row button accordion, the band instantly tightened up, and with Dopsie driving them along they steamed into a series of uptempo melodies that still had a little R & B feel, but the R & B was mixed with Louisiana two-steps, Cajun songs, plaintive Cajun blues, and the occasional strongly accented waltz for the dancers.

Dopsie sang every number with a high, piercing, half-shouting voice. Even with his microphone to help him he still had to work to make himself heard over the pounding of the band. He never stopped pumping his accordion, and sometimes I'd see him come off the stage leaving wet footprints from the perspiration that had soaked through his shoes as he played. When zydeco had first emerged only ten or fifteen years before, it was still a quiet acoustic style—mostly a singer playing a button accordion, accompanied by a friend who stroked a washboard. A steel washboard was considered to have the best tone. To carry the melodies, the musicians relied on their own sturdy voices. Within a few years the style, though, had picked up more of an R & B sound. A band like Dopsie's worked with six musicians—Dopsie's accordion, Major Handy's guitar, John Hart's tenor sax, the electric bass of "Morris" Francis, Dopsie's son Junior's drums, and the rubboard—now known by the French word *frottoir*—played by Chester Zeno, a small, rumpled, man who had been making music with Dopsie since they were both teenagers. Some of the bands that have followed the Twisters have added keyboards, a rhythm guitar, and a trumpet.

So much of the zydeco repertoire recycles the R & B mainstream of the 1940s and 1950s that the two styles would seem to be at least close cousins. But zydeco *sounds* different. The band might be doing a cover of the popular "Lawdy Miss Clawdy," but by the time the words have made the change into bayou French, the melody has been fitted to a button accordion, and at least one of the rhythms is being scraped out on a *frottoir*, what comes out over the loudspeakers has turned into a sound that is new and only half familiar. It's also too simple to characterize what the bands play as a local, bayou version of the R & B mainstream. Zydeco takes at least as much of its repertoire from the songs and dances of the surrounding French-speaking community. They swap the bouncy two-steps and the sentimental waltzes back and forth with the white Cajun bands of their neighbors. People who don't live in the southwest parishes use the term *Cajun* to include everything and everybody that's found there, but the cultural sources of what is locally termed "French music" are as complicated as the mix of influences that goes into the music.

Zydeco and Cajun, or French, music grew up in the same Louisiana countryside, but they have found their own paths, and they are different in as many ways as they are alike. The racial complexity of the American rural South is even more of a puzzle in Louisiana than it is in other states, and it's the presence of the Cajuns, descendants of a small group of late-arriving French immigrant settlers, that stretches the social canvas. The rural isolation created an uneasy situation in which two groups, living side by side in the Louisiana bayous, one white and one black, were each struggling to find some footing in the swamp of American racial relations. It isn't possible to understand the music of the zydeco musicians like Dopsie without having at least a beginner's knowledge of the people who own the next farm or who work at the filling station at the prairie crossroad where everybody stops for gas.

The term *Cajun* is itself a corruption, just as zydeco is a colloquial version of another term. *Cajun* began as the local way of saying the word "Acadian." Although the people were French speaking, they would probably be better described as Canadian than as French. They were the descendents of French settlers who had come as a group from the French provinces of Centre-Ouest in the 1600s to the new French colony in North America. They were self-sufficient, resourceful farmers, and they settled together on a large island off the Canadian east coast called Acadia. Like the other scattered groups of settlers in North America and

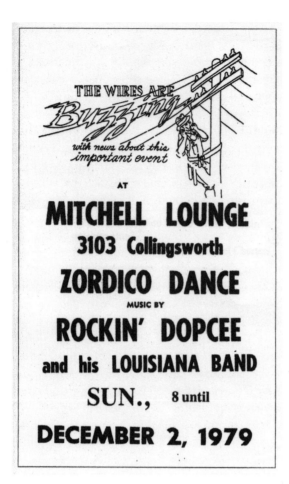

A poster for a "Zordico Dance" with "Rockin' Dopcee and his Louisiana Band."

the Caribbean, however, they were at the mercy of European politics, and they found themselves dealt back and forth, like playing cards in a game they had no power to control. In 1713, at the end of the War of Spanish Succession, Acadia was ceded to the British, who renamed it Nova Scotia, a latinate term for New Scotland. The Acadians were at first permitted to remain on their farms, but a few months after the outbreak of a new war between France and England in 1754, the British, uneasy with the presence of a large French-speaking group settled on a large island north of their own American colonies, demanded assurances from the Acadians that they would not join the French forces that at this time still occupied most of Canada.

The next year, when the British demanded oaths of allegiance to England, the Acadians refused, and large groups, often entire families, were seized, their homes burned, and their crops ravaged. It is estimated that in this first move against the Acadians six thousand people were forcibly removed and transported in crammed ships to the lower English colonies, where they were scattered in settlements the length of the Atlantic coast, from Maine to Georgia. Another group, also about six thousand people, fled to nearby Cape Breton Island, Prince Edward Island, and parts of New Brunswick, where for a brief period they organized in small armed groups that fought the British. They held out for more than a year, despite continuing attacks by the British fleet and desperate hunger and sickness in their new wilderness lands. When the resistance finally collapsed the survivors were herded into detention centers in Halifax, the renamed largest town of Nova Scotia. They were held in the centers until the war ended, five years later, in 1763.

The treaty that ended the war allowed the imprisoned settlers a period of eighteen months to return freely to French soil. The situation of the Acadians who had been left in the American colonies wasn't much better, since they had been considered potential traitors by the Americans who found them in their midst. Some of them were aware that to the west, in the Louisiana territories beyond the Mississippi River, the land was still controlled by the French. The first organized group of Acadians to try to reach Louisiana were remnants of the bands of fighting men who had tried to hold off the British in Halifax. They gathered together enough money to hire a ship to carry them to New Orleans and finally, after a stop in Santo Domingo in the Caribbean, arrived in the city in February, 1765. Probably the number of Acadians who stumbled off the ship's gangway was no more than twenty.

The total number of Acadians who finally reached Louisiana, some making the difficult journey overland from the American coastal colonies through Indian territory, is thought to be somewhere between five and ten thousand. With their dismal luck, however, they reached Louisiana at the moment when it was turned over to Spain by the French government. They had been away from France for more than a century, they had just endured several years as virtual prisoners in Halifax and in the American colonies, and now they faced a future as Spanish subjects. What saved them was the indifference of the Spanish, who were so desperate for settlers that they would have accepted virtually anyone who showed up at the New Orleans docks.

For the African Americans who also drifted into the flat farmlands west of the Mississippi River, the journey was not as complicated. Most were slaves who worked the large plantations that had been established along the Mississippi by the early generation of French planters. Sugar had also been planted on some of the land, but the nearby Caribbean islands produced so much sugar that for some time Louisiana's sugar production was not a major economic factor. At the end of the Civil War the freed slaves found themselves in a different situation from the large work-forces that had been tied to the cotton growing areas of Alabama and Mississippi. The French language that the slaves had learned from their owners put them at a disadvantage if they moved to an English-speaking area, so many of them stayed in western Louisiana, despite the poor soil, the isolation, and the lack of any kind of commercial enterprise. Since the same difficulties faced the Cajuns, the society that emerged was much more integrated economically than in other areas. Both groups, African American and French American, were poor, and in the small communities out on the flat, sparsely settled countryside they could share their poverty.

Dopsie was born in 1932 outside of Lafayette, on a farm close to Carencro, and in those hardscrabble Depression years there was never enough money for him to go to school, even if there had been much concern about educating young African Americans in rural Louisiana at that moment. Schooling was always an elusive goal for children like Dopsie. He spent some time in the classroom but he dropped out at a very early age and never learned to read or write. Although western Louisiana was never as racially restricted as the "cotton belt" areas to the east, black children still had the poorest opportunities for education. Like everyone who grew up in his part of the state, Dopsie spoke both French and English, and when he began playing, still a teenager, most of the songs he knew were the same French pieces that his neighbors knew.

The land today is still a patchwork of small farms and meandering narrow roads, many of them unmarked and some still unpaved. The dark nights, the unexpected rains, the condition of the roads, and the prevalence of heavy drinking have made automobile accidents a common tragedy. Three of the musicians I recorded in Lafayette in the 1970s were killed in accidents on wet roads within a few months of the sessions. In the beginning some of the Cajuns tried cattle raising, but many others turned to the same small scale farming they had done in Canada, and within two or three generations they found themselves trapped in a cycle of near poverty that lasted until the end of the Second World War and the boom in the oil industry along the Gulf Coast. Mingled with the freed slaves and the Cajuns was still a thin scattering of native peoples, but they soon disappeared. Along the dirt roads were scattered frame houses set in the midst of cleared fields, with a growth of trees close to the houses to provide some shade and a little privacy.

To someone driving on one of the back roads, there is not much to tell you which houses are white or black owned. Like the Cajuns, the

African Americans tried small scale farming, and they also found poorly paid employment in the same kinds of hauling, cleaning, repairing, and building services that emerged at the same time in the white communities. The cane fields west of New Orleans and south of the Mississippi also expanded, using labor that was almost entirely black. At the end of many dirt roads in southern Louisiana there are still small cane worker's villages, with a dusty, unpaved main street, a shabby grocery store, usually with a gas pump in front, and rows of weathered frame shacks that are home to predominately black families.

Although the music that came out of these isolated, poor, racially mixed communities west of New Orleans was called, with some pride, "French music," except for the French language of some of the songs there's nothing about the playing that's French. The Acadians had been away from France for a hundred years before they were driven out of Canada, and it was another century before the isolated communities began to develop a local consciousness following the defeat of the Confederacy. None of the dances that are characteristic of Cajun music, the two-steps and the waltzes, existed in France before the Acadians left their homeland. The most popular instrument, the accordion, first appeared in crude forms in Vienna in the 1820s, and although it passed through Louisiana in the wagons with German immigrants in the 1840s and 1850s, the instrument was still clumsy, and performers found it was difficult to play in tune with the Cajun fiddles. It wasn't until the early 1900s that cheap, dependable accordions appeared in the Cajun areas, and the instrument was gradually adopted by both Cajun and Creole musicians. The German settlers carried it farther west to Texas, where it became popular with the laborers from Mexico who found work in their fields. The most popular music today in northern Mexico is the accordion-based Norteños music that has obvious ties to the accordion styles of Louisiana.

Although there are only patchy descriptions of the music in southern Louisiana before the first recordings were made in the late 1920s, the Cajun musicians generally credit the African American musicians with creating many of the songs and the instrumental techniques that became popular in the little dance halls in the area. Among the first musicians to record was a slight, short, light-skinned accordionist named Amédé Ardoin, who became one of the legendary artists of the quiet countryside. Ardoin was born in 1898 to a mother and father who had both been slaves. His father had acquired a large farm, but he was killed in an accident only a few months after his son's birth. Ardoin continued to live with his mother until her death when he was in his twenties, and he then moved in with a brother. His first accordion was an instrument that had been purchased for another of his brothers, but it was Amédé, as the family's baby, who took over the instrument and taught himself to play it. When he registered for the draft in 1918 his occupation was given as "farmer," but he is remembered as spending most of his time playing his accordion. He managed to scrape out a living in poor country by staying on the move and playing for any kind of crowd he could find. Sometimes he traveled on horseback, sometimes he hitchhiked to get around, carrying his instrument in a flour sack.

Ardoin was popular for dances because he lent an indefinable swing to the familiar pieces, and in his singing he brought the intonations of the blues into the Cajun repertoire. He played for white audiences more than he did for black audiences, but it was an uneasy way of life as he tried to pick his way through the sullen undercurrents of racism that surrounded him. Although he pretended to deal with the situation casually, he was aware that in the isolated farm country he could never be sure he was safe from drunken violence. For many years he played in a duet with a talented white fiddler named Dennis McGhee, and McGhee's presence helped soothe some of the jealousies that his partner's playing aroused. They first recorded together in 1929, when Columbia Records brought them to their temporary recording facilities in New Orleans. The next year they recorded again for Brunswick Records, and there was another session in New York for Bluebird Records in 1934. On their recordings it was Ardoin who did the singing, in a high, emotional blues-tinged voice, with his accordion and McGhee's fiddle providing the accompaniment. Their arrangements of many of the traditional pieces are still performed today. For a final session, in New York in December 1934 for Decca Records, he recorded twelve songs, for the first time performing as a soloist.

A man named Vincent Lejeune, whose father ran a dance place in the country and who regularly hired Ardoin to play, described the crowds on the nights Ardoin appeared.

They'd come from Church Point, Lewisburg, Eunice, Opelousas, Basile. People would come from miles. Wagons, buggies, old Model T's, and horseback, every weekend. They'd charge the people twenty-five cents to come in to the dance, and Amede got seventy-five, eighty dollars some time. It was good money, because five or six dollars in those days for a musician, that was top money . . . Amede would sing anything he wanted. His voice would go through you. He could play some music, every woman in the dance hall would cry. They'd stop dancing. Sat down and wiped the tears. Oh yes sir, he made the women cry, and the men would hang their heads down.[1]

Although there is no agreement about the incident that ended his career, the most widely repeated story is that at a dance about 1949 a white woman lent him her handkerchief to wipe his perspiring face, and two men followed him into the darkness and beat him so savagely he was never able to play again. The story has also been denied or so altered in the telling that the truth will probably never be known. He might have suffered a beating, but whether it was over a borrowed handkerchief or even if it was the beating that caused his decline could never be established. As little is known about his death as about what happened to him that night on the way home from the dance. He seems to have died in the state asylum in Pineville three or four years later, but even this is uncertain.

What is clearer is that his recordings helped bring the accordion back into Cajun music. The popularity of western swing had led most of the local bands to modernize, adding the string bass and the electric steel guitar. The old style accordion didn't have the harmonic range or the smooth sound that the new bands wanted. For several years Cajun dance music was dominated by the fiddlers. In the complicated exchanges that have characterized the development of Louisiana music, it was a young white musician named Iry Lejeune, who picked up the blues influenced singing style and the rhythmic accordion accompaniment from Ardoin's recordings, and guided Cajun music back toward its older traditions. Lejeune was born in 1928 near Church Point, but he was virtually blind, and, like Ardoin, he was never able to do farm work. From Ardoin's recordings, Lejeune learned the blues vocal style that he in turn passed on to the younger musicians who heard his records. His first session was for a small local company in 1949. Lejeune's career ended tragically when he was killed in a roadside accident in 1955. He and the violinist J. B. Fuselier were coming back from a dance late at night when a flat tire stopped them on the road. While they were changing the tire in the darkness another car struck them, and Lejuene was thrown into a field, dying instantly. He was only twenty-six years old, and he'd had time to record only twenty-six songs.

Zydeco's roots lie in the entire spectrum of the music of the bayou countryside, but an earlier song style shaped some of the music's distinctive character. When older musicians, both black and white, were first interviewed, they still could remember a kind of singing they had known when they were children. It was a solo song style accompanied only by hand clapping called *juré*. The first juré recording was made by John Lomax and his son Alan on a journey through Louisiana in the 1930s. At a church gathering in 1934 in Lake Arthur they recorded a young man named Jimmy Peters, who sang a verse for them that included the phrase "les haricots sont pas salé." The song's sources were clearly an older Acadian folk song, but this verse was a recent addition. In his excellent study *The Kingdom of Zydeco* New Orleans writer Michael Tisserand discussed both the recording by the Lomaxes and the influence of juré songs on later Cajun music.[2] The term juré means, in French, sworn to testify, but Tisserand also points out that the name *bazar*, which refers to the church socials where the songs often were sung is sometimes also used to describe the style.[3]

In one of the many interviews Tisserand did with living musicians he discussed juré songs with the legendary black fiddler Canray Fontenot. In an earlier interview with Alan Govenar, which Tisserand quoted, Clifton Chenier, the king of the zydeco artists, talked about his groundbreaking 1965 recording of the classic zydeco anthem "Zydeco sont pas salé," which has a distinctive rhythmic and melodic style. "The beat came from the religion people," Chenier insisted.

When he was interviewed by Tisserand, Canray Fontenot recalled a conversation he had had with Chenier, and it may be the closest we can come to establishing the links between Acadian folk songs and the later forms of Cajun and zydeco music that have taken some of their form from them.

> One day me and Clifton was talking. He said, "Say, Canray, a long time ago, they used to have some *juré*." He said, "Did you ever go at one of them things?" I said, "No, Clifton, I never did." Because they used to have that where they didn't have no musicians, but I was born where they had some musicians. What was it, them *juré*, they didn't have no music, but them old people would sit down, clap their hands,and make up a song. And they would dance on that, them people. Around Basile there, they didn't fool with nothing like that. I kept saying I wanted to go around Mamou and Ville Platte, where they used to have them *juré*.
>
> But Clifton's daddy was an accordion player, and he said that his daddy played one of them *juré* songs, and they called that "Zydeco est pas salé," Which means the snap beans don't have no salt in them. So Clifton says, "That 'Zydeco est pas salé' song is good, but the way Daddy played that, that's the wrong speed."
>
> [Clifton] says, "I'm going to take that same song, and I'm going to put a different speed on it and them people are going to be able to dance that." And he did, too. And when he started, everybody wanted to play the accordion, everybody wanted to play what Clifton played.[4]

It was significant that Fontenot remembers that juré songs were sung in the church halls after services. In many rural churches, slaves, or after 1863 freed blacks, were permitted to be present on separate benches during church services and sometimes they could linger in the background at the after-church social gatherings. It was only in churches that this kind of contact between the races would be countenanced. The black worshippers could hear the accapella Acadian songs sung in the church halls, and they would have learned many of them themselves. As the newly freed men and women built their own churches they created these same moments of juré song, and it is here that the first steps in the interchange began. When a Cajun singer like Joseph Falcon talks about learning a song from his African neighbors, often it is a song that has its roots in the Acadian folk tradition. What Falcon heard was the new rhythmic style of the African American musicians as they performed the old songs. As Clifton Chenier described it, the black Creoles "put a different speed on it."

But with the song "Zydeco sont pas salé" we also come close to another of Louisiana's musical influences. The melody is chant-like, with many of the characteristics of African song. It is shaped around a continuous, repetitive melodic figure without any defined European harmonic pattern and with a close association to a gapped pentatonic scale. If it is slowed down to the tempo that Clifton remembers from his father's accordion version, the minor mode of its melody becomes more obvious. An older zydeco musician, Sidney Babineaux, told Tisserand that he remembered hearing the piece as a juré melody before 1895. The melody is still played today by every zydeco musician. Dopsie remembered playing it when he was working in little country juke joints for tips as a boy, and the only accompaniment was Chester Zeno's rubboard.

Nothing in vernacular music, however, remains fixed for long. Audiences change and their musical tastes change. The melody has stayed the same—one of the scant handful of melodies widely performed in the South that still have the distinctive sound of an African song—but even in the nearly twenty years that I recorded zydeco bands, the style of playing the piece continually changed. When I first heard Dopsie play it at a dance outside of Lawtelle he still performed it the old way with accordion and Chester Zeno's *frottoir*. The only addition was the drums. Since the other members of the band didn't have anything to play, they stood on the stage smiling and watching the swooping dancers. Then after a few months the bass player worked out a simple riff pattern to the melody. When John Hart, the tenor saxophone player who had been working with Clifton Chenier, came into the band he introduced an extended solo in the arrangement. When I heard the piece with Clifton's band two or three years later, a trumpeter, Warren Ceasar, was in the band, and both the tenor sax and the trumpet soloed. Most recently when I heard the song played in a New Orleans bar, the bass player had worked out a rudimentary harmonic pattern, and probably somewhere down the line the African melody will finally be drawn into the popular mainstream.

If you drive west out of New Orleans today, looking for music, the roads have improved, but there is still a wildness about the bayous, a worn shabbiness about the small towns. Just west of New Orleans you find yourself crossing miles of flooded land. Off the side of the elevated highway you look down into a darkly tangled cypress forest, and through the branches you can glimpse the moodily glistening surface of the water that floods much of the land. The occasional dry stretches of land are choked with brush and bayou grasses. Narrow, winding channels in the bayous open out like church aisles leading away from the large streams that meander across the hazy countryside. Along the wire fences close to the highway you see the hunched shapes of hawks, and in the air is a scattering of smaller birds gliding down into the canopy of trees and vines.

Past the swamplands, as you continue driving west, you come to drier ground, and a weave of narrow rutted roads that go back along the curving mounds of the earth levees that keep the bayous in their channels. Then you reach a stringy growth of cypresses that bring you to a longer, higher elevated roadway over the Atchafalaya Basin. The term *basin* suggests the size of the vast, almost lake-like, spreading stream of water that flows south from the Mississippi River, but it doesn't give an impression of the power of the water currents below you. If the system of levees closing it off eventually fails, the Atchafalaya will act out its ancient destiny, seizing the flooding waters on the other side of the artificial barriers and become the main channel of a newly directed Mississippi, leaving New Orleans without its river. At the center of the basin's moody currents you see off to the south almost to the Gulf, with the trees, their straight trunks half sunken into the water, looking as if they'd impulsively started to scatter somewhere in the swamp, then changed their mind and stayed where they were.

A few miles west of the basin you pass the turnoffs to Lafayette, and the land becomes drier and browner. The prairies stretch on either side of the car, the modest, small houses set back away from the road, the flat fields divided into grazing strips with rusted barbed wire. If you continue west, turn off the highway, and swing north to a small town like Mamou you find yourself in the old Acadia—a main street with a seedy hotel, a convenience store, two or three gas stations, and, in Mamou, the well-known bar Fred's Lounge. Its small door opens into a low-ceilinged barroom that for years broadcast a disorganized live Cajun radio show on Saturday mornings with a band led by the fiddler Sadie Courville and the guitarist Preston Manuel. The town's frame houses were built along a grid of rectangular streets laid out by surveyors when the prairie was opened a century ago. The houses line the neglected streets behind patches of bushes closing in the small lawns, half hidden by the growth of dark trees, their porches shrouded with rusting screens to fend off the mosquitoes.

The weekends when Dopsie and his Cajun Twisters drove over to Houston only occurred every couple of months. It was in this flat stretch of land, in the scattered small towns west of the basin, where the band did most of their playing. Sometimes there were jobs in Lafayette and they didn't have to travel. A school dance, a church hall social, a night on the band stand at the old Bon Ton Roulay before it burned, a shambling dance hall close to the center of the city. Not far from Dopsie's house was the frame building that housed the Blue Angel Lounge, the home club for Clifton Chenier's Red Hot Louisiana Band when he was able to play.

Dopsie drove the band to the jobs in his van, just as he'd done that weekend in Houston, picking them up at their scattered homes and getting them back at the end of the night. The longest drive was for saxophonist John Hart, who lived north of Lafayette in Opelousas. John was blind, so Dopsie's last hour of driving was always that empty stretch of road to John's home in a darkened Opelousas suburb. Dopsie was also aware that if he was doing the driving he knew where everybody was, and he wouldn't have any trouble with one of his musicians going off the road after a night of drinking on the bandstand.

On any Saturday night in the countryside between Lafayette and Lake Charles there could be a dozen zydeco bands like Dopsie's pulling up into the rutted parking lots behind the shadowy dance halls, hauling their amplifiers and microphones up on the battered band stands and laughing and shouting as they unwound cables, and strung out wires, while the drummer patiently screwed together cymbals and pedals. Buckwheat Zydeco, Fernest Arcenaux and the Thunders, Sampy and the Bad Habits, Nathan Williams and the Zydeco Cha Chas, John Delafose and the Eunice Playboys, The Sam Brothers Five, Boozoo Chavis, Beau Jocque and the Hi-Rollers—so many bands like them out in their vans. Some of the bands had a driver who helped them set up, but a driver had to get some kind of salary, and the jobs didn't pay much. A leader like Dopsie, to keep a band together, had to pay a weekly salary to his musicians, and anything extra came out of the leader's money.

Some of the dance halls where they played were well known, like Richard's, (pronounced REE-shards), outside of Lawtell, but despite its

Rockin' Dopsie and the Cajun Twisters performing at the Fort Spriggs club in Houston, 1983. John Hart and Alton Jr. Rubin are visible behind Dopsie.

illuminated sign close to the edge of the road even Richard's was hard to find in the darkness. The building is about the size and shape of the large sheds used for storing farm machinery, and at night the light over the doorway is the only thing that gives it a different appearance from the scattered large sheds along the highway that *are* used for storing farm machinery. Some of the other places are much harder to find, and even with instructions over the telephone from one of the band members you still can spend frustrating hours driving along the dark, twisting roads and at the end of the drive find yourself in a half-empty, unfamiliar barroom, with a tinny juke box and a line of regulars on bar stools looking around and wondering what you're doing there.

It was New Orleans that introduced me to Dopsie. There were clubs in the city like Tipitina's out on Magazine Street, or the Maple Leaf Club on Oak Street that were bringing the bands over from western Louisiana, so the zydeco musicians had some exposure to a larger world. One of the most popular places for dancing today is a bowling alley on Carrollton Avenue where the bands play over the rumble and clash of the bowling balls. The "Rock and Bowl," as it's called, was forced to close for several weeks after the hurricane, but it was already presenting its Thursday zydeco night less than three months later. New Orleans also presents its famed Jazz and Heritage Festival out on the grounds of the race track every spring. The festival tries to bring in every kind of Louisiana music—along with every kind of Louisiana handicraft and food. Dopsie played it for several years. On one of his appearances he was mentioned by a popular music journal, and a copy of the article, with the name of the band underlined, "Rocking Dopsie and his Cajun Twisters," made its way to the company I was working for as a producer. Why not go out to western Louisiana and look up that band with the colorful name? The band's name intrigued us as much as the few sentences about the music. I was going to the United States in a few weeks to do some work in a studio in Nashville and I'd already produced albums with the Cajun musicians who lived in the same small towns outside of Lafayette, so I could fit in a trip to Louisiana to find Dopsie.

The weekend after I finished in the studio in Nashville, Dopsie was advertised at Richard's Dance Hall, outside of Lawtell. Four of us drove out from New Orleans. For once there was some moonlight and it was a bright night, and the directions we'd been given took us to the right town. Richard's was just off the road in a pool of light that illuminated the potholed parking lot and the painted boards of the building's sides. If it hadn't been for the noise of the car's engine we would have heard the club when we passed on the highway. Dopsie's band was *loud*. The amplifiers were cranked up, the sound system turned Dopsie's voice into an emergency fire announcement, the drums sounded like someone was trying to break into the club by pounding on the walls, and the house loud speakers echoed the sound off the shadowy wooden spaces of the club's rafters. Once inside, we saw that it was a long, pinched, crowded room. The dancers had already taken all the tables close to the bandstand, so—still dealing with the volume—we pulled out hard backed wooden chairs at a table back by the door.

The tables *were* filled by the bandstand, we could see that much, but the only thing on the tables we could see were drink setups, plates of food, and coats hanging on the backs of chairs. Between us and the band, who were behind a painted wood railing ringed by the tight squeeze of tables, was a dance floor, and it seemed like everybody from every table was dancing. It was loose, energetic dancing. The men would break away to pull up one pant leg and go into a little country shuffle, a couple up by the bandstand would go into a swinging spin, couples around them would begin to dance with their knees bent, bodies swaying with their loud laughter, women would throw their heads back, pluck up their skirts, and go into their own grinning, eyes-shut circles.

The club was dark, but there were lights over the bandstand. Dopsie and his Twisters were in brightly colored, broad patterned shirts, except for a shorter man in a wrinkled suit in front of the bandstand, who was using a taped spoon to scrape at his ridged metal vest, the *frottoir* that had only recently replaced the old washboards that had hung from a string around the player's neck. Since Dopsie was leading the band, he had on a necktie, but he had pulled it around to the side of his shirt to keep it from tangling in the accordion. He was a medium-sized, broad-chested, muscular man, his hair cut short and his round, friendly face set in a serious expression until he straightened up and smiled to let us know how much he enjoyed seeing the dancing. On their tours later outside of Louisiana none of the bands ever got used to audiences that sat staring at them, even if there was a burst of applause when they finished a number. They had worked all their lives trying to get their audiences up on their feet, and if there weren't any dancers they always suspected that it was because the band wasn't giving them the music they wanted to hear.

There was no hesitation about the dancers jamming the crowded floor at Richard's. Dopsie played the club two or three times a month, and the crowd hadn't come out to sit and listen to a zydeco concert. Most of the couples were in their newest, brightest clothes. Hip tight, shining dresses, elaborate fringed blouses, jewelry and beads, high heels for the women; sport jackets over colorful shirts and slacks for the men. But

Rockin' Dopsie on stage; Major Handy is visible in the background.

once the dancing started it was too hot for the jackets, and the women took off any scarves or dressy jackets they'd been wearing. Now they were just dancing, letting the ice melt in drinks back at the tables and the food they'd spread out at their places go cold on the paper plates.

Dopsie's music was solidly in the middle of the zydeco repertory, which meant all the zydeco classics, like "Ma Negresse" and "Josephine," whatever current R & B hits the band had gotten around to rehearsing, Cajun two-steps, and waltzes sung in French with the same heavy one-two-three downbeat as the big zydeco two-steps. Their "Zydecosont pas salé" had the clattering rush of the wind throwing stones against the side of a building. It was just Dopsie, the *frottoir*, and the drums, but the sound pulsed and roared like the full band, while the dancing spun off into other dimensions in the shadows. I could see handkerchiefs waving, women's arms flinging in circles, men jumping up off the floor. In the middle of the second set the band even presented a little show. The rhythm went into a thumping riff and the worn little man playing the *frottoir* balanced a chair unsteadily upside down above his head, holding the chair's top rung clenched in his teeth while he kept up his beat on the *frottoir* with his spoon. When the band finally left the bandstand for a break, I went to find Dopsie. I had already decided to offer him a contract.

For the next several years Dopsie and the band and I spent hours in recording studios as scattered as Baton Rouge, or the small town of Crowley farther along the Interstate west of Lafayette, or, once, even in Oslo, Norway. There were completely unpredictable nights at clubs and music halls in places as unlikely as The Hague, in Holland, London, and Stockholm, along with gritty weekends around Lafayette, in the nearby small towns, and over to Houston. What happened to Dopsie over those years was only part of a sudden worldwide excitement over zydeco music. Every band, it seemed, was offered a recording contract, there were new audiences waiting at the end of every telephone call, and instead of church halls in Eunice, Louisiana, the musicians found themselves playing in concert halls in Paris or Berlin. When I'd sit with the Twisters back at one of the church halls in Louisiana and they'd meet members of other bands they usually wound up exchanging travel stories about airports in Switzerland or restaurants in France or hotels in Germany where they'd stayed on the latest tours.

The leaders of the bands all accepted their role as "princes" of zydeco, since there was never any question about who was zydeco's king. The king was Clifton Chenier, who had grown up on his father's sharecropper farm out in the countryside, then spent some years in Lake Charles and Houston after he began leading his band. Finally he had moved not far from Dopsie in Lafayette. It was Chenier, in the 1950s, who put together the first successful zydeco band out of the elements of all the styles he heard around him. With his brother Cleveland on rubboard he defined the zydeco sound, and for the last ten years he'd had a solid relationship with Berkeley's Arhoolie Records and its owner, Chris Strachwitz. To someone not from zydeco country the whole idea of kings and princes seemed like a sort of joke, but Clifton wore his large, glittering crown for years on his jobs, and after his death first Dopsie and then Boozoo Chavis, an accordion player and singer from Lake Charles, were formally given the title and played at least occasional jobs wearing their own shiny crowns.

It was still Chenier, at this time, who set the height of the bar for the rest of the musicians around the country areas where they all played, but he suffered from diabetes, and for long periods he couldn't perform. He and his wife tried to pay for his dialysis treatments with ideas like "barbecue breakfasts," selling barbecue sandwiches out their kitchen window on Sunday mornings. When Clifton didn't have enough jobs to keep his fine band together, Dopsie was able to replace his own saxophone player with John Hart, who had worked with Clifton for years. We called John when we were going into the studio for Dopsie's third album. We recorded it on a Sunday afternoon in Jay Miller's old Excello studio in Crowley, upstairs in a veteran brick building over a beauty parlor and an old Ford Model T assembly space. The idea was that if John fit in the band they'd try to work out something to bring him in for the rest of their jobs. After that first Sunday afternoon John never left.

Sometimes Dopsie tried to explain to me how his life had changed, but it was all beyond anything either of us could have imagined. In our first years of working together he was still holding his day job as a construction laborer. He could write his name—Alton Rubin—but he couldn't write anything else and he couldn't read. Construction work was what he could do, and for years he made himself stay awake on the drives back to his day job and then somehow hung on through a long day of erecting power poles at a new shopping center or breaking up cement to pave a parking lot. For the first few years that I recorded the band he didn't have a checking account, but when finally I insisted that I couldn't carry so much cash with me around Louisiana we went over to a bank not far from his house and asked to talk to the bank manager. The man came out immediately with a smile and shook Dopsie's hand. He'd danced to Dopsie's music for years, and on one of his construction jobs Dopsie had also laid the cement floor in the bank. I wondered later if it was the job he'd done on the floor that opened the bank's doors for Dopsie. In a moment he had his account.

Dopsie's musical background was as sketchy as his brief schooling. His brother had an accordion—a two-row button instrument—and Dopsie used to sneak it away so he could try to teach himself to play it. Since nobody showed him anything he picked it up upside down, and that was the way he played it all his life. He worked out all the zydeco melodies, but he never learned any chords, so his approach to the upside down chord buttons was to hit them in a rough, toneless rhythm that was generally covered by the sound of the rest of the band.

The problem for us with Dopsie's inability to read was that it was very difficult for him to learn new lyrics. For a new album I would come to Lafayette, check into a motel across town, and spend weeks working with him on the songs and doing arrangements with the band. Since I was in Lafayette for such long periods I spent almost as much time at Dopsie's house as I did at the motel. He and his wife Almina had eight children, and in Dopsie's life I could see reflected so many of the social changes that had come to the South. There had been no education for him, but all of his older children had gone on through high school, and they had continued on to colleges that, at least on the junior college level, had been integrated. When I first met him he was living with Almina and their children in a cramped house in a mixed neighborhood of mobile homes and small frame buildings on a street crowded with cars and trucks. After three or four years he bought a beautiful, modern home in the middle of the block in one of Lafayette's finest neighborhoods. His neighbors were white, but I didn't feel any of the wrenching hostility that had been part of my experience of the South when I first came to Louisiana in 1950. He and Almina had a new baby, a large, energetic one-year-old named Dwayne, and their next door neighbor, a young white mother with a baby about the same age, was in the house almost every afternoon so the two babies could work out some of their energy on each other.

In all of the rehearsing we did for any of the new albums, Dopsie was endlessly patient and tried to give me everything I was looking for. The musicians were actually pleased at having something new to play on their endless dance jobs. In their world, also, what we were working on was not the album that would reach some buyers in a foreign city the band might not ever see—what concerned them was that we might cut a song that we could release as a jukebox single and it could get them some local notoriety. Sometimes we rehearsed in a local barroom, with the instruments set up along the bar, and I would sit on the pool table as we went over the sketch arrangements. Everything had to be hummed or sung, since it wasn't a band that read music. Another place we used often was a small outbuilding on a nearby farm. It had a sink, so it probably had been used for cleaning chickens or washing vegetables. Since we were in the middle of the fields we could play as loudly as we wanted, and the rehearsals could go on until we were satisfied with what we were getting. The rehearsals for one of the albums showed me again how intertwined the musical traditions were in zydeco/cajun country.

I asked Dopsie if he'd like to do an album in the "French Style," with those pieces he'd grown up hearing when he was playing for local dances outside of Carencro.

"Sure, we got all that," Dopsie assured me.

"I'd like to bring in some of the Cajun players," I told him.

"Who you thinking of?"

I said I thought of calling up the well-known traditional Cajun fiddler, Dewey Balfa,

"Oh man, me and Dewey go way back! You go ahead and call him!"

For the rehearsal we were using the small building on the farm, and I asked Dewey to bring along some of his band as well. We'd also re-corded together, and I felt that anything in the new French style would have to include the steel guitar borrowed from the country and western groups that now had become standard with the Cajun bands. It was the tenor saxophone and the *frottoir* in Dopsie's band that identified their music as zydeco. I also asked Dewey to bring along his young nephew Tony, the son of Dewey's brother Rodney, to add the sound of the standard hollow body guitar. Rodney, a singer and guitarist in the Balfa Brothers Orchestra, had died in a car crash a few months before, along with a third Balfa brother, Will, a violinist, and Tony was determined to carry on the family tradition. Once everyone found the building and the instruments were set up, we found ourselves sitting in each other's laps. Since Jay Pelsia's pedal steel took up the middle of the room, and Dopsie's son's drums filled up one wall behind him, everyone else had to find some space that was still empty. The only way I could think of to start the rehearsal was just to name a tune they might know, and then begin to put some kind of arrangement together when the problems were clear. As a guess, I suggested a popular old dance piece, "Shopick Two-Step."

"What key do you play that in?" Dewey turned to Dopsie's guitarist, Charley Tyler. Charley called out the key, everybody nodded, Dopsie gave a count, and with a sudden, relentless rhythm the group swung into the tune. By the time they'd gotten through half a chorus it was obvious how closely they had all grown up with each other's music. Dopsie shouted out the vocal in his country French, solos flowed without a break over the loping rhythm, the guitarists Tony and Charley checked each other's fingerings on the chord changes, John Hart filled in the accompaniment with a saxophone riff he'd obviously learned when he was first starting out to play for dances, and Jay Pelsia's steel wove its familiar patterns through the dense instrumental texture. I had thought, when I suggested the idea to Dopsie, that I would be bringing together two traditions that had begun to go their own ways, despite their existing side by side in their small communities. What I realized after a moment was that the traditions had never really lost touch with each other. After the piece had gone on for three or four minutes and the musicians glanced quickly at each other and effortlessly tied their impromptu jam together in a bright final chord, Dewey looked around, catching his breath, and announced, as he always did when something he'd played had felt really good, "I just about sawed this old fiddle in half!"

It would be simple to say that Dopsie had no consciousness of any kind of the larger cultural role that his little band was filling as they traveled the Louisiana roads, since he didn't use the sort of language that translates ideas like these into sociological terms. Dopsie, however, just used other words to say the same thing. When I occasionally asked him about how he felt in his role he would smile his usual quick, warm smile and say something as comfortable as, "I'm just carryin' on. That's what I'm doing when I'm out there. There's something I got that only me and the other boys like me can keep going with. So that's all I'm doing—that's what we all doing—just carryin' on."

One night at one of the neighborhood clubs in Houston I was sitting at a back table with Dopsie while the band was setting up the amplifiers when we suddenly noticed a man in the corner of the dark room, talking in a low voice to the heavy-set man in shirt sleeves who owned the club. The man was in a good-looking jacket, but it hung on his shoulders and he had obviously lost some weight since he'd bought it. His hair was processed and he had an air of style about him. It was Clifton Chenier. He had clearly driven over to look for work, and that meant that he had put a band together again. He looked around the room as he talked, and he certainly saw Dopsie, even though he didn't give any sign that he was aware of him. He left without a glance behind him. Dopsie shook his head and sighed, "The times I've lent that man money."

For months Dopsie, like the others in the small zydeco community, had done what he could for Clifton, hoping he could go back on the road again.

Chenier had also ended his long relationship with Arhoolie Records. His records weren't selling the way they had been when he was playing regularly in California, but he chose to shift the blame for the shrinking sales onto Arhoolie's patient owner, Chris Strachwitz. Clifton put together a new band, sometimes playing harmonica, and then using a new Italian-built electronic accordion that didn't have to be pulled to make it sound. His brother Cleveland was still with him, and his son C. J. Chenier was playing either accordion or saxophone, depending on the arrangement. It was, as always with Clifton, a tight, exciting band. I followed them up to Chicago and heard them in a club there, and since Clifton was without a contract for the first time in many years I arranged to do an album with him.

Dopsie, with his usual generosity, didn't hold it against me that I was going to record Clifton. He had grown up with Clifton's music and he couldn't have formed his own band without following the path that Clifton had marked. Clifton and I worked out what might go into the album when I met him at jobs around the country, and we did the new album at a studio in Bogalusa, a small town northeast of New Orleans. Clifton was notoriously difficult to work with, but the band was sharp, they'd been out on the road, and he had some strong new material. I even managed to get a second take on at least one of the songs, and when he blustered about a payment larger than the contract we'd already signed I managed to face him down. The album wasn't his best, or the best record I'd ever done, but it won a Grammy award in 1983. Zydeco was now on the larger world music map.

For the next album with Dopsie we used a studio in Baton Rouge. It was in a neighborhood that looked no worse than I was used to, but the band knew better. They wouldn't let me outside the building without one or two of them walking beside me. We had the same problems with Dopsie and new lyrics, but we wanted him to do his version of a local hit by Rocking Sidney, who played out of Lake Charles. The song was a traditional children's piece, known under many different titles, but all of them with the general theme of "Down on the Farm." The humor of the song is that down on the farm everybody is asking for you. The pigs are asking for you, the cows are asking for you—in this new version the tomatoes ask for you, the potatoes ask for you, the corn asks for you. Dopsie was in an isolated booth for most of the session, so his accordion playing wouldn't bleed onto the other instrumental tracks, and I couldn't see him as he was singing. To my surprise he got the name of every vegetable, and he got them in the right order. I went out to the isolation booth to congratulate him and he opened the door with a broad smile.

Clifton Chenier at the Blue Angel Lounge, his home club in Lafayette.

"I got 'em right here! I didn't miss a one!"

In the morning he'd gone out to a local grocery store and bought one of every vegetable he was supposed to sing about. He had lined them up in front of the microphone and he waved at them, still smiling.

"Every one of them's there—and I got 'em! I got 'em all!"

The album was nominated for a Grammy the next year, and Dopsie made the trip to New York for what he was certain was the zydeco prize. To his acute disappointment, the Grammy went to folk guitarist Elizabeth Cotton. Dopsie called me with pain in his voice.

"That prize was supposed to go to zydeco, and they gave it to that old woman!"

Did zydeco change as the bands began traveling outside their bayou world? The essence of this language of song, this African-influenced musical language, is that it continually changes, and it is the artists themselves who carry on the process of change. Some of the zydeco musicians, like Dopsie and Boozoo Chavis, didn't change. Boozoo, three years older than Dopsie, a successful farmer and horse breeder who wore a plastic apron when he played to keep the sweat from his shirt away from the accordion, had a strong country attachment to his zydeco roots, and he didn't want to change any more than Dopsie did. Out in California, in the Louisiana community there, Queen Ida Guillory and the Bon Temps Band continued to perform in the old bayou style, but it isn't surprising that most of the younger musicians, like Clifton Chenier's son and his keyboard player Stanley "Buckwheat" Dural, as well as his trumpet player Warren Caesar, played a newer kind of zydeco. The influence now wasn't R & B, it was soul music. When Buckwheat first went on his own he featured an organ sound with his band and he could handle a smooth motel lounge job anywhere in the country. A few years later, with a contract with England's Island Records and a full brass section added to the arrangements, Buckwheat became zydeco's best-selling artist, with a blend of soul, R & B, and rock, all of it with a zydeco tinge. It is the natural progression with any music that grows from a culture that is continually changing and evolving.

The relentless pace of Dopsie's new life demanded too much from him, after so many years of long drives and the late nights. He suffered a serious heart attack when he was in his fifties. A final attack ended his life in 1993, at the age of sixty-one. Of all the memories I have of the years with Dopsie the one that still comes back the most often is a moonlit night in the islands off the east coast of Sweden. The record company had brought Dopsie and the band to Stockholm to help celebrate the company's twenty-fifth anniversary, and Dopsie was playing on a small, turn-of-the-century, steam-driven ferry boat that had been built to take Stockholmers out to their summer homes on the islands. The band was playing with fierce enthusiasm, and Dopsie was pulling his accordion on the jammed middle deck with the perspiration streaming down his face, his shirt and the tops of his trousers streaked with sweat. I went up onto the narrow little deck to catch my breath, and I heard someone calling up to me. I looked over the side and I saw a motor boat, slipping through the water beside us.

"What is that music?" the voice called.

I leaned over the railing and shouted "Rocking Dopsie!"

In the half darkness I could make out a head nodding. "Beautiful," the voice answered, "So beautiful!"

Then I straightened up and looked behind us. There in the moonlight, threading through the narrow channels between the islands, was a stream of small boats, all of them edging as close to the little steamer as they could, listening to Dopsie and his music. I could sense what the sound of Dopsie's voice meant to that shining night and to the people listening to him in the stillness, listening almost as though, at that moment, they had forgotten how to breathe.

13 ✳ ¿Como se llama este ritmo?

The Music of Cuba, Bebo Valdés, and the Buena Vista Social Club

"¿Como se llama este ritmo?" "What's the name of that rhythm?" I asked the tall, gray-haired man in a comfortable sweatshirt and sweat pants who was sitting by the CD speakers with me. My Spanish was a memory from my school days.

Bebo Valdés smiled and began to gesture with his long, elegant fingers, "It's a conga. You listen to the little beat there," and with his arm he picked up the second beat of the measure. The accent came a little before the beat—it was an almost imperceptible shift, and I hadn't heard it until he made me conscious of it. Now I could hear that the other two musicians on the recording were accenting the rhythm at just that same place and with just the same anticipation. It was that slight catch of breath that gave the arrangement its momentum. For most of the quiet afternoon in his apartment we had been going through a test pressing of his latest recording, a trio, with some arrangements including the saxophone and clarinet of Paquito D'Rivera, that I had heard him recording in a downstairs recording studio in Greenwich Village in New York the spring before. Bebo was the pianist, Cachao, one of the legends of the 1950s world of Afro Cuban music, was the bass player, a friend since their childhood days in Havana and a musician Charlie Mingus once described as the world's finest bass player. The congas player—the "congalero"—was the famed Patato, who had been a friend for almost as long.

"You listen, on this song, 'Romance en La Habana,' it's a bolero, and it's played like a rumba. I don't play the second beat in the rhythm, like the bolero, but I accent the next two beats like a rumba. Cachao, he's playing *doble*—double the rhythm." What I had first listened to, in the studio while they were recording it, was the gentle melody that Paquito had breathed through his brown wood clarinet. As Bebo showed me the rhythm with his fingers I still heard the melody, but now I also heard the subtle texturing of the other instruments. With the music of Cuba there is always this layering, this subtle texturing of tones and accents that makes us conscious again of the complexities of its many musical styles.

Afro-Cuban music today is a ripe blending of every style of music that has made its way onto the island, from the frenzy of the newest salsa bands to the stately assurance of the Buena Vista Social Club; from the irrepressible jazz-toned new music of Irakere, led by Bebo's pianist son, the multi-Grammy winner Chucho Valdés, to the fresh compositions of Paquito D'Rivera. In its most obvious manifestations Cuban music would seem easy to sort out. At one edge of the musical spectrum is the drumming of the religious groups, many of them of the Yoruba Santaría faith, with the drumming of their secret men's society, the Abakuá. With them, like the Santaría drummers of other Caribbean islands, it is almost meaningless to speak of their playing as Afro-Cuban or Afro-Haitian or Afro-anything—it is so close to African drumming that the only thing separating their styles today is the distance of the ocean between them. At the other edge of the spectrum is the emergence of experimental groups like Los Afrokanes, with their rhythm called *Mozambique*, that Pedro Izquierdo "Pello El Afrokán" developed in the 1960s. In between is what is often described as one of the most complex and rich harvest of African-influenced musical styles of any of the Western Hemisphere countries, a musical outpouring that has reached everywhere in the New World, and stretched back to effect the music of Africa itself.

Cuba, the United States, and Brazil usually are considered the three fountains of musical creativity that have flowed from the arrival of Africans in the new hemisphere, and everything that is characteristic of the assimilation of African elements into another musical culture is there in Cuban music. The persistence of polyrhythms, renewed continually by the influence of the drummers, has colored and shaped the melodies as they blend with the rhythmic shifts. Short repetitive phrases forming the harmonies are clearly at the root of the *montuno* piano rhythms of the orchestral arrangements. In song after song there is the call and response of the chorus, and for much Afro-Cuban music there is the irresolution of major and minor modes that is the characteristic reworking of the African vocal scales. Also, it is music shaped for dance and celebration, music that brings swirling crowds of dancers into the night clubs or onto the streets in festival times in a flow of movement that is a celebration of the body itself.

I don't know if I could have found my way through the elusive subtleties of Cuban rhythms without someone like Bebo Valdés. I think at the beginning, what everyone hears in Cuban music are pulsing rhythms we can count out as *one-two*—and for dancing we don't need to think of much else. Around the base of one-two there is another texture of beats—accented notes in the bass, hands elaborating the rhythms on drum heads, sticks scraping on scratched gourds, seeds rattling in smaller dried gourds, sticks clicking together, sticks pattering against the metal sides of a drum on a stand. It is in the accents and the texture that so much that is unique in Cuban music is created. As I listened to the arrangements I *heard* the rhythms through the pointing of Bebo's fingers. Over several months I spent many afternoons with him, listening to him rehearse with his son for a recording project we'd planned as they talked about Cuban rhythms and accents, but the three of us sometimes still laughed about the first afternoon we had met.

I'd only spoken to Bebo over the telephone in the suburb of Stockholm, where he has lived for more than thirty years, and in the spring of 1998, when we agreed to meet outside a downtown subway station, I suddenly realized I hadn't thought of asking him what he looked like. I am as used to a city that is filled with slim, pale Swedes as he is, and I thought I would have no trouble in the uncrowded subway entranceways finding a nearly eighty-year-old Afro-Cuban pianist. Instead, as I looked around the different entrances, I realized that Stockholm had changed in the years that Bebo and I had lived there. Any one of more than a dozen men I saw could be the person I wanted to find. So that I wouldn't have to go on asking strangers around the central plaza in downtown Stockholm if they were Bebo Valdés, I took a piece of paper that I'd brought to make notes and wrote the name

VALDES

on it in large letters. Beside a newsstand close to the doors leading to the plaza I saw a tall, dignified man, his short hair graying, his skin a light tan color. He was in neatly creased chinos, with a dress shirt and a light windbreaker jacket. He was thin, but I had a sense of a wiry strength. Beside him was a shorter, younger man looking nervously around at people walking past. His skin was lighter and his face thinner, but it was clear that the older man was his father.

This time when I held up my crude sign there was a nod. The gray-haired man studied my face, then said carefully, "That's me."

I had called Bebo because the Swedish record company I worked with for many years had asked me if there was a possibility he could do an album for them. Bebo said we should sit down at an outdoor hamburger restaurant not far from the newsstand and we could talk. With his son Rickard a few steps behind us, we walked to one of the tables, Bebo studying me intently to see who I might be. Like most veteran musicians he had picked up a workable English in his years of traveling, and his Swedish was even more helpful. The only sore point between us over the years has been that I don't speak Spanish well enough for us to talk as easily as he does with so many other friends. When we found a table and

Bebo Valdés. *Photograph by Ewa Stackelberg,*
Courtesy Gazell Records.

I brought over something to drink, Bebo asked me what the company
was, and what did we want. His expression was guarded, and he never
took his eyes off my face. It was a fall day, which means, in Sweden, that
it was chilly, and we were sitting on hard, cold iron chairs, but the day
was bright and sunny and there was a buzz of people clustered at other
tables and walking past on the edges of the plaza. Finally he gestured
to Rickard, who had been holding a small Walkman cassette player.
Rickard handed it across the table to me.

"Is this what you want?"

I put on the earphones, turned on the cassette player, and almost
fell off my chair. The music was one of the purest performances of a
traditional Cuban danzón I had ever heard. There was a freshness to
the playing and a clarity to the melody and rhythm that turned this old
Cuban style into a modern experience. It was a tape of Bebo performing
at a recent concert in Madrid, with Rickard accompanying him on *timbales*. Bebo saw the expression on my face, and he leaned back, smiling
for the first time.

"If that's what you want, then we have it!"

"When you play a *son* it's a very old rhythm. The song now, "Son de la
Loma," that's a *son*. The *bajo*—the bass—plays this." Bebo and I were

in his apartment, listening to another of the songs on his new CD. He sketched out the accents of the bass rhythm. "And the *güiro*, it plays this." His other hand moved in a scraping rhythm. "You have a guitar, and it does this." A strumming movement with the first hand, which somehow didn't interrupt the bass rhythm I still could see in front of me. "The *bongos* and the *claves*." His fingers fluttered with movements as light as the air. "Then the *tres*." And he made a brighter, more distinctly accented sound and his fingers picked at the air with a more decisive gesture. As his hands moved in the apartment's soft afternoon light he had somehow managed to give the polyrhythms of the *son* a physical shape. He leaned back with his short, high laugh. "So much to learn about Cuban music."

I shook my head and laughed with him. Some of the things that give the Cuban styles their distinctiveness I also could as easily have encountered in other places I'd traveled. If I hadn't heard the scraped gourd, the güiro, in Cuban music I would have heard it in other Latin music styles, since it's everywhere, and there was no confusion with *bongos* or *claves*. The *tres*, the guitar with three double strung sets of strings, was more Cuban, but so many of the world's instruments are familiar to us now. But the nuances of Cuban rhythms, the shifting texture of sounds—there is, as Bebo laughed, so much to learn.

If Bebo's life were not so filled with events, and if he didn't show a calm acceptance of whatever his life has brought him, his story could perhaps have been considered an unhappy one, and as we sat in his quiet apartment in a large suburban apartment block, I was conscious that he was willing to show me anything I asked him about Cuban rhythms because he was so isolated from Cuba. What happened to Bebo happened to virtually an entire generation of Cuban musicians, and the music of the island will always be affected by the absence of this generation. What happened to them was the Castro revolution. Whatever good came to Cuban workers and to peasants in the countryside from Castro's seizure of power in January 1959 and his subsequent turn to a Soviet-styled government, the change was catastrophic for Cuba's free-wheeling musicians, most of whom were employed in the tourist casinos, and who had their own touring itineraries. Bebo had been the pianist and arranger at the best known of the casinos, the Tropicana Night Club, for more than ten years, until the dangerous chaos of the period of the Revolution before Castro's fighters entered Havana forced him to begin working in a hotel that was better protected. By the early 1960s Bebo and many of the musicians he had worked with for so many years were gone.

In his comprehensive survey *Música cubana*, published in 1981, Dr. Cristóbal Díaz Ayala lists the important musicians who left the country in the months around 1960 and continued to flee over the next few years. Their difficulties began when the members of the casino dance orchestras and the singers and entertainers on radio and television were declared to be ordinary workers, like any others, with the same salaries and the same working conditions.[1] His list includes nearly ninety names, and ends with "etc." Among the names included are singer Celia Cruz, who toured with the Buena Vista Social Club, the singer Rolando La Serie, who left for Mexico with Bebo, the trumpeters El Negro Vivar and Chocolate Armenteros, from Bebo's El Sabor de Cuba orchestra, Cachao, Paquito D'Rivera, and Bebo himself. As Dr. Ayala himself emphasizes, at the same time as so many artists left, the Cuban musical climate was so fertile that there were other performers ready to take their places. But without tourists the new orchestras and singers didn't have the same kind of audiences to play for, and the musicians who remained faced long years of scuffling for work.

It is perhaps some kind of undefined compensation for what they faced that it was Cuban musicians who were at the center of the unexpected worldwide renewal of interest in Latin American music in the 1990s. When the American guitarist Ry Cooder traveled to Havana in 1993, planning to do an album combining African musicians with Cuban veterans, he found an older generation of brilliant musicians who had little work and little future. There were unexpected difficulties with travel visas for the Africans, but Cooder already had a recording team with him, so he decided to record a group of the Cubans he had just met. His recordings with them, as the Buena Vista Social Club, became a worldwide success. The album sold as jazz, as instrumental music, as a Latin collection, and as a popular release. In countries like Germany the album sold hundreds of thousands of copies on the pop charts.

A number of world tours followed, and when the group came to Stockholm I wondered how Bebo would feel about them. He had played in bands with some of their fathers, and he had employed many of them in his own orchestras. Would he envy their sudden fame? Marie, his wife, said that at their concert he didn't stop smiling, his long arms moving with the melodies, his hands sometimes pointing to the rhythms. He was as pleased for the men and women on the stage as if they'd been his own children, and they were as excited to have him in the audience. They talked so much about their former great band leader that people around him kept turning their heads to see where Bebo was sitting. On a later tour the band brought him on stage to accompany Celia Cruz, who had sung in his orchestra at the Tropicana in Havana forty years before. For the musicians in the group it was as much of a surprise to find Bebo there in Stockholm as it was for most of the excited people in the audience around him, who hadn't been aware that he had been living in their city since early in the 1960s.

If you begin to listen seriously to Cuban music you soon realize that every arrangement is shaped around a distinct rhythm. On the backs of the older LPs by Latin musicians there is almost invariably a concise listing of the rhythm for each piece—*guajira, danzón, bolero, mambo, mambo son, mambo descarga, son capricho, conga, cha cha chá*, along with a dozen other variants. On the LPs Bebo recorded with his El Sabor de Cuba Orquesta and his Havana Jazz All Stars, the brilliant, ground-breaking ensembles he led in the 1950s, the rhythms are appended to each song title. The variety of names is like a handful of bright flowers, bunched in a bouquet. Sometimes the names have descriptive subdivisions, like *rumba son*. The style Bebo introduced himself in the early 1950s, the *batanga*, is there—sometimes modified to batanga-montuno.

The names of the rhythms, however, don't help someone listening to the music for the first time. After a few years of playing rock and roll drums, Bebo's youngest son Rickard asked his father to teach him the Cuban rhythms, "to carry on the old tradition. You know," Rickard explained self-consciously. Months went into their afternoon rehearsals so that Rickard would be able to play with his father on the double CD we were planning. Rickard studied the rhythms his father had annotated on a collection of music scores and then tried to follow his father's play-ing on the *timbales*, a small drum mounted horizontally on a waist high drum stand, or on a small orchestra drum kit. When Bebo and other Cuban musicians talk about their style of playing they always emphasize the African roots that make Cuban culture so distinctive, and when he explains the rhythms or describes the styles himself Bebo invariably uses the term *Afro Cuban*.

"In our music you have to have polyrhythm. That's because it's Afro-Cuban. It comes from Africa. You can hear it in everything we play. What you hear in the rhythms is Africa, from the drums." Even though he'd spent years working as a solo pianist after his move to Stockholm in the 1960s, he couldn't consider doing any recording without Rickard's rhythm accompaniments. He shook his head emphatically at the idea.

"If you don't have polyrhythms you don't have Cuban music!"

The drums of the African-derived religions which play such an im-portant role in Cuban life are also part of the array of the island's percussion instruments. There are three types of drums, called *Bata* drums, used in the Santería ceremonies, with their close affinity to the

Yoruba ceremonies in Africa. They are sacred drums, shaped like an hour glass, with the heads attached to the wooden body of the drum with sinew. The drums have kept their Yoruba names—the lead drum, the largest, is called *Itotele*, the smallest is *Okonkolo*, and the middle drum is *Iya*. The Yoruba rattle is also part of the orchestra percussion. It is called *shekere*, a large gourd covered with an elaborate weave of beads that rattle against the hard surface of the gourd when it's shaken. Unlike the smaller maracas and güiros, the *shekere* is also struck on the bottom for a heavier sound. It is sometimes called by its Yoruba name *agbe*.

Two other instruments in the popular Cuban orchestras of the 1920s were also closely linked to Africa and the slave past. The string bass came late into the *son* orchestras, perhaps because it is a large, expensive instrument, and it isn't easy to learn. One of the substitutes was the *botija*, a large clay jug that came to the island filled with olive oil from Spain. It's played by blowing across its mouth, just as jugs were used in the novelty jug bands of the American South in the 1920s. The other substitute, which is still played today, is the *marimbula*, a version of the African thumb piano that has grown into a row of metal strips on the side of a wooden box. The instrument is so large the player sits on it. It is part of an older style called *changui*.

In the United States the drums of the jazz orchestras were never given the prominence of Latin drums. The jazz drummer is much more useful sitting behind the other musicians so the soloists can hear the beat. In the Cuban orchestras, rooted in the rich drum traditions, the *congoleros* and the *timbaleros* have taken center stage. At the height of the mambo craze in the 1950s Bebo was asked by a New York music publisher to introduce a collection of his pieces, some of them renamed to work *mambo* into the title, with a history of the mambo. In his short essay Bebo credits one of the modern Cuban musicians with bringing the drums into their central place in the orchestras.

An important contribution to the development of the Mambo was made by one of the veterans of Cuban music, ARSENIO RODRIGUEZ, the blind orchestra leader and composer. His "BRUCA MANIGUA" was a big hit, and although he named this new rhythm "DIABLO" (Devil) and not "Mambo," he added several of the important features of the Mambo of today. It was his idea to enclose in his band the "Tumbadora," the Mambo drums which today are the indispensable rhythm section of every mambo band.

Following Rodríguez's lead, the gleaming conga drums, often painted in bright reds and greens, are the first thing you notice when you see a modern Latin band.

In their months of rehearsals Rickard found that the one rhythm that was the most uncomfortable for him was also the oldest of everything his father played. It was the *danzon*, which doesn't flow with the loose sway of the other Cuban rhythms. Cuba's colonial culture was Spanish, and the continual adaptations of African rhythms to European song forms took on the coloration of the Spanish forms. The sources of the danzón, however, were French. The name itself was derived from the name of a popular French dance of the eighteenth century, the *contradanse*. In the composition of the Cuban slave population there were clear differentiations between many areas of the island. In the west of Cuba, which included Havana, the largest proportion of slaves came from the Ashanti areas in Dahomey, and their language and religion were Yoruba. In the eastern provinces of the island, however, centering around the city of Santiago, there were large numbers of slaves who had arrived later from Haiti.

As the slave revolt in the 1790s ravaged the Haitian countryside and the slave armies led by the charismatic Toussaint L'Ouverture succeeded in driving out the French rulers in 1803, many Haitian plantation owners fled to Cuba with their slaves. The contradance was the formal dance of the French masters, and as in all slave cultures, the musicians who played for the plantation entertainments were slaves themselves. The early contradance was performed first in a circle, then as a line dance. Finally danced with a partner, it became the formal dance of the Cuban upper classes. In his *Diccionario de la música cubana* Helio Orovio points out that both of the basic Cuban rhythmic innovations, the habanera and the danzón, derive from this earlier contradanse, which was called *la danza criolla*, "the Creole dance."[2]

This was the earliest new form of dance that was characteristically Cuban. With its subtly syncopated beat and thinly veiled African melodic elements it became wildly popular as the *habanera danza*—the nineteenth-century Habanera that inspired a wave of European and North American imitations. In South America it was the rhythmic foundation for the *tango*, which emerged in slightly different forms in Brazil and Argentina, each claiming to be first. In Europe it was the rhythm for the popular aria from Bizet's opera *Carmen*. The form that developed from the Cuban danza, which became known as *son*, became the music of the streets and public dance halls. As couples danced the danzón in upper-class parlors, the body was held stiffly and the dancers touched only each other's hands. The patterns of the rhythm guided the dancers' feet through the sequences of the dance. The accents of the *son*, on the other hand, flowed with all of the movements of the body. In an introduction to a collection of historical *son* recordings, John Santos summed

The streets around Calle Neptuno in Havana.

up many of the factors that led to the success of the new dance, including the popularity of the style with the small string ensembles of Havana.

. . . We can safely say that the Afro-Cuban *son* actually began to take shape towards the end of the 19th century, coinciding with the abolition of slavery in Cuba (1880s). The unique sound of the Cuban *son* is the result of the combination of stringed instruments and poetry used by the Spanish-descended Campesinos (rural peasant farmers) with African derived rhythmic elements. It is also an accurate microcosm of Cuba's cultural history since the ending of slavery. This is not to say that all of the rhythmic elements of the *son* are African, nor that all the melodic and linguistic elements are purely Spanish. It was mostly in the hands of Black and Mulatto musicians that the *son* took shape and emerged.[3]

Santos also emphasized that the origins of *son* lay in the east of Cuba, although then as now Havana drew to it the most talented and ambitious of the country's musicians. The earliest recordings of the *son* were made in 1912, and the first recordings of one of the small instrumental groups who were to become identified with the *son*, the Sexteto Habanero, were made in 1918. For a time Havana's polite society complained about the vulgarity and licentiousness of a dance with hips swaying and arms opening to an embrace, as well as the uninhibited social commentary of some of the *son* lyrics, but on Havana's streets and in its thriving dance halls, as everywhere else, it was soon the uninhibited rhythms of the new dance that prevailed.

Though Havana today is struggling with the long years of poverty that followed the collapse of the Soviet Union early in the 1990s, music is still part of the clamor of the streets. On a late afternoon walk in 2005 along Calle Neptuno, a long, clogged street that begins close to the Capitol building and rises to end at the steps of the university, I gave most of my attention to balancing safely on the narrow sidewalk as people crowded past me on their way home. The narrow street itself was choked with a stream of the picturesque old cars that function as taxis, and battered, three-wheeled mini-cabs that carry one or two passengers on the back of what looks like a gasoline driven bicycle with a handmade metal shell covering the passengers. The fumes and the noise of the laboring engines filled the street, and the worn engines of the old Detroit cars that are the favorite of tourists added more fumes to the heavy air. From time to time I had to take a chance with the traffic to get around the lines that still lingered outside the occasional small shop that had something new to offer on its dusty shelves, or to pass the knots of friends who occupied the sidewalk exchanging the day's news. Calle Neptuno, with all its life and excitement, is very poor, and whatever you encounter only insists on presenting you with a new face of the street's poverty. As the light faded, however, the traffic thinned, and the air stirred with the evening wind, and over the noise of the passing mini-cabs I could hear the rhythms and the melodies of Cuban music.

The sun was bright and the day was warm, but it was the Cuban winter and it was the last day of the year. Along Neptuno people were preparing for New Year's Eve. Part of the chaos along the street was the press of people returning early from their jobs, and up and down the street people were decorating their rooms, or hurrying to bring the food and the drinks for their family's party. The buildings along Neptune Street are the old, familiar stucco-front colonial buildings that perhaps are the most familiar image of today's Havana. They are two or three stories tall, most with balconies out over the sidewalk. Many of them are also in distressingly bad repair. Drying clothes dangle from the railings of the balconies overhead, and some of the side streets leading off Neptuno are still unpaved. They are strewn with rubbish and scattered building stones. Occasional streets are blocked with the rough wooden scaffoldings built haphazardly to complete repairs that have been under way for considerable time.

Along Neptuno, however, like everywhere in Havana, faces were smiling, voices called shrill greetings to neighbors across the street. Men with hair still glistening from a shower, in fresh T-shirts and pressed slacks, swung bottles of rum by the neck as they turned in a doorway. Women in bright skirts and ornate blouses edged carefully along the sidewalk carrying plates of food or decorated cakes under wrinkled sheets of cellophane in their outstretched hands. The old buildings are built against the sidewalk, and in most of the downstairs apartments the tall wooden shutters were left open. As I passed, I could see the modest paper decorations that had been carefully arranged on the table in the center of the room. The bulbs of the hanging chandeliers and the floor lamps had all been turned on, their light shining on the pictures tacked to the walls and the bright coverings on the best furniture. In some of the rooms the older women had already settled at the table and they were laughing at something with their daughters. In another room a new mother in a freshly laundered dress bent down to help her small baby through the complicated maneuver of turning from its back to its stomach.

I could hear music everywhere, some loud and piercing, some softly muted and thoughtful, drifting from the shadowy back rooms. The music came from small tape cassette players, or from the new, shiny gray cassette and CD players that had unexpectedly arrived in many of the shops for the holidays. *Bolero, cha cha chá, mambo, guäjiro, son.* Cuba's dance rhythms. From an upstairs apartment I could hear the metallic ring of a live band, the clatter of the *claves,* the wooden sticks that mark the rhythm for the dance orchestras, the brittle accents of the *bongos* rattling against the fronts of the buildings across the street. I often walked along Neptuno, and never felt any hostility from the people I passed on the sidewalk, even when I had to make my way around clusters of women and children with plastic buckets waiting for water from one of the battered communal water trucks or dodging into the traffic to get around the patient crowds waiting for bread that is passed out through the small window of the government bakery. What we all had to endure was the concentration of exhaust fumes, since at its lowest points Neptuno seems to act as a collector of the carbons spilling out of the laboring motors of the hordes of cars. Voices called out across the street, "Feliz Año! Feliz Año!" It was New Year's Eve, and the music coming from the open windows in the street was only a part of a cascading stream that was sweeping everything in the city before it.

I had already found that Havana offered music almost everywhere I turned. In the large plazas, in the restaurants, along the streets and outdoor markets where the tourists gather, classic ensembles perform traditional pieces in the older styles. The poverty of the city gives the music a nostalgic flavor since the bands don't have money for the microphones and amplifiers that would change the nostalgic character of their *sexteto* and *septeto* arrangements. All of the musicians still sing, they still alternate playing different instruments, and most of the groups still perform with a beautifully balanced acoustic sound. What you hear is the old natural style—six or seven voices blending in the familiar harmonies and the rhythms still defined by the sharp tick of the *claves*, the scratch of the *güiro*, and the light beat of the *bongos*. The solos of the *tres*, without any amplification, still mingle their distinct tone with the strummed rhythms of the guitars. With prosperity the sound will change—in the tourist hotels most of the groups are beginning to use electric bass guitars—but in Havana's older neighborhoods the music still echoes the city's past.

Closer to midnight I walked along La Rampa, a broad boulevard at the beginning of the hills around Havana University, stopping to listen to the sumptuous varieties of music playing for the cheerfully drunken young New Year's crowds who often begin to dance spontaneously on the dark sidewalk to any rhythms coming from a doorway. La Rampa was given its name, "The Ramp," since it slips down from the hills to the sea wall of Melecón. It is lined with restaurants, and it also offers downstairs jazz clubs. The crest of the hill is crowned with a modern, outsize tourist hotel, and across from the hotel is a small city park with a modern, many-leveled ice cream parlor that had lines of people waiting at what seems to be any hour. Walking down from the park and the hotel, with the soft night breeze feeling like the brush of a hand against my face, I passed crowds eddying in front of a half-dozen fashionable restaurants. The mood was just as elated as I'd felt in the poorer blocks of Neptuno, but this was a more upscale Havana, with brighter dresses, suit jackets on some of the men, and newer cars lining the curb.

I could choose music at any of the restaurants or dance clubs, with their brightly lit doorways interrupting the shadows along the sidewalk. At one slickly decorated restaurant with a wide window opening onto the street a trio was playing familiar *son* melodies, but they were performing on an electric keyboard, with amplified bongos and maracas. The musicians in the trio looked out toward the sidewalk with some anxiety in their expressions. The tables in front of them were empty. The crowds had gathered, instead, at the *cafetería* next door, with a classic *grupo* playing without amplification. The cafetería is a favorite for me. I had walked to it two or three times in the evenings to eat their stringy, but robustly

The orchestra at the Cafetería Sofía.

flavored fried chicken with rice. Though it is called a cafetería, the Cafetería Sofia is a casual restaurant with a small dining room at the end of a hallway for diners who want to avoid the noise of voices and laughter around the musicians. The large room beside the sidewalk where the band plays is open to the air, with only low railings as a barrier to the street. Young waitresses in dark trousers and white blouses, some looking like students, wait patiently beside the tables for the noisy parties to decide what they're going to order.

The band plays in the corner of the room, five nights of the week, standing in front of the jukebox that fills in behind the rush of talk when the group takes a break. The leader, an energetic man with a quick smile, about thirty-five, looked surprised at my question, then shrugged, nodded, and wrote down the group's name for me. *Grupo Marian Verdecia y Tradicion Cubana.* In all the hours that I'd listened to them their music had been comfortable and loose, and with an easy air of spontaneity, even though they performed favorite songs they'd played hundreds of times before. Night after night the group brought so much of the flavor of Cuban music to me. It wasn't because they were distinctive in any way, but because they were typical of the hundreds of small ensembles that kept the traditions of their music alive.

There were seven musicians in *Grupo Marian*, completely at ease with the classic arrangements. They'd obviously spent most of their nights playing in a group like this somewhere in Havana. They were all in florid orange shirts printed with a scene from an ocean shoreline. Dark outlines of palm trees reached to their shoulders, with the gray shapes of small boats and splashes of leaves along the bottom of the shirts. They did the usual doubling of instruments. The tall, dark-skinned flutist in gold-rimmed glasses played the *güiro* on some of the pieces. *Maracas* were handed around. The skin colors of the musicians were the usual Cuban spectrum. The güiro player–flutist was dark—tall and lanky, with gold-rimmed glasses. The guitarist was white, with a broad Spanish forehead, the *tres* player shorter and blockier, was light skinned, with a shaved head and an earring dangling from his left ear.

When you sit down in front of these *sexteto* or *septeto* groups a first impression is always that the sound will be heavily rhythmic, since usually there is only a flute playing the melody, with a solo by the *tres* somewhere in the arrangement. The rhythm is layered with the tonal kaleidoscope of bongos and the cow bell, bass, claves, guiro, rhythm guitar, and the *tres*, which also fills in the rhythm when it isn't soloing. For the trios and quartets that play in the lobbies of the hotels or restaurants, there is a pedal stand for the cow bell, like the stand for the sock cymbal of a dance band drum set, which one of the musicians, usually a guitarist, plays with one foot. The steady metallic pulse is one of the necessary elements of the sound. The rhythm, however, never dominates the ensemble. The voices act as the balance to the texture of the beat. All of the musicians sing, and they sing in chorus with a strong, thickly chorded, harmonic syncopation. It is a style that took the Cuban musicians many years to create, and its balances and nuances have been buffed to a high gloss, even in groups like the band at the Cafetería Sofia, that passes a basket for tips. It is difficult to imagine that the sound could be as strong, and at the same moment so personal and intimate, if it were strained through amplifiers and microphones.

The *Grupo Marian*'s midnight set opened with a sing-along—"Feliz Navidad"—which translates as "Merry Christmas," but did as well for New Year's Eve, since it had an uptempo beat and everybody knew the words. For the rest of the night the music was the usual selection of familiar melodies. For the moment Havana's problems were forgotten in the flow of song.

In the evenings when I stopped in the cafeteria for a quick supper I also heard, in everything the *grupo* played, the African rhythmic textures and the repetitions of the call and response choruses that characterized every melody. It was, however, not only the cultural factors of Cuban slavery that left their mark on Cuba's music. Just as in each of the areas in the New World with slave populations, the coincidences of history also played a decisive role. The island was only thinly inhabited when the Spanish landed, but it was one of the few places in the Caribbean where there was enough of a native population to supply some forced labor as slaves. Ninety percent of the island was thickly forested, and the first years passed as the tree cover was cleared away so crops could be planted. In islands to the south where the Spaniards had found native settlements, disease and resistance to the invaders quickly emptied the villages. In Cuba, however, enough of the people the Spaniards named *caribes* survived to be useful as slave labor. For a short period there was no immediate need for more African importation.

When the importation of slaves began, Cuba's farmers were growing tobacco as their main cash crop. Tobacco is grown on small plots of land, and much of its cultivation requires painstaking hand labor, which was shared between the individual farmers and the handfuls of slaves who shared their life on the farms. In its first century Cuban slavery was different from the gang labor on other Caribbean islands, and the differences were enough to shape a culture with a complex tier of social levels.

The Spanish government had as much difficulty colonizing Cuba as it did its other new lands, and very few single women could be persuaded to make the arduous journey from Spain. Whatever policies officially dealt with the question of racial mixing, the government tacitly understood that many of the early settlers would find wives among the natives or among the slaves. The accepted bargain was that generally the children of these relationships, and sometimes the women themselves, were finally freed. As a consequence, and also as the result of more lenient Spanish attitudes toward the custom of slaves earning their freedom through paid labor away from the plantations, Cuba had a large population of free blacks and children of mixed ancestry. It was one of a small number of Caribbean islands with a white majority. In 1792 the population was a little over 172,000, with 96,400 whites, more than 30,000 free blacks and mulattos, and 44,000 slaves.[4]

This racial mixture in Cuban society changed dramatically in the late

1700s when the plantations grew in size and turned to sugar as their main crop. Sugar was the cruel force that shaped slavery everywhere in the West Indies. The relentless labor that sugar demanded, and the wretched conditions of the crude dwellings where the slaves lived exacted a heavy toll—so heavy that it was necessary to import new slaves continuously to maintain a workforce. The phrase that was common in Cuba was *Se hacer azucar con sangre* ("Sugar is made with blood"). On all of the sugar islands during this period, sugar production was so profitable that the investment in the price of a slave could be balanced by the return on the slave's labor in only two or three years, if the slave survived. With the steady demand for hands in the cane fields and a life expectancy for the slaves of less than twenty-five years, the planters were unconcerned about the possible replacement of their workforce by children of the slaves. The slave ships that landed on the island brought many more men than women, contributing to the social turmoil created by slavery itself.

Between 1791 and 1810 the number of slaves landed at Havana and Santiago tripled, and the broad valleys that spread over the center of the island were planted in sugar. 91,000 slaves were imported during that period, and by 1820 another 131,000 slaves had been brought into Cuba and Puerto Rico, which also was turning to sugar cultivation. Between 1791 and 1870, when Spain finally yielded to the efforts by the British Navy to end the slave trade in the Atlantic, it is estimated that the number of slaves brought to the plantations was nearly 800,000. Cuba's population had been only a little more than 170,000 when the influx began, and at the end of the period a large majority of Cubans were of African ancestry.

The rapidly changing conditions in the Cuban countryside were reflected in chaotic shifts in Cuban society, aggravated by the armed struggles for independence from Spain which continued through most of the century. Many of the political leaders who rose to prominence in the struggle, like the great poet and exiled revolutionary José Martí, who eulogized the island's free peasants, both Spanish and African, were from these early arrivals who worked the small tobacco farms. With the continual rise in sugar prices, the individual landowners were pushed off the most desirable land by the hunger of investors, many of them foreign, for new lands to grow more sugar. Cuba's prosperity had become dependent on its black slaves. By 1817, only twenty-five years after Cuba had been one of the handful of islands with a white majority, Cuba had become more black. Of the population of 600,000, 224, 268 were slaves, and 115,691 were freed Afro-Cubans of mixed blood.

With this continuing flood of new workers to replenish the slave labor force, the cultures, religions, and ceremonies of Africa maintained a vital presence in Cuban everyday life. The Catholic Church also accepted the reality that the native religions brought to the island by the Yoruba people, *Lucumí* and *Santería*, flourished alongside the established church. Their ceremonies continue to have deep roots in the consciousness of the Cuban people today, and their ceremonies continue to attract new worshippers, even during this period of a socialistic economy led by Fidel Castro. The rich traditions of Cuban drumming reflect the importance of the religious sects, at the same time that they continue to nourish the language of song that binds the scattered people of the African diaspora.

I had come to Cuba because everything involving the African musical experience in the new lands interested me, but with Cuba there was the personal reality of my friendship with Bebo Valdés, who had not returned to the country since he fled the new social order nearly forty years before. In some ways I realized that I was seeing it for him. In other ways I was trying to see it through him.

Bebo, with his light, buffed brown skin, and his courtly manners, was from the older free Afro-Cuban society, with its middle-class aspirations. He was born in the city of Quivicán, then thirty miles south of Havana, but now almost within Havana's circle of satellite suburbs. He was born in 1918, and given the name Dionisio Ramón Emilio Valdés Amaro. As the first born son, he was given all of the family's names, ending, as is the Cuban custom, with the name of his mother, Caridid Amaro. "Bebo," is short for "Bebito," "little baby," and it is one of the most common Cuban names for young boys. He was the eldest of six children. When he was born his father worked as an accountant in the city offices, but the economic depression swept over Cuba a decade before it reached the United States, and Bebo's family was very poor. He remembered music in the town square, *orquestas típicas*, modest instrumental ensembles with trumpets, clarinets, violins, drum rhythm, sometimes a guitar. "No pianos." Bebo shook his head. "Pianos came later."

He looked back at Quivicán as a calm, comfortable town of quiet streets, houses with gardens, and friends. A family with children his age—the father managed the one local industry, a glucose factory—had a pianola and a radio that could bring in American stations. An older sister gave him his first piano lessons. This calm, settled background is still part of his quiet manner, even though he moved to Havana as a teenager, living with an aunt as he studied the piano at Havana's Conservatorio Municipal. In the capital he lived in a noisy apartment building, and only a few blocks away student demonstrators were shot to death by

The streets around Calle Neptuno in Havana.

soldiers in the street fighting that swirled around the general strike in the summer of 1933, when the corrupt president Gerardo Machado was finally forced to flee. For a few years there was social progess under the rule of one of the members of the group that had overthrown Machado, Fulgencio Batista, but it was ultimately Batista's increasingly corrupt rule that led to the revolution that brought Fidel Castro to power twenty years later.

What has always made Cuban music distinctive is its eclecticism. Cuban musicians use everything from their island's complicated cultural background, and whatever they perform has a brilliant technical sheen. The proximity to the United States meant that for the first half of the century the island was more or less under the control of American economic interests, but as a tourist destination, with lavish casinos, with gambling and drinking during the years of prohibition in the United States, and with flourishing brothels for every social class, Havana offered jobs for musicians everywhere in the city. Through the 1930s and

1940s Havana was something like what Las Vegas later became: an exotic, slightly tawdry, extremely popular place to find limitless pleasures. Bebo's studies at the Conservatory weren't preparing him for a concert career. He was looking for a job with a dance band.

His introduction to the African roots that underlie Cuban rhythms came when he moved into Havana in 1936 to stay with his mother's sister.

"My aunt in Havana was a Yoruba priest. She was also Catholic, but that didn't make any difference. You could be both. It was the same religion they had in Haiti. It was Lucumí, the Yoruba religion they had everywhere. So I already heard African music when I was living in Havana with her family. It was the drummers I heard first, then the song after that." Already in Quivicán, however, he'd begun listening to Miami radio on the set in his friend's living room. What he found was American swing music, the disciplined, jazz-influenced orchestras that dominated popular music in the United States. "Those arrangements! They played so well!" In his years as Cuba's most popular orchestra leader Bebo's continual ambition was to combine the rhythms and the unique musical sensibilities of the Cuban musicians with the professionalism of the bands he heard on the radio as a teenager. For a period he led a group in Haiti and when I asked him what influenced him the most of everything he heard there he grinned and said, "Stan Kenton!" The owner of the club where he was working had a large record collection, and it was the music of the avant-garde swing orchestra that excited him more than the drum rhythms or the ensemble styles he heard of the native Haitian bands.

For Cuban musicians like Bebo, the success that they hoped for was to become associated with one of the important casinos, and for more than a decade Bebo was an arranger and pianist of the most successful and lavish of the Havana casinos, the Tropicana Night Club. For much of the period he led a modern orchestra the emphasized jazz in its arrangements at a smaller restaurant in the large Tropicana complex. When I asked Bebo if he played for many tourists from the United States, he nodded.

"I think it was eighty percent Americans. It could be more. Miami was only forty-five minutes away. They came to the big clubs and the hotels where we had the orchestras"

Were they white? What about the orchestras?

"The orchestras—someone like myself, I was Afro-Cuban. Some of the musicians I had in the orchestra were dark, but the audience—it was American tourists with a lot of money, and they were all white."

What kind of people were they?

He held up his hands and laughed.

"Rich!"

I had read in a guide to Havana that the Tropicana still was presenting its musical revues, despite the initial restrictions of the new government, and it had once again become a major tourist goal—though not for tourists from the United States, who are still kept out of Cuba by their government's economic blockade. The blockade has isolated Cuba from United States citizens, although not from anyone else, for more than forty years. It was as much to see the Tropicana, after I had heard Bebo tell me about its shows so often, as it was to hear the small groups and to talk with Cuban musicians that I had made the journey to Havana. I had somehow an impression that the Tropicana would be along the waterfront, on the curving, once elegant Malecón boulevard, with its long seawall and its matchless view of the sea. Malecón today, however, is lined with crumbling buildings, only in scattered areas showing any effort at renovation, and the traffic fills the air with a stinging pall of exhaust. The Tropicana, I learned, was across Havana, in an out-of-the-way suburb, and the brochures I found in a tourist office close to the harbor pictured an outdoor theater, with a towering stand of tropical vegetation, bushes and trees, framing the opening to the night sky.

Once I'd found where the Tropicana was located, and I'd called for a reservation, I looked at my city map and decided that I would walk to find it. The route from my hotel near La Rampa followed a series of wide boulevards and side streets that would take me through more of the city than I could see any other way. Once I'd left the central district along Calle Neptuno and the crowded tourist areas, I found I was in a different Havana. The houses were small, one-story, occasionally two-story, they were set in small lawns, and newer cars were parked along the curbs. The neighborhood streets were relaxed, and the occasional people I passed sitting in front of the small stores smiled politely. It was a Havana I knew nothing about, a modest, secure way of life that was a world apart from the picturesque, but dismaying, poverty of the Neptuno district.

Some of the houses I passed needed a new coat of paint, but just as many had freshly painted trim and newly framed windows and doors. The buildings were a mix of stucco and wood, with the look of a suburb in a city of the American South from the 1940s and 1950s. The hours it took me to cross the city gave me more of a perspective on Havana and on Cuban life today than anything I had seen in the clogged streets of crumbling mansions and stifling traffic where I'd been walking before. The only overtly political signs were occasional banners praising the forty-fifth anniversary of the Revolution, which was just being celebrated, with portraits of Fidel and the ever-present Che Guevara. What I found even more pleasing were the great masses of flowers that blossomed everywhere.

The large signboard telling me I had arrived at to the Tropicana was on the corner of a small lot in the Playa district of the city. The streets around it were still part of the unprepossessing neighborhood of small bungalows and gardens that I'd been passing in my walk. When I entered the gated driveway I realized that nothing Bebo had told me about the famous club had prepared me for the reality. In its quiet neighborhood the Tropicana occupied four or five city blocks, hidden behind a high, unbroken masonry wall painted white. Inside the wall I found myself in a forest of palm and deciduous trees, with a winding series of drives that led past elaborate white-painted fountains of dancing women's figures glimpsed through the vegetation. Inside the elaborate entrance and past the carpeted lobby was a large, circular amphitheatre surrounding a black painted, round stage. Above me was the sky. I found later that as I sat at my table and waited in the darkness for the show to begin that it seemed as though the sky opened up above me into the limitless reaches of space.

I wasn't certain how the Tropicana, from its beginnings in 1939, had managed to survive the war years and then the changes in Cuban society since the Revolution, but the vast circular stretch of tables was nearly filled an hour before the show was to start. It was a gathering of tourists from everywhere in the world for the show, despite the blockade. The Tropicana had no gambling, there was only a small gift shop, and many of us at the tables had settled for a drink and appetizers. It was the brilliant staging and musical excitement of the presentation, with more than two hundred dancers and musicians, that filled the tables night after night for the two-hour performance. At a table of six, the bill for dinner and the show could come to $1,000, but I had no feeling that anyone left disappointed. My own more modest ticket, including a glass of champagne and appetizers, cost $75, and how could I complain about a brilliantly staged spectacle that used three stages (one high in the trees) that presented every style of Cuban music and dance, and for a moment let me try to dance beside one of the chorus in the aisle beside my seat. What was most surprising about the dancing was that the show had no nudity. There was more skin exposed on any of the nearby beaches, and even in the very abbreviated costumes the dancers wore for many numbers, they also had on a light body stocking. What the Tropicana was offering was simply an often breathtaking dance and theatrical spectacle with its roots in Cuba's rich cultures.

What would Bebo have thought of the new orchestra? He would have heard the same musicianship and flare for entertainment that was the hallmark of the Tropicana when he was playing in its orchestras himself. The three percussionists, swaying over their drums in front of the orchestra, played extended solos that were raw and exciting and at the same time models of precision and skill. In one of the numbers the three trumpeters passed the solos back and forth, in a Cuban "cutting session," and we could have been back in the great days when Bebo was on the bandstand with his favorite trumpeters, "El Negro" Vivar and "Chocolate" Armenteros, or trombonist "El Tojo" Jiménez. As the scenes passed and the cascade of music continued I understood Bebo's pride in what he accomplished himself before one life ended and a new life began, and I could share his pleasure at the achievement of Cuba's musicians themselves.

In the folder of family pictures that Bebo and his wife, Marie, keep in a drawer in their Stockholm apartment there are emotional scenes of Bebo being hungrily embraced by his Cuban daughter, Marya, who sang with the Grammy-award-winning group Irakere that was led by her brother Chucho. There are family poses with grandchildren whom Bebo has seen only in the photos he's been sent from Cuba. Two of his granddaughters traveled to Paris with their children so he could meet them when he was in France for a ceremony. Only his eldest son, Chucho, is able to maintain close ties. With his career as an internationally successful jazz pianist he often travels outside of Cuba, and he and his father are able to meet, and even occasionally to play together. If Chucho finds himself in Sweden on one of his tours he tries to find time to go out to the apartment to visit Marie and his Swedish half-brothers. Rickard still remembers his own shy nervousness at meeting his celebrated brother for the first time.

So many years have passed since Chucho drove his father to the airport in Havana, on what officially was to be a three-month orchestra director's job in Mexico. In an impulsive gesture Bebo emptied his pockets of Cuban money and handed it his son. They wouldn't meet again for eighteen years. So much has changed in Cuba, and in the world's attitudes toward Cuba and its flagging Revolution, that Bebo could visit Cuba again if he chose. Marie and his family in Stockholm sometimes try to convince him to make the journey, but he still feels too much anger over the compromises he was asked to make and at what he had to leave behind him. Also, after an absence of more than forty years he is too distant now from his early life there. If Marie or Rickard ask him about meeting the family he left behind, his mouth stiffens in a thin line and he shakes his head roughly.

"Never!"

As Cuba becomes more open to the rest of the world the question will continually arise, will any of the generation of artists who left return to become part of Cuban musical life again?

In March 2000 Bebo and I met for a few days in New York when he took part in the filming of the brilliant documentary *Calle 54*, by the Spanish filmmaker Fernando Trueba, which presented the generation of Latin musicians who had led the way creating the new instrumental styles. The film included a touching personal glimpse of Bebo and Chucho meeting for the first time in five years and performing a two-piano duet, each playing in his own style, but showing clearly their deep response to each other's musicianship. Bebo also filmed a sequence with an old friend, the bassist Cachao, with the two performing an old style bolero in their club tuxedos and with a gravity that seldom is part of a return to the musical past. Bebo and I met every night at the Carnegie Delicatessen after he'd finished either the filming or the recording sessions for an album he was making at the same time for the producer Nat Chediak. We always sat comfortably into the early morning, Bebo, in his early eighties now, complaining a little that he didn't like New York's cold winds, and that he perhaps would return earlier to Stockholm than he'd planned.

What neither of us could have foreseen was that the CD he recorded with Chediak would be awarded a Grammy, and the film would be seen by a young Spanish flamenco singer, "El Cigala," who would be intrigued enough with the old-fashioned bolero that Bebo and Cachao performed to ask to meet Bebo and sing with him. Fernando Trueba brought them together in his Madrid apartment, and after a few months of becoming familiar with each other's musical idiom Bebo and El Cigala recorded the album titled *Lágrimas negras*, which went on to sell nearly a million copies, was awarded a Grammy, and took them on almost two years of continuous touring. At eighty-four Bebo's career came to life again, and his appearances now are greeted with the kind of enthusiasm that usually is waiting for a rock star. His long fingers are as supple, his musical sensitivities as finely centered as at any point in his career, and after his final number at one of his appearances he always dances off the stage with a distinctive Cuban elegance.

In the winter of 2001 Fernando Trueba was invited to Havana to present a specially edited version of *Calle 54* that emphasized the role of the Cuban musicians. Trueba had an assistant film the screen from the back of the auditorium, capturing the audience's responses to the artists in the film. Bebo first appeared on the screen with his old friend Cachao, and as the two of them embraced at the piano, the tall, elegant Bebo and the short, heavy Cachao holding his bass, the audience in the Havana theater realized who they were and burst into spontaneous applause. Whatever anger had been felt many years ago by the Cubans who supported the Revolution toward men like Bebo, who had chosen to flee, there was now a respect and a consciousness of what their music has meant to a new understanding of Cuban culture.

Trueba sent a video copy of the film his assistant had taken at the Havana auditorium to Bebo, and one gray, lashing winter afternoon in his Stockholm apartment Bebo put it on the TV screen for me to see. He stood quietly looking at the screen, listening to the burst of applause when he and Cachao appeared on the stage. After a moment he looked away, out of the window at the streaking snow, at the gray curls of ice across the colorless grass. He looked back again at the screen as he and his son Chucho came to the stage for their piano duet and the Havana audience erupted in applause a second time. He listened to the duet with a satisfied smile, and then nodded as they finished and the applause rose again in the Havana auditorium. If I had asked him at that moment if he would ever see Cuba again, I know he would have said "Never," as he always does. But I wondered if this time it would take a moment for the word to come.

Carnival in Brazil's Black World

I think it was because my wife Annie and I had to shade our eyes against the shining sun glancing off the water of the broad channel, off the strips of rocks and sand beach just over the whitewashed balustrade, and off the antique stone fort that marked the limit of the small cove, that I found myself thinking of the line of towering vehicles parked along the curb beside us as a fleet of cargo ships from another century—as caravels lining an exotic sea front. The looming shapes pressed against the littered sidewalk of the city of Salvador's old port, Porto do Barra, on Brazil's northeast coast, as if they were seeking shelter from the sun in whatever shreds of shade they could find under the shining leaves of the trees on the edge of the sidewalk.

It was the scene's brightness and the steady bustle of activity along the sides of the giant sound wagons in the days before Bahia's Carnival that made me think of those insubstantial, small, unsteady ocean vessels, the caravels of the Portuguese navigators that had made the first journeys to this coast five hundred years before. The crowded vans and heaped barrows, the carts and wagons pushed up against the sides of the sound wagons could have been provisioning them for a voyage that would take them out onto the bay beyond the fort, then out through the mouth of the bay into the currents and tides of the Atlantic. The clanging metal doors of their storage spaces were thrown open to take on their supplies, even though their journey was going to be only through Salvador's night streets. The towering shapes were the celebrated *Tríos elétricos* of Salvador's Carnival celebrations, and the passengers on the elaborate sound stages that had been constructed on their elongated top decks would be the sweating musicians and dancers, the glittering stars, and the excited hangers-on of the Carnival nights.

The laborers in shorts and tank tops filling the street and the sidewalk were enduring the afternoon's heat to load the counters, shelves, and gaping refrigerators of the *tríos* with tons of ice, hundreds of cases of beer and soft drinks, food, and paper decorations.

Laborers in clammy overalls cleaned the toilets from the journey of the night before and swept the trash off the boards of the soundstages. At the side of one of the *trios* an amplifier was being winched up in a straining rope hoist. Workers in once white jackets and much handled aprons lifted trays of sliced meats, bags of bread rolls, toilet paper, towels, T-shirts, and medicine out of a bobbing sea of small trucks, loading whatever the people who would ride on the great vehicles thought they might need as they set out on their night journey. Crowds of spectators would fill the streets as the sun went down and the air turned cooler, and the atmosphere alongside the idling vehicles would become steadily more chaotic until with a roar of their engines, their lights would blaze out in the darkness and they would lumber their way into the pandemonium of the parade route.

It was still early. Sprawled figures of young men and women in shorts and sweaty T-shirts had taken over whatever shade the sound wagons had left. They were the *cordeiros*. With each *trio* came its own waves of dancers, and the cordeiros were lined along large loops of rope, hundreds of yards long, that they drew out in a large arc that reached out beyond the *trío* and followed in a smaller arc behind it. The youthful crowds of dancers who had paid to become members of the *trío*'s *bloco* (club) did their partying inside the rope, and the jam of the street crowds was kept outside. It was obvious that many of the cordeiros, who were mostly a discouraged assortment of Salvador's poor and its teenagers, had struggled with their ropes through the streets the night before. As they stretched aching legs and arms in the heat, they rubbed blistered places on their hands where even their cheap gloves hadn't helped protect them from the friction of the rope. Beginning at sunset they would straggle out into the streets again for another endless twelve hours, struggling against the weight of the crowds, the burning weight of the rope, and the pain of their blisters. They earned about ten dollars a night, which for Salvador, a poor city in Brazil's stricken northeast, was an acceptable amount of money. They tried to sleep in the shade for what was left of the afternoon.

It was impossible to feel entirely at ease beside the sound wagons. Annie and I stayed a few steps away as we skirted the crowd of delivery trucks and stepped past the sprawled bodies. In the darkness, with their garish flare of neon lights and thunderous music, they seemed like great lumbering, living creatures that threatened everything around them. As they bulled their way through the crowds they seemed to be pushing the dancers imprisoned inside their rope ahead of them, and dragging another captive crowd of dancers behind them. If you found yourself in the crush around one, the level of sound their amplifiers created was as frightening as their towering size.

Tríos Elétricos and the cordeiros, Carnival in Bahia, 2002.

Once in a crowd I was pushed close as a *trío* lumbered past. I could feel my chest pounding with the beat of an amplified bass drum. I had been caught in the pandemonium only twenty or thirty yards from the booming sound. I tried to elbow my way out of the crowd, afraid of what the sound might do to my body. When I had struggled fifty yards I had a group of dancing teenagers between me and the noise, but I still could feel the pounding in my chest. At seventy-five yards I was shielded by a police barricade, but the thunderous sound was still a physical blow that thudded in my chest every time the drummer stamped on his bass drum pedal. It wasn't until I was a hundred yards away, standing on the grassy slope in front of the old fort in Porto Barra that the sound was endurable. In front of me I could see families with children clinging to shoulders and legs, darting shirtless boys selling beer and soft drinks, and beyond them the glittering crowds choking the street. And I still could hear the electric boom of the drums.

Salvador's newspapers ran daily articles on the history and events of the Carnival and over breakfast I learned one morning that the *tríos elétricos* had been only *duettos eléctricos* when the first one appeared on Salvador's streets in 1950s. A "duetto" since the street orchestra only had two musicians. Like everything else about Carnival, however, the novelty had quickly taken on grander dimensions. The articles claimed that during the street celebrations a country-style duo decided to mount a loudspeaker on their battered car and play as they drove around the city. They were already well known locally, so their appearance attracted small crowds. The article included a photo of one of the early *elétricos* and it was a sedan convertible with two speaker horns mounted on the sides. Standing inside it were two musicians with guitars, staring into the camera with proud smiles. They had put on flamboyant shirts and they had dark mustaches. There was a group of onlookers around them, looking as pleased as if they were going to be performing themselves.

One of the musicians, a local "legend" named Osmar Macedo told the English music writer John Krich that it was he and his partner Adolfo "Dodô" Nascimento who had established the reign of the trios. "This was back in 'forty-seven, just after the war." Dodô, Osmar insisted, had invented the electric guitar, and he proudly showed Krich their first instrument, an elongated guitar neck with electric pickups. After their first trials in the streets as a *dupla*—a duet—they set out determined to change the style of music that was popular then in the Bahian carnival. "Soft gentle music was much in fashion then. At that time, we had been playing *chorhino* mostly with some *valsas* and *boleros*. But Dodô and I noticed what a stir had been made at the past Carnival by the Vassourinhos, a *frevo* group that came down from Recife. This music really made the crowds wild. It was so quick and so sharp. And with *frevo* you could really show your virtuosity. I mean you had to be good."

The two musicians decided that they would shake up the local Carnival, which seemed much too tame for Salvador. Osmar complained, "There was no wild dancing and no nudity. People threw confetti at each other." He described people watching the parades from rocking chairs that they set up on the parade route and then chained down so nobody would steal them. Osmar and Dodô's answer was to install a sound system in their old car and put a loudspeaker in the back seat. "Once we struck the very first note, it was an apotheosis. We were mobbed by people dancing on all sides. They almost turned the car over. *Meus deus!* We lost the sound many times. And then the police came, ordering us to stop."

The two men's first thought was that middle-class society—the "elite"—in Salvador was trying to stop them, conscious that if they went on playing, Carnival would never be the same again.

But the people were shouting, rioting, ordering us, "Toca, toca!" (Play, play!) So we played again. We quickly ran out of our repertoire. I think we even sang "La Marseillaise." By the time we got to Praça Castro Alves, there as such a mob following us that I was sure we'd be taken to prison. Horses reared and drivers were thrown. The mob shoved one another into the *acaraje* stands (deep-fried bean cakes) and many people were burned by the hot oil and cooking fires. We had lost our brakes by then, lost all four gears, but people kept pushing the car. Nothing stopped them. They didn't allow us to parade again for two years. But by then, we had a Chrysler. And the *trio elétrico* was established.[1]

The new sound wagons have kept the old name, but everything about them has become much grander. Instead of two or three musicians, the groups had swollen until I often counted fourteen or fifteen musicians on some of the popular *trios*, many with soundstages filled with jostling troupes of costumed singers and dancers. The ponderous modern vehicles are often as long as a Salvador city block, and the stages where the musicians perform are on the level of a third-floor balcony. The electric wires that straddle the street have been pulled away on the parade routes. The sides of the towering vehicles are ornately painted and decorated. One was in the shape of a vintage automobile, another shaped like a spaceship, painted in gray aluminum. Others were designed as desert oases of palm trees or flower-covered tropical islands. Ornate neon letters spelled out names of advertising products, names of the bands, slogans, and designs. Advertisements for Ford automobiles, soft drinks, and cigarettes brightened the sides, but the painting was done on a thin scrim that hung from the railing around the band's platform. Behind the scrim was a solid wall of dark loudspeakers hung in long rows. It's as though the *trios* were trying to shrug off their power by disguising it with florid paintings and swaying figures. When the microphones above them pick up the sound of the drums, the scrim trembles like a leaf in the thunder.

Sometimes, as I tried to confront the blast of sound, I felt as though I were in a stadium rock concert, only the stadium was slowly, ponderously making its way past me. It can take a *trio* forty-five minutes to push its way around a jammed street corner. In the side panels of many of the vehicles are open windows for the dancers to buy more beer, and there are unsteady narrow stairways for them to climb up to the toilets under the band platform. The stairways also lead to cramped spaces where dancers who have had enough of the party can rest for a while. These gaps in the screen of speakers along the sides lighten some of the thunderous sound, but the backs of the *trios* are rigged with a solid area of speakers from the level of the wheels up to the platform three stories above them, delivering a thudding crash of sound over the crowds of dancers following them.

As the vehicles move unsteadily forward, the *cordieros*, heaving on their ring of rope, struggle to keep some street space clear for the *bloco* members who have paid for a chance to dance to the music. From time to time, shouting and waving to each other, the dancers hang back during one of the songs, giving the people straining with the ropes space to make an opening ahead of them, and at the climax of the melody hundreds of them rush forward together, waving their arms and leaping in a simultaneous wave. From the sidelines of the parade it looks as though the street has suddenly exploded, with the flailing arms and bodies leaping into the dazzling lights and colors.

If the pressing crowds brought me too close to one of the wagons I found the sound was deafening, but the dancers didn't seem to feel anything. As I looked at their shining, grinning faces, I wondered if they were depending on the beer to protect their hearing. Most of the cordeiros wore some kind of earplugs. The ones who had forgotten to wear gloves were using folded pieces of newspapers or sodden rags to protect their hands. In the afternoons, when we walked past the line of *tríos* taking in supplies, these were the people who lay in huddles in the shade. If they spoke to each other, their voices were a hoarse whisper.

The music that drifted from the high platforms in the dawdling afternoons was different from the thunder of the night processions. Most of the sound wagons had awnings strung over the music stages to provide a little shade as the supplies were loaded, and some of the musicians came early to tune their guitars or adjust their amplifiers. The music of the afternoons had softer, floating rhythms. A guitar would pick out one of the old bossa nova classics while below them the sweating workers dragged in tubs of ice and cases of drinks.

It is everywhere evident during Carnival that Brazil is one of the three cultural areas, along with Cuba and the United States, that have given the world much of the music that has been created out of the diverging currents of the African diaspora. Brazil's musical culture is perhaps the most richly varied of the three, since it had so many more people of African heritage. Not only did slavery in Brazil last longer than in the United States, there was a much greater influx of slaves. At least five million is a common estimate, compared to North America's fewer than half a million. Cuba, with more than a million slaves, also was inevitably drawn to the experience of African music, with waves of later arrivals and their African religious expression. Brazil, however, has

Tríos Elétricos and the cordeiros, Carnival in Bahia, 2

embraced many other cultures, and each of them has played a role in shaping the flood of melody that is a part of Brazilian life.

In the streets of Salvador during the noisy Carnival week I was always conscious that it was Brazilian music sounding in the air around me. From the sound wagons and from the radios that filled the streets during the daytime, the only music I heard was Brazilian. The only time I noticed a different kind of song was one afternoon as I was walking along the Porta Barra sea wall and heard a radio station playing "Dancing Queen" by the Swedish group ABBA. Another year a spangled young guitarist on one of the *tríos* announced defiantly that he was going to play a hit by the British heavy metal band Led Zeppelin, and he crashed into one of Jimmy Page's familiar riffs. The crowds found after a moment that as far as they were concerned, the music wasn't anything they could dance to, so they shrugged along in their rope enclosures, laughing and passing their beer back and forth until the band gave up and went back to one of the Bahia favorites.

For most of the world it is the Brazilian harvest of song that has spread the furthest and reached the largest audiences, sparked by the enthusiastic response to bossa nova. Rio de Janeiro has named its international airport for one of its songwriters. When your plane comes into Rio you find yourself landing at the Antonio Carlos Jobim International Airport. "Tom" Jobim, as he is known to all Brazilians, composed the bossa nova anthem "The Girl from Ipanema," along with many other classic songs, and in Brazil a song can give its composer the immortality of the greatest novelists or sports stars. Today's best-known Brazilian musicians are its older generation of songwriters and singers: Gilberto Gil, Caetano Velosa, Chico Buarque, Milton Nascimento, Marie Bethânia, Gal Costa, and Jorge Ben, who are only a handful among many brilliant artists. Veloso and his sister Maria Bethânia grew up in a small town outside of Salvador, and Gil is from Salvador itself.

Part of the uniqueness of Brazil's music lies in its history, and a crucial difference, certainly, is that of all the New World countries with a rich African-derived culture, it was the only one that was Portuguese. At the root of a thousand modern Brazilian melodies is a Portuguese style of song called the *modinha*, and it was the mingling of the melodies of the *modinha* with the rhythms from Africa that gave this new world of song its character.

It was only through an error in geographical reckoning that Brazil became part of the Portuguese Empire. The purpose of the Line of Tordesillas, which was promulgated by Pope Alexander VI in 1494, was to determine which areas of the world would be dominated by Spain and which by Portugal. The Portuguese had already explored Africa's west coast, and in the wake of Columbus's first voyage the concern of the church was that the two Catholic Powers, Spain and Portugal, would become bitter rivals for the new lands that had been discovered. In 1493 Spain was granted the rights to all the lands to the west of an imaginary line drawn in the Atlantic Ocean 100 leagues (about 300 miles) west of the Azores and the Cape Verde Islands. The Portuguese protested the limit, and the next year the Spanish consented to shift the line 370 leagues farther west. As the historian Boris Fausto characterized it, with the new treaty "The world was divided into two hemispheres separated by an imaginary line 370 leagues west of the Cape Verde Islands. The land discovered west of the line would belong to Spain, that to the east of it would belong to Portugal. The division lent itself to controversy, since it was never possible to establish exactly where the line of Tordesillas was."[2]

The Portuguese had never turned their caravels toward the New World, so the line was intended to define the Portuguese presence on the west coast of Africa. There was no realization on anyone's part that within this demarcation was a massive bulge of the South American continent far to the east of what the Spanish voyagers had explored in the Caribbean and on the northern Venezuelan coast. The first Portuguese landfall on what is now known as Brazil was on April 22, 1500, by the fleet commanded by Pedro Alvares Cabral. For many years the new land was thought to be a large and rather poor island, and the interest lay in the two large rivers, the Amazon in the north and the Plate in the south. There were optimistic conjectures that they might be the long-sought passage to the East Indies, and the continual disagreements over the Tordesillas demarcation concerned the two rivers. Were the mouths of the great streams within Spanish or Portuguese dominion?

As the Portuguese had extended their presence down the African west coast they lacked the human resources to attempt any kind of colonization. Portugal's population was small, and the country had one of Europe's poorest economies. What they established along the coast were armed trading posts called *feoritas*, giving them access to trading for raw materials and for slaves intended for sale in Portugal as domestic servants. They continued the same pattern in Brazil. To encourage the production of food crops for sale outside of the new colony, the Portuguese crown granted vast landholdings to individuals who were in favor in the court, rather than small land parcels which could have been offered to individual families or to small groups to make them self-sufficient. It was not until a large party of nearly a thousand settlers led by Tome de Sousa landed in Salvador in the 1540s that the Portuguese made a serious effort to colonize the land, and Salvador was named the capital of the struggling colony.

The lands around Salvador were fertile and easily cultivated, and the new settlers almost immediately planted their newly cleared fields with sugar. Just as in every other part of the new continents where sugar was the main crop, the growers faced an immediate crisis as they tried to secure labor, and like every other sugar economy, they turned to slaves. Slaves were not only profitable, they were readily available. In an archive in Denmark there are a series of large, brilliantly conceived and detailed paintings of the natives of Brazil and the lands they were settling done by a Dutch artist in Salvador in the 1640s. Among the paintings are two portraits of Africans in the uniforms of high officials. They were ministers sent to Brazil by the government of the Congo, and one of them had as his responsibility the signing of an agreement concerning the number of slaves that the Brazilians wished to import. The Africans who controlled their part of the trade continued to ship slaves for the next two hundred years. By the end of the period of importation, the journey from Africa could take as little as three weeks, and the captains had become more skillful at landing with much of their cargo still healthy enough to

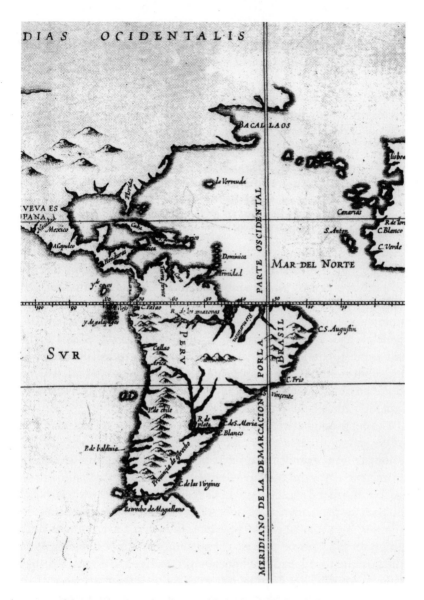

A map of the Western Hemisphere published in a book titled *Description of the West Indies* (1601) by Antonio de Herrera, taken from an earlier Spanish map of 1575. The vertical double line marks the division by the Treaty of Tordesillas (1494) of the newly discovered lands between Portugal and Spain and shows the error that gave Brazil to the Portuguese.

command high prices. It was on the sugar plantations that the appalling living conditions took their toll of the slaves' lives. There was an average yearly decline of 5 to 8 percent in the slave population because of the high mortality rate, and the planters continually had to replace them. The life expectancy of the slaves was about twenty years. Although the average Brazilian didn't live much longer, their average life expectancy was about twenty-seven years. In contrast, in the United States a slave could live to the average age of thirty-five.

For nearly a century the gently rolling hills around Salvador were the world's richest sugar-growing area, and for some decades Salvador was probably the wealthiest city of the New World. The signs of its affluence can still be seen in the crumbling neighborhoods of colonial streets and plazas, in the once elegant tiled house facades and the half-restored cathedrals of Peroulinho, the old section of the city that has survived on a group of hills overlooking the harbor. The city was built on the heights as a defense against pirates and raiding naval squadrons that roamed the coast. In the first years, most of the slaves who reached the city were from the northern tribes, among them Yorubas, Ewes, and Hausas. The principle trade item used for their purchase was Brazilian tobacco. In the last decades of the slave trade, as new areas of development opened up to the south around Rio de Janeiro, the sources of the slaves shifted to the south, to Congo and Angola, and a major trade item for the purchases was Rio's white rum *cachaça*.

The depth and richness of the African survivals that are characteristic of the music of Bahia reflect the racial imbalance. There were so few colonists from Portugal itself that Brazil from its beginnings was in many crucial ways an African—or in some rural areas an Afro-Indian—society. When the Brazilians declared their independence from Portugal in 1822, the population of Salvador was 79 percent black and mulatto, in contrast to Rio de Janiero's 64 percent. In each of the areas with large groups of slaves there were also large numbers of free Africans. As in Cuba, slaveholders had been encouraged to free slaves, or to permit them to work to earn the purchase price for their freedom. Nearly half of the Africans in Salvador were free, and large numbers of those still enslaved were employed as "slave earners," who worked independently and paid a portion of their earnings to their owners.

The racial imbalance was corrected to an extent in the early 1700s with the discovery of gold in the mountainous areas to the north of Rio de Janeiro. More than 600,000 people emigrated from Portugal and the Atlantic Islands to work in the mines, which continued to be productive for several decades. Brazil, however, is a huge country, and the European influx didn't spread up the coast to Salvador. The local sugar growers had already lost much of their advantage to the newer plantations of the Caribbean, and as the economic balance of the colony shifted to the mountain areas, with Rio as their major outlet to the sea, it was decided to move the capital. Salvador had been the dominant Brazilian city for two hundred years, but in 1763 it lost its financial base as the government and its personnel moved south to Rio de Janeiro, and the city in many ways has never recovered.

At the time the government was moved to the broad harbor at the base of the picturesque mountains surrounding Rio, each of the cities had about forty thousand inhabitants, but Rio quickly outgrew its northern competitor. The districts that still survive from Salvador's colonial era are the largest remainder of the older culture in the hemisphere, but with the city's poverty, many of the buildings may not be preserved. Some renovation has been completed, but the streets are narrow and cobbled and difficult for traffic. Houses still with remnants of their elaborate tiled facades are falling into ruin, and many of the younger people now finding employment prefer to move to the scattered new high-rise complexes to the north of the city center.

Modern Salvador is a city of almost 2.5 million people, but during the Carnival season it feels as though its population has doubled. Brazilians have long argued about the comparative excitements of Carnival in Rio and Salvador, and the usual conclusion is that although Rio has more elaborate staged pageantry, Salvador is closest to the African soul of the Carnival celebrations. In the week before the celebration the airport is jammed with new arrivals, many of them students and young couples from other Brazilian cities. I had found a hotel close to the old fort in Porto Barra, and everyday I had to push my way through steadily growing crowds if I wanted something to eat or needed to shop in the mall that was several blocks away through a neighborhood of small bungalows and narrow streets. Across the street from the hotel was the low seawall that continued half a mile to the old fort. My wife and I had walked along the wall to watch the *trios* lined up to be supplied with food and drinks for their night's journey through the city streets. Below the wall, close to the hotel, was a small beach, and on the hot afternoons it was so densely packed it was difficult to see any place for someone new even to stand up, much less try to unfold one of the canvas chairs that were for rent, and stretch out in the sunlight.

From the fort, which marked the mouth of the broad harbor, the coastline stretched to the north, and a wide boulevard followed its sweeping turns. Most of the coast, however, was a ragged barrier of dark rocks, the lower strata, where the tide flowed, slick with weeds and speckled with the shells of the marine life of the shallows. The Atlantic swells surged against the rocks, there were few footholds to get down to the water, and only occasional hardier swimmers crept out to the deeper pools by edging along a ridge of stones that would take them far enough from the low edges of the headlands to swim with some safety. On a map the coastline might look like a swimmer's paradise, but at Porto Barra there was only the enclosed cove by the Fort and its small beach. Teenaged boys swam close to the rocks below the weathered wall of the fort, and in the bright sun their glistening dark skins against the blue-green of the water, with the small scale, stiffly shaped colonial building in the background, was a scene that could have been out of Salvador's oldest days as a colony.

The area of Porto Barra close to the beach was very small, and it was at the base of a steep bluff. City buses strained up a long street past walled villas and newer apartment buildings as they carried the visitors to the center of the city. The benches along the tree-lined streets were filled with the school crowds who had the days off for the celebration and with the visitors who had brought their party with them. Late at night it still was possible to buy something to eat at three or four food shops whose lights were a bright splash in the darkness. Since it was set off from the rest of Salvador that towered above it on the bluff, Porto Barra had little through traffic, and the side streets had blossomed with small clubs and informal restaurants. They were filled day and night, and the crowds were noisily pleased to be there to celebrate Carnival, and later, when the beach was empty, the clubs also had music. It wasn't the thunder of the *tríos*, or even the bright dance rhythms of the street orchestras in the center of the city. The performers played guitars and sang to their own accompaniment, drawing on the great repertoire of song that is one of the enduring expressions of Brazilian life.

Although all popular music is a complex amalgam of styles and influences, a modest style of song from Brazil's history has given its music much of its identity. The song was the fresh, popular expression, the *modinha*. The *modinha* was already a fixture in the life of the Portuguese court by the late 1700s. Its most colorful exponent was a mulatto priest from Rio named Domingo Caldas Barbosa, who called his songs *cantigas* and accompanied himself singing them with a steel stringed guitar. In his valuable booklet to a CD collection re-creating the nineteenth-century *modinha*, the pianist and musicologist Manuel Viega quoted a complaint about the new songs that appeared in 1763.

[They are] love songs talking of sighs, of flattering words, of refined affairs and frivolous rambling. It is with this they delude young girls, it is what they teach children, it is what the lads sing and maids have on their lips. What great maxims of modesty, temperance and virtue they learn in these songs! Today this plague is general since Caldas began using them in his poetry and began writing verses for women.[3]

The *modinha*, as it first developed in Portugal and was widely circulated in popular printed song collections, was a simple melody, usually written for two voices in close harmony, with an accompaniment that generally only notated a figured bass—a melody with symbols indicating the harmonies, which an experienced performer was expected to use as a basis for an improvised accompaniment. As pianos began to replace the older forms of the harpsichord in many families, the songs were published with keyboard accompaniments and arranged for a single voice. The first piano reached Salvador in 1810. The clumsy instruments gradually were carried by mule train from the port city to the sugar plantations in the surrounding countryside, but already by that time the *modinha* had evolved into a style accompanied by native guitars, flutes, and small string ensembles. The songs became so popular for suitors to sing at their mistress's windows that Viega suggests with only a little sarcasm that the first decline in the general popularity of the songs was the result of the introduction of street lamps in the middle of the 19th century. A verse from a typical *modinha* that Viega included in the album alludes to the night serenades.

In the evening, when you come to the window,
A loose braid where the wind sighs,
My soul kneels in contemplation of you
While my thoughts go to lament at your feet.

In the introduction to his study of contemporary Brazilian composers *Masters of Contemporary Song*, Charles A. Perroni noted the steady rise in the *modinha*'s popularity, comparing its spread to the relative decline in general acceptance of a more African-influenced song form called the *lundu*.

Around 1870 the *modinha* began to be adopted more regularly by popular musicians outside the salon context. The serenade was a common setting for its use. While the *lundu* was eventually absorbed into other forms, *modinhas* spread throughout Brazil and underwent a process of folklorization, entering the cycle of oral tradition. In the 1910s and 1920s, Catulo da Paixão Cearense (1866–1946) revitalized the *modinha* in Rio de Janeiro; he brought stylized rural variants to "nice" society, establishing the acceptability of the guitar as the instrument for accompaniment, and initiated a "backland vogue" in both song and poetry. Historically, the *modinha* is particularly important in Brazil because it was cultivated for an extensive period and was popular at all levels of society.[4]

It was not until a new vocal samba style became popular in the 1930s, the *samba-canção*, that the lyric forms of the modest Portuguese colonial song lost their distinctive place in Brazilian culture, though the *modinha* continued to be at the root of the compositions of the new generations of song writers. Part of the style's continuing attraction was that it had first become popular as a domestic entertainment. The melodies were set in a comfortable vocal range for the daughters of the plantation owners who sang them for gatherings in the family parlor, and they were as useful as a courting song for the daughters' admirers, who sang in the shadows by their windows. The emphasis of the lyrics was always love, and the mood was usually a simply expressed longing. There were similarities to the classic Portuguese song form, *fado*, but fado is more intense, more expressive, and the mood is more despairing. Like fado, the melodies of the modinhas were generally in a minor mode, which accommodated itself easily to the minor modalities of much African influenced song. Listening to the older modinhas today, it is remarkable how close the mood and the melodic content are to much of contemporary Brazilian song. The most significant newer adaptation is the syncopation of the rhythms, reflecting the influence of the *lundu*. Much of the older song form survived its journey to the colony, but it also changed inevitably as the years passed.

Even though the Atlantic Ocean separated the Brazilian colonists from their homeland, as the role of the modinha in modern Brazil suggests, Portugal continued to play an important role in Brazil's culture and growth, again because of circumstances that were unique to the country. For an extended period of its history, Brazil *was* Portugal. The tumultuous history of Europe during this period decisively shaped Brazil's history. In 1807, in the midst of the long war between England and France, Napoleon invaded Portugal to seal its ports and complete his blockade of the continent against British commercial interests. The British Navy, anticipating his move, acted more quickly. In two days, between November 25 and 27, they aided the Portuguese royal court and civilian government in their flight from the French armies. Between ten thousand and fifteen thousand people crowded into a fleet of ships and sailed from Lisbon, making the crossing under the protection of a British naval squadron. The ships first landed in Salvador, where the royal passengers were dismayed at the backward conditions, but they immediately requisitioned the best homes and began to set up a temporary government. They had brought everything they needed with them. In the ships that left Lisbon were the government ministries, the justices of the Supreme Court, and the important religious leaders. Crammed in the cargo holds of the fleet were the royal treasury, the government archives, a printing press, and cases of books, enough to establish the National Library in Rio de Janeiro. The mercantile policies of the government had attempted to assure the colony's economic dependency on the home country by denying the colonists the right to import printing presses—or pianos.

Brazilian ports had also been closed to foreign commerce as part of the mercantile policies, but in gratitude to the British naval squadron that had saved the Portuguese court, one of the first acts of the new government was to open the country to trade with friendly nations. After the government had moved to Rio, the next step, in 1808, was to open the country to industrialization. Rio quickly swelled to a city of more than 100,000 people, creating a wave of cultural excitement. Music, theater, and literature marked a new birth of Portuguese culture in Brazil, and among the many influences that became established was the little song, the modinha.

Often through the din on the streets I could hear one of the gentler modinha melodies in a song the musicians were blasting from the top of one of the *trios*, but the newest bands have turned to anything from the broad flow of Brazilian rhythms that will bring the crowds of thousands to a dancing frenzy in the Carnival nights. On some of the vehicles I counted as many as fourteen drummers sweating in the lights along the edges of the soundstages. It was also obvious as I watched that it is difficult work for the musicians to keep the music together on the tops of the wagons as they are jerked along the streets through the crowds, and the punishing level of volume also had its effect on them. John Krich, who interviewed the pioneers of the *trio elétrico*, managed to hitch a ride on one of the trios as it paraded on a holiday that preceded Carnival itself.

> With perseverance, I get my crack at climbing the ladder which ascends up the side of the band's truck through the balanced black blocks of amplifiers. This close, I can feel each thud of the electric bass reverberating in my chest cavity. Riding a *trio elétrico*'s moving juggernaut, sandwiched between a half-dozen groupies waving pom-poms, a couple of bodyguards, and one of the three percussionists, I discover what's true about most everything in Brazil. The view from the top isn't as compelling as the vision gained in the midst of the pack.
>
> Along with an intense headache, I get the feeling of how difficult the work of a Carnival musician must be. Given that the work is seasonal, the *trios* have got to take as many jobs as they can get, at whatever meager rate is offered. Yet even in this warm-up, the trucks inch along at a block an hour, and it can take them up to twelve hours to cover the main

parade route. Most of the bands are kept busy until dawn at balls and block parties.

Nonstop frenetic energy is required. There are no "slow dances" in Bahia, no thirty minute sets. Luckily, the guitar pickers are brawny long hairs who wear rings of sweatbands like medals earned in battle. Their playing looks as unrehearsed as it is, for want of a better word, electric.[5]

The rhythms are usually fast, particularly with popular younger groups like Chiclete com Banana. The extended polyrhythmic patterns are blurred, since they need a slower basic pulse to be effective. When Chiclete plays on the streets the tempo is built on the leader's guitar, which fires rapid chords in a jagged sequence of a quick down beat on the first beat of the measure, a rest on the second beat, an edgy, quick triplet on the third beat, then a rest on the fourth. Against this, the bass plays a steady four beats to the measure, and the drums create shifting patterns usually built on triplets. Despite the surging tempos and the electric sounds of the groups' rock-style instrumentation, their music still has a clear African voice.

What has preserved the older Carnival in Salvador, what continues to make Salvador's festival a feast of older styles and musical customs, is simply the width of the city's streets. The *trios* are too big to drive into Pelourinho, the old colonial section that is still the heart of the city, with its narrow cobbled streets and twisting lanes. On a Carnival afternoon you can look back from Pelourinho at the dense crowds filling the Avenida Sete de Setembro in the heart of the business district, surrounding the *trios*. For the last days of Carnival the street has taken on the appearance of a construction site. Virtually every store window and building entrance has been boarded up with sheets of plywood, painted—for no reason I could discover—a reddish pink. Down the slope from Pelourinho I could see swelling crowds streaming out of the plazas and side streets along the avenue toward the thunderous music and the gleaming neon decorations.

In Pelourinho Carnival has a different character. The Carnival spilling through the cobbled streets and squares in the old quarter has its own crowds, its own excitements, its own discomforts, its own strains and confusions, and it fulfills the promise of a Brazilian musical panorama with its roots in its African past. Without the thunder of the *trios* to overpower them the other voices of Brazilian music can be heard. The center of the excitement, a broad plaza named the Largo de Pelourinho, is crowded with metal tables and much used chairs set up around large, steamy tents selling beer and heaped plates of food and soft drinks. Not far from it, on a broad street leading to the colonial cathedral, a low stage has been set up with towering wooden figures of the proud women of Bahia wearing their native dress. Many of the city's families bring their children to spend the day in the plaza and to have the children's pictures taken on the stage, posed stiffly against the skirts of the figures. Often the children have been dressed in modest, homemade costumes, while the adults are in jeans or shorts, T-shirts or tank tops—anything that's comfortable in the heat. Annie and I stood at the edge of the crowd and watched a procession of children whose faces were solemn, frightened, or excited—or all three at once—as they took their turns in front of the statues. For many Bahian families a succession of photographs from year to year is probably their strongest memory of Carnival and their childhood.

One year a stage was erected in a large open space near the entrance of the plaza and a vocal group—twenty men and women in comic variations of the costumes of the street serenaders, with guitars and small drums—sang Bahian melodies that everyone around me knew. The next year Annie and I found an elaborately choreographed water fountain with splashing jets that filled the space. Suddenly a group of young dancers wearing Brazilian versions of African dress burst from a side street. They were an informal association called an *afoxe*, and the lead figures in the group carried a painted banner with their name, *Bloco Art Cia*. The first dancers were women who swirled into the plaza with brightly flowered cloth skirts and latex tops. Behind them were lines of wiry, perspiring shirtless men, in mud-colored grass skirts. The muscular dancing surged in waves across the crowded street. In the middle of the waving arms and gesturing hands of the dancers a stilt walker covered in white feathers stamped to the drums that pressed closely after him. The first drummers were a line of teenaged boys and girls who beat on small drums with thin sticks in a sharp, clattering rhythm. Two other teenagers lustily added to the noise with European instruments, a bugle and a valve trombone. Behind the two horns a new line of drummers played elongated, slim drums attached with cloth belts to their waists, and after them came a line of thick shouldered men pounding on their large bass drums. The fierce energy of their dancing felt like it must leave a visible aura in the air over our heads.

As we joined the noisy, laughing crowd dancing behind the group, they turned down the street, toward the Avenida, filled with the crowds around the *tríos*. The towering sound wagon closest to us had stopped for a moment at the end of its route, and as the dancers in their African dress came closer to them, the musicians on the high music platform noticed the dancers and their musicians. One by one the *trío*'s musicians

Carnival in the
Pelourinho, 2002.

fell silent so the crowds around them could hear the street drummers,
and for a suspended moment the rhythms of the two groups mingled.
We stopped in the street in surprise. We could hear that it was all the
same music. The drummers on the sound wagons were playing faster
and the songs had been lifted to a new level of energy, but their melodies
and the rhythms wove seamlessly into the pulse of the street drumming.
We were all dancing to one rhythm and one song.

At the corner of another narrow street, as we made our way back to
the plaza, there were new sounds. We found a group of men lounging
around a battered small truck with speakers mounted over the driver's
cab. It could have been an early version of the *trío*. The men were playing a dance-like rhythm pattern on small sets of two-toned African bells
known in Brazil as *agogôs*. The sound was a light, metallic tinkling, but
it had an intense lift that matched the drumming we could hear in the
distance. The men were obviously waiting to follow the truck out into the

street, and they were playing for themselves, holding the curved metal rod that joined the two bells in one hand and striking them with a stick in the other. There was no singing. They were listening intently to each other, and if one of the men subtly altered the accents of what he was playing the others followed him in the new rhythm.

Across the street from the *agogôs* musicians, under a dingy arcade, there were clusters of women waiting, and we realized that they would be the dancers who could come onto the street accompanied by the bells, and they would form a procession with the small sound truck and its small rope enclosure. The ropes had gotten hopelessly tangled, and a dispirited group of *cordeiros* was sitting on the street, attempting to unravel them as the musicians and dancers waited with obvious impatience. Most of the women under the arcade were older, and their skin was dark. Many were heavy, and they were wearing the traditional Bahian costume—long white skirts bellied out with an inner frame and layers of white underskirts, white turbans with starched tips, white blouses and pink sashes—everything newly washed and ironed. Each of them was also wearing a long string of beads that they tucked into cloth belts. The banner that two of the women were holding, as they waited for the struggling *cordeiros* to sort out the ropes, proclaimed the name of their group, *Korin-Efan*.

When the ropes finally were drawn into their bowed curve along the street, the men playing the light-sounding bells spread out in lines behind the truck. The women streamed from the arcade in wavering lines ahead of the truck and as they stepped off the curb onto the street they began dancing with slow, grave, stylized movements out of some earlier century. Their arms, in their white sleeves, wove patterns in the air, as though they were describing something to us, using only gestures and self-conscious smiles. As the truck lurched ahead, a woman in bright robes stepped to the microphone on a platform that had been built on the truck bed and began singing a high-pitched chant. It was one of the religious chants that still are part of the Bahian *candomblé* rituals. Beside her a second robed woman joined her in shrill, high-voiced responses.

On another Carnival night I was out on the streets alone and I found myself in the plaza in a crowd that grew steadily larger as it got later. There was a heavy press of people filling the narrow Pelourinho streets and alleyways behind me, so I decided that I would walk back to Porto Barra along the Avenida Sete de Setembro. I'd walked it two or three times in the fierce sunlight, and at least the darkness was a little cooler. But by the time I'd walked only a few blocks, I had been swept into the masses of dancers around the *trios*. Around me everyone was

Carnival in the Pelourinho, 2002.

tirelessly jumping up and down, shouting hoarsely at some choruses, then waving their arms at the choruses that followed. It was a kind of wild, unpredictable street choreography. The sound of the voices and the thunder of the musicians on the tops of the swaying *tríos* was deafening. I soon found that I been pressed into the crowds without any way to get off the street. I was lifted in the sea of bodies from the packed mass around one of the *trios* and carried two or three hundred yards to the next. At times, even with their great bulk, the wagons were powerless to push ahead themselves. I could have been a stick on a wave, but the wave was desperately unpredictable, and I was helpless to move in any other direction. If I was pushed against one of the light poles along the street I was stranded until the *trio* and its surging group of dancers in the *bloco* lurched past me. The heavy shape moved so slowly that it could take thirty minutes for it to move past where I was trapped.

I was able to tell the time that was passing because I still was wearing my wristwatch. I had realized earlier in the evening, as several people had called out to me to ask the time, that I was the only one I could see who was wearing one. The crowds were a magnet for thieves. On one Carnival night Annie and I were trapped in the crowd and six young pickpockets descended on us, cutting her purse straps with a knife and going through our pockets until our shouts frightened them off. There was so much street theft during Carnival that most of the people who came out into the streets to celebrate stripped themselves of everything except a small amount of money hidden in their shoes or under their skimpy shorts to buy something to drink and to get them home. I was struggling as much against my rising fear as I was against the press of people pushing me toward another *trío*, the sweating arms around me swaying like branches in a wind. I began pushing and straining to pry myself loose from the crowd's clutch, and finally I stumbled against a flight of steps. Beyond the fringe of bodies lined against a building I could see shadows and an uneasy darkness.

When I stumbled down the steps I found myself in a different world. At the bottom was a clogged, narrow alley. The alleyway and the small squares that opened up every hundred yards ahead of me were filthy and only sporadically lit with dim streetlights and lanterns. Beside me was a line of raggedly dressed men and women sitting on boxes or piled sacks, offering small piles of fruit or bread or cans of soft drinks for sale. Occasionally I passed people clustered around small, crude iron presses that looked as though they might have come on one of the first ships to the colony. The press's owner, his shirt wet with perspiration, was crushing lengths of sugar cane and draining the sweet sap into a metal cup he held out to the next waiting hands. Old women in African-styled robes, much worn and faded, sat at battered stands, without expression on their wrinkled faces, slicing vegetables by lantern light. Small fires were set back against the house fronts, metal grills over them holding roasting meat. An acrid pall of smoke hung in the air. Beer was selling steadily out of metal boxes filled with ice, and the procession of men moving along the center of the alleyway wavered when several of them dropped off to urinate against the wall.

As I went farther along the alleyway I began to hear a different musical sound. Behind me was the echo of the crashing rhythms from the bands on the *tríos*, but at shadowy corners two or three blocks from each other young men had set up small sound systems, and the music they were playing was the classic slow beat reggae of the 1960s. The voice of Bob Marley filled the shadows. Around each of the cheap sets of speakers, thin, serious young men, shirts stripped off, danced with slow, measured movements. The music had drawn them into its own ceremony. There was a muted restraint in their grave movements as they gestured with outstretched arms, and their legs lifted in the ritualized patterns I had seen in Marley's concerts, when he handed off his guitar and moved across the stage with a kind of dance that also suggested a moment of contemplation.

On Carnival day itself the cobblestoned streets of Pelourinho were bright with the sound of music everywhere, and Africa was a continual presence in the layering of the rhythms and the tone of the voices. The plaza was still a place for families. Children in their handmade costumes ran everywhere, laughing as they sprayed their parents and each other with a white foam that came from brightly colored cans for sale at every corner. It fell like snow and then—like summer snow in this tropical heat—melted in three or four minutes, leaving no trace. The only adults in conspicuous costumes were the turbaned and robed members of *Os Filhos de Gandhi*—The Sons of Gandhi—an organization with more than five thousand members, with its spiritual roots in the teachings of the Indian leader and whose members were brightly dressed enough to add to the spectacle of the people milling in the plaza.

The costumes of the Sons of Gandhi had been influenced by Indian models: white, Indian-styled tunics, arms bare except for beaded bracelets, white sandals and blue socks, heads draped in white turbans made of toweling. Some of the men who hurried late to the plaza took turns sewing the intricate turbans into place for each other. To complement their costumes they were draped with long strands of beads in the same blue and white colors of their costumes. The colors represented Oxal and Ogum, two spirits of the Candomblé faith. The costumed figures were a striking presence everywhere in the city. Their own lavish night procession struggled through the crowds under the spiritual guidance of the leader of their organization, an older man who wore a dhoti and had a startling resemblance to Gandhi. Part of their procession was a float with a life-sized, somewhat tattered white papier-mâché baby elephant, and on a separate float an even more battered stuffed camel.

As the night turned cooler, more and more people came into the plaza at Pelourinho, but the crowds never turned into the crush of bodies that had engulfed me the night before. The plaza grew steadily noisier, but the sound levels never achieved the deafening thunder of the *trios*. I stood on a corner, a few feet from a row of elegant, imperious women in their traditional white costumes who were cooking pots of food, the classic Bahian dishes, and I let the music sweep over me. As the hours passed I felt as though four hundred years of Brazil's African-inspired musical styles had made their way into the swaying lights of the plaza, and

Carnival in the Pelourinho, 2002.

I heard all of it without walking more than a few steps from the corner where I stood.

Other drum groups passed me, some only irregular collections of teenage boys wearing matching T-shirts and playing an assortment of much-dented metal drums painted with bright African colors. Each of the groups had a leader who strutted ahead and abruptly lifted an arm to indicate changes in the clanging rhythms. Anything vaguely African was a source for ideas for the costumes. Some dancing groups spun past dressed in woven clothes of dried grasses that had been sewn into skirts and headdresses. In one group the young woman who twisted and sang in the center of the lines of drummers was wearing only a skirt and a turbaned covering on her head. She had sprayed her body with silver paint, so with her silver covering she could dance on the streets with her breasts bare. She shone with perspiration, her body's nakedness seeming as natural as the bare chests of the young men pounding on the drums around her.

On a brightly lit sidestreet only a few yards away I found music from a different century, but with as much of Africa's influence in its syncopations. Sitting around one of a row of tables that had been set up under strings of lights along the edge of the street were several men playing acoustic string instruments and hand drums. Two of them were playing small European-style banjo-ukuleles, one a guitar. Others were playing a kind of scaper called a *reco-reco*, or a small drum held in one hand and hit with a stick—the *tamborim*. There were the unmistakable animal grunts of the *cuínca*, a friction drum that makes a sound when the player rubs a wet cloth attached to a stick on the inside of the instrument. A joke among Brazilian musicians is that the best moistener to use is their drink cachaça. I was familiar with the distinctive style of instrumental music of the small acoustic groups that had come out of the favelas of Rio, the brilliant, irresistible style called *choro*, but this was an idiom shaped around shifting chords and the muted sound of fingers and thumb on the tambourine-like *pandeiro*.

As the hours passed, small, informal processions swept up and down the steep Pelourinho streets. I could hear the shrill exhortations of brass bands. Some passed me in bright matching T-shirts and white pants of varying lengths, like the ordinary clothes of many of the people who were following them, but usually the band members were in distinctive costumes. One band straggled past in striped convict's clothing, the number 171 sewn onto their chests with a red patch. Another band wore red tunics and white caps with green head bands. The largest of the brass bands, performing on a rough stage set up in front of the old house of the famed Brazilian author Jorge Amado, had settled for blue and white flowered shirts and yellow or red visored caps, while a new band pushing through the crowds not far from them was outfitted in garish sateen women's blouses, with women's turbans in matching colors tied on their heads.

As I clung to my corner it seemed at moments that bands were streaming toward me from all directions. I felt like I was hearing every half-forgotten musical expression of the old Portuguese culture. The brass bands themselves were a memory of the colonial past, as they filled the streets with irregular lines of trumpets, saxophones, and trombones—some with only four or five horn players, but always with a gathering of drummers. The largest of the bands—the one on the stage in front of the Amado house—included a dozen horn players, anchored by the stentorian tones of a tuba. The melodies were still European—short, simple phrases played in ragged unison over and over, just as this kind of band music at village festivals in Portugal repeats these same melodies with the same fervor. From Africa came the dense thicket of rhythms clattering behind the horns, and the fierce tempos and the rushing energy of the playing. Some of the bands had quickened their tempos, in the style

Carnival in
the Pelourinho,
2002.

of the Rio bands, so the crowds trailing after them had to follow with
choppy, running steps, arms clenched, their heads swaying from side
to side in the glaring lights.

I finally left my corner. Even through the din of the crowds I could
hear that the energy was running thin for some of the musicians. I
trailed after a stream of families with tired children in their arms down
to the bottom of the hill at the exit from Pelourinho. I wasn't going to
repeat my attempt of the night before and walk into the dense crowds
on the Avenida. Taxis waited in a line that trailed out of sight on the
dark, twisting street. A driver ferried me back to Porto Barra at death-
defining speed, careening around laughing groups of people still out on
the streets everywhere in the city. He was rushing to get back to the old
town for a new fare. But once back at the hotel, with my ears still ringing
with the music I'd heard, a late swim in the hotel pool didn't feel like
the end of Carnival.

I dried myself off, pulled on a dry T-shirt and shorts and went back on the streets. I followed the street beside the beach toward the old fort, where the last *tríos* waited to begin their voyage through the city's streets. It was almost one in the morning, but there was still a press of people on the grassy slope in front of the fort. The last few babies were sleeping soundly on their father's shoulders. The procession on the street had a momentary lull, but already the swollen shapes of advertising balloons and the straining figures of the first cordeiros for the next vehicle were moving up to fill the space. With a diffident silence the *trío* made its way toward us, imposing in its hulking, still dark presence. It hadn't turned on its lights or begun its music. Then with a burst the lights blazed on—a flare of neon and bright band spotlights—and the musicians swept into a cascading street samba. Standing in the lights there above us, his arms outstretched, a guitar hanging from his neck, his name spelled out in large green neon letters below him was one of Bahia's—and Brazil's—most loved artists. What the lights spelled out was

GILBERTO GIL

His home was in a neighborhood not far away, and this was a journey that Gil made every year through the delirious streets. When he finally passed us, a half an hour later, I felt that at last the Carnival was over.

I walked slowly back along the line of *tríos* that had finished their voyage and rested silently in dark shadows. The street was littered with trash and discarded bottles. It was suddenly very quiet. I could see in the faces of the people who passed me that the fierce joy of the Carnival had found its way inside them. What they were bringing back as they straggled home along the emptying street, and what I would take with me when I finally caught my plane back to Rio, would be enough of its sounds and its music and its energy to carry us through the long months of another year—or perhaps forever?

1 A Griot's Art

1. Charters, *Roots of the Blues*, 71.
2. Quoted in Green, *Collection of Voyages*, 714.

2 Canaries, *Canarios*

1. Alzola, *Brief History of the Canary Islands*, 70.
2. Arbeau, "Canarie," 5.
3. Siemens Hernández, *Orígenes y devenir del baile llamado "El Canario."*
4. Hudson and Little, "Canary."
5. Siemens Hernández, liner notes to Millares, *Clásicos canarios*.

3 Go Down, Chariot

1. Kemble, *Journal of a Residence on a Georgia Plantation*, 51.
2. Ibid., 15.
3. Ibid., 30.
4. Ibid., 106.
5. Ibid., 127.
6. Ibid., 218.
7. Parrish, *Slave Songs of the Georgia Sea Islands*.
8. Ibid., 9.
9. Ibid., 237.
10. Ibid., 32.
11. Hurston, *Go Gator and Muddy the Water*.
12. Hurston, *Folklore, Memoirs, and Other Writings*, 870.
13. Kemble, *Journal of a Residence on a Georgia Plantation*, 80.

4 Skiffles, Tubs, and Washboards

1. Reitz, liner notes to *Jailhouse Blues*.

5 Red Clark's List

1. Friedlander, *Jazz People of New Orleans*, 70.

2. *Daily Picayune*, February 25, 1885.

3. Interview by author, 1956.

4. Quoted in Al Salaam, liner notes to *What You Gonna Do for the Rest of Your Life*.

6 A Dance in Ragged Time

1. Preston, *Scott Joplin*, 55.

2. Reproduced in Ware, *Ragtime Ephemerelist*, 28.

3. Jasen and Jones, *That American Rag*, 37.

4. Ibid., 38.

5. Ibid., 48.

6. Quoted in Charters and Kunstadt, *Jazz*, 47.

7. Southern and Wright, *Images*, 19.

8. Abbott and Seroff, *Out of Sight*, 448.

9. Ibid., 449.

10. Whitney Balliett, interview, quoted in Scotti, liner notes to *American Beauties*.

11. John Keen, quoted in Ware, *Ragtime Ephemerelist*, 216.

12. Interview, *Joseph Lamb*.

13. Folkways interview, *The Music of the Bahamas*, vol. 2.

7 Gal, You Got to Go Back to Bimini

1. Quoted in Charters, *Day Is So Long*, 73.

2. Barratt, *Grand Bahama*, 54.

3. Charters, *Day Is So Long*, 91.

8 Pretenders, Caressers, Lions

1. Ottley, *Calypsonians from Then to Now*, part 2.

2. Ottley, *Calypsonians from Then to Now*, part 1, 123.

3. Roberts, *Black Music of Two Worlds*, 123.

4. *Jamette* is an old term that can mean someone of lower class, or even a prostitute.

5. Liverpool, *Rituals of Power and Glory*.

6. Ottley, *Calypsonians from Then to Now*, part 2, 18.

7. "Shadow, Stalin Rule at Kaiso House," *Express* (Port of Spain), January 23, 2002.

9 Like Thunder If a Man Live Close

1. Ottley, *Calypsonians from Then to Now*, part 1, 23–24.

2. Liverpool, *Rituals of Power and Glory*, 394.

3. Grant, *Ring of Steel*, 25.

4. Ottley, part 1, 23.

5. Ottley, part 1, 22.

10 Reggae Is a New Bag

1. Roberts, liner notes to *Caribbean Island Music*.
2. Barrow and Dalton, *Rough Guide to Reggae*, 166.
3. Quoted in liner notes to Marley, *Catch a Fire*.
4. Ibid.

11 To Feel the Spirit

1. Allen, Ware, and Garrison, *Slave Songs of the United States*, x.
2. Levine, "Slave Songs and Slave Consciousness," 220.
3. Ibid., 220–21.
4. Ibid., 221.
5. Smylie, "Camp Meeting."
6. Ward, *Dark Midnight When I Rise*.
7. Ibid., 110.
8. Quoted ibid., 110.
9. Quoted ibid., 115.
10. Ibid.,
11. Parrish, *Slave Songs of the Georgia Sea Islands*, 173.
12. Jackson, *White Spirituals in Southern Uplands*.
13. Downey and Oliver, "African American Spiritual," 192.

12 A Prince of Zydeco

1. Quoted in Tisserand, *Kingdom of Zydeco*.
2. Ibid., 11.
3. Ibid., 15.
4. Ibid., 72.

13 ¿Como se llama este ritmo?

1. Diaz Ayala, *Música cubana del areyto a la nueva trova*.
2. Orovio, *Diccionario de la música cubana*.
3. Santos, liner notes to *Sones cubanos*.
4. Sherlock, *West Indian Nations*, 230.

14 Bahia Nights

1. Quoted in Krich, *Why Is This Country Dancing?*, 160.
2. Fausto, *Concise History of Brazil*, 10.
3. Viega, liner notes to *Modinhas brasileiras*.
4. Perroni, *Masters of Contemporary Song*, xvi.
5. Krich, *Why Is This Country Dancing?*, 151.

Abbott, Lynn, and Doug Seroff. *Out of Sight*. Jackson: University Press of Mississippi, 2002.

Allen, Ray, and Lois Wilcken. *Island Sounds in the Global City*. New York: Folklore Society, 1998.

Allen, William Francis, Charles Pickard Ware, and Lucy McKim Garrison, eds. *Slave Songs of the United States*. New York: Dover, 1995 [1867].

Al Salaam, Kalamu y. Liner notes to *What You Gonna Do for the Rest of Your Life*. Columbia Records 7464-47383, 1991.

Alzola, José Miguel. Trans. Ann Ruddock. *A Brief History of the Canary Islands*. Las Palmas: Museum of the Canaries, 1989.

Ancelet, Barry Jean, text, and Elmore Morgan Jr., photos. *Cajun and Creole Music Makers*. Jackson: University Press of Mississippi, 1999.

Appleby, David P. *The Music of Brazil*. Austin: University of Texas Press, 1993.

Arbeau, Thoinot. "Canarie." In *Bonniers Musik Lexicon*. Stockholm: Bonniers, 1978.

Barratt, Peter. *Grand Bahama*. 2nd ed. Newton Abbot, U.K.: Macmillan Caribbean, 1989.

Barrow, Steve, and Peter Dalton. *The Rough Guide to Reggae*. London: Rough Guides, 2001.

Bernard, Shane K. *Swamp Pop*. Jackson: University Press of Mississippi, 1996.

Bremer, Fredrika. Trans. Mary Howitt. *The Homes of the New World*. New York: Negro Universities Press, 1968 [1853].

Browning, Barbara. *Samba*. Bloomington: University of Indiana Press, 1995.

Charry, Eric. *Mande Music*. Chicago: University of Chicago Press, 2000.

Charters, Samuel. *Jazz, New Orleans, 1885–1963: An Index to Negro Jazz Musicians of New Orleans*. 2nd rev. ed. New York: Oak, 1963.

———. *The Roots of the Blues*. London: Marion Boyars, 1981.

———. *The Day Is So Long and the Wages So Small: Music on a Summer Island*. London: Marion Boyars, 1999.

———. Trans. Olle Thörnvall. *Mambo Time: Historien om Bebo Valdes*. Stockholm: Ars, 2001.

———. *New Orleans: Playing a Jazz Chorus*. London: Marion Boyars, 2005.

———, and Leonard Kunstadt. *Jazz: A History of the New York Scene*. New York: Doubleday, 1962.

Clinton, Catherine. *Fanny Kemble's Civil Wars*. Oxford: Oxford University Press, 2000.

Cowley, John. *Carnival, Canboulay and Calypso.* 1st paperback ed., 1998. Oxford: Oxford University Press.

Diaz Ayala, Cristóbal. *Música cubana del areyto a la nueva trova.* San Juan, P.R.: Cobanacán, 1981.

Downey, James C., and Paul Oliver. "The African American Spiritual." In *The New Grove Dictionary of Music and Musicians,* ed. Stanley Sadie, vol. 10. London: Macmillan, 2001.

Fausto, Boris. *Concise History of Brazil.* Cambridge: Cambridge University Press, 2000.

Foster, Chuck. *Roots Rock Reggae.* New York: Billboard, 1999.

Friedlander, Lee. *The Jazz People of New Orleans.* New York: Pantheon, 1992.

Grant, Cy. *Ring of Steel.* London: Macmillan Education, 1999.

Green, John. *Collection of Voyages.* London, 1745.

Hasse, John Edward. *Jazz, the First Century.* New York: William Morrow, 2000.

Hill, Donald R. *Calypso Calaloo.* Gainesville: University Press of Florida, 1993.

Hudson, Richard, and Meredith Ellis Little. "Canary." In *The Grove Dictionary of Music and Musicians.* London: Macmillan, 1967.

Hurston, Zora Neale. *Folklore, Memoirs, and Other Writings.* New York: Library of the Americas, 1995.

———, ed. With biographical essay by Pamela Bordelon. *Go Gator and Muddy the Water.* New York: Norton, 1999.

Jackson, George Pullen. *White Spirituals in Southern Uplands.* Chapel Hill: University of North Carolina Press, 1933.

Jasen, David, and Gene Jones. *That American Rag.* New York: Schirmer, 2000.

Joseph Lamb: A Study in Classic Ragtime. Recorded by Ann and Samuel Charters. New York: Folkways Records FG 3562, 1959.

Kemble, Fanny. *Journal of a Residence on a Georgia Plantation.* London: Green, Longman, Roberts and Green, 1863; New York: Harper and Brothers, 1863.

Krich, John. *Why Is This Country Dancing?* New York: Simon and Schuster, 1993.

Lemann, Nicholas. *The Promised Land.* New York: Vintage, 1992.

Levine, Lawrence. "Slave Songs and Slave Consciousness." In *Cultural Resistance Reader,* ed. Stephen Duncombe. New York: Verso, 2002.

Liverpool, Hollis "Chalkdust." In *Rituals of Power and Rebellion.* Chicago: Research Associates School Times, 2001.

Manuel, Peter. *Caribbean Currents.* Philadelphia: Temple University Press, 1995.

Marley, Bob. *Catch a Fire.* Deluxe ed. New York: Universal Island Records, 2001.

Marre, Jeremy, and Hannah Charlton. *Beats of the Heart.* New York: Pantheon, 1985.

McGowan, Chris, and Ricardo Pessanha. *The Brazilian Sound.* New ed. Philadelphia: Temple University Press, 1998.

Morris, Dennis. *Bob Marley: A Photography.* London: Plexus, 1999.

Olivier, Rick, photographs, and Ben Sandmel, text. *Zydeco!* Jackson: University Press of Mississippi, 1999.

Orovio, Helio. *Diccionario de la música cubana.* 2nd rev. ed. Habana: Editora Universitaria, 1965.

O'Shaughnessy, Hugh. *Around the Spanish Main.* London: Century, 1991.

Ottley, Rudolph. *Women in Calypso.* Part 1. Arima, Trinidad: Rudolph Ottley, 1992.

——. *Calypsonians from Then to Now.* Part 1. Arima, Trinidad: Rudolph Ottley, 1995.

——. *Calypsonians from Then to Now.* Part 2. Arima, Trinidad: Rudolph Ottley, n.d.

Parrish, Lydia. *Slave Songs of the Georgia Sea Islands.* New York: Creative Arts, 1942.

Perroni, Charles A. *Masters of Contemporary Song.* Austin: University of Texas Press, 1942.

Preston, Catherine. *Scott Joplin, Composer.* New York: Chelsea House, 1988.

Reitz, Rosetta. Liner notes to *Jailhouse Blues.* Rosetta Records RR 1316.

Roberts, John Storm. *The Latin Tinge.* New York: Oxford University Press, 1979.

——. *Black Music of Two Worlds.* 2nd rev. ed. New York: Schirmer, 1998.

——. Liner notes to *Caribbean Island Music.* New York: Nonesuch Records, 1998.

Rogozinski, Jan. *A Brief History of the Caribbean.* Rev. ed. New York: Facts on File, 1999.

Salewicz, Chris, and Adrian Boot. *Reggae Explosion.* New York: Harry N. Abrams, 2001.

Santos, John. Liner notes to *Sones cubanos.* El Cerrito, Calif.: Arhoolie Records CD 7003, 1991.

Schreiner, Claus. Trans. Mark Weinstein. *Musica Brasiliera.* London: Marion Boyars, 1993.

Schuller, Gunther. *Early Jazz.* New York: Oxford University Press, 1968.

Scotti, Joseph R. Liner notes to *American Beauties: The Rags of Joseph Lamb* (CD). New York: Koch International Classics, 2000.

Segal, Ronald. *The Black Diaspora.* London: Faber and Faber, 1995.

Sherlock, P. M. *West Indian Nations.* Kingston, Jamaica: Macmillan, 1973.

Siemens Hernández, Lothar. Liner notes to Totoyo Millares, *Clásicos canarios* (CD). Gran Canaria: Centro de la Cultura Popular Canaria, 1978.

——. *Orígenes y devenir del baile llamado "el canario."* Las Palmas: Museum of the Canaries, 1999.

Smylie, James H. "Camp Meeting." In *Encyclopedia Americana.*

Southern, Eileen, and Josephine Wright. *Images: Iconography in African American Culture (1770s–1920s).* New York: Garland, 2000.

Stewart, Earl L. *African American Music.* New York: Schirmer, 1998.

Sutton, Allan, ed. *Cakewalks, Rags and Novelties: The International Ragtime Discography (1894–1930).* Denver: Mainspring, 2003.

Tisserand, Michael. *The Kingdom of Zydeco.* New York: Avon, 1998.

Vianna, Hermano. Ed. and trans. John Charles Chasteen. *The Mystery of Samba.* Chapel Hill: University of North Carolina Press, 1999.

Viega, Manuel. Liner notes to *Modinhas brasileiras.* Wyastone Leys, U.K.: Nimbus Records, 1997.

Ward, Andrew. *Dark Midnight When I Rise.* New York: Farrar, Straus and Giroux, 2000.

Ware, Chris, ed. *The Ragtime Ephemerelist*, no. 3. Oak Park, Ill.: Chris Ware, 2000.

Page numbers in italics refer to illustrations.

Samuel Charters is an independent scholar. He is the author of *A Trumpet Around the Corner: The Story of New Orleans Jazz* (2008); *Walking a Blues Road* (2005); *New Orleans: Playing a Jazz Chorus* (2006); *Mambo Time: The Story of Bebo Valdés* (2001); *The Day Is So Long and the Wages So Small: Music on a Summer Island* (1999); *A Country Year: A Chronicle* (1992); *Elvis Presley Calls His Mother after the Ed Sullivan Show* (1992); *The Blues Makers* (1991); *Louisiana Black: A Novel* (1986); *Jelly Roll Morton's Last Night at the Jungle Inn* (1984); *Mr. Jabi and Mr. Smythe* (1983); *The Roots of Blues* (1981); *Spelmännen* (The Swedish Fiddlers) (1979); *Sweet as the Showers of Rain* (1977); *The Legacy of the Blues* (1975); *Robert Johnson* (1973); *From a Swedish Notebook* (1972); *Same Poems/Poets: Studies in American Underground Poetry since 1945* (1971); *As I Stand at This Window* (1970); *To This Place: Poems* (1969); *The Bluesmen* (1967); *Days, or Days as Thoughts in a Season's Uncertainties* (1967); *The Poetry of the Blues* (1963); *The Country Blues* (1959); *Jazz: New Orleans, 1885–1958: An Index to Negro Musicians of New Orleans* (1958/1963); also with Leonardo Kunstadt, *Jazz: A History of the New York Scene* (1962). He is the author with Ann Charters of *Blues Faces* (2000); *I Love: The Story of Mayakovsky and Lili Brik* (1979). He also edits with Ann Charters *Literature and Its Writers: An Introduction to Fiction, Poetry, and Drama* (1997; 5th edition, 2009).

Library of Congress Cataloging-in-Publication Data

Charters, Samuel Barclay.
A language of song : journeys in the musical world of the African diaspora /
Samuel Charters.
p. cm.
Includes bibliographical references and index.
ISBN 978-0-8223-4358-5 (cloth : alk. paper) — ISBN 978-0-8223-4380-6 (pbk. :
alk. paper)
1. Charters, Samuel Barclay—Travel. 2. Music—African influences.
3. Music—United States—African influences. 4. Music—Latin America—
African influences. I. Title.
ML423.C494.A3 2009
780.89′96—dc22   2008055237